Mestizo International Law

The development of international law is conventionally understood as a history in which the main characters (states and international lawyers) and events (wars and peace conferences) are European. Arnulf Becker Lorca demonstrates how non-Western states and lawyers appropriated nineteenth-century classical thinking in order to defend new and better rules governing non-Western states' international relations. By internalizing the standard of civilization, for example, they argued for the abrogation of unequal treaties. These appropriations contributed to the globalization of international law. With the rise of modern legal thinking and a stronger international community governed by law, peripheral lawyers seized the opportunity and used the new discourse and institutions, such as the League of Nations, to dissolve the standard of civilization and codify non-intervention and self-determination. These stories suggest that the history of our contemporary international legal order is not purely European; instead they suggest a history of a mestizo international law.

ARNULF BECKER LORCA is a visiting member of the International Relations Program at Brown University, Rhode Island, USA, and fellow at the Institute for Global Law and Policy at Harvard University. His research traces the global intellectual history of international law focusing on the role non-Western international lawyers have played in the construction of the international legal order between the second half of the nineteenth century and the first half of the twentieth century.

CAMBRIDGE STUDIES IN INTERNATIONAL AND COMPARATIVE LAW

Established in 1946, this series produces high quality scholarship in the fields of public and private international law and comparative law. Although these are distinct legal sub-disciplines, developments since 1946 confirm their interrelations.

Comparative law is increasingly used as a tool in the making of law at national, regional and international levels. Private international law is now often affected by international conventions, and the issues faced by classical conflicts rules are frequently dealt with by substantive harmonization of law under international auspices. Mixed international arbitrations, especially those involving state economic activity, raise mixed questions of public and private international law, while in many fields (such as the protection of human rights and democratic standards, investment guarantees and international criminal law) international and national systems interact. National constitutional arrangements relating to 'foreign affairs', and to the implementation of international norms, are a focus of attention.

The series welcomes works of a theoretical or interdisciplinary character, and those focusing on the new approaches to international or comparative law or conflicts of law. Studies of particular institutions or problems are equally welcome, as are translations of the best work published in other languages.

A list of books in the series can be found at the end of this volume.

Mestizo International Law

A Global Intellectual History 1842–1933

Arnulf Becker Lorca

CAMBRIDGE
UNIVERSITY PRESS

CAMBRIDGE
UNIVERSITY PRESS

University Printing House, Cambridge CB2 8BS, United Kingdom

Cambridge University Press is part of the University of Cambridge.

It furthers the University's mission by disseminating knowledge in the pursuit of education, learning and research at the highest international levels of excellence.

www.cambridge.org
Information on this title: www.cambridge.org/9780521763387

First published 2014

A catalogue record for this publication is available from the British Library

Library of Congress Cataloging in Publication data
Becker Lorca, Arnulf, 1971– author.
Mestizo international law : a global intellectual history 1842–1933 / Arnulf Becker Lorca.
pages cm – (Cambridge studies in international and comparative law ; 115)
Based on author's dissertation (SJD – Harvard Law School), 2010.
ISBN 978-0-521-76338-7 (hardback)
1. International law – History. 2. Legal polycentricity. I. Title.
KZ1242.B42 2014
341.09′034 – dc23 2014032244

ISBN 978-0-521-76338-7 Hardback

para mis mestizos Milo, Benno y Melchor

Contents

Maps

Acknowledgements

A book of this scope could only have been written with the help, advice and support of many friends and colleagues from around the world. Long time ago, back in Chile, I became interested in thinking about international lawyers as political actors. I thank Cecilia Medina and Amparo Menéndez-Carrión for that initial encouragement. This project developed first as a SJD dissertation at Harvard Law School. I thank the members of my thesis committee, Duncan Kennedy, Roberto Mangabeira Unger and Susan Silbey. My main supervisor was and continues to be a great source of inspiration: David Kennedy not only shaped the way I see international law, but also created at HLS a uniquely cosmopolitan environment without which adopting a global approach to the history of international law would have been impossible. At Harvard I was also extremely fortunate to use the international and foreign law collection at the law library before it was dismantled. I thank Stephen Wiles and all the staff at the library for allowing me to dig deep in the collection. In Cambridge MA, I also found a group of friends who listened to various versions of the stories recounted in this book: among others I thank Jane Bestor, Paulo Barrozo, Julieta Lemaitre, Roni Mann, Moria Paz, Carlos Portugal Gouvêa, Anna di Robilant, Hengameh Saberi, Alvaro Santos, Hani Sayed, Holger Spamann, Talha Syed, Philomila Tsoukala and Raef Zreik.

This project took shape as a book at King's College London. It was Susan Marks who first made me think about my disparate stories about non-Western international lawyers as a unified book. I thank Susan and my friends at King's: Christoph Kletzer, Federico Ortino and Lorenzo Zucca. I also benefited from London's vibrant international law scene. Among others I thank Matt Craven, Andrew Lang and Ralph Wilde.

The book was finished while teaching for the International Relations Program at Brown University. I thank Mark Blyth, Claudia Elliot and Anita

Nestor for their hospitality, Nathaniel Berman and Julio Ortega for enriching my understanding of global cultural trends and Richard Snyder for inviting me to present the Latin American stories in this book at Brown's Center for Latin American and Caribbean Studies. Thanks to Hannah Koenig for designing the maps. Teaching international law and a seminar based on this book to intellectually curious college students has been very gratifying. I thank my students for challenging me to improve the way I tell the different stories in the book.

A book on the intellectual history of international law would have been unthinkable without the paths opened by Toni Anghie and Martti Koskenniemi. I am grateful for their comments and support. I have been fortunate also to participate in Martti Koskenniemi's 'international law and empire working group' at the University of Helsinki. Presenting parts of the book in front of a fantastic group of intellectual historians and international law scholars was extremely useful.

I borrowed from Duncan Kennedy the idea that legal thought can be seen as a linguistic structure that has globalized in a classical and modern form. This heuristic provided a useful blueprint to explore a global history of international law. In some respects I was driven to this project in order to challenge Duncan's narrative in which legal thinking flows mainly from centre to periphery. I thank Duncan for the inspiration and the many lunches to report progress on the book.

Trying out hypotheses with historians interested in the history of international law was crucial to the development of the book. I am grateful to David Armitage, Benjamin Coates, Douglas Howland and Caroline Reeves for useful conversations. I thank Stacie Hanneman for organizing a panel at the 2102 Social Science Historical Association Conference where I presented parts of the book.

A shorter version of Part II of the book was published as 'Universal international law: histories of imposition and appropriation, 1850s–1900s', *Harvard International Law Journal*, 51 (2010), 475–552. Rein Müllerson, Bill Alford, Steve Harris and Karen Knop offered useful comments, as well as participants in presentations at the International Law Association British Branch–University College London international law seminar, King's College London School of Law staff seminar, Center for Transnational Legal Studies London Transnational Law Colloquium, Elizabeth Batelle Clark Legal History Colloquium at Boston University, and the Harvard-Stanford International Junior Faculty Forum. An earlier version of Chapter 5 was published as 'Sovereignty beyond the West: the end of classical international law', *Journal of the History of International Law*, 13 (2011), 7–73; I thank Douglas Howland and participants at the International Law and World Order Conference at Wisconsin-Milwaukee. A very short overview of Part III was published as 'Petitioning the international: a prehistory of self-determination', *European Journal of International Law*, 25 (2014), 497–523; I thank Anne Orford, Dino Kritsiotis, Mattias Kumm and participants at the second annual junior faculty forum for international law at the University of Nottingham.

As a member of a larger group of international law scholars gathering mostly around David Kennedy's Institute for Global Law and Policy, I have been able to test and develop the ideas explored in the book. For years, every student or scholar of international law from the non-Western world that I encountered was subjected to a long list of questions about the first international lawyers of his or her country. I thank these countless students and scholars, since these informal conversations were fundamental to realize the global scope of international legal thought and practice.

In particular, conversations with Liliana Obregon, Jorge Esquirol and Rodrigo Gallindo enriched my understanding of international law in Latin America. Mekondjo Kaapanda introduced me to the Pan-African movement's petitions. My understanding of Africa and Ethiopia also benefited from conversations with Rose Parfitt. Hani Sayed has always been willing to listen to my semi-peripheral stories; Hani and Michael Fakhri offered helpful context to understand Syria and Lebanon under the French mandate. My grasp of Japanese international lawyers benefited from conversations with Doug Howland, Sookyeon Huh and Koji Nishimoto. Conversations with Pasha Hsieh, Chen Li Chen and Stefan Kroll contributed to my understanding of international law in China. Paul McHugh introduced me to the Six Nations' petitions.

While writing the book I had very useful conversations with Nathaniel Berman about Abd-del-Krim, with Mark Toufayan about Armenia, with Saptarishi Bandopadhyay about India, with Boris Mamlyuk about Russia, with Umut Özsu about the Ottoman Empire and with Stavros Gadinis and Thomas Skouteris about Greek international lawyers. Finally, many others gave me feedback on general questions of history and theory of international law. I thank Alan Nissel, Luigi Nuzzo, John Haskell, Justin Stein, Ignacio de la Rasilla, Akbar Rasulov and Mikhail Xifaras.

Finally, thanks to my boys Melchor, Benno and Milo for their love. And thanks to Anna: I counted on her influence, love and support at every stage of this long process. Without them there would be no book.

Introduction

It was 1878 when for the first time a Chinese and Japanese delegate attended a professional meeting of international lawyers. That year, Kuo-Taj-In (Songtao Guo) and Kagenori Wooyeno (Ueno), attended a session of the Association for the Reform and Codification of the Law of Nations, later renamed International Law Association. Founded in 1873 in Brussels by a group of liberal lawyers, reformists and philanthropists, the International Law Association exists until today as one of the profession's more important organizations. The founding, at the end of the nineteenth century, of this and other professional organizations like the *Institut de Droit International* marked the beginning of international law as a liberal reformist project.[1] Advancing the rule of law in international relations, this project involved the enactment of international rules and the creation of international courts and organizations. It also involved the emergence of an autonomous international legal profession, progressively separated from diplomatic circles and from the representation of the interests of individual states.

The late nineteenth century international lawyer, departing from diplomatic practice and state interest, sought to transcend the European balance of power as the principle organizing interstate relations. Instead, liberal international lawyers believed in an international community governed by law. Transcending sovereign self-interest, this was a cosmopolitan project. Was it also a cosmopolitan project in relation to the participation of non-Western delegates in international law meetings and conferences like the one of 1878, and more importantly, was it

[1] M. Koskenniemi, *The gentle civilizer of nations: the rise and fall of international law, 1870–1960* (Cambridge University Press, 2002), pp. 39–41, 57–67.

cosmopolitan in relation to the inclusion of non-Western nations into the realm of international law? Was the international community to be governed by law European or universal? If the international community had in fact boundaries, what were the rules governing inclusion and exclusion? And what were the rules governing relations between states and polities beyond the realm of international law?

In 1878 there were no clear answers to these questions. In the inclusion of non-Western members to the International Law Association, however, we may find some initial answers suggesting international law's cosmopolitan vocation. Among its founding members the Association counted not only renowned European lawyers such as Auguste Visschers from Belgium, Johann Caspar Bluntschli from Switzerland or Travers Twiss from Britain, but also David Dudley Field from the United States and Carlos Calvo from Argentina, two delegates from extra-European nations. Moreover, the Japanese minister at Rome, Masataka Kawase attended the second meeting and a Russian, Vladimir Bezobrazov, joined the Association at its third meeting.[2] It was in 1878, at the sixth meeting held in Frankfurt, that Songtao Guo and Kagenori Ueno, the Chinese and Japanese delegates, addressed the Association for the first time.

Kagenori Ueno (1845–1888) was extremely aware of the importance that his participation had as a sign of the inclusion of Japan into the international community and as a sign of the universality of international law.[3] Ueno opened his speech as follows:

> I desire to take the first occasion which presents itself to assure you the pleasure and honour which I feel in having been permitted to join your admirable and useful Association. Its aims are cosmopolitan, the benefits it seeks to distribute are cosmopolitan. It is therefore right that its members should be chosen from among all the nations of the world.[4]

On the other hand, the experience that Guo had acquired as China's first minister to Britain and France had made him very conscious not only about the inconsistencies between the unequal treatment to which China was subjected and international law's principle of sovereign equality, but

[2] *Association for the Reform and Codification of the Law of Nations Report of the Conference*, 1 & 2 (1873–1874), 53; *Association for the Reform and Codification of the Law of Nations Summary of the Proceedings* 3 (1875), 36.

[3] *Association for the Reform and Codification of the Law of Nations Report of the Conference* 6 (1878), 38–41.

[4] *Ibid.*, 38–9.

also about the possibilities that international law could offer to overcome unequal treatment.[5] Guo affirmed:

I am very desirous of attaining a knowledge of this science [international law], in the hope that it will be beneficial to my country. I think it my duty to express the high esteem which I entertain for this Association and my great pleasure in joining it, and hope that by this means the relations of China with other countries may be improved.[6]

The first words of both the Chinese and Japanese delegates were introductory words of courtesy, followed by high hopes on the possibilities international law could offer to confront their states' main preoccupation, that is, securing the abrogation of the treaties concluded with Western states that had imposed unequal terms and extraterritorial jurisdiction.[7] Hopes were rapidly shattered.

Immediately after Guo and Ueno concluded their remarks, David Dudley Field, an American lawyer, reformer and one of the founding members of the Association, asked to take the floor. The proceedings of the meeting reports Field observing that:

In many Eastern countries ... it was necessary to uphold the capitulations, owing to the procedure and modes of punishment used by the native tribunals being intolerable to citizens of the West. He instanced that, until recently, crucifixion downwards had been common in Japan. In China, he said, he had himself seen the torture applied ... So long as there was not something like a parity of civilisation in the East and West, the consular courts, or some analogous institution, must be maintained.[8]

Field's defence of the superiority of Western civilization was as unsurprising as was his readiness to deduce legal consequences out of cultural differences. That capitulations and inequality had to be maintained was a predictable answer for someone like Field. For the international law that emerged during the late nineteenth century was predicated on the distinction between civilized and uncivilized nations and on the exclusive recognition of sovereign autonomy and equality to nations believed to be civilized, namely Western nations. In fact, as Luiggi Nuzzo has shown, Field did travel to China and around the world and moreover invoked his experience to sustain the standard of civilization in the well-known

5 J. D. Frodsham, *The first Chinese embassy to the West; the journals of Kuo-Sung-T'ao, Liu Hsi-Hung and Chang Te-Yi*, translated by J. D. Frodsham (Oxford: Clarendon Press, 1974).

6 *Association for the Reform* 6 (1878), 40–1. 7 *Ibid.*, 38–41. 8 *Ibid.*, 41.

1875 report by the *Institut de Droit International* on the applicability of European international law outside the realm of Christian nations.[9]

Were Guo and Ueno invited to Frankfurt only to be reminded about the exclusively Western character of the international community? That is what emerges from Field's response. Late nineteenth century international law was not cosmopolitan. In the eyes of late nineteenth century jurists, the international community governed by law was a community of civilized nations. Western international lawyers, furthermore, assigned to themselves – as Martti Koskenniemi has put it – the role of 'the legal conscience of the civilized world'.[10]

Legal scholarship has only lately and slowly come to terms with the colonial and imperialist legacies of international law. The story about Field's response would fit well within this trend showing the colonial and imperialist origins of key international law concepts and doctrines, such as sovereignty, *uti possidetis* or the standard of civilization.[11] However, the exchange between Ueno, Guo and Field shows something more than Western lawyers simply formulating the rules and doctrines justifying unequal treatment vis-à-vis non-Western sovereigns, and something more than non-Western international lawyers accepting these rules and doctrines as fixed and given. This was in fact an exchange of opinions, for Ueno replied to Field declaring that: 'crucifixion was now happily abolished in Japan, and that that country was quickly mastering the enlightened notions of the West'.[12] Ueno did not contest the idea of a standard of civilization deriving from international law, as any official would have argued prior to the arrival of Western powers ready to use force in order to open to trade a non-Western nation. But Ueno was part of Meiji era Japan, which after defeat was undergoing rapid modernization, including the appropriation of international law. Ueno does not contest the standard, but contested Japan's place among uncivilized nations. This was an exchange of opposing views articulated in a common language of international law.

As the end of the century was approaching, exchanges like this, in which non-Western actors used the language of international law to resist foreign domination, became more and more common. The participation of

[9] L. Nuzzo, *Origini di una scienza: diritto internazionale e colonialismo nel XIX secolo* (Frankfurt am Main: Vittorio Klostermann, 2012).

[10] Koskenniemi, *Gentle civilizer*, pp. 11–97.

[11] See Koskenniemi, *Gentle civilizer*, pp. 98–178 and in general A. Anghie, *Imperialism, sovereignty, and the making of international law* (Cambridge University Press, 2005).

[12] *Association for the Reform* 6 (1878), 41.

non-Western lawyers and diplomats, internalizing and appropriating the international legal discourse, and finally becoming international lawyers marked a significant departure in the history of international law. It was obviously not the first time that scholars, lawyers and politicians debated and disagreed about the legality of Western domination in the non-Western world. Remember, for example, the famous Valladolid dispute (1550–1). Summoned by Carlos V, Bartolomé de Las Casas and Juan Sepúlveda debated over the Spanish titles in the New World.[13] But during the sixteenth century, natural law offered a universal language only in theory. In practice, although the dispute considered the nature of the indigenous and the titles over native-American lands, the convener, the audience and the opponents were all Europeans.

The exchange of 1878 was similar to the Valladolid dispute in that both were conveyed in the language of law, a universal language offering, at least in theory, an arena for social resistance. An arena that, unlike other realms of social life, is defined by its formal commitments to logical consistency, generality and impartiality, constraining rulers and ruled and affording to the ruled concrete avenues to sustain social struggle and resistance.[14] The 1878 exchange was different because only during the course of the nineteenth century international law became a regime with a global geographical scope. Moreover, it was only towards the end of the century that non-Western elites appropriated the Western international legal discourse and became versed international lawyers. Only then could international law become an actual arena for resistance and only then a global history of international law was truly inaugurated.

The trajectory of Guo, who attended the Frankfurt meeting as China's minister to Britain and France, offers a good example. Songtao Guo (1818–1891) one of the leading reformist figures in the diplomatic circles of late Qing China (1644–1912), became in 1876 the first permanent diplomatic representative of China in the West.[15] Almost thirty years before, in 1842, following the defeat of China in the First Opium War (1839–42), Britain and China signed the treaty of Nanjing, opening a number of Chinese ports to foreign presence and trade. While Qing officials of the time were

13 See L. Hanke, *All mankind is one; a study of the disputation between Bartolomé de Las Casas and Juan Ginés de Sepúlveda in 1550 on the intellectual and religious capacity of the American Indians* (Northern Illinois University Press, 1974).

14 E. P. Thompson, *Whigs and hunters: the origin of the Black Act* (London: Penguin books, 1975), pp. 258–69.

15 I. C. Y. Hsü, *China's entrance into the family of nations: the diplomatic phase, 1858–1880* (Cambridge, MA: Harvard University Press, 1960), pp. 206–7.

troubled by the fact that the Queen of England, 'a female barbarian' was named alongside the Emperor, unequal terms such as tariffs and extraterritorial jurisdiction passed unnoticed.[16] Only later, during the 1870s, did the perception of the treaty of Nanjing and other similar treaties change, in great part due to the influence exercised by Guo, who openly expressed that 'the West should treat China as equal' and that 'Westerners in China should fall under the jurisdiction of the Chinese local authority'.[17] Thus, these treaties began gradually to be seen as a humiliation and half a century later began to be described as unequal treaties.

This transformation was not only gradual, but also entailed a slow process of learning and appropriating international legal thought. Guo's first steps were followed by the Zongli Yamen (Tsungli Yamen), the first centralized office of the Qing Court to deal with foreign affairs, established in 1861 under Prince Gong. In 1864, under the auspices of the Zongli Yamen and Prince Gong, the first international law book, Henry Wheaton's *Elements of International Law*, was translated and published.[18] W. A. P. Martin, the American Presbyterian missionary in charge of the translation was later appointed to teach the Law of Nations at the Tongwenguan, the Interpreters College, becoming China's first professor of international law. In 1898, when the Imperial University of Peking replaced the Tongwenguan, Martin was appointed as the president of the university and international law gained an exceptionally pre-eminent role.[19] The first Chinese lawyers undergoing Western legal training joined the foreign office, like Wu Tingfang, a Hong Kong lawyer trained in the University of London and called to the bar at Lincoln's Inn.[20] Many others followed, including most prominently Vi Kyuin Wellington Koo (1888–1985), who studied in Columbia University, was enlisted by the Republic to give legal advice to the Chinese delegation at the Paris Peace Conference of 1919 and later became judge at the International Court of Justice (ICJ). Although the path opened by Tingfang and later by Koo was followed by many others,

[16] D. Wang, *China's unequal treaties: narrating national history* (Lanham, MD: Lexington Books, 2008), p. 24.

[17] *Ibid.*, p. 25.

[18] L. Liu, 'Legislating the universal: the circulation of international law in the nineteenth century' in L. Liu (ed.), *Tokens of exchange: the problem of translation in global circulations* (Durham, NC: Duke University Press, 1999), p. 136.

[19] P. L. Hsieh, 'The discipline of international law in Republican China and contemporary Taiwan', unpublished paper (2013), pp. 9–10.

[20] *Ibid.*, p. 7.

the attempts by the Chinese government and their lawyers to abrogate unequal treaties failed until the Second World War.

This book explores this and many other stories about the expansion and appropriation of international law outside the West as well as instances in which Western and non-Western international lawyers interacted and disagreed about the interpretation of international rules and doctrines. From the disagreement about who had met the standard of civilization in the nineteenth century, as the exchange of 1878 shows, to the meaning of non-Western states' sovereign autonomy and equality at the turn of the century, in the interventions of Luis Drago and Ruy Barbosa, the Argentinean and Brazilian delegates to the Second Hague Conference of 1907, who respectively defended the autonomy and equality of smaller states, to the disputes about extending the scope of self-determination to non-Western nations under foreign rule during the first decades of the twentieth century, in the petitions sent to the Paris Peace Conference of 1919 and then to the League of Nations, by lawyers and activists ranging from W. E. B. Du Bois from the Pan-African movement, to Deskaheh, Chief of the Six Nations, to Abd-el-Krim, leader of the Rif insurgent nation and Ras Tafari, Crown Prince of Ethiopia, as well as other leaders of nationalist parties from Egypt, India, Korea or Syria; these stories narrate a history of international law from the point of view of the interactions between Western and non-Western nations and their international lawyers, from the point of view of the interactions between the centres and peripheries of the world.

This history begins in 1842 with the signing of the treaty of Nanjing and ends in 1933 with the adoption of the Montevideo Convention. These two treaties signal the beginning and culmination of an era. Nanjing marks the beginning of an era in which a particular European discourse, the international legal discourse of the nineteenth century, was appropriated and then transformed by non-Western states and their lawyers. Montevideo marks a culmination in the appropriation of international law thinking, in that appropriation of the modern discourse was followed by the semi-peripheral transformation of basic rules of international law.

The year 1842 symbolizes the opening of the non-Western world to trade and foreign presence, by force – the Opium war – and law – the treaty of Nanjing. This treaty is a token for the series of unequal treaties imposed from Japan to the Ottoman Empire as well as the regime of diplomatic protection operating in Latin America and beyond. The law that justified the opening of non-Western nations under unequal terms, nineteenth century classical international law, was detrimental to the non-Western world. Moreover, after a show of force or actual military defeat, semi-peripheral nations had little room for manoeuvre. It was under this predicament that semi-peripheral nations sought to internalize, use and appropriate international law. Doing just that, however, semi-peripheral transformed international law into a universal legal discourse and regime. The year 1933, on the other hand, symbolizes the successful appropriation and transformation of international law, for the Montevideo Convention marked the dissolution of the standard of civilization, replaced by a formal definition of statehood and doctrine of recognition. This book is about what happened between 1842 and 1933: what follows are some of the main stories.

PART I · *MESTIZO* INTERNATIONAL LAW

This is a history of international law. It explores the origins and development of the international legal order we live in today. But the stories that follow are different from those narrated in conventional histories. The stories retold here are different in at least three respects. They are part of a *global* and *intellectual* history of a *mestizo* international law.

Conventional histories of international law are deeply Eurocentric.[1] Centred in the West, conventional histories not only have defined borders: from Grotius to Lauterpacht, from the Thirty Years War, to the World Wars, from the Treaty of Westphalia, to the Treaty of Paris, to the League and the United Nations, but also present a teleological trajectory: from a European to a universal international law.[2]

This book delves into a different, non-Eurocentric account of that same story. It does not restrict the gaze to a few European states and Western jurists, who have devised and set up rules and institutions to govern international relations, but examines the trajectories and contributions of a larger number of nations and lawyers across the globe. Therefore, no

[1] Martti Koskenniemi has recently described the Eurocentric nature of the history of international law: 'Europe served as the origin, engine and telos of historical knowledge'. M. Koskenniemi, 'Histories of international law: dealing with Eurocentrism', *Rechtsgeschichte*, 19 (2011), 152–76, 158.

[2] Among others, German historian Wolfgang Preiser has noticed the Eurocentric nature of the history of international law. In a book where he sets out to study the history of non-Western legal orders, he states: 'Up to now, the history of international law has been predominantly preoccupied with the law that in the European world developed into an interstate order, and that from there has, since the beginning of modern times, expanded over the world'. W. Preiser, *Frühe völkerrechtliche Ordnungen der außereuropäischen Welt: Ein Beitrag zur Geschichte des Völkerrechts* (Wiesbaden: F. Steiner, 1976), p. 7. Non-European international legal orders are only considered relevant if they came into contact with the European world: *ibid*., p. 8.

references will be made to international law's deemed founding fathers, be they Vitoria, Grotius or Vattel, in the sixteenth, seventeenth and eighteenth centuries. On the contrary, we will explore the work and life of non-Western jurists. Some of them are quite renowned, like Friedrich Martens, the nineteenth-century Estonian/Russian jurist, after whom the 'Martens clause' was named, or like Alejandro Alvarez the famous twentieth-century ICJ dissenter. Others are more known as politicians or activists, than as players in a history of international law, like Nobuaki Makino, the Japanese plenipotentiary to the Paris Peace Conference who put forth the racial equality clause, and Marcus Garvey, the Pan-African intellectual from Jamaica who sent several petitions to the Peace Conference and the League of Nations. Yet others are relatively unknown, like Gustavo Guerrero, Constantin Sipsom and Chao-Chu Wu, the Salvadorian, Rumanian and Chinese delegates to the 1930 Hague Codification Conference who defended, against Western delegates, a restrictive doctrine of state responsibility, and like the Iranian delegate to the League of Nations, Arfa-ed-Dowleh who, advocating a more inclusive organization, helped the Six Nations and other delegations in their attempts to be heard at the League's Assembly.

None of these stories goes back to the time of the conventional founding fathers. As already mentioned, this history starts in 1842, at the time when international law started to acquire a global geographical scope. Before that, if there is history of international law, it is the history of different – geographically and culturally disconnected – regional legal orders. This book explores how an international legal order and discourse circumscribed to Europe universalized. In this sense, it is a global history that takes an 'international turn' to explain the history of international law.[3]

Narrating a global history of international law demands neither identifying a starting point in Europe (or in another distant past outside Europe), nor studying how the original idea unfolded because of the involvement of Western states, their lawyers and thinkers. Instead, this book suggests that international law emerged out of the interaction between Western

[3] I take this definition of global history as 'the history and pre-histories of globalization, the histories of objects that have become universalized and the links between sub-global arenas' from David Armitage, who furthermore identifies a 'desire to go above or beyond the history of nationally defined states and state-bounded nations' among historians taking an 'international turn': D. Armitage, *Foundations of modern international thought* (Cambridge University Press, 2013), p. 18.

and non-Western sovereigns, as well as from the professional rapports and debates between Western and non-Western international lawyers, in exchanges like the one of 1878 and many others; it suggests that international law has a *mestizo* history. But why should one care about a history like this?

1 Why a global intellectual history of international law?

Let's say that you are an international lawyer, an international relations student or scholar, a diplomat, or even like myself a historian of international law, and we have not heard about Songtao Guo, Gustavo Guerrero or Arfa-ed-Dowleh. We have also never seen in a history of international law noted politicians or intellectuals such as W. E. B. Du Bois, Ras Tafari Mekonnen (future Emperor of Ethiopia Haile Selassie), Abd-el-Krim, or Marcus Garvey.[1] If we have rarely seen or heard about the history of international law beyond the West, have we missed something?

If it happens that you are also one of the many international lawyers who have studied, practised or lived somewhere outside the West, or if you are simply curious about the non-Western world, you might have asked yourself about the history of international law in your own, or adoptive, non-Western country or region. Sometimes, in front of your Western colleagues, you might have invoked a number of contributions that lawyers from your own place have made to the development of international law.[2] At other times, you may have evoked the ideas of your local predecessors, to proudly distance yourself from the darkest passages of our discipline's Western past. But most probably, you have hardly thought about the history of international law in your own non-Western country or region and about the international lawyers that have preceded you, as part of the history of international in general – the real history unmediated by contributions and unapologetic about its darkest passages.

[1] See Maps 3 and 4.

[2] Latin Americans are particularly apt to praise their regional contributions. Just to mention two examples, see J. M. Yepes, 'La contribution de l'Amérique latine au développement du droit international public et privé, *RdC* 32 (1930/II), 691–799; M. Kohen, 'La contribución de América Latina al desarrollo progresivo del derecho internacional en materia territorial', *Anuario de derecho internacional*, 17 (2001), 57–77.

One may think about the history of international law in Africa, Asia, Latin America or Russia as minor or local histories. Since there are many non-Europeans in the international field, these histories may be valuable as a kind of non-Western cultural heirloom. Retrieving histories about lesser-known lawyers whose work has been forgotten, could serve to redress a historical injustice. But if we end up only with local narratives, we would have to leave the writing of the general history to others. We would have to leave the real history to those like Wilhelm Grewe – the influential post-World War German diplomat and historian of international law – who, adopting the perspective of the Western centres of power and prestige, write the universal history of international law.[3] This book deals with the matter of local stories, but shows that local stories are part of a common history of international law in which the centres and peripheries of the world are intertwined in relations of domination and resistance. It shows that the international law we deem universal and Western is in fact heterogeneous and global. One should therefore care about these stories because they explain the general history of international law.

For example, while conventional histories of international law mention only in passing the Second Hague Peace Conference of 1907 as a step towards the institution of international tribunals, I will retrieve a debate ensuing during the conference between Western and non-Western jurists. Western jurists advocated a court with larger representation of judges from Western great powers. Non-Western international lawyers opposed the court since the proposed method of selection of judges violated the principle of sovereign equality. I will suggest that the professional disputes between supporters and opponents of the court, between the American and Brazilian delegates, James Brown Scott and Ruy Barbosa, as well as the critique of Barbosa's position that followed, by prominent jurists like John Westlake and Max Huber, were central to the development of international law, and crucial in understanding the transition from classical to modern international law. Huber and others blamed Barbosa's exaggerated reliance on absolute sovereignty for The Hague's failure to establish the first permanent international court. Thus, a consensus emerged around the idea that a critique of absolute sovereignty, an essential element of modern international law, was needed if permanent international organizations had to be established. Remembering the

[3] W. Grewe, *Epochen der Völkerrechtsgeschichte* (Baden-Baden: Nomos, 1984), *The epochs of international law* (trans. and rev. Michael Byers, Berlin: Walter de Gruyter, 2000).

story about Barbosa will help to dispel conventional narratives in which the move from absolute sovereignty to the critique of sovereignty, and generally the shift from classical to modern international law, comes as a progression towards a more developed and peaceful international society. It suggests that the transition from classical to modern international law was in the interest of the great powers and it explains why the modern legal discourse was detrimental to the non-Western world, since, for instance, rather than limiting sovereignty in relation to military interventions outside the West, it added new justifications in the name of the interests of the 'international community'.

This book advances three broad claims regarding the relevance that interactions between Western and non-Western states, more specifically, between centre and periphery, had for the general history of international law. First, the book explains the geographical expansion of international law; showing that during the second half of the nineteenth century, non-Western jurists appropriated classical international law, transforming European international law into a universal regime. Second, it explains the transition from classical to modern international law, at the turn of the century, as a process in which state sovereignty was reconceptualized to make room for international organizations, not just to prevent war, but also to justify imperialism. Third, the book explains the fall of the standard of civilization, during the interwar period, through semi-peripheral engagements with modern legal thought. The dissolution of the standard is crucial to understand, for it allowed later during the second post-War, the re-emergence of a right to self-determination.

Each of these three claims disputes conventional wisdom about the history of international law. The first challenges the idea that international law became a legal regime of global validity by way of simple geographic expansion when new states were admitted after meeting membership requirements, or by way of imperial imposition. The second claim challenges the idea that the transition from classical to modern international legal thought marked progress after international lawyers' realization that classical international law failed to prevent the First World War. And the third claim challenges the idea that during the interwar period self-determination did not become a reality because it was only a political postulate. There is a common thread in these three challenges. Whereas the conventional view gives greater prominence to Western protagonists, in the stories behind these three claims, roles are reversed. In these stories non-Western nations and states and their lawyers, activists and politicians have agency. We will see them using international law to resist and in the process we will see them transforming international law. But we will also see the limits of international law, for we will see the efforts to realize law's emancipatory potential again and again defeated.

The fact that we are quite ignorant about these non-Western stories of international law's past is revealing today. In this regard, as the editors of one of the most ambitious works in our contemporary discipline, Bardo Fassbender and Anne Peters, have put it, a '"living bond" between past and present' emerges.[4] This 'living bond' surfaces not just when we finally learn that some of the present international ideas and doctrines have non-Western origins and contributors, although, this realization may offer interesting lessons for those who continue using international law in non-Western locations today. More importantly, the 'living bond' exists between a silent past and the nature of contemporary international law; it is about understanding that the ignorance of our non-Western past is not accidental. The conventional historical narrative about the history of international law is politically relevant today, for it performs an ideological function, it universalizes and legitimizes the particular Western standpoint. If the stories in this book succeed in challenging the Western standpoint from which the past is conventionally written today, they may clear up space for new and more emancipatory international legal practices tomorrow.

An intellectual history: ideas to change rules

A history of the relationship between Western and non-Western states and lawyers, between centre and periphery, could certainly adopt different forms. Some, for example, have presented chronological successions of authors and schools of thought within a general narrative of progression.[5] Others, particularly popular among international lawyers and diplomats, write monographs on a history of an individual international legal norm,

[4] B. Fassbender and A. Peters, 'Introduction: towards a global history of international law' in B. Fassbender and A. Peters (eds.), *The Oxford handbook of the history of international law*, (Oxford University Press, 2012), p. 3.

[5] See e.g. A. G. de Lapradelle, *Maitres et doctrines du droit des gens* (Paris: Les Editions internationals, 1950); E. Reibstein, *Völkerrecht; eine Geschichte seiner Ideen in Lehre und Praxis* (Freiburg: K. Alber, 1958); A. Truyol y Serra, 'L'expansion de la société internationale aux XIXe et XXe siècles', *RdC*, 116 (1965/I), 89–179. For a more recent example, see D. Gaurier, *Histoire du droit international: auteurs, doctrines et développement de l'antiquité à l'aube de la période contemporaine* (Presses universitaires de Rennes, 2005).

doctrine or institution, to which they have devoted most of their careers.[6] Less frequent, though probably more influential are works that subordinate the development of international law to the dynamics of international power, thus presenting a history of the involvement of powerful states in the development of international law.[7] More recently, the field of international law in general has witnessed a turn to intellectual history. Shifting the attention away from states, rules and institutions, leading scholars have turned to historical explorations of the international legal profession or discipline of international law.[8] These works have revitalized the study of the history of international law, exploring international lawyers' professional sensibilities and political dispositions, that is, how jurists and practitioners have, at different historical moments, conceived and understood international law and their own professional projects.[9]

This book is part of this trend in international legal scholarship, but it is an intellectual history with a different purpose. It considers the intellectual footprint of non-Western international lawyers in relation to the transformation of concrete international rules and institutions. Non-Western international lawyers had no special interest in international legal thought as such. They rather appropriated the discourse of international law and intervened in professional debates with the intention of changing existing international legal rules, doctrines and institutions. Late nineteenth-century Japanese legal scholar Tsurutaro Senga,

[6] Let me just offer one example taken from the field of international adjudication. A significant number of studies about the history of international adjudication have been written by international judges, practitioners and diplomats, who with a strong presentist bent construct a narrative of the past based on the standing of international judicial institutions today. See e.g. S. Rosenne, *The Hague Peace Conferences of 1899 and 1907 and international arbitration: reports and documents* (The Hague: T. M. C. Asser, 2001); R. Higgins, 'The Hague Peace Conference as a milestone in the development of international law' in Y. Daudet (ed.), *Topicality of the 1907 Hague conference, the second peace conference (Actualité de la conférence de La Haye de 1907, deuxième conférence de la paix)* (Leiden: Nijhoff, 2008), pp. 29–40; A. Cançado Trindade, 'The presence and participation of Latin America at the Second Hague Peace Conference of 1907' in *ibid.*, pp. 51–84.

[7] Grewe, *Epochen*; A. Nussbaum, *A concise history of the law of nations* (New York: Macmillan, 1954).

[8] On the turn to intellectual history, see I. Hueck, 'The discipline of the history of international law. New trends and methods on the history of international law', *Journal of the History of International Law*, 3 (2001) and R. Bandeira Galindo, 'Martti Koskenniemi and the historiographical turn in international law', *EJIL*, 16 (2005), 539–59.

[9] See Koskenniemi, *Gentle civilizer* and D. Kennedy, 'International law and the nineteenth century: history of an illusion', *Nordic Journal of International Law*, 65 (1996), 385–420.

for example, offered an internal critique of the standard of civilization, highlighting its scientific inconsistency, in order to denounce the regime of consular jurisdiction in Japan.[10]

Western jurists, in turn, repeatedly opposed the legal ideas held by the newcomers as well as their attempts to change international rules and doctrines. Edwin Borchard (1884–1951), an American professor at Yale who had extensively written about diplomatic protection, for example, openly rejected the report Gustavo Guerrero drafted for the Codification Conference of 1930, which limited small states' scope of responsibility. The differences between Borchard and Guerrero were not just conceptual differences about the scope and nature of state responsibility. They reflected, I will argue, the different positions they inhabited, the position from the core and semi-periphery of the world.

Seen from the peripheries

Unlike conventional Eurocentric histories, this book has been written from the specific perspective of the non-Western world. More specifically, the book looks at semi-peripheral states, diplomats, activists, politicians, rebels and of course international lawyers. The semi-periphery occupies a particular position in the international system. From a world system perspective, the organization of the international world depends on the establishment of a global division of labour.[11] States at the world's core not only set the terms of global production and exchange, but also reap most benefits through surplus extraction. Conversely, the periphery encounters the world division of labour as given, producing the primary goods that the centre requires, with narrow profits, for these goods are subjected to unfavourable terms of exchange. The relationship between centre and periphery is not fixed, but historically fluid. The semi-periphery specifically describes those states that have acquired some margin of autonomy to insert themselves strategically in the global economy and that aspire to move upwards, but that because of geopolitical or economic reasons still do not amass enough power to become part of the world's core. The

10 T. Senga, *Gestaltung und Kritik der heutigen Konsulargerichtbarkeit in Japan* (Berlin: R. L. Prager, 1897).

11 On world system theory I have followed: I. Wallerstein, *World-systems analysis: an introduction* (Durham, NC: Duke University Press, 2004) and F. H. Cardoso and E. Faletto, *Dependency and development in Latin America* (Berkeley: University of California Press, 1979).

concept of a world system, with its centres, peripheries and semi-peripheries, does not predetermine every single event happening within the international structure. These are rather analytical categories to understand the international political economy in its totality. By the same token, I heuristically use these categories to shed light on international law's global historical patterns.

For law to govern interstate relations on a global scale, economic or political interactions had first to develop between polities across the globe. It was during the nineteenth century that international relations intensified and attained global scope, when European states, especially Britain, and the United States led the expansion of the modern world economy. Through economic and military means, states at the centre of the world system extended their influence globally. Yet, these states also made use of legal discourse to give stability, predictability and legitimacy to their global expansion and to the privileged position they had attained. Publicists belonging to states located at the centre reconceptualized the law of nations to tackle the new international reality, moving legal thinking in the direction of positivism and developing doctrines to justify unequal treatment vis-à-vis the periphery. I will use the idea that the world system has a centre to describe this reality, that is, the reality of international legal thought has been developed to shape the rules and doctrines that sustained and legitimized the privileged position of states that were behind the expansion of the world system. It also describes the production and circulation of knowledge, for international legal thought produced at the centre becomes the dominant thought, as scholars from the core become the most important international law thinkers.

On the other hand, peoples at the periphery have been coercively inserted into the world economy in a position of dependence, they have experienced international law as bare embodiment of Western power. Giving legal basis to the acquisition of overseas territories and colonial rule, in relation to the periphery, the history of international law includes some of its darkest passages – let us recall only the partition of Africa in the Berlin Conference of 1884–1885.[12] To the periphery, international law did offer limited, though important avenues for resistance. Using international law made sense only to peoples under a colony, mandate or protectorate who were able to fight against direct foreign rule, organizing

[12] See Anghie, *Imperialism*, pp. 90–114.

a diplomatic offensive against the foreign power using international legal arguments, through their own activists or legal experts, or hiring lawyers, and, as we will see, mostly to support the resort to violent resistance.

This book explores some of the rather exceptional cases in which international law could be actively used in peripheral locations: we will see, for example, Rif rebel leader Abd-el-Krim appealing to the international community and the League, and making use of international legal arguments, in order to legitimize armed resistance and internationalize the struggle for independence against Spain and France. This book, however, focuses mostly on semi-peripheral states and their international lawyers. In the semi-periphery, international law played a distinctive role.[13] Relative economic and military strength, geographical distance, geopolitical irrelevance, or other contingent reasons, meant that semi-peripheral nations were able to prevent or resist direct and formal colonial subjugation. Yet core states were left with a vast margin to exercise informal power over semi-peripheral states, including direct force if necessary. The latter states turned to international law in the hopes of narrowing the scope of power core states could legitimately exercise over their territory. For example, European states regularly intervened in the semi-periphery, exercising diplomatic protection over their nationals, at times using direct military force, as in the 1900 allied intervention in China to quell the Boxer rebellion and the 1902 Venezuelan blockade to recover debt. Latin Americans, as we will see, turned to international law to resist, codifying the principle of non-intervention in the Montevideo Convention of 1933.

Why did semi-peripheral elites turn to international law, rather than turning inwards in the search of domestic discourses to resist foreign intervention? There is an obvious reason in that international law was used by the very same powers intervening in the semi-periphery. Chances of resisting by playing according to the rules of the powerful were certainly higher than treating international law as a regional discourse – as it actually was – and thus seeking redress in local political or moral traditions, based for instance on a tributary system or even in peaceful coexistence. However, there were additional reasons why internalizing international law was a preferred choice.

Foreign law as well as international law was not unfamiliar for semi-peripheral elites. Participating at intermediate points in global chains of

[13] I will use the term 'peripheries' in plural, to refer to the periphery and semi-periphery taken as a whole, and will use the singular to refer to each of the two as distinctive spheres.

exchange, as producers of primary commodities and basic manufacture and services, the fortunes of the semi-periphery were deeply intertwined to the core through dependent relations of trade, finance and investment, which, once established, were governed by law.[14] But more importantly, semi-peripheral elites across the globe were generally modernizing elites, for which internalizing international law was simply part of a wider strategy to confront Western technological and military dominance by reforming traditional state and society.

In semi-peripheral locations where the coalition of forces in favour of modernization was strong, reform went beyond establishing links with the world economy, reaching political and social institutions. In particular, legal reform entailed not just introducing modern laws, but also training elites, at home and abroad, to become experts in Western law, including international law. Meiji Japan, as we will see, was the paradigmatic example.

The interaction between core and periphery has not been commonly used to examine the history of international law. Mainstream lawyers rarely consider the dynamic between law and politics in the development of the international legal order. Antônio Cançado Trindade, a renowned Brazilian scholar and ICJ judge, for example, reflecting on the inclusion of peripheral states in the Hague Conferences as indication of the universality of international law, rejected the idea of 'periphery' as a useful category. Cançado Trindade declared: 'to my mind, "peripheral States" is an expression for political scientists, not for jurists. In my understanding, it is the principles and norms, the rights and obligations, rather than the interests and strategies that are proper concern of jurists.'[15]

Let me therefore defend the idea that understanding international politics, interests and strategies matter to understand the history of international law. The exploration in this book suggests that the international lawyer, although working with a discourse that claims universality, sees the world from the prism of the particular geopolitical location where situated, and thus understands international law differently, if situated

[14] See L. Benton, *Law and colonial cultures: legal regimes in world history, 1400–1900* (Cambridge University Press, 2001).

[15] Cançado Trindade, 'The presence and participation', pp. 111–12. Otherwise, Cançado Trindade incorrectly believes centre and periphery to be geographic categories: 'as the earth is round, depending where you look from at the *mappa mundi*, all the regions of the world may appear peripheral' (*ibid.*).

at the core, periphery or semi-periphery.[16] Exploring the strategic use of international legal arguments in the peripheries of the world, the book argues not only that international law was used by peripheral states in order to pursue their particular interests, but also that through these peripheral uses, specifically through the appropriation of international legal thinking, fundamental rules and doctrines of international law changed. Sometimes changes in rules and doctrines improved peripheral states' position in the world system, challenging and limiting the impact of economic and military power in international relations, for instance, abrogating unequal treaties, or codifying non-intervention.

Let me also caution that adopting a semi-peripheral perspective follows simply heuristic purposes. There is no interest in determining with absolute certainty the position of different states in the world system. Rather the interest lies in the stories that a peripheral perspective allows us to discover, namely the stories illustrating the impact that the interaction between centre and peripheries had in the development of international law. The history that emerges is the history of an international law with hybrid origins and multiple sites of articulation, an international law holding the promise for a better future for smaller nations while repeatedly breaking that promise: this I will call *mestizo* international law.

A *mestizo* international law

The term *mestizo* evokes international law's hybrid origins without ignoring the privileged position the Western legal tradition has occupied and the role Western power has had throughout its history. *Mestizo*, in its common usage, refers to the ethnic groups originating during the conquest and colonization of the new world by the mix between European and indigenous peoples. With a European father and an indigenous mother, the situation of the *mestizo* is riddled by questions of identity and belonging.[17] In cultural terms, a vivid token of colonial domination in the eyes of his mother's indigenous people, a return to pure pre-colonial worldviews is for the *mestizo* either impossible or at most purely rhetorical. The rejection of the mixed child by the European father only increases

[16] I have worked out the legal implications that taking a semi-peripheral orientation into account would have for a current international problem: A. Becker Lorca, 'Rules for the "global war on terror": implying consent and presuming conditions for intervention', *New York University Journal of International Law and Politics*, 45 (2012), 1–95.

[17] L. Zea, *Pensamiento positivista latinoamericano* (Caracas, Venezuela: Biblioteca Ayacucho, 1980), vol. I, p. xiv.

the eagerness and determination of the *mestizo* to master and plant into new solid the paternal Western tradition.

The expression *mestizo international law* reminds us of the historical association between Western colonial expansion and European international law. While the world was drawn together by Western forces, European international legal thought offered a discourse to justify and give stability to European expansion. But *mestizo* captures another aspect of the history of European expansion, namely, the hybrid origins of the international law that emerged with the encounter between the Western and non-Western worlds and the globalisation of European international legal thinking. *Mestizo* conveys one of the central arguments of the book: international law became an order of global geographical scope throughout the appropriation of the European legal tradition by non-Western jurists.

As international law became global, not only new states became members of the international society, but also a new type of practitioner entered the discipline of international law. Let us imagine the situation of Ueno and Guo, dressed in Western attire, participating for the first time in international conferences. Or let us picture Greek, Latin American or other non-European lawyers proudly affirming to be more European than Europeans themselves. We might interpret the situation of the non-Western international lawyer as similar to the experiences of rejection and belonging common to the *mestizo*. For example, V. K. Wellington Koo, the most prominent Chinese international lawyer involved in the revision of the unequal treaties, was regarded as both a foreigner and Chinese: 'Westerners think of Koo as a Chinese, and Chinese think of him as a Westerner'.[18]

Foregrounding the peripheral location of non-Western jurists will explain their modernizing and Westernizing ideology, their faithful attachment to the international legal tradition, their obsession with achieving recognition at home and contributing to the international legal tradition. The fascination at the prospect of contributing to the development of international law, as shown below, is not the monopoly of Latin Americans. This trait, I would suggest, is characteristic of the semi-peripheral jurist at large, an expression of the unstable and contradictory affiliations of someone like Koo or Alvarez.[19] Peter Holquist,

[18] P. Chu, *V. K. Wellington Koo: a case study of China's diplomat and diplomacy of nationalism, 1912–1966* (Hong Kong: Chinese University Press, 1981), pp. 3 and 11.

[19] See A. Becker Lorca, 'Alejandro Alvarez situated: subaltern modernities and modernisms that subvert', *Leiden Journal of International Law*, 19 (2006), 879–930.

for example, in a study of nineteenth-century international law in Russia finds that: 'Martens frequently overstates his own role in international affairs – following the Second Hague Conference, he was crushed when he failed to receive his anticipated Nobel Peace Prize'.[20] Similarly, Lauri Mälksoo's work has suggested a linguistic and mental divide between Western and Russian international legal scholarship, which gives the impression of Russian jurists as living under the illusion of Russia's intellectual self-sufficiency. The flipside effect of the mental and linguistic divide is Russian scholars' overemphasis of the contribution of Russia to the development of international law: 'The ever-returning *Leitmotiv*, especially since 1917, is that Russia and Russian scholars were "at least as good as scholars in the West", and generally "played an important role" in the history of international law and its scholarship.'[21]

The term *mestizo* might capture not only the dialectic of rejection and belonging, but also the hopes that peripheral international lawyers have placed on a new syncretism guiding their efforts to build an international legal order more attentive to the cultural, political or economic particularities of smaller and less powerful states, a legal order which will lay the foundations for a more just and peaceful world.

Between centre and periphery, between the international and the local

Overcoming the narrow Eurocentric outlook of most histories, this history brings to the present a *mestizo* international law. A Eurocentric perspective generates a distortion in the historical narrative, a distortion that overemphasizes the centrality of Western contexts of practice – including authors, ideas, and events – and underemphasizes the practice of international law outside the West.[22] But this history is not simply about a greater number of non-Western nations and lesser known lawyers; it tries to correct the Eurocentric distortion by examining the interaction between the centre and the semi-periphery in the history of international law.

[20] Peter Holquist, 'The Russian Empire as a "civilised nation": international law as principle and practice in imperial Russia, 1874–1878', The National Council for Eurasian and East European Research (2004), 11.

[21] L. Mälksoo, 'The history of international legal theory in Russia: a civilisational dialogue with Europe', *European Journal of International Law*, 19 (2008), 215.

[22] See A. Becker Lorca, 'Eurocentrism in the history of international law' in Fassbender and Peters, *Oxford handbook*, pp. 1034–1057, 1053.

The interaction between centre and peripheries is marked by a specific tension of great historical significance. This tension emerges when nations located at the centre and the semi-periphery pursue, through the language of international law, different goals and interests. We will see many examples of this divergence. One of these was the striking disparity between semi-peripheral hopes that the Paris Peace Conference of 1919 could deliver self-government to those under foreign rule and the unwillingness by the great powers to recognize self-determination beyond the West. But this tension not only reflects divergent interests and goals. It arises because international lawyers located at the centre and the peripheries see the world with different eyes.

For example, we will explore the work of French jurist Albert de Lapradelle supporting a right of intervention by Western powers in China. Lapradelle based this right not on selfish reasons, such as protecting foreign residents, but as a social duty deriving from an interdependent international community. Lapradelle's discussion of a right of intervention was consonant with the way he perceived China and the West to be radically different: 'Western civilisation, which is movement and progress, runs up against the Oriental civilisation, too contemplative for not being sluggish, too fatalistic for not being dull.'[23] Semi-peripheral lawyers are generally well aware of the role that perceptions about the non-Western world have on the foundation and interpretation of legal rules and institutions. Wellington Koo's book on the legal status of aliens in China, for example, tackles directly this problem. Although in recent years several monographs have appeared – Koo notes in the preface – 'I am not aware of any work' treating the position of foreigners 'from the Chinese point of view'.[24] Throughout the book Koo sets out to dispel various misconceptions. If extraterritorial judicial privileges enjoyed by aliens were based on the alleged 'sanguinary injustice' of Chinese law, Koo corrects the misperception, pointing out that 'penal laws of China, as enforced in the eighteenth and the first part of the nineteenth century, were no severer than those in force in England during the same period'.[25] Koo concludes the book with a call for cooperation between the Chinese government and the treaty powers to revise the extraterritorial regime. However, Koo's argument does not depend only on the invalidity of extraterritoriality based on the modernization of Chinese penal law. In his conclusion Koo also

[23] A. de Lapradelle, 'La Question Chinoise', *RGDIP*, 8 (1901), 272–340, 277.
[24] V. K. W. Koo, *The status of aliens in China* (New York: Columbia University, 1912), p. 8.
[25] *Ibid.*, pp. 80, 89.

brings to life an image of China diametrically different from the image pictured by Lapradelle:

> in spite of their frequent allegations that the Chinese are exclusive and anti-foreign, foreigners in China enjoy very many rights and privileges which are not accorded to aliens in other countries... It is true that this special status is guaranteed to them by treaties... yet... their peaceful enjoyment... has been made possible only by the favourable disposition... of the Government and people of China.[26]

There is a simple reason why, in addition to doctrinal arguments, international lawyers at the core and semi-periphery, like Lapradelle and Koo, are ready to invoke different images about the world. Extraterritoriality, the international community, sovereign autonomy, self-determination, a right or duty to intervene, etc. are all political principles as well as legal institutions subject to a wide range of interpretations. These terms can be seen and interpreted from the centre and the peripheries. The discussion of the 'Chinese question' by Lapradelle and Koo illustrates this type of indeterminacy and the use of images and perceptions to produce interpretative stability. Eurocentric histories are unable to recognize this type of indeterminacy because they assume international law to be one and universal. For example, the late Ian Brownlie, a renowned British international lawyer, defended the unity of international law in a discussion about 'the role of the ASIL [American Society of International Law] in the further development of the existing college of international lawyers'.[27] Brownlie warns about the 'need to reduce the fissiparous tendencies of different political groupings of states, tendencies that threaten the very existence of general international law'.[28] Recalling the main representative of this threat, Alejandro Alvarez, the Chilean ICJ judge who defended the existence of a regional Latin American international law, Brownlie affirmed that 'in practice such regional tendencies prove insubstantial and small in extent'.[29]

Even if international law is believed to be one, even if international lawyers have conventionally thought about it in universal terms, namely deracinated from the particularities of domestic history, politics or culture, international lawyers are not in fact uprooted from the local context they inhabit and thus completely acculturated in a neutral international

[26] *Ibid.*, p. 350.

[27] I. Brownlie, 'The President's roundtable', *American Society International Law Proceedings*, 13 (2001), 13, 14.

[28] *Ibid.* [29] *Ibid.*

sphere. The international sphere is not sustained in a vacuum. It resides in places. Even if international lawyers share a cosmopolitan professional identity, enacting, interpreting, applying or disregarding international legal norms, all these professional activities occur in concrete locations with their own history and with their own social, political and cultural particularities.

For example, confronting an international crisis, a controversy between states, or a doctrinal problem, the international lawyer, let us assume, will overcome the particularities of strategy and interest and will, as judge Cançado Trindade would like it, focus on 'principles and norms', 'rights and obligations'.[30] To do so, the international lawyer will consult some renowned scholar, most probably a professor writing in a European language, whose authority will most probably be guaranteed by the prestige of the European university where she, but most probably he, is based. Perhaps, the name of some Western city will be brought up, a metonymy for a rule of international law – Paris, Utrecht, Locarno, San Francisco. Perhaps, an ICJ precedent will be cited, or a contribution by an international organization will be remembered. Each of these authorities, rules and institutions are part of the international world. But, in addition to a universal life, legal concepts, rules, authorities or institutions have also an ordinary life of politics and interest.

In The Hague, for example, the ICJ delivers justice to the world. In practice, however, Alain Pellet, a prominent French practitioner, describes his work representing states in front of the ICJ in much more mundane terms: 'In the small world of public international law we may at present speak of the "mafia" of the International Court of Justice... There is only a small number of persons who revolve around the World Court... The statistics show, on a purely empirical basis, the indisputable existence of an "invisible Bar" of the International Court of Justice.'[31] That international law and the international legal profession are actually embedded

[30] Cançado Trindade, 'The presence and participation', p. 111.

[31] A. Pellet, 'The role of the international lawyer in international litigation' in C. Wickremasinghe (ed.), *The International lawyer as practitioner* (London: British Institute of International and Comparative Law, 2000), p. 147. Interestingly (*ibid.*): 'This quasi-monopoly of a dozen of persons is sometimes criticized – and I can understand that colleagues, who are excellent international lawyers but have never appeared before the Court, aspire to do so. Not only for financial reasons [...] but also and first of all because of the legal, political, historical and intellectual interest [...] At the same time, I advocate some continuity... as a result of my experience: acting as Counsel before the World Court is a profession.'

in concrete contexts is an obvious point. What is interesting are the ways in which international lawyers have understood the relationship between the international sphere and the profession's concrete contexts of articulation. For most international lawyers the relationship between the international and the local is generally smooth and passes unnoticed, for they imagine their own context to be within the universal. The closer to the world's centres of political power and intellectual prestige, the likelier it is for the international lawyer to experience that overlap.

Famously, Oscar Schachter coined the term 'invisible college' to describe a professional community of international lawyers, including both practitioners and scholars, that, though dispersed throughout the world, have been in fact united under the common endeavour of extending internationalist ideas into governmental channels.[32] Conventionally, international lawyers have considered that differences between various schools of thought or approaches have not undermined the unity of this invisible college, for they express methodological or theoretical preferences, rather than cultural, religious or ideological discrepancies.[33] Given that fundamental ideological disagreements are ruled out, and that the most important schools of thought are founded on methodological or theoretical debates driven by European and American international lawyers, the invisible college's intellectual horizon seems to be confined within the limits of the centres of the Western world.[34]

Moreover, international lawyers at the core tend to construct the cosmopolitan ideal of the international in the narrow geographic and intellectual coordinates of their own locations of practice. For example, in 1997 the *Institut des Hautes Etudes Internationales* and *EJIL* convened a conference in Paris, to discuss the current state of international law and

[32] 'The professional community of international lawyers . . . though dispersed throughout the world and engaged in diverse occupations, constitutes a kind of invisible college . . . [that] extends into the sphere of government, resulting in a *pénétration pacifique* of ideas from the nongovernmental into official channels . . . acting in the dual capacity of objective scientist and governmental advocate.' O. Schachter, 'The invisible college of international lawyers', *Northwestern University Law Review*, 72 (1977–8), 217–18.

[33] See D. Kennedy, 'When renewal repeats: thinking against the box', *New York Journal of International Law and Politics*, 32 (2000), 335–500.

[34] In 1999, for example, ASIL organised a 'Symposium on method in international law'. Scholars representing a variety of approaches – from legal positivism, to international relations, feminist jurisprudence, etc. – were invited to contribute. See S. Ratner and A. Slaughter, 'Appraising the methods of international law: a prospectus for readers', *AJIL*, 93 (1999), 291. Scholars representing approaches without roots in the European and American intellectual and professional milieu – like Third World Approaches to International Law (TWAIL) – were conspicuous by their absence.

celebrate the work of Wolfgang Friedmann. A French jurist, Charles Leben, director of the *Institut*, explains that the idea of organizing a symposium bringing together a group of European and American scholars, came from the perception that 'international legal culture had become less "plural", less diversified, less truly "international" than in Friedmann's time'. This is how Leben describes Friedmann's internationalist outlook:

> this man of culture . . . an author equally at ease in the French school of exegesis, the German school of public law, or in British and American legal scholarship, exercised great fascination over the students. Similarly, his [book] *The Changing Structure of International Law*, where George Scelle is cited and discussed just as much as Jessup, Lauterpacht as well as Kelsen, Brierly and Geny, and where judgments of the *Conseil d'Etat* are referred to as often as those of the United States Supreme Court or the House of Lords, offered a model of an internationalist who, to paraphrase Dworkin, took the adjective 'international' in the expression 'international law' seriously.[35]

Stretching from both shores of the north Atlantic to both banks of the Rhine, the conventional contours of the international sphere are in fact quite narrow. Though not narrower than the borders one could delineate if considering, for example, the international law books that are reviewed in the discipline's main journals, in terms of publishers, academic affiliations of the authors, or the languages in which these books have been written. And Leben's narrow outlook is not unique.[36]

These examples suggest that international lawyers at the core do not experience the interaction between the international and the local as a relevant dimension of their professional practice, for they experience their local contexts as embodying the universal. Although lawyers like Brownlie or Pellet have routinely advised and represented peripheral states in

[35] C. Leben, 'The changing structure of international law revisited. By way of introduction', *EJIL*, 8 (1997), 399–400 (footnote omitted). Leben's narrow internationalism is puzzling if one remembers that he is director of the *Institut des Hautes Etudes Internationales* which was cofounded by Alejandro Alvarez, the Chilean jurist who became famous for defending the existence of a regional Latin American international law.

[36] E.g. Armin von Bogdandy and Sergio Dellavalle have described the main conceptual positions held by contemporary international lawyers as divided in two competing paradigms: 'particularism and universalism'. Although they recognize that the two paradigms represent theories 'primarily coming from the Western tradition', they see no problem in exploring them 'to support intercultural dialogue on international law' and advocating universalism 'for all humans to strive for an international public order that efficiently safeguards universal principles and solves global problems': A. Bogdandy and S. Dellavalle, 'Universalism and particularism as paradigms of international law', IILJ Working Paper (2008/3), pp. 1, 57.

front of international tribunals, lawyers at the core have only exceptionally realized that the peripheries exist as a distinctive context of practice and that semi-peripheral international lawyers may pursue their own legal projects independently from their influence.

The semi-peripheral finds an own voice and the core jurist becomes anxious: the debate about international law's origin

Only occasionally core jurists realize that the peripheries exist as a distinctive realm of international legal practice. As Brownlie's remarks about Alvarez suggest, this occurs when semi-peripheral states or semi-peripheral jurists articulate legal ideas or interpretations that challenge dominant understandings about international law in the core. When Cançado Trindade defends the pre-eminence of norms over interests, he will be seen as an international lawyer who happens to be Brazilian. In fact, there has been no shortage of semi-peripheral judges at the ICJ, or semi-peripheral members at the *Institut de Droit International* and the International Law Association, for their presence reassures the universal character of the court and professional organizations. But when another Brazilian like Ruy Barbosa who at the Hague Conference of 1907 opposes and finally defeats the project to create the first permanent court, because the equality of smaller states is not respected, or when an ICJ judge like Alvarez invokes a Latin American international law to base his dissenting opinion, the international lawyer at the core tends to downplay the semi-peripheral ideas as deviations. Regional tendencies proved insubstantial – responded Brownlie. Another British international lawyer, John Westlake, as we will see, harshly criticized the participation of newly admitted states at The Hague Conference of 1907. Quoting a newspaper account describing Barbosa's closing speech as a 'fierce' exposition of equality, Westlake sarcastically remarked: 'perhaps it might have been less fierce if the conception had not been pampered'.[37]

Historians of international law have been particularly irritated by semi-peripheral lawyers' attempts to challenge the received historical canon. Studies disputing the idea that international law had an exclusively Western origin appeared during the 1960s and 1970s, mostly by authors from

[37] J. Westlake, 'The Hague Conferences' in *The collected papers of John Westlake on public international law* (Cambridge University Press, 1914), 531–67, 537 (originally published in the *Quarterly Review*, 414 (1908), 224–51).

newly independent nations.[38] A Dutch jurist and historian Jan H. Verzijl, for example, responded to the challenge, affirming with vehemence that international law is 'essentially the product of the European mind' and that in consequence, it has been '"received"... lock, stock and barrel by American and Asian states'.[39] Moreover, Verzijl largely ridiculed the idea that reception could be anything more than non-Europeans adopting '*en bloc* the traditional law of nations as it had developed throughout the course of Western European history'.[40] Verzijl explicitly considers international law outside Europe to be a misrepresentation of the original:

> This historic manifestation [the dominance of Western European ideas] is accentuated by the fact that we see the new constellation of Asian States operating with legal concepts extracted from, or lying at the basis of, modern international law without having first duly mentally digested them, which necessarily results in the distortion and misunderstanding of elementary legal issues such as the limitations of national sovereignty and the sphere of domestic jurisdiction.[41]

As international law's scope of validity expanded, Western international lawyers had to adapt to a new reality. The irruption of new states and jurists from the non-Western world opened international law to new cultural horizons that could potentially lead to new understandings and interpretations. For many Western lawyers, this was a source of great apprehension. At the beginning of the post-war period and even before decolonization, Alfred Verdross, the famous Austrian jurist, for example, believed that the expansion of international law represented a danger because new states that never belonged to the Christian-European culture may follow legal attitudes that diverge from the Western concept of law.[42] Similarly, Belgian Charles de Visscher believed that international law's expansion weakened the unity of the traditional legal community.[43] More recently, former ICJ judge and British scholar Robert Jennings worried that international law's capacity to harmonize differences between states that share a common cultural substratum could be undermined by the admission of new states. For in a multicultural world, an international law

[38] E.g. T. O. Elias, *Africa and the development of international law* (Leiden: A. W. Sijthoff, 1972). See, in general, Becker Lorca, *Eurocentrism*, pp. 1042–50.

[39] J. H. W. Verzijl, 'Western European influence on the foundations of international law' in J. H. W. Verzijl, *International law in historical perspective* (Leiden: A. W. Sijthoff, 1968), vol. I, p. 442 (originally published in *International Relations*, 1 (1955)).

[40] *Ibid.*, p. 445. [41] *Ibid.*, p. 443.

[42] A. Verdross, *Völkerrecht* (Wien: Springer, 1950), pp. 39 ff.

[43] C. de Visscher, *Théories et réalités en droit international public* (Paris: A. Pédone, 1953), p. 182.

of 'indubitably European and Christian' origin is strained by ideological, economic, religious and cultural differences.[44]

Others worried that the privileged position bestowed by classical international law to Western sovereigns could be lost after the admission of non-Western nations. The German conservative thinker Carl Schmitt, for example, invoked a distinct Western *nomos* to support the claim of European origin and Western nature of international law. More than a system of rules, Schmitt considers the public law of the European interstate system the order of a 'family' of European royal houses, states and nations, a domestic community (*Hausgenossenschaft*) of European peoples. Schmitt bitterly resented that universalization entailed not simply a geographical expansion, but the radical transformation of European public law, the *Jus Publicum Europaeum*, into the 'spaceless universalism' of a liberal international legal order that no longer discriminated between Western and non-Western nations.[45] Even an advocate of sociological jurisprudence like Julius Stone believed that the expansion of international law brought 'a continuous dilution of its content, as it is reinterpreted for the benefit of newcomers'.[46]

Writing a historical narrative centred in the West was one of the core lawyers' defence mechanisms. While semi-peripherals understood the universalization of international law to be a hard-fought victory that had to be secured, in part through a non-Eurocentric historical narrative challenging the historical centrality of the West, finding a European origin was one of Western lawyers' strategies to preserve normative monopoly over international law. A historical narrative about Western origins became central to the claim of the Western nature of international law. For example, in addition to Verzijl, Wilhelm Grewe argued that in spite of its geographic expansion, there is no doubt that Western Christianity forms the core of the international legal community.[47] Grewe articulated a strong

[44] R. Jennings, 'Universal international law in a multicultural world' in M. Bos and I. Brownlie (eds.), *Liber Amicorum for the Rt. Hon. Lord Wilberforce* (Oxford: Clarendon Press, 1987), pp. 40–1.

[45] C. Schmitt, 'Die Auflösung der europäischen Ordnung im "International Law" (1890–1939)' in C. Schmitt, *Staat, Großraum, Nomos. Arbeiten aus den Jahren 1916–1969* (Berlin: Duncker, 1995), pp. 372–87, pp. 373 ff and, generally, C. Schmitt, *Der Nomos der Erde im Völkerrecht des Jus Publicum Europaeum: Im Völkerrecht des Jus Publicum Europaeum* (Berlin: Duncker, 1988), pp. 111–86.

[46] J. Stone, *Quest for survival: the role of law and foreign policy* (Cambridge: Harvard University Press, 1961), p. 88.

[47] W. Grewe, 'Vom europäischen zum universellen Völkerrecht. Zur Frage der Revision des "europazentrischen" Bildes der Völkerrechtsgeschichte', *Zeitschrift für Ausländisches*

defence of his position to counter semi-peripheral criticism of Eurocentric histories of international law.

For example, C. H. Alexandrowicz, a legal scholar and historian of international law who studied at the University of Cracow, moved to London during the Second World War, practising at the Bar by Lincoln's Inn and lecturing at the University of London, and then was appointed professor at the University of Madras where he stayed for ten years, singled out the East Indies as one of the regions where international law originated.[48] South Asian powers governed their interactions based on a tradition that compared to the European – Alexandrowicz argued – was more ancient 'and in no way inferior to notions of European civilisation'.[49] Moreover, Alexandrowicz maintained that between the seventeenth and the eighteenth centuries, East Indian and European sovereigns interacted on relatively equal footing. The series of treaties governing these interactions reflected mutually agreed principles of inter-state dealings, which not only shaped the content of the Law of Nations, but also shaped international law's doctrinal outlook, influencing the intellectual legacy of what is conventionally believed to be a purely European tradition.[50] Western historians have not only neglected these interactions and the influence they exerted on international law. Alexandrowicz points out: 'The orthodox eurocentric view . . . is that most of the Afro-Asian countries joined the Family of Nations as full and equal members only recently, anyhow, not before World War I'.[51] But also, Western historians have vigorously rejected Alexandrowicz's effort to historicize the selfsame notion of an exclusively European law of nations. In particular, they have ignored the claim that before the nineteenth century, international law developed through the legal interactions between European and non-European sovereigns. According to Alexandrowicz, it was only during the course of the nineteenth century, when international law shifted from natural law into positivism, that European international lawyers reconceived international law as exclusively European.[52]

Öffentliches Recht und Völkerrecht, 42 (1982), 449–79, 453 and, in general, Grewe, *Epochen*, Chapter Two, Part Four and pp. 541 ff.

[48] W. A. Steiner, 'Charles Henry Alexandrowicz', *BYIL*, 47 (1975), 269–71.

[49] C. H. Alexandrowicz, *An introduction to the history of the law of nations in the East Indies* (Oxford Clarendon Press, 1967), p. 224.

[50] *Ibid.*, p. 2 and *passim*.

[51] C. H. Alexandrowicz, 'The Afro-Asian world and the law of nations (historical aspects)', *RdC*, 123 (1968), 117–214, 121.

[52] Alexandrowicz, *History East Indies*, pp. 9–10 and 237.

Grewe's answer to Alexandrowicz illustrates the ideological nature of Eurocentric and non-Eurocentric histories. While Alexandrowicz characterizes legal rapports between East Indian and European sovereigns as treaties, Grewe describes them as treaties between 'European seafaring and trading nations' and 'exotic rulers' (*exotischen Herrschern*).[53] Alexandrowicz believed that these treaties, under the universalism of a natural law substratum, influenced the development of international law. Grewe believed that the conception of a law with global validity was necessary to conclude these treaties. But these treaties, Grewe believed, did not change a manifest awareness of European distinctiveness. All European nations, in their inter-governmental relations as well as in cultural (*geistigen*) and political life, believed international law to be primarily an order of the Christian-European family of peoples, valid to govern the conduct between their members.[54] The difference between Alexandrowicz and Grewe – between conceiving polities as sovereigns or as exotic rulers, between interpreting an agreement as a treaty or as an accord of convenience, between understanding the *Jus Publicum Europaeum* as a regional regime or the normative foundation of international law – is not based on a disagreement about the historical material, but a difference on how to read and interpret that material: the difference is ultimately political.

Our ideas about the origin and nature of international law are shaped by historians like Alexandrowicz and Grewe. This narrative is then reproduced in the discipline's main textbooks. Let us briefly focus on one treatise by Lassa Oppenheim (1858–1919), one of the most influential treatises in the English-speaking world. The various editions of Oppenheim's international law offer a good diachronic example.[55] From the first edition of 1905 to the seventh edition of 1948, we may see the progressive expansion of the 'dominion of the Law of Nations', while the Western nature of international law remains constant. As late as 1948, Oppenheim's textbook continues to affirm that 'international law as a law between sovereign and equal states based on the common consent of those states is a product of modern Christian civilisation'.[56]

In 1905, Oppenheim defines international law as the body of rules 'which are considered legally binding by civilised States in their

[53] Grewe, 'Vom europäischen', 452. [54] *Ibid.*

[55] See Map 6 for a visual representation of the expansion of international law according to the definition of the international community in different editions of Oppenheim's treatise.

[56] L. Oppenheim and H. Lauterpacht, *International law, a treatise*, 7th edn, 2 vols. (London: Longmans, 1948), vol. I, p. 68.

intercourse with each other'; adding immediately, in the paragraph that follows, that in its origin, international law is 'essentially a product of Christian civilisation'.[57] Here Oppenheim was repeating the conventional wisdom of the nineteenth century that had the standard of civilization as the doctrine determining membership in the 'family of nations'.[58] At the beginning of the twentieth century it still seemed obvious that the standard of civilization was equivalent to Western civilization. However, determining who was civilized had by then become less obvious. Oppenheim had thus to determine the scope of international law. The list of states admitted into the family of nations included Turkey and Japan.[59] Although making it very clear that 'the Law of Nations is a product of Christian Civilisation' and that it 'originally arose between the States of Christendom only'.[60] On the other hand, Oppenheim rejected the admission of states like Persia, Siam, China, Korea and Abyssinia. Nations that, although having reached a significant level of civilization, their development was deemed insufficient for membership to be granted, for their governments – Oppenheim claims – do not 'understand and carry out the command of the rules of international law'.[61]

In subsequent editions we see new nations being admitted, and at times some reverting back to semi-civilized status, and overall we see the standard of civilization being eroded and international law achieving universal validity. While the 1928 edition prepared by Arnold McNair affirmed that Turkey's position was anomalous, for 'her civilisation fell short of that of the Western States', the seventh edition prepared by Hersch Lauterpacht in 1948 affirms that: 'religion and the controversial test of degree of civilisation have ceased to be, as such, a condition of recognition of the membership of the "family of nations"'.[62] However, the phrase reaffirming the Western origin of international law survived all through the seven editions.[63]

How did the standard become a 'controversial test'? There is, in Oppenheim's treatise, no explanation about the demise of the standard of

[57] L. Oppenheim, *International law, a treatise*, 1st edn, 2 vols. (London: Longmans, 1905), vol. I, pp. 3–4.

[58] *Ibid.*, p. 31. [59] *Ibid.*, p. 33. [60] *Ibid.*, p. 30. [61] *Ibid.*, p. 33.

[62] L. Oppenheim and A. McNair, *International law, a treatise*, 4th edn, 2 vols. (London: Longmans, 1928), vol. I, p. 40; Oppenheim and Lauterpacht, *International law*, vol. I, p. 47.

[63] 'International Law as a law between Sovereign and equal States based on the common consent of these States is a product of Christian civilisation, and may be said to be hardly four hundred years old': Oppenheim, *International law*, vol. I, p. 45; Oppenheim and Lauterpacht, *International law*, vol. I, p. 68.

civilization. *Mestizo* international law offers a historical explanation about the dissolution of the standard, an explanation that focuses on petitions to the Paris Peace Conference and then to the League of Nations demanding self-governance or the end of mandate rule. This explanation also examines the rules developed to admit semi-peripheral states to the League and culminates in the drafting of a definition of statehood in the Montevideo Convention of 1933.

Oppenheim's treatise illustrates one of the problems Eurocentrism imposes on the narration of history. Even though at the beginning of the twentieth century international law governed interactions between civilized states – rather than Christian states as the standard of inclusion was previously defined – even though mid-century international law governed relations between nations admitted according to a formal doctrine of recognition – rather than the standard of civilization – international law continued to be described as a product of Western civilization. That international law's expansion is accompanied with an affirmation of international law's Western origin has practical consequences for the narration of history. The relevant contexts of practice, authors and events all belong to the Western centres of power and intellectual prestige. Thus, we will not learn much about the demise of the standard of civilization if we consult conventional Eurocentric histories. For, the dissolution of the standard – *Mestizo* international law argues – happened in part because of peripheral interventions.

A history of two semi-peripheral sensibilities

This book changes the perspective from which to write a history of international law. It explores the interaction between polities and lawyers from the core and peripheries, and more specifically the interactions in relation to the articulation of international legal thinking. Changing the perspective, one discovers a common semi-peripheral international legal discourse. I will argue that between 1842 and 1933, international lawyers from the semi-periphery developed two distinctive legal discourses and shared two distinctive disciplinary sensibilities. These two sensibilities, as I will explain, correspond to but are also different from the two periods – classical and modern – that are commonly distinguished in the intellectual history of international law. In fact, I will suggest that the two semi-peripheral discourses, that is, a legal consciousness, disciplinary style or professional sensibility, are the semi-peripheral versions or appropriations of nineteenth-century classical international law and twentieth-century modern international law. Between 1842 and 1907, semi-peripheral lawyers shared a sensibility that I describe as *particularistic universalism*. In 1919 this disciplinary sensibility was replaced by another sensibility lasting until the end of the post-war, which I describe as a modernist *style of resistance*.

The classical international law of the nineteenth century, as we will see, was an idea of law governing relations between civilized sovereigns as individuals are governed by contracts. Its central pillars were the principle of sovereign autonomy, the standard of civilization and positivism. Semi-peripherals appropriated the classical discourse, emphasizing the universality of international law for those who fulfilled the requirements of participation. Emphasizing universality, jurists like Carlos Calvo or Kagenori Ueno celebrated their own presence in the professional centres of the West as a sign of the inclusion of their polities.

The classical discourse declined at the turn of the twentieth century when semi-peripheral states no longer succeeded in invoking absolute sovereignty to protect their autonomy and equality or internalizing the standard of civilization to revise unequal treaties. Rather than foregrounding the interests of individual sovereigns, the modern international legal discourse that replaced classical international law foregrounded the interests of the international community. This was not necessarily a welcomed change for semi-peripheral states. For example, interventions in the non-Western world could now be justified under the interests of the international community. Modern semi-peripheral lawyers and activists, however, appropriated again the modern legal discourse in support of the struggle for independence; in doing so they developed a professional *style of resistance*.

PART II · UNIVERSAL INTERNATIONAL LAW

2 Appropriating classical legal thought

The idea that there is or should be law in the international world has inspired a multiplicity of intellectual, professional and institutional projects. At the most basic level, this idea implies that there should be one international law: a single set of legal rules, principles and institutions governing interstate behaviour on a global scale. International law, however, became a global legal order only during the course of the nineteenth century.[1] Before that, according to the prevalent view, international law's range of validity was circumscribed to the interaction between European sovereigns. For international law – both as an idea and as a concrete legal order – was born and developed in seventeenth-century Europe. In consequence, most international lawyers understand that the process through which international law became global involved the expansion of European international law.[2]

[1] One dimension of the geographic expansion of international law is the global treaty-making pattern. Taking Great Britain as an example, Map 1 and Map 2 suggest that treaty relations between Western and non-Western polities increased markedly during the nineteenth century. Map 1 shows that during the 151 years between 1648 (the year when the Treaty of Westphalia was concluded, which is conventionally understood as the treaty inaugurating the European interstate system) and 1799 (the last year of the eighteenth century), Great Britain (England and then Great Britain) concluded seventy treaties with non-European states (excluding the United States and including multilateral treaties between European and non-European states). Map 2 shows that during the nineteenth century, during the hundred years between 1800 and 1899, Great Britian concluded 474 treaties with non-European states. Maps 1 and 2 include treaties between Great Britain and non-European polities regarded as states. The number of treaties would be even greater if treaties are included between Western states and polities regarded as non-sovereign entities (for example, treaties establishing protectorates).

[2] See generally Grewe, 'Vom europäischen' and Grewe, *Epochs*, pp. 445–82 and specifically, for a description of the process of expansion and a typical list of new states, see *ibid.*, pp. 462–3.

This perspective is widely reproduced not only in international law textbooks written by Western authors, but also in the scholarship of non-Western international lawyers. On the former, for example, the ninth edition of *Oppenheim's International Law*, prepared by Robert Jennings and Arthur Watts, affirms:

The old Christian States of Western Europe constituted the original international community within which international law grew up... But gradually the international community expanded by the inclusion of Christian states outside Europe (such as various former colonies of European states in America) as they became independent...and...by inclusion of non-Christian states. Particularly significant was the express acknowledgement of Turkey's membership of the international community.[3]

On non-Western international lawyers, consider for example Chinese lawyer Tieya Wang, affirming that: 'modern international law has its origin in western civilisation. It has, however, been expanding to the whole world'.[4] Although the explorations by Western and non-Western lawyers arrive at the same result, there is considerable divergence in the description of the events leading to the emergence of a universal international law.

For some, international law expanded when non-European states were admitted as new members of the international community.[5] For others, it expanded when international legal rules, doctrines or ideas were imposed outside Europe to enable and justify formal or informal colonialism.[6] Followers of the first interpretation assume that international law is a legal order that governs relations between states, an order including rules and doctrines to attribute international legal personality.

[3] L. Oppenheim, R. Jennings and A. Watts, *Oppenheim's international law*, 9th edn, 2 vols. (London: Longmans, 1996), p. 87. Similarly, 'the prevailing view in the study of international law is that it emerged in Europe in the period after the Peace of Westphalia ...': M. Akehurst and P. Malanczuk, *Akehurst's modern introduction to international law*, 7th edn (London: Routledge, 1997), p. 9.

[4] T. Wang, 'International law in China: historical and contemporary perspectives', *RdC* 221 (1990-II), 195–369, 204. Assuming the Western nature of international law, semi-peripherals tend to focus their effort into transforming contemporary international law into a more multicultural legal order. See e.g. Y. Onuma, 'When was the law of international society born?' *Journal of the History of International Law*, 2 (2000), 1–66.

[5] I. Brownlie, 'The expansion of international society: the consequences of the law of nations' in H. Bull and A. Watson (eds.), *The expansion of international society* (Oxford: Clarendon Press, 1984), pp. 357–69.

[6] Anghie, *Imperialism*, pp. 32–40.

International law thus achieves universality when a significant number of new states acquire membership in the international community; such membership was determined by the standard of civilization in the nineteenth century and is now determined by the doctrine of recognition. Followers of the second interpretation assume that international law manages cultural differences between Western and non-Western polities. Thus, when the non-European world was colonized or subjected to informal imperialism, international law expanded but did not become universal. Although international law recognized the sovereignty of Western states, it denied legal personality to non-Western polities, legalizing the acquisition of overseas territories, on the basis of discovery and occupation, or through treaties in which these polities ceded sovereignty or jurisdiction to Western powers.

The discrepancy between these two interpretations is not trivial. It illustrates two sharply different realities at the root of the international legal order that have developed up until today. More importantly, these two accounts are contradictory; each one portrays the expansion of international law as the geographical extension of an international legal regime of a diametrically dissimilar character: a legal order valid between sovereign equals or a set of legal relations sanctioning inequality. We will explore the history of international law in the nineteenth century as containing both regimes of equality and inequality, both conferring and denying sovereignty.

From geographical expansion to a universal international law

When we assume that international law has a European origin and look back at the progressive inclusion of non-Western states, we think that European international law expanded. However, delving into the discrepancy between the ideas of expansion through admission and expansion through imposition, that is, acknowledging the coexistence of the regimes of equality and inequality, offers a glimpse into a very different story. This is the story about how international law became universal.

Nineteenth-century international law achieved global geographical scope by including two separate regimes: one governing relations between Western sovereigns under formal equality, and the other governing relations between Western and non-Western polities under inequality, granting special privileges to the former.[7] International law changed radically when the doctrines erecting the boundaries between these two regimes, the doctrine of recognition and the standard of civilization, were reinterpreted so that some semi-peripheral sovereigns were admitted into the international community and thus became governed by the regime recognizing formal equality.

Changes in the rules used to attribute international legal personality, however, resulted in a transformation deeper than the geographical expansion of international law's range of validity. In the nineteenth century, international law became universal. The transformation of the doctrinal structure of international law was not a Western concession (i.e. expansion through inclusion), but the reinterpretation of rules by non-Western states, supporting their admission into the international community. This reinterpretation was possible because a generation of semi-peripheral international lawyers had appropriated Western international legal thought. After becoming versed in Western legal discourse, these semi-peripheral lawyers used it to engage in disciplinary debates, arguing for rules and doctrines that served the interests of their states. These particular uses of international law and engagements with the classical legal tradition produced a distinctive semi-peripheral legal consciousness. I will examine and interpret this semi-peripheral version of classical international legal thought as a form of a *particularistic universalism*.

Consideration of semi-peripheral international lawyers' engagement with Western international legal thought invites us to rethink the meaning of universality as a term describing the transformations that the international legal order underwent during the nineteenth century. The term universality, I would suggest, reflects not only changes in international law's doctrinal outlook – reducing the scope of the doctrines that limited inclusion of non-European sovereigns – but also points at the global professionalization of international lawyers, articulating a transnational legal discourse. Furthermore, it describes a profound transformation in the nature and function of the international legal order itself: although international law continued enabling Western powers' global, political and economic intervention, it also began regulating and to some extent

[7] See Map 2 showing a significant increase during the nineteenth century in the number of treaties concluded between the British Empire and non-Western states. Many of these treaties contained unequal terms.

limiting the power of Western states, governing the interactions between independent political organizations on a global scale.

European international law expanded along with the global, economic and military expansion of the West. Semi-peripheral jurists internalized European legal thought in order to change rules. In changing the rules, however, they also transformed international law. International law became universal, I would argue, only when non-Western jurists internalized European legal thought, transforming nineteenth-century international law in the abovementioned doctrinal, professional and normative dimensions.

The central contention of this chapter, that international law became universal through semi-peripheral appropriation, will be supported by showing a correlation between changes in legal thought and changes in international rules and doctrines. I will suggest a correlation between semi-peripheral elites' engagement with international law – by becoming international lawyers, publishing, participating in conferences, etc. – and the inclusion of semi-peripheral states in the international community, within the regime where states are considered formally equal. In some cases this correlation was strong: in 1894 Japan renegotiated the unequal treaties it had concluded with Western states, signing the first treaty under equality with Great Britain.

To understand the plea of semi-peripheral states to be governed under international law's regime of equality, we should grasp the nature and development of the diverse legal rules and principles governing the interaction between Western and non-Western sovereigns at the beginning of the nineteenth century, especially the ones establishing unequal treatment. I will explain the diversity of these rules by examining the international legal regimes governing ideal typical interactions between Western and non-Western states.

Unequal regimes in nineteenth-century international law

Even though international law attained global geographical reach in the nineteenth century, a stable treaty-making pattern and a rather dense legal regime had already conjoined some European and non-European powers for centuries. We have already seen that Alexandrowicz identified a thick net of treaties governing relations between European sovereigns and sovereigns in the East Indies.[8] Moreover, Italian jurist Roberto Ago

[8] Alexandrowicz, *History East Indies*, pp. 101–10 and 158–77.

argued that, at the beginning of the ninth century, an international community of coexisting sovereigns developed in the Euro-Mediterranean area, which after two centuries included interactions governed by treaties between sovereigns belonging to the Roman Christian, Byzantine and Islamic worlds.[9]

Although several of these regimes were old and well-entrenched, Western international lawyers of the first half of the nineteenth century ignored these legal connections and developed the idea of an exclusively 'European law of people' by marking out the conceptual and doctrinal apparatus developed by an array of European thinkers and schools of thought.[10] This redefinition of international law as *Jus Publicum Europaeum* was in part brought by the nineteenth-century academic study of the history of international law. These were basically studies on the history of European ideas. In the words of a German historian, Wolfgang Preiser, these works largely offered 'international legal theory, i.e. the repetition and explanations of schools of thought in international law' in contradistinction to 'a history of the law of nations as such, i.e. a history of law as had developed and had been applied in practice to govern the peaceful and hostile relations between States and State-like entities'.[11]

Western international lawyers and diplomats, representing their merchants' interests or their states' expansionist policies, deployed the idea of an exclusively European international law in order to justify the exclusion of non-European entities from the privileges of an international legal order based on sovereign equality. The doctrinal shift from naturalism to positivism transformed a universal law of peoples into a regional European international law.[12] Rather than expansion, the

[9] R. Ago, 'Pluralism and the origins of the international community', *Italian Yearbook of International Law*, 3 (1977), 3–33, 3, 13 and 21–26; see in general P. Guggenheim, 'Das Jus publicum europeum und Europa, *Jahrbuch des Öffentliches Rechts der Gegenwart*, 3 (1954), 1–14, 1–2.

[10] See Map 1 showing that treaties concluded between Western and non-Western polities were not unknown prior to the nineteenth century.

[11] W. Preiser, 'History of the law of nations: basic questions and principles' in R. Bernhardt et al. (eds.), *Encyclopaedia of public international law* (Amsterdam: North-Holland, 1984), vol. VII, pp. 126–32. Similarly, McNair noted that 'most history of international law is either a history of its literature, or a history of international relations . . . It is difficult to find much history of the content, that is, the actual rules of law as applied in practice': A. McNair, 'Aspects of state sovereignty', *BYIL*, 26 (1949), 6–47, n. 1.

[12] Alexandrowicz, *History East Indies*, pp. 9–10 and 235–7.

nineteenth-century re-conceptualization of international law as a positive social phenomenon, that is, law as an expression of the juridical consciousness of a homogenous international community of civilized states, resulted in the reduction of international law's geographical range of validity.[13]

International lawyers from the core thus gave legal support to formal colonialism or unequal treatment, respectively; for example, by redefining oversees territories as *terra nullius* – that is, territories that are not subjected to the authority of any sovereign and thus can be acquired through occupation – or by exempting their nationals from local law through consular jurisdiction.

On many occasions, European states conquered new territories and incorporated them as colonies. In this case, international law's geographical sphere of validity enlarged only to the extent that it developed rules to justify conquest overseas, regulating controversies between European states with conflicting claims over the same territory. But in terms of the interactions between the metropole and its colonies, international law did not expand since the legal regulation between them was integrated into the metropole's colonial administrative law. As a result, the use of international legal arguments to resist expansion was limited to pushing forward a right to self-determination, and the materialization of a genuinely universal international law largely had to wait until twentieth-century decolonization.

At other times Western expansion was informal: that is, Western states opened new areas of the world to international trade without integrating them into their own dominions. In this case, Western and non-Western states signed treaties establishing formal international legal relations that occasionally sanctioned formal equality, but mostly instituted unequal treatment. Most of these treaties were signed under duress, following military defeat or the exercise of armed or diplomatic coercion. Nonetheless, semi-peripheral lawyers saw the formalization of their dealings with Western states as an opportunity to bring to bear the notion of international law as law between sovereign equals, and thereby challenge the rules that were unfavourable to them.

[13] Juan Antonio Carrillo Salcedo, 'Aspectos doctrinales del problema de la universalidad del derecho de gentes', *Revista Española de Derecho Internacional*, 17 (1964), 3–15, 5–10. Grewe has disputed the idea that international law reduced its scope of validity, arguing that until the nineteenth century international law was a legal order between the Christian nations of Europe: Grewe, *Epochs*, pp. 451–2, 456, 469–70.

The fact that Europe extended its power and influence under different forms (colonial and informal), and therefore elicited different strategies of resistance (ideological, involving the use of armed force, or legal) suggests that the term 'European expansion' is inaccurate if it is employed to describe a single process through which international law achieved global validity. The claim that international law became universal after semi-peripheral appropriation and use of European international legal thinking, which I advance here, therefore involves a redefinition of the historical context in which the use of international law was possible. Looking at both the regimes of equality and inequality, I argue that international law was relevant in governing both intra-Western interstate relations and relations between Western sovereigns and semi-peripheral polities.

The next chapter examines relations between core and peripheral states regarding three different ideal types describing interactions in which the latter, semi-peripheral states, did not fall under direct colonial rule, either because they were too powerful, too large, or not geopolitically important enough, or because of other historical contingencies.[14] Consequently, in each of these cases there was greater room for strategic use of international law by non-European actors. The first ideal type describes formal equal interactions between Western sovereigns and non-European states; the second, unequal interactions in both political and legal terms; and the third, interactions involving non-European states that participated politically in the European concert, but whose international personality

[14] David Strang has offered an explanation why some non-Western states were able to avoid formal colonization in the nineteenth century, an explanation based not only on Western power but also on an institutional analysis of the state system and the language of sovereignty and recognition. Strang identifies three situations in which non-Western polities successfully constructed their claim to sovereignty, thus achieving recognition by Western states. First, when the non-Western state was able to both defend its territory militarily and frame that use of force within the Western rules of war so that it would not jeopardize its civilized status, thus decreasing the chances of other Western states to intervene (e.g. Japan, Ethiopia). Second, when direct competition between two or more Western states with interests in the same territory impeded formal colonialism and supported the maintenance of the non-Western state's sovereignty (e.g. the Ottoman Empire, China, Persia). Finally, Strang identifies a form of 'defensive Westernization', primarily in the case of Japan and to a lesser extent in Siam, in which 'explicit imitation of Western political and administrative institutions led to the abrogation of the restrictive treaties imposed by the West'. D. Strang, 'Contested sovereignty: the social construction of colonial imperialism' in T. J. Biersteker and C. Weber (eds.), *State sovereignty as social construct* (Cambridge University Press, 1996), pp. 22–49, 40. Whereas Strang emphasises 'defensive Westernization', in this study of the work of non-European jurists I show that imitation meant not only mimicry, but also appropriation of the legal ideas that transformed international law.

and enjoyment of formal equality was contested.[15] Appropriating international law was a strategy available for states in these three ideal types. Semi-peripheral lawyers supported changes in the rules sanctioned in these regimes by reinterpreting central concepts and doctrines of the European international law tradition. The appropriation of this intellectual tradition to overcome the doctrinal barriers European lawyers had developed to bar equal treatment was not simply academic; it was also a political and legislative project.

Semi-peripheral jurists

It was neither in the interest of European powers and the United States, nor in the sight of most Western international lawyers, to expand beyond the West the scope of European international law, understood as a law sanctioning sovereign equality among peoples sharing a common juridical consciousness.[16] It was rather in the antipodes where the project of invoking and internalizing the European concept of international law led to its globalization. A generation of non-Western international lawyers studied European international law with not only the purpose of learning how to play by the new rules of international law that Western powers sought to impose on them, but also with the aim of changing the content of those rules.[17] I will explore the work, life and professional trajectory

[15] I use ideal types, in the conventional Weberian sense, as heuristic devices to draw historical comparisons between different non-Western political entities that established international legal relationships with European powers. The construction of ideal types does not entail the analysis of all the cases fitting under them. I have therefore excluded or given marginal treatment to the appropriation of classical international law in places like Ethiopia, Persia or Poland.

[16] Jörg Fisch argues that expansion came along only after the progressive weakening of European states' power in the international world: J. Fisch, 'Power or weakness? On the causes of the worldwide expansion of European law', *Journal of the history of international law*, 6 (2004), 21–6. The argument is sustained on a wide-ranging historical study. See J. Fisch, *Die europäische Expansion und das Völkerrecht: Die Auseinandersetzungen um den Status der überseeischen Gebiete vom 15. Jahrhundert bis zur Gegenwart* (Stuttgart: Steiner, 1984).

[17] In consequence, I supplement the interpretation put forward by Fisch arguing that diminishing power does not completely explain the expansion of European international law. The decisive appropriation of international law by semi-peripheral lawyers also contributed to the expansion. Although one can identify a general trend in international power relations explaining European economic and military expansion and the use of international legal arguments by non-European states to resist, there was considerable diversity in the strategies and outcomes of semi-peripheral international lawyers' appropriations of international law. Sometimes they challenged the content of the rules by invoking underlying principles; at other times they contested the fact that

of this generation of semi-peripheral lawyers who visited or moved to Europe during the second half of the nineteenth century. Among the lawyers included in Map 3, consider the following sample from various semi-peripheral nations: Carlos Calvo (Argentinean, 1822–1906); Etienne Carathéodory (Turk (ethnic Greek), 1836–1907); Fedor Fedorovich Martens (Russian (Estonian), 1845–1909); Nicolas Saripolos (Greek, 1817–1880); Tsurutaro Senga (Japanese, 1857–1929).[18]

These lawyers were as prolific as they were strategic. At home, they published hornbooks and general studies intended to teach international law in their own languages and to demonstrate the assimilation of European international law. However, they also wrote specific monographs in French, English or German, which were published in Europe and intended for Western audiences. These works engaged with Western authors and their ideas, thereby appropriating the conceptual and doctrinal machinery that European thinkers had developed both to distinguish an exclusively European law of nations and to demarcate within its boundaries the range of validity of law between sovereign equals. Throughout their writings, semi-peripheral internationalists pursued a distinctively non-European interpretation of the classical European law of nations, in which they re-signified and redeployed its fundamental elements – positivism, the standard of civilization, and absolute sovereignty – to advocate for a change in extant rules of international law and to justify the extension of the privileges of formal equality to their own states in their interactions with Western powers.

This group of semi-peripheral international lawyers converged in Europe not simply as a result of individual efforts, but also as a consequence of wider political patterns within the nineteenth-century world system. Notwithstanding differences in nationality, culture or religion, the similarity of these lawyers' paths responded to a common historical imperative defined by the economic and military expansion of Europe and the resistance opposed by non-European peoples. At least since the

the rules applicable within the West did not apply to them, from partial success (formal recognition as a sovereign equal) to partial failure (renegotiation of treaties under unequal treatment).

[18] In light of the professional relevance attained by these lawyers, it seems contradictory to qualify them as semi-peripheral. I have dealt previously with the problem of interpreting the work, professional trajectory and contributions of semi-peripheral lawyers situated at the intellectual and political centres of the world. See Becker Lorca, 'Alvarez situated', 927, 929.

fifteenth century, Europe had expanded overseas by opening trading posts or incorporating new territories as colonies. By the nineteenth century, imperialistic expansion integrated vast areas of the globe into a world economy centred in Europe.[19] Resistance to European expansion adopted various forms, including not only popular revolt and organized military campaigns, but also modernization projects pursued by reformist national movements.

While the role international law played in the European expansion was not homogenous, the strategies lawyers used to articulate resistance through international legal arguments were similar. Let us look at this similarity by examining the appropriation of the basic elements of classical international law by a number of jurists from the semi-periphery.

The semi-peripheral appropriation of classical international law

The global expansion of the great European powers and the United States was economic, political and military. Legal relations also developed when Western expansion into overseas territories was accompanied by the establishment of diplomatic relations and international agreements. However, the international legal regimes that governed relations between Western and non-Western states during the nineteenth century do not explain why Japanese, Latin American, Turkish or Russian lawyers engaged with the European international legal tradition. Neither doctrines nor legal concepts travel by themselves. Non-European elites had to convince themselves that mastering European international legal thinking was included in the project of national modernization, in which the recognition of international legal personality became a proxy for civilization. Additionally, they had to persuade traditionalist opponents at home of the usefulness of international law (for example, to tame Western incursions). Treatises had to be translated and legal doctrines had to be taught. Thinking and acting like an international lawyer requires instruction and practice. When national elites in Turkey, China or Latin America decided to use international law and engage with the European tradition of international legal thinking, aiming to improve their bargaining position vis-à-vis Western powers, they had to import legal knowledge. Consequently,

[19] On the continuities and changes between the earlier period of European colonial empires and nineteenth-century imperialism, see H. L. Wesseling, *The European colonial empires, 1815–1919*, Diane Webb trans. (Harlow: Pearson Longman, 2004).

some of their lawyers and diplomats had to become European-fashioned international lawyers.

To acquire knowledge about international law, non-European governments sponsored the translation of foreign textbooks: remember the case of the American Presbyterian W. A. P. Martin, hired to translate the first international law treatise in China. These governments also directly hired foreign international lawyers. Japan, as we will see, employed an Italian and German-Swiss international lawyer, Alessandro Paternostro (1852–1899) and Otfried Nippold (1864–1938). In 1874, French international lawyer Paul Pradier-Fodéré (1827–1904) was hired by the Peruvian government to teach international law and serve as a legal adviser. Gustave Rolin-Jaequemyns (1835–1902), renowned Belgian lawyer and cofounder of the *Institut de Droit International*, after accepting a personal invitation by the king of Siam, served as a counsellor to the crown between 1892 and 1902.[20]

A profession beyond the West

By the nineteenth century it had become increasingly common for non-European intellectual elites to migrate to Europe in the search for high culture, knowledge and gains in their individual social capital. International lawyers rapidly followed suit.[21] After completing legal education in their home countries, lawyers from different regions of the world moved to Europe's intellectual and political centres. Japanese were at the forefront, but were not the only lawyers congregating in Europe.[22] Some entered the foreign office and served in diplomatic missions accredited in Europe;

[20] W. Tips, '*Gustave Rolin-Jaequemyns and the making of modern Siam: the diaries and letters of King Chulalongkorn's general adviser* (Bangkok: White Lotus, 1996), pp. 1–2.

[21] See V. Karady, 'La migration internationale d'étudiants en Europe, 1890–1940', *Actes de la recherche en sciences sociales*, 145 (2002), 47–60.

[22] For example, according to Shigeki Miyasaki, during mid-nineteenth century, Japanese Shin-ichiro Tsuda and Shusuke Nishi were sent to Leiden University and Takeaki Enomoto to Holland, while Chinese Chien-Chung Ma (Jianzhong Ma) studied international law at the University of Paris. See S. Miyasaki, 'History of the law of nations regional development: Far East' in R. Bernhardt et al. (eds.), *Encyclopaedia of public international law* (Amsterdam: North-Holland, 1995), vol. II, pp. 802–9, 806. Also, Japanese lawyers Tsurutaro Senga and Shingo Nakamura studied during the end of the nineteenth century at the University of Berlin. See I. Fuji, 'One hundred years of international law studies in Japan', *Japanese Annual of International Law*, 13 (1969), 19–34, 28. Japanese Sakutaro Tachi studied in France, Germany, and England between 1900 and 1904. See *Annuaire de l'Institut de Droit International*, 43 Tome II (1950), 517. Russian Andre Mandelstam took courses with Renault in Paris between 1897 and 1898: *ibid.*, 483.

others accepted European governmental positions with the explicit purpose of learning European international law. Others, supported by their family fortunes or independently financed, moved to Europe to pursue advanced legal studies and remained there while working for their home countries. Most of them combined more than one occupation, serving as legal advisers or diplomatic agents while in Europe and taking on academic and political positions once back in their home countries.[23]

By the end of the nineteenth century, there was a significant community of international lawyers from semi-peripheral countries who had pursued doctoral studies in law or informal studies under the guidance of prestigious international law professors in Europe. This trend increased throughout the first decades of the twentieth century. This migration of lawyers and law students during the second half of the nineteenth century was part of a broader phenomenon in which non-European elites, intellectuals, diplomats and international lawyers converged in Europe, which contributed to making Paris, Berlin, London, Brussels and The Hague global centres of international culture and politics.

During the nineteenth century, the international world transformed rapidly and dramatically. International law adapted and changed in response to the new global economic order that emerged from European and US-American expansion, becoming very different from the law governing intra-European relations and from treaties regulating the interaction between Western and non-Western sovereigns. In the context of shifting definitions, central concepts, doctrines and rules of international law were embodied not only in treaties but also in treatises. Semi-peripheral jurists sought, writing treatises, to change the rules contained in the treaties that governed the relationship between their polities and core states. These writings should therefore be considered as legislative acts in nineteenth-century international law.

I explore and draw comparisons between the work and professional trajectories of a number of international lawyers from the semi-periphery and suggest that the migration of non-European legal intellectuals to Europe, their appropriation of European international legal thinking,

[23] Onuma has argued that one of the reasons nations entering the 'Eurocentric international society' as 'later-comers' shared similar characteristics is the small size of their elites, so that a single individual had to play double or triple roles: Y. Onuma, 'Japanese international law in the prewar period: perspectives on the teaching and research of international law in prewar Japan', *Japanese Annual of International Law*, 29 (1986), 23–47, 42.

and the general circulation of international legal ideas and doctrines transformed international law into a global legal discourse. It also led to the emergence of a common professional style or legal consciousness among semi-peripheral international law practitioners.

This shared disciplinary consciousness was shaped by the tactical assimilation of extant international law through the selection of some of its features: positivism (over naturalism as international law's normative source), doctrines that substantiated an absolute notion of sovereign autonomy and equality (over doctrines that made sovereignty permeable) and the internalization of the standard of civilization as the attribute granting international legal subjectivity (over, for example, the use of the maxim *ubi societas ibi ius*). These broad conceptual commitments are undoubtedly the same elements defining the European synthesis out of which nineteenth-century classical international law came into being.[24] Non-Western international lawyers mimicked their Western colleagues, but they assimilated international law in their pursuit of objectives that differed from the ones usually at the centre of European international law. Consequently, classical international law itself acquired atypical attributes. That is, pulling international legal resources to sustain the recognition of legal personality of non-European states made international law different from the law safeguarding the European balance of power in the case of bigger powers, or securing legal equality in the case of small European states, whose legal personality was not contested.

I now describe how the general characteristics of classical international law – i.e. positivism, an absolute concept of sovereignty and the standard of civilization – were appropriated by semi-peripheral authors and channelled to produce a similar but different international law that responded to their distinctive interests. In the next chapter, I map the diversity of modes in which classical international law was imported and assimilated

[24] David Kennedy, however, suggests that the idea of the nineteenth century as characterized by the triumph of positivism and the centrality of sovereignty was itself a result of the critique of sovereignty and positivism advanced by modernist international lawyers during the first half of the twentieth century. Kennedy's study sheds light on the reasons why contemporary liberal internationalists see sovereignty and positivism as backward elements of the legal tradition that should be overcome and thus why the nineteenth-century history of international law has remained mostly unexplored: Kennedy, 'History of an illusion', 386–7, 412–13 and *passim*. In this study, I suspend the preconceptions about the nineteenth century identified by Kennedy and examine the rationale behind non-Western jurists' support of a legal theory and disciplinary sensibility that would seem problematic to contemporary observers.

as a result of local differences in the historical contexts of each of the three ideal types.

Positivism

Explanations of the predominance that legal positivism attained in nineteenth-century international law commonly point at the general influence this trend exerted in the field of jurisprudence and philosophy.[25] Alternatively, positivism is thought to have developed in the nineteenth century as the conceptual framework in consonance either with a period characterized by relative peace and material progress or with an age defined by imperialism and the concomitant need to offer legal justification to colonialism.[26] Either way, positivism gave conceptual coherence to a new reality: international law as rules, emanating from states and governing interstate relations.[27]

If the nineteenth century consequently marked the resolution in favour of positivism of the prolonged dispute with naturalist theories of international law, it should not be surprising that international lawyers from the semi-periphery followed the positivist trend.[28] Semi-peripheral jurists'

25 According to Kunz: 'it is against the long predominance of the "classic" natural law and its extravagances that, at the beginning of the nineteenth century, positivism came as a reaction in Europe': J. Kunz, 'Natural-law thinking in the modern science of international law', *AJIL* 55 (1961), 951–8, 952.

26 Kunz, for instance, revising the history of the debate between naturalism and positivism, argues that positivism provides a better theoretical framework during periods of peace, because of its emphasis on interpretation and codification of existing law, as opposed to periods of change and wars, when problems of law-making and the politics of law make positivism too rigid. See Kunz, *ibid.*, 953–4. In contrast, Anghie has revealed the historical and conceptual interconnections between positivism and colonialism: see Anghie, *Imperialism*.

27 See e.g. B. Kingsbury, 'The international legal order' in Peter Cane and Mark Tushnet (eds.), *Oxford handbook of legal studies* (2003), pp. 271–97. Kingsbury argues that since the late nineteenth century, the international lawyer, combining the roles of both scholar and practitioner, has followed a dispute settlement focus combined with a practice-oriented positivist jurisprudence, a model that emphasized the materials generated by recognized sources of law. According to Kunz, positivism 'stood for the predominance of the state, for the dualistic construction, for the will of the state as the only basis of international law, for the unquestionable right of every sovereign state to go to war, against third-party judgment, against progressive development of international organisations, and so on': Kunz, 'Natural-law thinking', 957.

28 E.g. 'In the science of international law, the nineteenth century was the great era of positivism. This means, first of all, that the conception of the law of nature and the kindred one of just war were to all intents and purposes abandoned': Nussbaum, *A concise history*, p. 232.

positivism might be characterized as the default position into which non-Western legal experts subsided in the course of their appropriation of international law, precisely at the time when the positivist school became dominant.[29]

Semi-peripheral international lawyers' positivism, however, could be more accurately described as an answer to the new international legal doctrines the positivist framework had systematized. To be precise, semi-peripheral international lawyer's positivism countered the legal doctrines that European and US international lawyers developed to provide their states with a greater scope for legal interventions in non-European states, changing the international legal regimes that regulated their interactions with non-Western states. Non-European international lawyers were therefore positivists not because of an unabashed position in the debate on the nature and normative foundations of international law, but rather because of pragmatic and strategic reasons.

On the one hand, non-Western lawyers confronted a pragmatic rather than theoretical problem when striving to make sense of the rules of the regimes governing the interaction between Western and non-Western powers. In the Japanese context, for example, Kinji Akashi has argued that international lawyers' practice-oriented attitude toward the idea and concept of international law responded to the daring situation faced by Japan once opened by Western powers. Japanese jurists were indifferent to the long-lasting European debate between positivism and naturalism: 'it is highly probable that the question whether it [international law] was natural or positive should have been a peripheral issue'.[30]

[29] Jacobini, for example, studies Latin American international lawyers in terms of their disposition towards positivism as the dominant trend of the epoch. H. B. Jacobini, *A study of the philosophy of international law as seen in works of Latin American writers* (The Hague: Nijhoff, 1954). Renowned non-European international lawyers like Russian Martens became central figures in the shift towards positivism. See Nussbaum, *A concise history*, pp. 179–85. See also F. Martens, *Völkerrecht: das internationale Recht der Civilisirten Nationen: systematisch dargestellt*, C. Bergbohm trans. (Berlin: Weidmann Buchhandlung, 1886); Baltic German/Estonian international lawyer Carl Bergbohm's (1849–1927) work became a classic in the positivist tradition: C. Bergbohm, *Staatsverträge und Gesetze als Quellen des Völkerrechts* (Dorpat: C. Mattiesen, 1877). On Bergbohm as a positivist in the Russian and Estonian context, see L. Mälksoo, 'The science of international law and the concept of politics. The arguments and lives of the international law professors at the University of Dorpat/Iur'ev/Tartu 1855–1985', *BYIL*, 76 (2005), 383–502, 420 ff.

[30] K. Akashi, 'Japanese "acceptance" of the European law of nations: A brief history of international law in Japan' in M. Stolleis and Y. Masaharu (eds.), *East Asian and European perspectives on international law* (Baden-Baden: Nomos, 2004), pp. 1–21, 19.

The professional sensibilities of semi-peripheral international lawyers, who mostly worked as legal advisers and diplomats, generally coincided with the positivist perspective because of their proximity to concrete state behaviour and the imperative to work with the sources of international law directly emanating from that practice. For example, limiting the grounds for a *de jure* justification of inequality between Western and non-Western nations was a central practical problem faced by non-Western international lawyers. Discussing the capitulation treaties that Japan had signed with various Western powers, Japanese lawyer Tsurutaro Senga maintained that the basis for Western states' exercise of consular jurisdiction was laid down exclusively by the treaties signed by Japan, and that its application was consequently entirely determined by their provisions. All matters not covered by the capitulations, Senga adamantly affirmed, should be resolved by rules of international or municipal law, that is, neither by the theory of extraterritoriality professed by some European publicists, nor by analogy to the institution of consular jurisdiction as forced on Turkey or on other Asian or African states.[31]

On the other hand, positivism might be described in hindsight as strategically chosen by semi-peripheral international lawyers to give preponderance to the sources of law that unequivocally expressed the will of their sovereign as well as to the theory of international law that circumscribed its scope within the realm of inter-state relations, rather than making inroads into the domestic realm. Positivism was indeed the theoretical approach more amicable to Senga's efforts to reduce the latitude to interpret unequal treaties beyond Japan's sovereign will and as such opposed the use of natural law doctrines to limit the sovereign autonomy of non-Western states. In the nineteenth century, equality was denied not only on the basis of the standard of civilization but also, some lawyers, like Scottish James Lorimer (1818–1890), denied equality on the basis of natural law principles.[32] Therefore, for instance, Martens insisted that international law is composed of juridical rules and not moral or religious laws.[33]

[31] The absence of solidarity between jurists from different non-European states is typical of the legal consciousness of this first generation of semi-peripheral international lawyers. See T. Senga, *Gestaltung und Kritik der heutigen Konsulargerichtsbarkeit in Japan* (Berlin: R. L. Prager, 1897), p. 10.

[32] J. Lorimer, *The institutes of the law of nations: a treatise of the jural relations of separate political communities* (London: W. Blackwood and Sons, 1883).

[33] F. Martens, *Traité de droit international*, A. Leo trans. (Paris: Librairie Marescq Aine, 1887), p. 24.

While not entirely dominant, the natural law remnants that carried on to the mid-nineteenth century were particularly detrimental to the interests of non-European nations. James Lorimer followed the basic tenets of naturalist doctrine when arguing that positive law is declaratory of the law of nature. The law of nations, in turn, is discovered through inferences from the basic facts of nature, which according to Lorimer are essentially power relations. Elevating the fact of power and the inequality between states to an alleged 'de facto principle', Lorimer rules out the possibility of formal legal equality among states that are unequal in fact, a difference that confers to European states unilateral rights to expansion and conquest.[34]

Semi-peripheral international lawyers therefore welcomed positivism's break with the naturalist tradition, for positivism confined law to the rules emanating from sovereign will while displacing detrimental rules deduced from general naturalist principles. Moreover, this break was crucial to overcome international law's Christian theological underpinnings and therefore useful to substantiate the inclusion of non-Christian political entities as international legal subjects on a morally neutral basis. For example, only the first attempts to assimilate international law at the beginning of the nineteenth century in China and Japan depended on drawing parallels between international law as natural law and Confucianism, which, as some have argued, was only a strategy to breach linguistic and cultural gaps.[35] As soon as professional international lawyers took over the legal aspects of the interaction with Western powers, latter generations of intellectuals opted for positivism. In the Latin American context, for example, the first international law textbook by leading man of letters Andrés Bello published at the beginning of the century follows a naturalist approach. At the end of the century, Argentinean international lawyer Carlos Calvo articulates the turn to positivism.[36]

[34] On the 'de facto principle', see J. Lorimer, *The institutes of law: a treatise of the principles of jurisprudence as determined by nature* (London: W. Blackwood & Sons, 1880), *passim*, in specific relation to international law see pp. 260–1, and on the application of the theory of 'de facto principle' to the doctrine of recognition, see p. 104.

[35] O. Hirohiko, 'Japan's early encounter with the concept of the "law of nations"', *Japanese Annual of International Law*, 13 (1969), 35–65. But see Akashi, 'Japanese acceptance', p. 19.

[36] A. Bello, *Principios de derecho de jentes* (Santiago de Chile: Imprenta de la Opinión, 1832); C. Calvo, *Le droit international théorique et pratique: précédé d'un exposé historique des progrès de la science du droit des gens* (Paris: A. Rousseau, 1896), vol. I, p. 154.

The continuing purchase of naturalist doctrines constituted a threat to the independence of non-European states even after Western governments had recognized their legal personality. Under natural law's argumentative plasticity, just war theory could justify Western military intervention in China, Turkey or Latin America. Semi-peripheral jurists thus realized the need to develop a comprehensive critique of natural law on 'scientific' grounds. Carlos Calvo, for example, did not simply join the positivist trend, but also described the distinction between natural law and positive law and the corresponding differentiation between customary law and conventional law as outdated.

Declaring that the distinction between naturalism and positivism had lost purchase in modern discussions and affirming that it is only proper to 'ancient publicists', Calvo shifted the attention toward elucidating the principles of justice on the basis of which international law is founded and that ought to precede interstate relations. After reviewing the positions of a long list of authorities, Calvo summarizes his opinion:

> [W]e recognize that the general idea of justice can transform the relations of states for the better and in their common benefit; however, in the course of our work we will stick with preference to the principles defined in treaties, to the rules naturally and logically deduced from particular conventions, or from the diverse cases resolved in practice, in short to the established jurisprudence.[37]

Calvo only enters the discussion about justice to distance himself from the debate on the naturalist/positivist theories of international law. But he also eschews a thorough discussion of the principles of justice, centring the analysis exclusively on the positive sources of law. In this manner and in similar fashion to Senga, Calvo gave theoretical leverage to a practice-oriented form of positivism. For instance, in 'the language of facts' Calvo reveals the practical character of his definition of the sources of international law, limiting it to valid treaties rather than emphasizing their moral or rational foundation.[38]

I have so far shown that semi-peripheral jurists were positivists in the sense of engaging with the central ideas of the positivist school of thought. Semi-peripherals supported positivism because the doctrines and legal arguments associated with the positivist school were seen as more beneficial to their interests than the doctrines and arguments linked to the

[37] Calvo, *Le droit international*, p. 154. For a similar opinion, see Martens, *Völkerrecht*, p. 24.
[38] Calvo, *Le droit international*, pp. 159–60.

naturalist school. However, there is another way to understand the positivist outlook of nineteenth-century international law. In addition to a school of thought based on a shared legal theory, positivism can also be grasped from the perspective of the modes of legal reasoning it foregrounds. In this sense, positivism is identified with the abuse of deductive reasoning, that is, positivism seen as legal formalism.[39] Semi-peripheral lawyers were formalists when supporting a variety of legal propositions or doctrines – from non-intervention, to the illegality of the use of force to recover public debt, to the abrogation of consular jurisdiction – by way of presenting them as deductions from the principle of sovereignty. In particular, we will examine in greater detail semi-peripheral jurists' appeal to sovereignty to defend the equality and autonomy of their states. For example, Greek international lawyer and scholar Michel Stavro Kebedgy (1865–1947) relied on this mode of reasoning when writing on the principle of sovereign autonomy and equality:

> *Sovereignty* is the fundamental attribute that the juridical conscience of peoples and the science of international law recognize to the distinct moral persons that form the society of nations and that we call states. It has as a necessary corollary the *juridical equality* of all states and their mutual *independence*. Sovereign states, by their very definition, hardly recognize any person above them. It evidently follows that they all are on the same ground *equal* and *independent*. That is true whatever may be the geographical extent, material power, or the constitutional form of each state ...[40]

We will explore these and other examples of formalist legal reasoning by semi-peripheral authors. These writers, however, did not define themselves as formalists. For obvious reasons, they characterized their approach as positivist.[41] Instead of expressing their conceptual views on the nature of law, semi-peripheral authors invoked positivism in their

[39] See Kennedy, 'History of an illusion', 385–420. I am using the notion of 'abuse of deduction' in Duncan Kennedy's phenomenological sense, that is, the difference between what is experienced as deduction and as abuse of deduction, depends on the 'blocking level', on the level of abstraction in which a proposition is experienced as permitting deduction. The blocking level varies over time according to usage rather than logical accuracy. Duncan Kennedy, *The rise and fall of classical legal thought* (Washington DC: Beard Books, 2006 [1975]), p. xviii.

[40] M. Kebedgy, 'Principes du droit des gens', *Zeitschrift für Schweizerisches Recht*, 19 (1900) 84–103.

[41] Formalism, as a sign of dogmatism or excessive idealism, has long been used to discredit the views of adversaries. However, formalism, as both designating a critique of the mode of legal reasoning characterized by the abuse of deduction and calling for a renewal of thinking in the direction of contextualist or outcome-oriented modes of

legal arguments, envisioning not a natural law oriented opponent, but the conservative European classical international lawyer. Also a positivist, this classical lawyer recognized special rights to the great European powers and thus would favour an international legal order based on inequality. In contrast to the Western lawyers' politically infused opinions, which supported the great powers' privileged position, the semi-peripheral scholar invoked positivism as a way to emphasize the objective, dispassionate and scientific character of his argument. Another Greek lawyer, Georgios Streit (1868–1948), for example, adopted this position in his 1898 inaugural lecture to the international law chair at the University of Athens. In the lecture, published in the *Revue de droit international et de législation comparée*, Streit begins by announcing the continuation of the tradition instituted by his predecessor, who based his entire analysis on two principles: 'he has conceived and taught international law as positive law; he has clearly separated the science of that law from politics.'[42] Accordingly, Streit could not only characterize his study on the position of great powers under international law as scientific, but also defend the juridical equality of all states.

Semi-peripheral jurists were positivists in the sense that they subscribed to a legal theory and a mode of legal reasoning. Affiliation to the theoretic stance or school of thought, however, did not animate their positivism; rather, it was their will to assimilate international law into practical knowledge. To meet Auslin's challenge against the conceptualization of international law as law, semi-peripheral authors did not pursue a scientific approach in the manner that European, and in particular British, positivist international lawyers did.[43] Positivism instead proved useful to non-Western states by defining their revocation of certain international legal rules, such as widespread international legal customs, principles and doctrines legitimizing unequal treatment of non-European states, as expressions of their sovereign will. Therefore, rather than subscribing to positivism per se, semi-peripheral international lawyers used the positivist claim to scientific knowledge as support for their practical reconstructions of international legal doctrines, among them the

legal thinking, as we will see, emerged only during the first decades of the twentieth century, during the transition from classical to modern international legal thought.

[42] G. Streit, 'Les grandes puissances dans le droit international', *RDI*, 2 (1900), 5–25.

[43] See generally M. Lobban, 'English approaches to international law in the nineteenth century' in M. Craven et al. (eds.), *Time, history and international law* (Leiden: M. Nijhoff, 2007), pp. 65–90, 66.

reinterpretation of the meaning of absolute sovereignty and the standard of civilization.

Absolute sovereignty

Semi-peripheral internationalists endorsed an absolute notion of sovereignty that emphasized both the rights to autonomy and equality. First, they stressed the domestic autonomy of a polity to constitute itself, rather than the factual independence vis-à-vis other sovereigns. For example, in his treatise Carlos Calvo reviews Vattel's definition of sovereignty as the capacity of the nation to govern itself, regardless of form, as along as it remains independent from any foreign people. Calvo then contrasts this definition with his own: 'the essential character of a state's sovereignty does not rest on being more or less independent from another state, rather it rests on the power that it has to give itself a constitution, establish its laws, establish its government, without any intervention of a foreign nation'.[44]

Second, unlike their Western counterparts, semi-peripheral publicists understood absolute sovereignty to include the rights of states as well as the obligations vis-à-vis other sovereigns. Emphasizing this dyad, semi-peripherals affirmed the formal equality between sovereign states and derived from it a series of principles that safeguarded the political independence and preserved the territorial integrity of their nations. Calvo, for instance, argued that absolute sovereignty necessarily implies complete independence. Hence for states, as moral persons, it implies a primary right, that of pursuing freely the achievement of their own destinies, and a no less pressing obligation of recognizing and respecting the sovereign rights and the absolute independence of other states.[45] More importantly, however, non-Western lawyers ventured to delineate the doctrinal contours of sovereignty by narrowing the range of potential exceptions to the rule, including the most imperious ones of intervention and consular jurisdiction.

Aiming at delimiting intervention as an exception to sovereign autonomy, Carlos Calvo, for example, devotes several pages to international law authorities that both justified the right of intervention and that supported the principle of non-intervention. He lists a number of conflicting views, sufficient enough to conclude that: 'there are almost as many different opinions as there are authors'.[46] Though asseverating

[44] Calvo, *Le droit international*, p. 171. [45] *Ibid.*, p. 264. [46] *Ibid.*, p. 278.

the dissatisfaction that comes from theoretically defining the right of intervention, Calvo instead focuses on interventions in the historical record from ancient times to the nineteenth century. This turn to history then allows him to highlight a distinction between interventions within European states and interventions by European states in the internal affairs of the states of the Americas. As regards the former, Calvo argues that in modern times, especially since the independence of Greece, intervention has followed high principles of international politics, such as the equilibrium among nations and the protection of moral or religious values.[47] The legitimacy or illegitimacy of intervention, according to Calvo, is therefore not intrinsic but subordinate to the situation of the country involved and the international impact that it produces. In the European cases, having followed 'sound reason and equity', interventions have been 'favourable to the development of civilisation'.[48] In contrast, on the basis of an examination of the French (1838–1840) and Anglo-French (1843–1850) interventions in Rio de la Plata, as well as the Anglo-French-Spanish intervention in Mexico (1861–1868), Calvo strongly affirms: 'regardless of the point of view adopted, it is impossible to discover a single serious and legitimate reason that could justify up to a certain point the European interferences in the domestic affairs of the Americas'.[49]

Interventions, Calvo laments, have been either politically motivated or, in the case of demands for pecuniary compensation, justified under the pretence of protection of private interests, with no inquiry whatsoever as to their authenticity. Regarding politically motivated interventions, if American as well as European states are independent nations and thus owe each other reciprocity in their treatment, Calvo concludes that the assertion of a right of Europeans to interfere in the domestic affairs of the New World would in turn give way to an equivalent right by the states of the Americas to intervene in Europe. That situation would render impossible the preservation of amicable and peaceful relations between habitants of both continents. Considering economically motivated interventions, Calvo points out that the recovery of debts or pursuance of other type of private claim has never justified the use of armed force by one European

[47] *Ibid.*, pp. 322–4.

[48] Apart from the British and Russian interventions in the independence of Greece, Calvo also mentions the French intervention in Italy as a contributing factor to the latter's unification: *ibid.*, p. 323.

[49] *Ibid.*, p. 348.

state against another, and concludes that no reason exists to change that rule in relation to the states of the New World.[50]

But if intervention becomes a legal principle equal to the non-intervention principle of the law of peoples, the question Calvo asks is which of them then becomes the rule and which the exception. Historically, Calvo maintains, non-intervention has in general prevailed in the political relations between states. Thus, he concludes by affirming that the absolute principle of non-intervention is a corollary to the principle of nationality, admitting exceptions only when a state freely appeals to another state for assistance in defending or recovering its autonomy when threatened by a foreign power.[51]

On the other hand, consular jurisdiction posed challenges similar to intervention, in the sense that delimiting the scope of this exception to sovereign autonomy elicited analogous responses. Japanese Tsurutaro Senga addresses the issue. Whereas it is undeniable that all limitations to the fundamental rights of the sovereign state are exceptional – German-speaking Senga reminds his European readers – the attempt to justify consular jurisdiction by appealing to its normal character in Asia and Africa in contrast to its non-existence in Europe is untenable.[52] In this manner, Senga unpacks the contention that European international law's validity outside Europe depended on the extent to which the social and consequently legal relations between the European and non-European states were immediate enough. For instance, German publicist Holtzendorff classified legal duties among states into four groups, according to which consular jurisdiction was justified in Turkish lands, Africa and Asia on grounds of the weak European relationship with these nations.[53] Senga opposed this interpretation by distinguishing two issues that he interpreted as separate: the possibility of identifying regional groupings around a similar class of legal bonds, on the one hand, and the limitation of sovereign autonomy, on the other. If regular and actually shared

[50] *Ibid.*, pp. 348–51.

[51] Note how Calvo takes on the principle of nationality at the centre of reconstruction of Europe to give it a twist: *ibid.*, pp. 351–5.

[52] Senga, *Gestaltung und Kritik*, p. 134.

[53] These four groups included: relations between European states, between European and American states, between Christian-European states and Turkish lands, and between European and Asian and African states. See generally F. von Holtzendorff, *Handbuch des Völkerrechts: auf Grundlage europäischer Staatspraxis*, 4th edn (Berlin: Habel, 1889); Cf. J. Westlake, *Chapters on the principles of international law* (Cambridge University Press, 1894) and Lorimer, *The institutes of the law of nations*.

particularities exist in the international legal relations within a group of states, Senga reasons, the differentiation in the conventional rights held by them must conform to the distinctive economic or social relations of their respective continents. Senga asserts that these variations of the rights applicable to legal interactions, however, remain within the realm of each group of states. Thus, distinctions between regional groups do not justify restricting the absolute rights belonging to each sovereign as an international legal subject. Namely, it does not make it lawful for European states to discriminate against Asian states, as is the case in the inequitable treaties establishing consular jurisdiction.[54]

Consular jurisdiction in Japan, Senga concludes, is in contradiction with the principle of sovereign autonomy.[55] Highlighting the contradiction was not enough to assure the success of the legal argumentation in Japan's favour, however, for Senga had to also show that Japan was actually sovereign. Japanese publicists, in consequence, had to confront the standard of civilization, that is, the yardstick used by Western international lawyers to justify or deny the recognition of international legal personality.

The standard of civilization

The doctrine of the standard of civilization has a particular genealogy. As the law of peoples, emerging in the sixteenth century under a natural law conception, international law shifted progressively to become a formalized legal order underpinned by positivist legal thought. In response, Western legal scholars developed the doctrine of the standard of civilization to delimit international law's scope and validity.[56] Moreover, nineteenth-century positivist international law of civilized nations did not include any formal procedure to determine the 'civilised status', leaving the admission of new members to the determination of international legal scholars.[57]

54 Senga, *Gestaltung und Kritik*, pp. 134–5.

55 Specifically, consular jurisdiction violates the state's constitutional sovereignty (*Staatsrechtliche Souveränität*), the sovereignty of the head of state (*Fürstensouveränität*), and international legal sovereignty: *ibid.*, pp. 107–9, 123.

56 For studies exploring the construction of the standard by Western international lawyers, see generally G. Gong, *The standard of 'civilization' in international society* (Oxford: Clarendon Press, 1984); see also Anghie, *Imperialism*.

57 G. Schwarzenberger, 'The rule of law and the disintegration of the international society', *AJIL* 33 (1939), 56–77, 64.

However, the standard of civilization did not emerge simply as a consequence of a shift in scientific debates. Positivism and the distinction between civilized and uncivilized peoples served the interest of Western imperialism and colonialism.[58] There is, however, another story running parallel to the imposition of European international law. At the same time Western international lawyers developed the standard and Western states used it to legitimize their overseas expansion, semi-peripheral intellectuals internalized the standard of civilization, developing legal arguments to justify the recognition of their countries as sovereign states. Semi-peripherals internalized the standard by demonstrating the civilized status of their respective nations. Alternatively and less frequently, lawyers challenged the standard as not scientifically sound and therefore legally useless to recognize or deny international legal subjectivity.

Not only did non-European jurists accept the civilization standard as a prerequisite to sovereignty and hence to membership in the 'family of nations', they also consented to the position that adoption of political institutions, particularly in regard to the domestic law of Western states, was the most visible indicator of a country having satisfied the standard. Accordingly, since non-European states adopted the Western standard of civilization, one might think that semi-peripheral lawyers passively imported Western legal thought, and that European international law was hence globalized. However, this appropriation was strategic; although not without problems, it served the interest of semi-peripheral states by allowing their jurists greater room for agency.[59] First, as argued above, in comparison to natural law doctrines, such as just war theory, the standard of civilization limited the realm of discretion left to Western states in their interaction with the extra-European world. With the standard, the link between Christianity and international law softened, and a non-Western sovereign's international legal personality came to depend on whether it was capable of assuming binding international commitments

[58] See generally G. Schwarzenberger, 'The standard of civilisation in international law', *Current Legal Problems*, 8 (1955), 212–34; Schwarzenberger, 'Rule of law'; Gong, *The standard of 'civilization'*; and Anghie, *Imperialism*.

[59] It is important to note that surveying the ways in which semi-peripheral jurists internalized the standard of civilization in the context of the modernization and westernization of their countries does not entail a positive, either political or normative, assessment of the consequences that this strategy imposed on their respective peoples. In fact, this type of critique should be levelled against both semi-peripheral as well as Western international lawyers.

and protecting the life and property of Western foreigners.[60] Second, lawyers from nations trying to achieve or secure recognition of their international personality did not simply submit to European determinations of who had met the standard of civilization. On the contrary, they were actively engaged in both European diplomatic circles and the international law professional scene, arguing for the recognition of their civilized status.[61]

Writing on the legal aspects of the interaction between their own state and Western states, semi-peripheral international lawyers strove to demonstrate not only their understanding of international law, but also the allegiance of their governments to international legal precepts. As such, they hoped to prove that their governments behaved as civilized and thus sovereign states. Non-European publicists saw their publications in Europe – books and articles in prestigious European law journals, mainly in French, the dominant language of the period, but also in English, German and Dutch – as underscoring the inclusion of their states in the society of civilized nations.

Following conventional wisdom, semi-peripheral international lawyers included both domestic and international facets in their efforts to substantiate their respective states' compliance with the standard of civilization.[62] The enactment of laws and introduction of legal institutions guaranteeing basic rights to nationals and foreign citizens alike were a central demonstration of their progression and modernization. In other words, while the idea of civilization was utilized by Western publicists to justify colonialism over 'uncivilized peoples' and special rights on 'quasi-sovereign' nations, such as consular jurisdiction, lawyers from countries in the latter situation, exercising only limited or formal sovereignty, appropriated the standard to overcome its legal consequences and to assert full sovereign autonomy. That is, non-European political elites not only imported and enacted Western law and institutions, but also

60 Schwarzenberger, 'Rule of law', 220; Schwarzenberger, 'Standard of civilisation', 62–6.

61 Carlos Calvo, for example, was a founding member of both the *Institut de Droit International* and the International Law Association.

62 Gong's study offers a useful enumeration of the requirements included in the standard: (1) guarantee of basic rights of foreign nationals, life, property, freedom of travel, commerce, religion; (2) organized political bureaucracy; (3) adhesion to generally accepted international law; (4) fulfilment of international obligations and diplomatic relations; (5) conforming to the accepted norms and practices of the "civilized" international society, including prohibition of polygamy and slavery. Gong, *The standard of 'civilization'*, pp. 14–15.

invoked these transplants as justifications for holding Western residents accountable under the law governing the territory, rather than the foreigner's national law applied by the consul.

First, semi-peripheral jurists internalized the domestic facet of the standard by enacting Western law as a would-be expression and proof of sovereignty. For example, Kentaro Kaneko (1853–1942), a renowned Japanese jurist and diplomat who in 1874 had earned a law degree at Harvard where he was a tutee of Oliver Wendell Holmes, Jr, writes in the *Revue de droit international et de législation comparée* that 'for certain countries that have already entered the concert of universal civilisation since some years, the question to be examined is if the modifications in the organisation of the courts have taken place in order that their jurisdiction can be applied without hindrance to subjects of Christian powers'.[63] Kaneko answers in the affirmative: 'Such is notably the case of the Japanese Empire, whose laws and institutions are at present at the level of the ones of the states of Europe and America'.[64] Kaneko enumerates the new laws and institutions that modernized the Japanese legal system: a new constitutional regime (Kaneko himself had participated in the drafting of the constitution of 1889), the law establishing the organization of the judiciary and a series of new codes of criminal procedure and civil procedure, a civil code, and commercial code. Kaneko concludes: '... together they constitute a legislative monument that has called the attention of the scientific community'.[65]

Kaneko goes on to suggest that the introduction of Western law in Japan positioned its judicial institutions on equal footing with the ones of the peoples of Europe and America. Kaneko's argument is subtle, for he implies that a Western legal system is not a sufficient sign to assert a country's status of civilization, but rather a justification for shifting the basis on which jurisdiction is exercised from the nationality principle to the territorial principle. Moreover, to grasp the full extent of the successful reception of Western law and institutions in Japan, Kaneko argues, one must understand Japan's extensive history, which he sets out to introduce to Western readers.[66] Giving an interpretative twist – typical of non-European thinkers – to the idea of Western law as a

[63] K. Kaneko, 'Les institutions judiciaires du Japon', *RDI*, 25 (1893), 338–56, 338–9.

[64] *Ibid.*, 338. [65] *Ibid.*

[66] Kaneko reviews four periods of Japanese institutional history: primitive, ancient, middle ages and modern: *ibid.*, 342–4.

European site-specific historical phenomenon and therefore to the ineluctable requirement of its importation, Kaneko presents a story in which the long history that preceded the imperial restoration of 1867 ripened Japanese legal institutions for modernization and successful assimilation of Western law.[67]

This mode of internalizing the standard of civilization was not uncommon. Other semi-peripheral jurists identified the standard with European civilization while claiming non-Western roots that confirmed the respective state's meeting of the standard. Another Japanese lawyer, Sakuyé (Sakuyei) Takahashi (1867–1920), illustrates this method: 'it must be confessed that this generosity [of applying the standard] is chiefly owed to European civilisation, which was introduced thirty years ago, but in general it may be said that if the graft was from Europe, the stock was an ancient one, deeply rooted in Japan from the earliest times'.[68]

Kaneko, on the other hand, points out that nineteenth-century codification was not the first time that compilations of laws had been enacted in Japan.[69] Furthermore, since the reorganization of the judiciary undertaken by the Japanese Empire in the year 660 AD, Japanese courts evolved in a fashion similar to European courts.[70] Accordingly, Kaneko defends the historical legacy enjoyed by Japanese courts, their modernization and the professional expertise of its judges, all of which made it quite difficult to compare the legal education or experience of Japanese judges with the competences of foreign consuls, who were simply elected by foreign merchants.[71] With a functioning Western legal system, Japanese lawyers could plead in favour of Japan's meeting the standard of civilization and consequently for the recognition of its sovereignty. They could then launch a critique of the legality of the unequal treaties, particularly with respect to consular jurisdiction.

In similar fashion, showing civilized behaviour, Latin American lawyers internalized the standard by asserting that, although sharing with the West the same cultural roots, civilization in Latin America had a history of its own. Carlos Calvo complained resentfully about Europeans' ignorance of the civilization of the 'peoples of the Latin race' in the Americas: 'Latin America has been discovered, conquered and populated by Europe, however, she is not known as it should be'. In order to correct European

[67] *Ibid.*, 341.
[68] S. Takahashi, 'Le droit international dans l'histoire du Japon', *RDI*, 3 (1901), 188–201, 200.
[69] Kaneko, 'Les institutions', 341. [70] *Ibid.*, 356. [71] *Ibid.*, 353.

neglect, Calvo published a monumental compilation of historical and statistical data about Latin America.[72] Calvo's revision of a vast record of laws and political institutions since colonial times onwards, on the one hand, and the cultural and political progress made by Latin American republics since independence from monarchic Spain and Portugal, on the other, allowed him to base the claim to sovereignty and civilization on solid foundations.[73]

Second, as soon as semi-peripheral international lawyers contended to have fulfilled the domestic prerequisites to count their legal systems and therefore their nations within the civilized world, they also had to supplement their assertions by demonstrating that the international facet of the standard was also met. Thus, they sought to demonstrate compliance with international law and civilized behaviour at the international level.

Japanese jurists, for instance, directed attention to Japan's record of compliance with the general principles of international law and with the rules and obligations contained in a series of universal treaties signed by all 'civilized nations' during the nineteenth century.[74] Japanese adherence to basic international agreements, as Douglas Howland has argued, was used to show its civilized status and thus to revise unequal treaties.[75] Compliance was not enough, however, for Japanese internationalists also had to show that Japan behaved like a civilized state in its international

[72] C. Calvo, *Recueil complet des traités, conventions, capitulations, armistices et autres actes diplomatiques de tous les états de l'Amérique latine, compris entre le golfe du Mexique et le cap de Horn, depuis l'année 1493 jusqu'à nos jours* (Paris: A. Durand, 1862), p. i. Dedicated to Napoleon III as an expression of gratitude of the peoples of the Latin race and published in Paris, Buenos Aires and Madrid, both in Spanish and French, and in eleven volumes between 1862 and 1868, this work collects legal documents and various figures on geography, populations, and commerce, from discovery to mid-nineteenth century.

[73] See also C. Calvo, *Annales historiques de la révolution de l'Amérique latine, accompagnées de documents à l'appui. De l'année 1808 jusqu'à la reconnaissance par les états européens de l'indépendance de ce vaste continent*, 5 vols. (Paris: A. Durand, 1864–7).

[74] In particular, Japan signed the treaties that laid the foundations of the laws in war. For example, in 1886, Japan acceded to the 1864 (First) Geneva Convention for Amelioration of the Condition of the Wounded and Sick in Armed Forces in the Field and in 1887 acceded to the Paris Declaration of 1856 on maritime law in time of war.

[75] D. Howland, 'Japan's civilised war: international law as diplomacy in the Sino-Japanese War (1894–1895)', *Journal of the History of International Law*, 9 (2007), 179–201, 183–4, 188. Similarly, Onuma has argued that 'scrupulous compliance' with the 'law of war was thought to contribute to the recognition of Japan as a "civilised nation" . . . prerequisite to abolishing extraterritoriality and restoring tariff autonomy': Onuma, 'Japanese international law', 34.

dealings.[76] In this regard, the standard was internalized in a manner similar to the nineteenth-century European practice, namely by recognizing a barbarian other in relation to whom a civilized status could be discerned. Sakuyé Takahashi exemplifies this attitude when distinguishing between Chinese 'barbarian' behaviour and Japanese 'law-abiding spirit' during the Sino-Japanese war of 1894–5.[77] Similarly, Nagao Ariga (1869–1921), linked the political and social reforms implemented by Japan with the declaration of the empire to carry on hostilities against China respecting the law of nations. Ariga affirmed that while the laws of war were based on reciprocity, Japan raised herself above the minimum legal duty, staying firm in her 'gracious commitment' to comply with international law, notwithstanding recurring violations of the laws of war by the Chinese.[78] Respecting the laws of war – Ariga concludes – Japan became civilized.[79]

Latin Americans also represented the process of acquiring civilization in contradistinction to other nations.[80] In Latin America, however, the civilized/barbarian dichotomy was projected less into countries of other regions and focused instead on the indigenous peoples of the Americas, in

[76] Japanese jurists presented Japan's conduct, in the war against China, as civilized: Howland, 'Japan's civilised war', 193–8.

[77] 'So barbarous was the conduct of the Chinese authorities that if reprisal were the prevailing principle of International Law, Japan need have stopped at nothing in revenging herself. But Japan refrained from revenge, for it was her intention, in spite of the nature of her opponent, to set an example of generosity by carrying on hostilities in an enlightened fashion': S. Takahashi, *Cases on international law during the Chino-Japanese war* (Cambridge University Press, 1899), p. 3.

[78] N. Ariga, *La guerre sino-japonaise au point de vue du droit international* (Paris: Pedone, 1896), pp. 1–5.

[79] 'Japan can be proud to have taken such a noble and dignified resolution at the occasion of an event determinant of its destiny. However, my intention here is not to incite universal admiration, either from the public nor historians; I simply want to draw general attention on this point as a legal question. The Chinese, from the point of view of the laws of war, can be compared to the Turks, Arabs and rough countries. The Japanese Empire, in its war against such a nation, wanted nevertheless to follow the laws that would apply to France, England or Germany': *ibid.*, p. 9.

[80] Calvo affirmed, for example, that from a positivist perspective of international law, international law is limited only to the states of Europe and the Americas: Calvo, *Le droit international*, p. 155. Furthermore, Calvo resented that Latin America is either frequently confused with other uncivilized regions of the world or still mistakenly identified with the period of colonial domination, disregarding the incessant progress Latin America had made since independence. To him, America was seen as conserving its primitive and savage state: 'its civilised and intelligent habitants are considered as the Indians or the blacks from Africa, going all naked or covered with feathers'. Calvo, *Recueil des traités*, p. ii.

respect to which Latin American elites had claimed an exclusive right of guidance to civilization.[81] Similarly, in the Ottoman as well as the Russian Empire, the internalization of the standard of civilization was redeployed domestically to justify the policy of modernization and Westernization and to attach the label 'barbarian' to the groups opposing reform. For example, Etienne Carathéodory, an ethnically Greek international lawyer at the service of the Ottoman rulers, is recalled to have championed for the internalization of the civilized/barbarian dichotomy in order to move Turkey towards the West, expressing that 'Turkey will be rescued, if she ceases to be pan-Islamic and becomes truly European'.[82]

It is interesting to note that the Japanese framed their own ancient history and culture as the fundamental source for the modernization and the progression that occurred in the latter part of the nineteenth century. Latin American lawyers have, at times, also made rhetorical use of the pre-Colombian, Inca and Aztecan Empires' civilization to distinguish the region from others populated by 'uncivilized tribes', regions that, in that period, were falling under the occupation of European states. Rather than a challenge to the idea of a Western standard of civilization on the basis of which to measure non-Western social organizations, locating civilization in an ideal and distant past, continued to be a rhetorical move to internalize that standard of civilization.[83] Evoking Latin America's pre-Columbian civilizations was rhetorical not only because by the time of independence only tenuous ties existed between the elites and the indigenous peoples, but also because the Creole elites were committed to positivism and modernization.

A critique of the standard

Nineteenth-century semi-peripheral international lawyers rarely critiqued the standard of civilization. The encounter between Western and non-Western peoples brought about a clash over different standards of civilization.[84] However, appealing to a non-Western normative system

[81] See L. Obregón, 'Completing civilization: nineteenth century *criollo* interventions in international law', unpublished SJD dissertation, Harvard University (2002), pp. 18–32, 93.

[82] G. Streit, 'Notices nécrologiques, Etienne Carathéodory', *Annuaire de l'Institut de Droit International*, 22 (1908), 342–5, 345.

[83] See e.g. A. Alcorta, *Droit international publique* (Paris: Larose et Forcel, 1887), pp. 202–13 and A. Alcorta, 'El derecho internacional en las antiguas civilizaciones americanas', *Nueva Revista de Buenos Aires*, 1 (1881), 82.

[84] Gong, *The standard of 'civilization'*.

#602 25-08-2016 10:19AM
Item(s) checked out to KALPOUZOS, IOANNI

TITLE: International law
BARCODE: 3500800538580[illegible]
DUE DATE: 01-09-16

TITLE: Cases and materials on internatio[illegible]
BARCODE: [illegible]
DUE DATE: [illegible] 09 16

TITLE: [illegible]
BARCODE: [illegible]
DUE DATE: [illegible] 12 16

remained exceptional.[85] For, semi-peripheral elites' appropriation of the international legal discourse began with a process of faithful learning of existing law during the first half of the century. It then shifted towards using existing rules and arguments to support their own interests and only then, towards the end of the century, an internal critique of the standard of civilization became possible.[86] For example, Tsurutaro Senga criticized the predominant view that limited the full enjoyment of the fundamental rights of sovereignty to states meeting a standard of civilization. Considered from an ethnographic standpoint, the standard was 'unscientific and deceitful' since – according to Senga – it assumes the existence of various stages of civilization.[87] It is quite remarkable that following this comment, Senga's sharpest criticism comes in the form of a dense and two-and-a-half pages long footnote:

> It is to be regretted that modern international law authors use in their works such an unscientific expression as 'civilisation' (resp. 'culture'). The definition of civilisation evidently lies beyond [the competence of] jurisprudence. But which science has defined this expression? None![88]

Following a rhetorical strategy familiar to semi-peripheral jurists, namely pointing at inconsistencies between ideas of different Western lawyers, Senga's footnote recounts an extensive list of lawyers who have used the expression 'civilisation' in a variety of ways. On the basis of this appraisal, Senga concludes by affirming:

> [E]ach one arbitrarily bestows to the expression 'civilisation' a subjective sense after their own Weltanschauung, so that each religious denomination or philosophical school cherishes a peculiar conception of civilisation. When European international law scholars speak about 'civilisation' or 'civilised states', they do so likewise from the subjective standpoint of their own Weltanschauung.[89]

Senga then identifies subjective considerations and logical inconsistencies in the use of the notion of civilization by prestigious international lawyers like Martens and von Holtzendorff, which is probably why he kept his critique within a lengthy footnote. Senga finds the standard of

85 For example, Henry Richardson has shown that Africans and African Americans advanced claims 'outside law' to challenge the legality of slavery: H. Richardson, *The origins of African-American interests in international law* (Durham, NC: Carolina Academic Press, 2008), pp. 3–34.

86 An external critique, in the sense of a critique based on alternative non-European normative systems, appeared only in the twentieth century, when semi-peripheral international lawyers called upon their own Latin American, Islamic, African or Third World traditions to challenge Western international law.

87 Senga, *Gestaltung und Kritik*, p. 135. 88 *Ibid.* 89 *Ibid.*, p. 136.

civilization not only scientifically useless, but also ideologically charged, since it disguises the subjective preferences of the lawyer who invokes it. In Senga's view, it is thus untenable to use the idea of civilization to limit the sovereign rights of states and the geographical range in which international legal relations are governed under equality.

A critique of the standard of civilization was exceptional among nineteenth-century semi-peripheral internationalists. Otherwise, Senga shared with them the same professional sensibility. He expressed this classical sensibility through his commitment to scientific legal analysis, articulation of a legal position or interpretation that reflected the interests of its own local polity and the consolidation of its modernizing nation-building project, and readiness to engage with the international legal doctrines produced at the political and intellectual centres of the profession.

Regardless of Senga's classical semi-peripheral sensibility, by challenging the use of the standard of civilization, Tsurutaro Senga set himself apart from most semi-peripheral international lawyers who instead internalized the standard. This challenge is also exceptionally powerful since it is articulated from within the premises of the European intellectual and legal discourse, inaugurating a mode of critique adopted by semi-peripheral internationalists ever since. It is extremely important to uncover this unique critique of the standard of civilization, for it amounts to a patent demonstration of the purposive and strategic appropriation of international law by non-European practitioners facing the challenges of nineteenth-century Western imperialism. Resistance, therefore, is not exclusive patrimony of third worldist international lawyers who were active during the 1960s decolonization. Defying the Eurocentric assumptions of international legal scholarship is not an exclusivity of contemporary international lawyers acquainted with postcolonial literature. Widespread interpretations of nineteenth-century history of international law prove inadequate as well. An account in which international law appears as an intra-European affair is not complete if the debate between European and non-European international lawyers – over consular jurisdiction or intervention for instance – as well as the use of their arguments in international disputes are ignored.[90] Interpretations

[90] Most studies share this type of Eurocentrism. For example, in Grewe's long history of international law there is nothing to say about consular jurisdiction, nor is there much about non-European lawyers' attempts to reduce the scope of intervention. See Grewe, *Epochs*.

that underscore the mutually constitutive relationship between international law and formal/informal colonialism, however, are problematic if they assume Western publicists' hegemony in the configuration of the discourse of international law, erasing the role of non-Europeans in the mutual constitution of the discourse itself.[91]

[91] Some TWAIL (third world approaches to international law) scholarship, I would argue, also falls under this type of Eurocentrism, since it fails to recognize, and therefore study, the counterhegemonic use of international law by non-Western jurists.

3 The imposition and negotiation of rules: hybridity and functional equivalences

Non-European jurists located in different parts of the world appropriated classical international law in a similar fashion, not simply because they faced similar challenges to the autonomy of their polities and similar strategic choices to use international law in their diplomatic negotiations with Western powers. Semi-peripheral lawyers also had to deal with nearly identical or functionally analogous rules of international law, so in similar fashion they internalized, adapted and used the arguments advanced by Western international lawyers. Semi-peripheral lawyers and diplomats who started negotiating treaties rapidly became occupied with the interpretation of the treaties' underlying legal doctrines, concepts and principles. Soon thereafter, as they became involved in the reformulation of these legal doctrines, concepts and principles, they engaged with, appropriated and transformed the intellectual tradition of international legal thinking in Europe, making it universal.

Let us examine the different international regimes valid in the semi-peripheral world as well as the functional equivalences between them. I distinguish between three ideal typical interactions between core and semi-peripheral sovereigns.

Three types of international regimes

The first ideal type describes formally equal interactions between Western sovereigns and non-European states whose international personality was recognized. It includes international relations between newly independent states and European states: that is polities that, due to a mix of domestic factors and political contingency between big powers, achieved independence during the nineteenth century (Latin America and Greece, for example).

The second ideal type is based on relationships between Western sovereigns and non-European states treated unequally both in political and legal terms. It encompasses relations between non-Western powers strong enough to oppose some resistance to their incorporation into the world capitalist system's commercial flows, so that they did not become colonies (China, Japan, Siam, and others), and Western powers (mainly European and the United States) who forcefully 'opened' the former.

The third ideal type represents interactions between Western sovereign states and non-Western states that even though participating politically in the European concert, their international personality was questioned and thus did not always fully enjoy legal equality. It considers the transformations that long-standing political and commercial relations between Europe and some of its powerful neighbours, that is, the Russian and Ottoman Empires, experienced during the nineteenth century, so that the latter had to 'apply' for re-entry into the 'family of civilized nations'.

With the help of this typology, I explore the local or regional specificity of a global trend. Nineteenth-century European colonialism and imperialism as well as the various forms in which non-Western nations handled and resisted foreign expansion defined the common historical context that led to the construction of a global international legal order. The appropriation of international law was a strategy available for states in these three ideal types, but the particularities of each historical context shaped the success, failure and modes in which international legal thinking was internalized and legal arguments used. Particularly important are the international legal regimes governing the relationship between Western and non-Western states that were in place up until the middle of the nineteenth century. Semi-peripheral lawyers supported changes in the rules sanctioned in these regimes by reinterpreting central concepts and doctrines of the European international law tradition such as the doctrine of recognition. The appropriation of this intellectual tradition to overcome the doctrinal barriers European lawyers had developed to bar equal treatment was consequently not only an academic but also a political and legislative project.

International legal relations between European and non-European polities were not new in the nineteenth century. However, as the world was drawn together into one global market, the number of treaties signed during the nineteenth century between European and non-European sovereigns increased exponentially. As a result, by the end of the century, a dense network of treaties developed between European sovereigns and sovereigns situated around the globe, including in Asia, Africa, Eastern Europe, Latin America, and the Pacific Islands.[1] The nature of the legal interactions instituted by these treaties varied: some treaties established equal relations between sovereigns, while others established unequal treatment between states. Still others instituted the end of international legal relations by sanctioning the cession of sovereignty and the colonial annexation of non-European territories.[2]

Although European and non-European states signed general bilateral treaties, which enacted rules covering a broad range of issues including the regulation of traditional diplomatic relations, international trade and the rights of foreign residents, no single treaty governed all interactions between the states. Instead, these relations were governed by a series of rules emanating from a series of treaties agreed over time, customary rules, or rules stated in the decisions of local authorities or tribunals. When international relations between a European and a non-European state became relatively stable and wide-ranging in scope, the series of international law rules governing their interaction, though emanating from different sources, instituted a consistent international regime.

Nineteenth-century international legal regimes were not only bilateral; on many occasions, a type of regional legal regime developed between a number of European and non-European states. As a result of the inclusion of the most favoured nation clause in each treaty concluded between a non-European state and a Western state, the specific bilateral treaty with the deepest concessions and thus the most favourable treatment had legal effects on other states, not just the signing parties. This particular treaty then represented the international legal regime governing the interaction between the non-European party and all other Western states with which that party had established legal relations.

At other times, when a particular bilateral treaty became the blueprint for subsequent negotiations and drafting of treaties, the rules of the treaty had an impact beyond the original parties. This was not an infrequent occurrence since, in the foreign offices of the nineteenth century, only a few lawyers had participated in multiple negotiations and gave legal advice on new issues. For example, as shown below, the convention

1 See Map 2.

2 For a study of these treaties see Fisch, *Die europäische Expansion* and for a study of protectorates see Anghie, *Imperialism*, pp. 54–7.

signed in 1535 between the Ottoman sultan Suleyman and Francis I of France, served as a first model that was followed by later treaties between the Ottoman rulers and other Western states.[3] Moreover, the capitulations Western states signed with the Ottoman Empire after the 'Near Eastern Crisis' of 1838–40 became blueprints for the negotiation of international agreements with those non-Western polities that, while not subjected to colonial domination, were opened to global trade by force. This model was consolidated and replicated in later treaties with Japan, Siam and China. In fact, the same British diplomat, John Bowring, participated in the negotiation of various treaties with the Ottomans, China and Siam.[4]

Consequently, to explore the legal relations governing the interaction between core and semi-peripheral states, let us now examine the legal regimes in each of the three abovementioned ideal types of international relations. Specifically, let us look at the international legal regimes in force in the Ottoman Empire, China and Latin America. The examination shows that these legal regimes were not simply imposed on semi-peripheral states and that rules and doctrines, such as extraterritoriality, were not simply Western, but had hybrid origins.

The Ottoman capitulations

Conventionally, international lawyers think that during the nineteenth century, international law began to regulate the relations between the Ottoman Empire and Western states following the imposition of capitulations, and that the treaty of Paris, signed in 1876, sanctioned Turkey's

[3] Phillip Brown, for example, maintains that the treaty of 1535 'may be considered as the real commencement of the regime of the Capitulations . . . Certainly all subsequent treaties were closely modelled on this treaty; and other nations have claimed as favourable treatment as therein accorded to France. In fact, it is stated in the body of this compact that the King of France reserved the right on behalf of the Pope, the King of England, and the King of Scotland, to adhere to the treaty should they so desire'. P. M. Brown, *Foreigners in Turkey; their juridical status* (Princeton University Press, 1914), pp. 33–4. Other lawyers and historians have also recognized the role of the treaty of 1535 as a model for subsequent capitulations. See e.g. L. E. Thayer, 'The capitulations of the Ottoman Empire and the question of their abrogation as it affects the United States', *AJIL*, 17 (1923), 207–33, 211 and T. Naff, 'The Ottoman Empire and the European states system' in H. Bull and A. Watson (eds.), *The expansion of international society* (Oxford: Clarendon Press, 1984), pp. 143–70.

[4] See Richard Horowitz, 'International law and state transformation in China, Siam, and the Ottoman Empire during the nineteenth century', *Journal of World History*, 15 (2004), 445–86.

admission into the international community. The history of capitulations, however, reaches far back into the sixteenth century when Western governments and Russia established regular diplomatic representations in the Ottoman court, and when treaties were subsequently concluded that created a *protégé* system for foreigners residing in the territories under Ottoman rule as well as for certain non-Muslim Ottomans.[5] However, well before the rise of the Ottomans, local authorities within the Byzantine Empire granted certain privileges to foreign merchants, including jurisdictional exemptions.[6] These grants were not only a matter of customary practice, but also privileges embodied in innumerable legal agreements concluded between sovereigns whose merchants participated in the commercial network connecting the Mediterranean basin.[7] Therefore, by the beginning of the nineteenth century the extraterritorial regimes that the capitulations established were not only of common usage, but also were well entrenched in the intellectual tradition of the laws of nations.[8]

By the mid-nineteenth century, however, capitulations had acquired an exceptional character, both conceptually and in terms of their impact. Conceptually, the jurisdictional concessions contained in capitulations became an exception when the international order progressively moved towards the principle of territorial sovereignty, which coalesced once the European political order abandoned the personal link between sovereign

[5] S. Sonyel, 'The protégé system in the Ottoman Empire', *Journal of Islamic Studies*, 2 (1991), 56–66.

[6] A. H. de Groot, 'The historical development of the capitulatory regime in the Ottoman Middle East from the fifteenth to the nineteenth centuries', *Oriente Moderno*, 83 (2003), 575–604.

[7] See in general Ago, 'Pluralism'. This interpretation is not novel. Travers Twiss, for example, argued in his late-nineteenth-century treatise that after the dismemberment of the Western Roman Empire, and in the absence of a common law or religion, merchants abroad have been governed by their own personal laws. Latin Kings of Jerusalem, for example, had, since the eleventh century, concluded with Genoa, Venetia and Pisa treaties conferring extraterritorial privileges. Also the Byzantine Empire had entered into agreements with Genoese and Venetian granting privileges to their merchants, including also to Muslim subjects. Moreover, these agreements were confirmed by the Ottomans after conquering Constantinople. T. Twiss, *The law of nations considered as independent political communities. On the right and duties of nations in time of peace* (Oxford: Clarendon Press, 1884), pp. 448–9.

[8] Late-nineteenth-century treatises included considerable sections on capitulations and consular jurisdiction. For examples from the British, French and German traditions, see respectively: Twiss, *The law of nations*, pp. 441–69; Henry Bonfils, *Manuel de droit international public* (Paris: Rousseau, 1898), pp. 174–5; Johann Ludwig Klüber, *Europäisches Völkerrecht* (2nd edn., by Carl Morstadt, Schotthausen, Hurter, 1851), pp. 30–6.

and subject as a basis for political organization.[9] At the same time, the impact of capitulations depended on shifts in the equation of force between the states exercising extraterritorial prerogatives and the states subjected to extraterritoriality. Prior to the nineteenth century, the exercise of extraterritorial jurisdiction was widespread and, in the case of Turkish capitulations, some agreements were in fact reached in the Ottoman Empire's own interest, and on occasions following the defeat of European powers.[10] In contrast, at the beginning of the nineteenth century, during the rise of European colonial expansion in general and the weakening of Ottoman rule in particular, the concession of privileges deeply eroded the power of local authorities.[11]

In brief, unlike international law scholarship, the specialized literature on Turkish capitulations provides a longer time span in which to contextualize capitulations. This literature suggests that the ordinary interpretation followed by international lawyers about the imposition of European international law during the nineteenth century should be qualified. 'Imposition' is a term that might accurately describe the shifts in power conferring to Western powers greater leverage to determine the terms and impact of the covenants signed with the Ottoman rulers and with other non-Western governments during the nineteenth century. It is not entirely correct, however, to use 'imposition' to describe the long-term evolution of the rules applicable to the relations between

[9] 'Treaties of this character [recognizing extraterritoriality] are not of novel device, as their origin may be traced back to a period, when race or nationality rather than territory was the basis of a community of law.' Twiss, *The law of nations*, p. 444. Compare treatises as late as Vattel's or Wheaton's, defining sovereignty as people and government with less importance given to territory. In this sense the extraterritorial regime instituted by the capitulations constituted a remnant of legal conceptions of the later Roman Empire: Edwin Pears, 'Turkish capitulations and the status of British and other foreign subjects residing in Turkey', *Law Quarterly Review*, 21 (1905), 408–25.

[10] Maurits H. van den Boogert argues that, at the beginning, the Ottoman Sultan unilaterally issued capitulations granting trade privileges to the sovereign countries that had sent envoys. The main purpose of capitulations was to stimulate trade with the West and regulate the presence of foreign merchants. M. van den Boogert, *The capitulations and the Ottoman legal system qadis, consuls, and beraths in the 18th century* (Leiden: Brill, 2005).

[11] Roderic Davison argues that in the nineteenth century the Sublime Porte, as a weaker party, sought refuge in international law in front of Western powers. For example, since the treaty of Paris signed in 1876 established a territorial settlement that was relatively favourable to Turkey, Ottoman diplomats supported the observance of international law and the principle of *pact sunt servanda*. R. Davison, 'Ottoman diplomacy and its legacy' in Carl L. Brown, *Imperial legacy: the Ottoman imprint on the Balkans and the Middle East* (New York: Columbia University Press, 1996), pp. 174–99.

the West and the non-Western world because the term implies that the expansion of international law exclusively flowed from core to periphery.

The Ottoman Empire routinely entered into peace agreements – *ahdnames* – with Christian states.[12] First, and at the peak of Ottoman power, these pacts included unilateral and non-reciprocal concessions that the Sultan granted to the foreign state, thus reserving for himself the right to abrogate the covenant at will if, for example, the condition of maintaining peaceful relations was breached.[13] Consequently, as İnalcık has shown, the Sultan conceded privileges in exchange for reciprocal advantages, under which non-Muslim Ottoman subjects engaged in commercial operations in Europe, for example.[14] On some occasions and in particular when the power of the Ottoman Empire declined, these accords were also signed in the form of bilateral agreements or peace-settlements conferring reciprocal rights to both signatories.[15] At the same time, the *ahdnāme* as the document itself, as a type of *berat*, namely a decree or edict issued by the Sultan, contained the trade privileges granted to individual

[12] '*Ahd-nāme*' was one of the official terms used by Ottomans for treaty. See J. M. Landau, '*Mu'ahada*' in P. J. Bearman and Marc Garborieau (eds.), *Encyclopaedia of Islam*, 2nd edn (Leiden: Brill Online), http://brillonline.nl/entries/encyclopaedia-of-islam-2/muahada-COM_0766. Specifically, according to Halil İnalcık, '*ahd-nāme* was the document subscribed to confirm the covenant (*ahd*) guaranteeing protection (*amān*) to an enemy (Ḥarbī). See H. İnalcık, '*Imtiyāzāt*' in Bearman and Garborieau (eds.), *Encyclopaedia of Islam*, http://brillonline.nl/entries/encyclopaedia-of-islam-2/imtiyazat-COM_0371.

However, according to Feroz Ahmad, Ottomans used also the term *imtiyazat*, which means privilege or concession for foreigners, to refer to the capitulations: F. Ahmad, 'Ottoman perceptions of the capitulations 1800–1914', *Journal of Islamic Studies*, 11 (1) (2000), 1–20.

[13] These documents were also called *ahd-nāme*: Landau, '*Mu'ahada*'; Thayer, 'The capitulations', 224.

[14] İnalcık, '*Imtiyāzāt*'.

[15] Scholars of the nineteenth and early twentieth centuries heatedly discussed the unilateral or bilateral character of '*ahdnāmes*', for the reason that Turkey could only legally abrogate capitulations if they were conceptualized as unilateral concessions. Panaite has noted how the distinction has inconsistently been drawn by using modern juridical criteria on documents of the fifteenth to the seventeenth centuries. Panaite also shows that on several occasions the Ottoman terminology, phrasing the agreements as unilateral concessions, contradicted the Latin, Italian or French translations depicting capitulations as bilateral treaties. V. Panaite, *The Ottoman law of war and peace: the Ottoman Empire and tribute payers* (Boulder: East European Monographs, 2000), pp. 239–42. See also V. Panaite, 'Notes on the Islamic-Ottoman law of peace', *Revue des études sud-est européennes*, 41 (2003), 191–206.

foreign merchants first and then to states.[16] In Western languages, bilateral peace agreements and unilateral concessions as well as the document issued came to be known as capitulations, having originally no association with the idea of surrender or imposition, but making reference to the agreement's division in chapters.[17]

The term 'capitulation' was first used to describe a treaty concluded with France in 1535, the first covenant in which the Ottoman Emperor addressed a European sovereign as *padishah*, i.e. emperor, and thereby treated him as a sovereign equal.[18] The concessions granted in 1535 (renewed in 1673) were confirmed, extended and systematized into a complete list of privileges by a 1740 treaty. This regime evolved through usage and interpretation, subsequent treaties with other Western powers and the widespread inclusion of the most favoured nation clause extending the privileges to other nations. This general corpus of rules governed the relationship between the Ottoman Empire and Western powers and Russia, and determined the legal status of foreigners within the Ottoman Empire and of certain Ottoman subjects.[19]

Salahi Sonyel has shown how the original practice of protecting foreign nationals expanded to also include the non-Muslim subjects of the Ottoman Empire, becoming a significant threat to the existence of

[16] In Panaite's terminology these are Imperial charters *ahdnames-i hmyn*. Viorel Panaite, H-Net Reviews 2 (2003), www.h-net.org/reviews/showrev.php?id=7325.

[17] Late-nineteenth-century international lawyers were well aware of this. See e.g. G. Pélissié du Rausas, *Le régime des capitulations dans l'empire ottoman*, 2 vols. (Paris: A. Rousseau, 1902). Twiss pointed out that the use of the term 'capitulation' referred to discrete portions of treaties: Twiss, *The law of nations*, p. 463. See generally Panaite who has compared the use of terminology in Turk and Western languages in various treaties concluded between Western sovereigns and the Ottoman rulers: Panaite, *The Ottoman law*, p. 240.

[18] Once the struggle for the Holy Roman Emperorship between Charles I of Spain and Francis I of France was resolved in favour of the former with his coronation as Charles V in 1521 and the latter's capture in 1525, the French resumed negotiations with Suleyman to forge an alliance against the Habsburgs. Although the military agreements came to nothing after peace between Charles and Francis was imposed, the relation of friendship and cooperation between France and the Ottomans continued. See Naff, 'The Ottoman Empire', pp. 146–7.

[19] Other Western nations that pushed Turkey to include in their capitulations the most-favoured nation treatment in order to enjoy the privileges granted in the French Capitulations of 1535 and 1740 included: England (1579), Holland (1579), Austria (1615), Russia (1711), Sweden (1737), Denmark (1756), Prussia (1761), Spain (1782), Sardinia (1825), United States (1830), Greece (1854), and Brazil (1858). Brown, *Foreigners in Turkey*, pp. 40–3.

the empire. Along with the privileges conferred on Western merchants under capitulations, some treaties also claimed religious protection for non-Muslim Ottomans.[20] Moreover, when Ottoman authorities granted to accredited ambassadors a number of *berats* (patents or warrants), that is, jurisdictional exemptions and tax and commercial privileges to individuals serving in the foreign legations as interpreters (*dragoman*), commercial agents, or employees, European and Russian ambassadors, in turn, either sold these patents to affluent Ottoman Greeks, Armenians and Jews, or widely conferred nationality on them. In this manner foreign ambassadors immensely expanded their protective role over Ottoman subjects.[21]

As a result, no single set of legal texts codified the scope and nature of privileges. Instead, their scope and nature depended on the invocation of rules, customs and precedents in particular diplomatic or consular negotiations. Furthermore, a significant gap separated the formal privileges conceded in the capitulations from their implementation. Maurits van den Boogert, in his study on the practice of the capitulatory regime in the eighteenth-century Ottoman legal system, describes this gap and argues that capitulations offered a general framework requiring negotiations between Ottoman authorities and Western representatives each time a controversy ensued.[22]

No single capitulation treaty contained a complete list of the privileges instituted by the international legal regime valid in the Ottoman Empire. Thus, authors have looked at the historical development of this international regime and distinguished between personal, economic and jurisdictional privileges.[23] Under the first type, capitulations granted foreigners permission to visit and reside in Ottoman territories, and included freedom of movement, worship, commerce, and the exercise of professions. Capitulations also granted foreigners the privilege to hold private religious services, to send and receive letters unopened by Turkish

[20] According to Sonyel, by the eighteenth century, French had claimed protection over Catholics, British and Prussians over small Protestant communities and occasionally over Jews, and Russians over Greeks and Armenians: Sonyel, 'The protégé system', 58–9.

[21] Sonyel claims that by 1860, in Istanbul alone, around fifty thousand Ottoman subjects enjoyed foreign national status: *ibid.*, 58, 64.

[22] See generally van den Boogert, *The capitulations*.

[23] See, e.g., N. Susa, *The capitulatory régime of Turkey, its history, origin, and nature* (Baltimore: Johns Hopkins Press, 1933), pp. 70–88 and Altuğ Yılmaz, *Turkey and some problems of international law* (Istanbul: Yenilik Basımevi, 1958), pp. 22–31 adding administrative privileges such as post offices operated by capitulatory powers, the establishment of schools, hospitals and monasteries.

authorities, and to have an inviolable domicile.[24] In addition to the general freedom of commerce, foreigners enjoyed economic privileges, such as exemptions from direct taxation, from internal taxes on foreign goods and on goods in transit, and from the regulation of import and export duties, maximums being fixed by the capitulatory powers.[25] Foreign powers also controlled the Turkish financial system through the *Dette Publique Ottomane* institution created in 1881 to protect the interests of the foreign creditors by allowing them to supervise the collection of revenues and other fiscal matters of the empire.[26] Finally, jurisdictional privileges were extremely complex and subject to many changes throughout time.[27] In general, consuls had absolute jurisdiction to resolve civil and criminal cases involving foreigners of the same nationality, and special mixed tribunals were established for cases involving foreigners of different nationalities.[28] Civil cases between foreigners and natives fell under the jurisdiction of local tribunals typically as long as a *dragoman* was present, while criminal cases originally followed the same rule, but were later passed to the exclusive jurisdiction of the consul.[29]

Turkish capitulations were first and foremost international treaties, and as such they regulated traditional interstate matters, from the conduct of ordinary diplomatic relations to the implementation of the European concert's political settlements.[30] Capitulations redrew boundary lines, guaranteed the right of navigation in rivers (e.g. Danube), or neutralized maritime spaces (e.g. the Black Sea). As peace agreements, capitulations declared the end of hostilities, established demilitarized zones, and determined war compensations. In addition to typical interstate matters, Turkish capitulations also contained a number of rules securing the integration of local markets into the international economy and the concession of privileges to foreigners and to some Ottoman nationals. Such rules were central to the constitution of a legal regime of vast scope and impact and led to the radical transformation and Europeanization of Turkish legal and institutional order.[31]

[24] Thayer, 'The capitulations', 215, 217; Susa, *The capitulatory régime*, pp. 70–2.
[25] Susa, *The capitulatory régime*, pp. 72–5. [26] *Ibid.*, pp. 75–7.
[27] See generally van den Boogert, *The capitulations*, pp. 159–79, 207–24.
[28] Thayer, 'The capitulations', 216. [29] *Ibid.*, 217.
[30] The Paris Treaty of 1856 included Turkey in the European concert of nations. General Treaty for the Re-Establishment of Peace between Austria, France, Great Britain, Prussia, Sardinia, and Turkey, and Russia, March 30, 1856, 114 Consol. T.S. 409.
[31] See E. Örücü, 'The impact of European law on the Ottoman Empire and Turkey' in Wolfgang J. Mommsen and Jaap de Moor, *European expansion and law: the encounter of*

The Chinese 'treaty port system'

The international law rules enacted in the Turkish capitulations were similar to the rules sanctioned in the unequal treaties concluded in Eurasia.[32] In 1842, following China's defeat in the Opium War of 1839, Britain and China signed the Treaty of Nanking.[33] Other Western powers rapidly followed suit, forming the first set of agreements that instituted a comprehensive legal regime between China and the West. Since the legal regime opened a series of Chinese ports to foreign trade, it was also known as the 'treaty port system'. The Tientsin treaty of 1858, signed under new threats of war after the Arrow incident, revised and extended the previously granted privileges.[34] It increased the number of treaty ports. It also included a series of personal privileges enjoyed by foreigners, including 'the right of residence, of buying or renting houses, of leasing land therein, and of building churches, hospitals, and cemeteries'.[35] Judicial privileges included the typical extension of foreign consuls' jurisdiction to adjudicate on controversies arising between British subjects, and in relation to crimes committed by British subjects in Chinese territory.[36] Economic privileges, such as the tariffs fixed in the Treaty of Nanking, were confirmed. However, special norms were incorporated to address particular complaints that British merchants made about the operation of the treaty port institution[37] as well as particular rules relative to the context and resolution of the Arrow incident.[38]

European and indigenous law in 19th- and 20th-century Africa and Asia (Oxford: Berg, 1991), pp. 39–58.

32 This similarity was well known to international lawyers of the first half of the twentieth century and to contemporary historians. See e.g. Horowitz, 'International law and state transformation', 460–1. Among lawyers, see e.g. F. B. Sayre, 'The passing of extraterritoriality in Siam', *AJIL*, 22 (1928), 70–88, 70; Y. Tseng, *The termination of unequal treaties in international law; studies in comparative jurisprudence and conventional law of nations* (Shanghai: The Commercial Press, 1933).

33 Two annexes and a supplementary treaty concluded in 1843 complemented the Treaty of Nanking. For an analysis of their rules, see D. Wang, *China's unequal treaties.*

34 This regime was further expanded after the Boxer rebellion and reaching the peak of influence in the 1920 and 1930s: Gong, *The Standard of 'Civilization'*, p. 140.

35 Treaty of Peace, Friendship and Commerce between China and Great Britain, Article XI, June 26, 1858, 119 Consol. T.S. 167.

36 Treaty of Tientsin, Articles XV and XVI.

37 To prevent local officials from imposing taxes beyond the treaty ports officials when they collect inland transit duties, Article 28 granted foreign merchants the right to pay a single charge and obtain a transit pass exempting them from further taxation. It also allowed Chinese authorities appointed to oversee the collection of duties to declare the tax rates. Treaty of Tientsin, Article XXVIII.

38 The treaty, for example, proscribes the use of the Chinese character 'I' in reference to the Government or subjects of Her Britannic Majesty. This character means both foreign

The treaty port system, like capitulations, instituted a complex legal regime consisting of a succession of agreements and supplementary conventions. This regime was also transformed by subsequent interpretation and usage as well as in its interaction with domestic politics, legal culture and institutions. As in the capitulatory regime, the impact of the treaty port system depended less on the formal privileges that the agreements contemplated than on the practical compromises that Chinese and Western officials reached. In John Fairbank's words, the treaty system became a 'joint Sino-foreign arrangement, a compromise or hybrid device, to which both parties had to contribute and which neither could control alone'.[39] The Chinese treaty port system, therefore, was not simply a product of unequal treaties imposed by the West. From a global perspective, on the one hand, the regime that emerged in China had historical links with the Ottoman capitulatory regime, since Turkish capitulations provided models for governing the interstate relationship with non-European countries. It was also significant that British envoys, for example, who had diplomatic experience in the Ottoman Empire were subsequently appointed to special missions in Asia. From a Chinese viewpoint, on the other hand, capitulations were a compromise between their own tributary system and Westerners' international law. Again in the words of Fairbank, 'the treaty system in its earlier decades from the 1840's to the 1880's was not merely a device for bringing China into the Western world; it may equally well be viewed as a Ch'ing device for accommodating the West and giving it a place within the Chinese world'.[40] Moreover, as in Turkey, extraterritorial institutional arrangements were not alien to Chinese legal culture.[41]

Similar to Turkish capitulations, the treaty port system also fulfilled traditional international functions. By displacing the existing tributary

and barbarian, which was in part at the root of the Arrow incident. For a general list of privileges, J. C. Vincent, *The extraterritorial system in China: final phase* (Cambridge: Harvard University Press, 1970).

[39] J. K. Fairbank, *Trade and diplomacy on the China coast: the opening of the treaty ports, 1842–1854* (Cambridge: Harvard University Press, 1964), p. 317.

[40] J. K. Fairbank, 'The early treaty system in the Chinese world order', in J. K. Fairbank and Ta-tuan Ch'en (eds.), *The Chinese world order; traditional China's foreign relations* (Cambridge: Harvard University Press, 1968), pp. 257–75, 258.

[41] For example, studying the Mixed Court in Shanghai, Pär Cassel argues that there was a continuity between the traditional Qing legal system and the extraterritorial aspects instituted by the treaty port system, since the norms that regulated extraterritoriality were borrowed and adapted from Qing legal concepts that had previously developed to grant certain legal privileges to Manchus. P. Cassel, 'Excavating extraterritoriality: the "judicial sub-prefect" as a prototype for the mixed court in Shanghai', *Late Imperial China*, 24 (2003), 156–82.

systems in China or Japan, the treaty port system laid out the basic legal rules governing interstate relations on the basis of diplomatic representation under horizontal equality. In the Treaty of Tientsin, for instance, signatories agreed to appoint ambassadors and other diplomatic agents to the Court of Peking 'in accordance with the universal practice of great and friendly nations'.[42] However, unequal treaties also contained the rules that made it possible to incorporate China into the global markets. In addition to the mentioned privileges, the treaty port system contained rules for Western organizations to operate and manage radio, telegraph, mining, railway, and industrial establishments.[43] Furthermore, in 1854, a foreign-manned and administered institution, the Foreign Inspectorate of Customs in Shanghai, was established, and had an impact in the control of revenues and the financial market, in the same way the Turkish Debt Administration did in the Ottoman Empire.

However, in terms of the progressive weakening of Chinese power and because of the fact that it lasted until 1949, the treaty port system arguably had a greater impact than the Turkish capitulations. Along with the concession of the typical personal, economic and juridical privileges, unequal treaties also granted compulsory and perpetual leases to establish various Western facilities, including the stationing of police, naval and military forces, along the coast and the Yangtze River, thereby sanctioning the operation of gunboat diplomacy.

General treaties of peace, commerce and navigation in Latin America

The international legal regimes in force in Turkey or China were certainly different from the regimes that developed in nineteenth-century Latin America. Unlike Turkish capitulations and the Chinese treaty port system, the agreements signed between Western and Latin American states established formal equal treatment. European powers and the United States recognized the newly independent governments of Latin America as full and sovereign members of the international community much

[42] Treaty of Tientsin, Article II. Moreover, diplomatic agents, their family and establishment could take permanent residence in the capital: Treaty of Tientsin, Article II. This treaty also imposed rules of protocol that would reflect the recognition of equal standing: [the ambassador] 'shall not be called upon to perform any ceremony derogatory to him as representing the Sovereign of an independent nation on a footing of equality with that of China'. Treaty of Tientsin, Article III.

[43] Tseng, *The termination of unequal treaties*, p. 16.

earlier than they recognized Turkey and China. In spite of this difference, the historical contexts and international legal regimes in force in Turkey, China and Latin America have significant parallels. These parallels explain a shared imperative among semi-peripheral lawyers in these three locations to internalize and use European international legal arguments to manage and improve the interaction of their states with the Western powers that dominated global politics and the emerging world economy.

First, capitulations, unequal treaties and the treaties negotiated under sovereign equality had a significant number of similar rules. For example, there were rules that opened the local markets to foreign trade, granted foreigners the right to travel, reside and commerce, imposed limits on import duties, determined the conditions for coastal shipping, and established most-favoured nation treatment. These privileges were generally conferred under reciprocity in the case of Latin America and unilaterally in the case of China and Turkey.

Second, some rules of international law from the capitulations and the treaty port system were formally different but functionally similar to rules in force in the international legal regimes governing the interaction between Western and Latin American states. For example, most international agreements concluded with Latin American governments did not grant jurisdictional powers to foreign consuls. Although consular jurisdiction, the most controversial aspect of unequal treaties, was absent from the international legal regimes in Latin America, extant classical international law doctrines granted broad diplomatic protection, giving foreign diplomatic representatives vast room for action. Thus, after the conclusion of general treaties and the establishment of diplomatic relations, European governments and the United States aggressively used diplomatic protection, not only representing their citizens' claims against Latin American governments – imposing for instance the settlement of disputes by mixed commissions – but also threatening or using force to secure the payment of compensation to injured foreigners and to collect public debt.

Third, while the doctrine of the standard of civilization mediated and limited the admission of Turkey and China into the international community and justified unequal treatment, it was the doctrine of recognition that performed an equivalent function in Latin America. Western states did not use the standard of civilization to refuse or qualify a Latin American state's admission into the international community or to deny reciprocity in the privileges and general norms of international conduct established in subsequent treaties. However, as I show below, Latin American publicists' strategies to achieve recognition were analogous to Chinese or Turkish lawyers' efforts to internalize the standard of civilization. The discussions regarding the scope and meaning of the standard of civilization determined the nature of the rules enforced by the Turkish capitulations or the Chinese treaty port system. Similarly, the negotiation between Western states and the new Latin American sovereigns concerning the recognition of the latter's international personality created controversy about the type of economic and personal privileges that foreign residents would receive and the conditions under which they would be conferred: unilaterally, under reciprocity, or with preferential treatment for the newly independent nations.

International rivalries, national self-interest, and political contingency played out in the negotiation of general treaties of peace, commerce and navigation between Western and Latin American governments, and explained the various classes of legal relations sanctioned by them. Most international agreements established commercial and maritime reciprocity, which was arguably more beneficial to the merchants and economic interests of the United States, Britain and other European states, than to the new states of Latin America. As a result, the Western states probably extracted them from the Latin American states in exchange for recognition, as a sacrifice to gain access to foreign markets or to obtain foreign loans, or under local elites' own commitment to the freedom of commerce.[44] It was therefore unusual that Britain received from Brazil, and to a lesser extent from Colombia and Rio de la Plata, non-reciprocal preferential treatment as well as economic and judicial privileges. Conversely, but also exceptionally, Mexico obtained from Britain preferential treatment in the form of reduced duties as well as a broad definition of Mexican commercial ships that favoured the development of coastal shipping. This range of international law rules can be illustrated in a brief review of the treaties signed between the governments of Spanish America and Brazil, and the most powerful states involved in the region's independence, Britain and the United States.

As soon as the United States recognized Latin American states in 1822 and articulated the Monroe Doctrine the year after, it started to negotiate agreements to promote its commercial interests in the

[44] See D. A. G. Waddell, 'International politics and Latin American independence' in L. Bethell (ed.), *The independence of Latin America* (Cambridge University Press, 1984), pp. 195–232.

region.[45] The United States granted recognition not only to support the emerging republics and to oppose the re-establishment of monarchies in the continent, but also to obtain access to the new markets to the south, making sure that the old colonial monopolies were definitely broken. However, the United States was unwilling to enter into a continental multilateral agreement, as proposed in 1826 by Bolivar at the Congress of Panama. When Britain obtained preferential treatment from Latin American governments at the Congress of Panama, the United States initiated a diplomatic offensive to conclude bilateral agreements with the governments of Spanish America and Brazil.[46]

In the context of Anglo-American commercial rivalry over Latin American markets, the United States sought to obtain strict reciprocal treatment in its relationships with Latin American states. Without much success at the beginning, the United States concluded its first treaty in 1824 with Colombia.[47] But the treaty of 'Peace, Amity, Commerce and Navigation between the Central American Federation and the United States', signed in 1825, became the model for later treaties, since it contained a complete catalogue of rules governing political and commercial relations, including full reciprocal treatment.[48]

[45] See A. P. Whitaker, *The United States and the independence of Latin America, 1800–1830* (New York: Russell & Russell, 1962), pp. 546–63.

[46] For example, in the twenty years following recognition of Spanish American governments in 1822 (1824 in the case of Brazil), the United States concluded treaties with: Colombia, 1824, 74 Consol. T.S. 455; Colombia, March 16, 1825, 75 Consol. T.S. 161; Central American Federation, December 5, 1825, *ibid.*, 433; Mexico, January 12, 1828, 78 Consol. T.S. 35; Brazil, December 12, 1828, *ibid.*, 249; Brazil, June 15, 1829, 79 Consol. T.S. 453; Colombia, November 25, 1829, 80 Consol. T.S. 225; Mexico, April 5, 1831, 81 Consol. T.S. 381; Chile, May 16, 1832, 82 Consol. T.S. 413; Mexico, April 3, 1835, 85 Consol. T.S. 101; Venezuela, January 30, 1836, 86 Consol. T.S. 1; Mexico, April 20, 1836, *ibid.*, 103; Peru-Bolivian Confederation, November 30, 1836, *ibid.*, 257; Mexico, April 11, 1839, 88 Consol. T.S. 397; Ecuador, June 13, 1839, 89 Consol. T.S. 63; Chile, July 7, 1840, 90 Consol. T.S. 263; Peru, March 17, 1841, 91 Consol. T.S. 301.

[47] Until 1825, negotiations or ratification of treaties had generally failed, sometimes because of domestic instability (as in the case of Chile and Peru) and other times because of British influence (in the case of Mexico). See Whitaker, *The United States*, pp. 586–7. The treaty with Colombia of 1824 included a most-favoured nation clause, which put an end to the preferential treatment afforded to Britain: *ibid.*, p. 588.

[48] General Convention of Peace, Amity, Commerce, and Navigation between the Central American Federation of the Centre of America, December 5, 1825, 8 U.S.T. 1867. The treaty contained a most-favoured nation clause (Article II). It placed commerce and navigation on the basis of perfect equality and reciprocity, granting mutually the right to 'frequent all the coasts and countries of the other and reside and trade there, enjoying the rights and privileges that native citizens enjoy' (Article III). The treaty also established religious liberty, conferred reciprocity on import and exports duties,

In contrast, Britain's recognition and negotiation of general treaties with Latin American states followed a slow and intricate course. Internal politics, namely, the King's support of the principle of legitimacy, as well as international politics, primarily the need to protect the relationship with Spain in their alliance against France, explains Britain's cautious policy vis-à-vis Spanish American governments. Consequently, Britain signed its treaties with the Spanish American republics much later than the conventions concluded with Brazil.

The first treaty signed between Brazil and Britain in 1827 granted non-reciprocal extraterritorial privileges in favour of Britain. Because the treaty includes consular jurisdiction, it is remarkably analogous to the unequal treaties concluded in Turkey, Siam, Persia and China. But, for the same reason, this treaty was an exception in Latin America, an exception explained by the traditional alliance between Britain and Portugal and the Brazilian Emperor's willingness to reciprocate for the assistance provided during the move of the Portuguese court to Brazil in the wake of Napoleon's occupation of the Iberian Peninsula.

In contrast, it was equally exceptional for Britain to grant preferential treatment to a Latin American state. For example, the treaty signed in 1826 with Mexico established reciprocal freedom of commerce and allowed citizens of each state to freely 'come, remain and reside in the respective territories'.[49] The treaty also conferred national treatment on import duties and on any other charges imposed on vessels entering their respective ports, and provided a narrow definition of British and Mexican vessels.[50] Two additional articles to the treaty somewhat mitigated the narrow definition of Mexican vessels, since Britain granted Mexico preferential treatment for a ten-year period, in which national treatment was limited and a wider definition of Mexican vessels was in force.[51]

granted their respective citizens the power to dispose of personal goods according to law and gave special protection to the persons and property of the citizens of each other, according to law and access to justice. *Ibid.*

49 The Treaty of Amity, Commerce and Navigation between Great Britain and Mexico, December 26, 1826, 77 Consol. T.S. 39, Article II.

50 *Ibid.*, Articles V, VI and VII.

51 According to Jaime Rodríguez, British diplomats agreed to grant preferential conditions because of the Mexicans' uncompromising position during negotiations. The post-independence excitement of Mexican politicians led them to refuse 'to grant special privileges to any nation, even Great Britain. The new republic would assume her place as an equal among the great powers of the earth': J. Rodríguez, *The emergence of Spanish America: Vicente Rocafuerte and Spanish Americanism, 1808–1832* (Berkeley: University of California Press, 1975), p. 91.

However, most treaties signed between Britain and Spanish American states instituted strict reciprocity.[52] These agreements were concluded in the form of general treaties of amity, commerce and navigation. In general, as was the case for covenants reached with the United States, these treaties opened up trade, limited tax on export and imports, secured the protection of the property held by foreigners as well as their lives and private liberties, and guaranteed most-favoured nation status. Although these treaties established reciprocal conditions, formally equal treatment did not mean substantive equality in the interactions between Britain and Latin American states. Equal treatment meant asymmetrical relations, not only because England's greater economic development reinforced a world division of labour that was detrimental to Latin American interests, but also because foreign proprietors secured the protection of their own interests through the exercise of diplomatic intervention, which could escalate to the imposition of coercive measures and demonstrations of force.

The Turkish, Chinese and Latin American regimes compared

We are unfortunately too familiar with complaints of the delay and inefficiency of the courts in the South American republics. We must, however, continue to repose confidence in their independence and integrity, or we must take the broad ground that these states are like those of oriental semi-civilised countries.[53]

[52] A brief review of one of these treaties illustrates the typical norms governing the relationships between Latin American states and Britain. For instance, the Treaty of Amity, Commerce and Navigation between Great Britain and Rio de la Plata, signed in Buenos Aires on 2 February 1825, established in Article 2 'reciprocal freedom of commerce', according to which the citizens of each party 'have liberty freely and securely to come, with their Ships and Cargoes, to all such Places, Ports, and Rivers . . . to enter into the same, and to remain and reside in any part of the said Territories . . . to hire and occupy houses and warehouses, enjoy the most complete protection and security for their Commerce; subject always to the Laws and Statutes of the two countries respectively'; Article 3 extends to British overseas territories the freedoms granted to citizens of Rio de la Plata; Article 4 establishes reciprocal most-favoured nation treatment on import and export duties as well as on import and export prohibitions; Article 10 appoints consuls for the protection of trade. Treaty of Amity, Commerce and Navigation between Great Britain and Rio de la Plata, February 2, 1825, GR. BRIT. – UNITED STATES PROVINCES OF RIO DE LA PLATA, 3 H.C.T. 44 (1841).

[53] Note from Mr Seward, Sec. of State, to Mr Burton, Min. to Colombia (Apr. 27, 1866) in J. B. Moore and F. Wharton, *A digest of international law* (Washington: Government Printing Office, 1906), p. 660.

This quotation shows that nineteenth-century diplomats were well aware of the existence of parallel international regimes. Unlike their colleagues in the past, contemporary international lawyers have only occasionally studied the Turkish capitulations, the Chinese treaty port system and the general treaties of amity and commerce concluded in Latin America – international regimes that strike most of them as historical remnants of a bygone era.[54] The relative absence of research on these international legal regimes explains most authors' tendencies to overemphasize the role of Western imposition of international law as the main cause explaining the global expansion and consequent transformation of European international law into a universal legal order. The history of international law in Turkey, China or Latin America calls this interpretation into question.

First, these non-European histories show that semi-peripheral lawyers did not merely implement Western powers' dicta, but that they had some leverage to negotiate the content of the international agreements they signed. In the midst of adverse power relations, semi-peripheral lawyers and diplomats relentlessly negotiated with Western states to advance their own foreign policy objectives.[55] Though these treaties were not simply imposed by Western states, it was still the case that most rules of international law served Western interests. Occasionally, non-European states extracted favourable terms from Western states, as in the British-Mexican treaty of 1826. Yet a majority of treaties enforced either rules

[54] Note that the previous discussion of these three international legal regimes has mostly relied on the research carried out either by diplomatic and legal historians, or by international lawyers of the late nineteenth and early twentieth centuries. The main histories of international law give only cursory treatment to unequal treaties. See generally Nussbaum, *A concise history*; Grewe, *Epochs*; Karl-Heinz Ziegler, *Völkerrechtsgeschichte: ein Studienbuch*, 2nd edn (Munich: Beck, 2007). By the same token, until recently, none of the major encyclopaedias of international law had entries on unequal treaties. Matthew Craven and Anne Peters stand as lonely exceptions. M. Craven, 'What happened to unequal treaties? The continuities of informal empire' in M. Craven and M. Fitzmaurice, *Interrogating the treaty: essays in the contemporary law of treaties* (Nijmegen, The Netherlands: Wolf Legal Publishers, 2005), pp. 43–80; A. Peters, 'Unequal Treaties' in Rüdiger Wolfrum (ed.), *The Max Planck encyclopedia of public international law* (Oxford University Press, 2012), pp. 38–50. The omission of unequal treaties in contemporary studies of the history of international law reflects the exceptional character that these treaties had conceptually and in terms of their impact. The absence also expresses a general indifference regarding the history of the rules of international law. Remember Arnold McNair's criticism of most history of international law as 'either a history of its literature, or a history of international relations': McNair, 'Aspects of state sovereignty', 6, n. 1.

[55] See e.g. M. Auslin, *Negotiating with imperialism: the unequal treaties and the culture of Japanese diplomacy* (Cambridge: Harvard University Press, 2004), p. 4 and *passim*.

instituting unequal treatment – most importantly consular jurisdiction – or rules under conditions of reciprocity formal equality that arguably benefited the more powerful states rather than weaker ones.

These treaties, however, were negotiated and signed by semi-peripheral authorities who had in sight the broader international political situation. Consenting to rules that were unfavourable in the short term would be nonetheless acceptable to pursue long-term goals, such as achieving recognition, gaining access to foreign markets, obtaining loans or military supplies.[56] Moreover, when Western states signed treaties, they limited, at least formally, their autonomy vis-à-vis non-Western states. Furthermore, Western powers had to push for diplomatic negotiations to revise existing treaties, rather than resorting to threat or actual use of force.

Second, even when international power relations were such that Western states could impose their own terms, the scope and impact of the rules enacted in treaties concluded with non-European governments depended on domestic institutions and informal practices. The abovementioned studies uncovering the mediating role that domestic authorities had in Turkey, China and Latin America, illustrate how the rights enjoyed by foreigners were not fully determined by the formal rules contained in the treaties concluded with foreign powers. The actual scope of the rights enjoyed by foreigners depended both on their ability to put forward their contentions to the representatives of their home governments and on the resolution of the conflicting claims advanced by consular authorities (under extraterritorial jurisdiction or diplomatic protection) and local political actors.[57]

Third, the history of nineteenth-century international legal regimes in Turkey, China and Latin America demonstrates that central rules of international law, both in respect to their content and nature and regarding

[56] For example, Bethell writes, 'Commercial treaties were imposed on Mexico, Colombia, Argentina and other independent Spanish American republics (with little possibility of negotiation) as a precondition for much-sought-after recognition': L. Bethell, 'Britain and Latin America in historical perspective' in V. Bulmer-Thomas (ed.), *Britain and Latin America: a changing relationship* (Cambridge University Press, 1989), pp. 1–24, 4.

[57] In addition to the literature quoted above, Richard Chang has challenged the interpretation that consular jurisdiction always favoured the interest of foreigners: R. Chang, *The justice of the Western consular courts in nineteenth-century Japan* (Westport: Greenwood Press, 1984), p. 135. On the role of the interaction between foreign citizens and authorities of their respective home governments in shaping the extraterritorial regime in China, see E. Scully, *Bargaining with the state from afar: American citizenship in treaty port China, 1844–1942* (New York: Columbia University Press, 2001), pp. 21–23 and *passim*.

their conceptual outlook, were much more hybrid than one would have expected given the stereotypical view of this period, as characterized by the imposition of international law (an order with an exclusively European origin). Rules and institutions sanctioned by these treaties had roots in the legal history and cultures of both parties. Extraterritoriality, for instance, was not alien to Turkey or China. In fact, extraterritorial jurisdiction as sanctioned in both the Turkish capitulations and the Chinese treaty port system had been in force prior to the nineteenth century in both the Ottoman and Chinese domestic legal orders, such as in the tributary relations with foreign polities, including at times European sovereigns.

Fourth, these international legal regimes came into force in the context of the economic and political interactions that followed the formation of a world economy. They gave stability and regulated the incorporation of non-European states into the global economic order. As part of a global trend, the series of treaties signed between core and semi-peripheral states contained either nearly identical rules or functionally analogous rules even though they were concluded in different and distant locations around the world. These treaties secured and governed the opening of the entire territory or some ports of China, Japan, Latin America and Turkey to international trade, including rules that gave foreign citizens the right to reside and travel, to acquire property, to conclude contracts, and to hire nationals. Some rules with dissimilar content, included in treaties signed with different non-European states, performed analogous functions. Although these treaties considered some non-Western states to be sovereign equals while others treated non-Western states unequally, the operative legal doctrines in both types of treaties – diplomatic protection and consular jurisdiction respectively – similarly enabled and mediated the presence and impact of European merchants and citizens in places as diverse as Argentina, Siam, Japan and Egypt.

This chapter provided a historical background on the nature and trajectory of the rules of international law that semi-peripheral states confronted in their interaction with Western states. Examining and comparing a series of international regimes ranging from absolute inequality to formal equality explains why semi-peripheral elites felt the pressure to learn the discourse of international law. Even when international law purely reflected power imbalances, the expression of such unequal treatment in the language of law gave semi-peripherals a starting point for resistance because rules set out in treaties or general principles written down in treatises set a baseline that semi-peripheral jurists could invoke in case of further encroachment by Western powers. This baseline of rules and doctrines could be reinterpreted by semi-peripherals to justify better treatment. From this starting point, semi-peripheral jurists sought to change the rules and doctrines governing their interaction with the West, replacing the regimes instituting unequal treatment with formal equality.

This chapter also offered a more complete picture of nineteenth-century international law, making apparent two important aspects. First, international law was plural. It consisted of a variety of international regimes with different rules and historical trajectories. At the same time, functional equivalences between different regimes as well as a single conceptual and discursive apparatus supporting the legality of diverse regimes suggest the existence of one international law, one legal discourse governing the relations between Western and non-Western states and allocating different degrees of equality. Semi-peripheral appropriations of international legal thought in support of a change of rules for semi-peripheral states – in particular, the legal consciousness that developed out of these appropriations – reflected the plural and singular character of international law.

4 The expansion of nineteenth-century international law as circulation

When semi-peripheral international lawyers appropriated classical international law and the European legal tradition, they advanced a series of doctrinal positions, reinterpreting positivism, absolute sovereignty and the standard of civilization. But this appropriation was not only doctrinal. At the same time, it entailed the construction of a deeper set of assumptions – assumptions about the nature of an international world dominated by Western powers, about the fate of non-Western polities as newcomers, about modernization as an answer to the Western challenge to semi-peripheral independence and about international law as part of the modernizing and nation-building project. I would suggest understanding these assumptions as well as the mode of thinking about them through the language of international law as a distinctively semi-peripheral legal consciousness.[1]

This semi-peripheral form of classical legal consciousness might be described as a *particularistic universalism*. Semi-peripheral jurists faithfully believed in the universality of international law as neutral and scientific knowledge and as a legal order where instituting sovereign autonomy and equality should attain validity on a global scale. However, semi-peripheral jurists' specific articulation of the universal rendered international law particular. Given their eagerness to be faithful to their own representations of international law's universality, in addition to the fact that international legal doctrine was a channel to support modernization or

[1] I borrow the concept of legal consciousness from Duncan Kennedy. 'The notion behind the concept of legal consciousness is that people can have in common something more influential than a checklist of facts, techniques and opinions. They can share premises about the salient aspects of the legal order that are so basic that actors rarely if ever bring them consciously to mind': Duncan Kennedy, *The rise and fall*, p. 5.

nation-building projects defined by the specific political predicaments faced in different parts of the globe, semi-peripheral lawyers' international legal thinking acquired a local or regional distinctiveness.

In other words, the distinctive semi-peripheral recombination of the central elements of classical international law – absolute sovereignty, positivism and the standard of civilization – contained a tension between the believed universality and neutrality of a scientific outlook and the centrality given to their respective national standpoints and interests. The former pulled the semi-peripheral internationalist towards a universalist jurisprudential approach to construe the meaning and definition of international law, and the latter pulled him in the opposite direction towards a particularist perspective from which to evaluate the impact of international legal doctrines and rules. For example, when Argentinean publicist Amancio Alcorta (1842–1902) challenged Carlos Calvo for neither giving adequate treatment to Argentinean interests nor recognizing the existence of American principles of international law, Calvo retorted:

> these words entail a reproach that is not comprehensible for an Argentinean jurist who follows the world's scientific movement... As Argentinean I comply with the law of my country, but as an author of a book of universal jurisprudence, I have had to situate myself under a scientific point of view, seeking, if not a mode to uniform the principles, at least to reconcile the interests of all peoples.[2]

The desire to improve the international position of their respective polities by means of international law drove nineteenth-century semi-peripheral lawyers' hurried and faithful acquisition of knowledge about international law. As a result, semi-peripheral publicists adopted central tenets of the international legal tradition at face value, only subsequently adjusting the uses and interpretations to serve particular and local interests. Consequently, their belief in the universality of international law as the law between civilized states, for example, remained intact. This had a great impact on their professional sensibilities. In particular, the strategy of internalizing (rather than rejecting) the standard of civilization by demonstrating the civilized status of their countries in contrast to other non-European nations contributed to the absence of ideological cohesion between international lawyers from different nations and regions of

[2] C. Calvo, 'Polémica Calvo-Alcorta', *Nueva Revista de Buenos Aires*, 7 (1883), 629, 632–3. For a description of the disputes between universalist and particularist international lawyers in the Latin American context, see A. Becker Lorca, 'International law in Latin America or Latin American international law? Rise, fall, and retrieval of a tradition of legal thinking and political imagination', *Harvard Journal of International Law*, 47 (2006), 283–305.

the semi-periphery. The absence of bonds of solidarity resulted from the structure of the argument adopted by semi-peripheral publicists; that is, unequal treatment applies not to 'us' but to other 'less civilized nations'. As a result, I would argue that Latin Americans set themselves apart from their indigenous peoples; Japanese from the Chinese; Russians from the Ottomans; Ottoman elites from their own Islamists.

Non-European international lawyers who evaluated the history of their own political, legal or cultural contexts to demonstrate their participation in the civilized world were less inclined to recognize commonalities with other regions or states of the semi-periphery. Thus, the generation of semi-peripheral lawyers who accepted international law under the classical synthesis during the second half of the nineteenth century saw no reason to establish bonds of solidarity with one other, which is one of the features that set them apart from the generation of modern semi-peripheral international lawyers that followed. Assimilating the knowledge and mastering the arguments that would contribute to the task of getting European nations to recognize the legal personality of their states fostered a pragmatic sensibility that put non-European international lawyers under significant professional pressure. Once this pressure lifted, later generations of lawyers had more latitude to risk departing from the dominant perspective by deploying interpretations of international law that explicitly responded to the particularities of the history, culture and problems in their specific location. This partial detachment from European intellectual influence bolstered semi-peripheral international lawyers' confidence and made it possible to bond professionally and politically with international lawyers from other regions. This is the reason that I reserve use of the notion of *modernist resistance* to describe the legal consciousness of peripheral international lawyers of the interwar period and describe semi-peripheral classical international lawyers of the second half of the nineteenth century as *universal particularists*.

I have thus far emphasized the global trends that explain the transformations international law underwent during the nineteenth century. I have highlighted the influence that European expansion and the consolidation of global markets had on the international legal regimes regulating interactions between Western and semi-peripheral states across the globe. I have also indicated that both the functional equivalences in the rules enacted by these legal regimes and European international lawyers' development of doctrines sustaining the inclusion of unequal rules in them explain the global character of the appropriation of European international law thinking in the semi-periphery.

The global character of this trend is not an excuse to forget that the appropriation of international law in places as dissimilar as Japan, Turkey, China, Russia or Mexico served a plurality of interests and agendas. That is, the specific characteristics of each context where this global trend was articulated explain the particularistic aspect of the semi-peripheral legal consciousness. International lawyers supported the modernization and Westernization of their polities, but the significance, impact and politics of these processes varied dramatically. To understand these differences, I now turn to a comparative study of the historical contexts in which European international legal thought was appropriated and in which international law became universal. Let us look at the three ideal types explored in the previous chapter. Considering them in chronological order, let us examine: first, the inclusion of newly independent sovereigns under formal equality; second, Western expansion through the forceful opening of weakened empires under legally and politically unequal relations; and, third, the effort of non-Western empires to seek re-admission to the international community.

Inclusion of newly independent states through recognition

Political elites in the semi-periphery, especially in the colonial territories that won the various wars of independence waged during the first half of the nineteenth century, considered the discourse of international law to be a fundamental building block in their nation-building projects. Once military means had secured independence, the authorities of the new states sought recognition of their sovereign autonomy as members of the international community from the main European powers and the United States. The desire for recognition primarily occurred following the partial dismemberment of the Spanish, Portuguese and Ottoman empires that created the Latin American republics and Greece.[3]

In contrast to Japan, Turkey and China, where the standard of civilization limited their admission into the international community and

[3] The wars of independence at the beginning of the nineteenth century put an end to Spanish rule in Latin America and resulted in the creation of a number of new countries. Compared to Spanish America, Brazil followed a different trajectory, when in 1822 and with far less struggle it became a monarchy separate from Portugal. On the other hand, another group of independent countries (Greece, Montenegro, Romania) emerged from the defeat of Ottoman forces in the Greek war of independence and the Russo-Turkish war of 1877–8. However, I will only explore the use of international legal language to obtain recognition in relation to Latin America.

justified unequal treatment, in Latin America or Greece the doctrine of recognition performed an equivalent function. Recognition had vital political consequences. Western states did not grant recognition as a gratuitous concession. Instead, Spanish American states and Brazil had to vigorously pursue recognition of their statehood by European governments and the United States. By the 1820s, after declaring independence but during war against Spanish loyalists, some Spanish American governments had sent special envoys to London and Washington. These envoys fought arduously to establish formal diplomatic relations with European states and then, as we have seen above, to conclude treaties of friendship, commerce and navigation.

European recognition, in particular by Britain, was crucial to undercut support from the Holy Alliance for a Spanish incursion to regain control of its former colonies. Spanish American states also wanted recognition in order to increase European trade and investment as well as to improve the conditions under which they procured loans and arms from European bankers and merchants. Moreover, Spanish American envoys sought to establish diplomatic relations and sign general treaties not only with Britain and the United States, but also with France and other smaller European states.[4]

International politics were evidently at centre stage in the diplomatic struggle to obtain recognition and to determine the rules of international law that would regulate the interaction with governments that had been newly admitted to the 'family of nations'.[5] Both their victories of the new Latin American republics and Greece in their wars of independence and their post-bellum success depended to a great extent on the self-interest of the great powers and particularly on the ascending role of Britain. For example, to prevent a relapse into colonial rule under the auspices of the Holy Alliance, Canning devised a policy of cooperation with the United States to recognize the Latin American republics under the latter's hegemony, as expressed in the Monroe doctrine.[6] Similarly, Britain allying with Russia secured the independence of Greece from the Ottoman Empire.

[4] Rodríguez, *Spanish America*, p. 93 and *passim*.

[5] See generally Waddell, 'Latin American Independence', pp. 225–6.

[6] See J. Davis, 'Britain and the European balance of power' in C. Williams (ed.), *A companion to nineteenth-century Britain* (Oxford: Blackwell Publishing, 2006), pp. 34–52, 37 and Waddell, 'Latin American Independence', pp. 213–15 ff.

However, the fight for recognition was also a diplomatic dispute fought on legal grounds.[7] On the one hand, recognition challenged the Vienna Congress' principle of legitimacy as well as the conventional understanding of the doctrine of recognition itself. On the other hand, Latin American diplomats created a new dimension of controversy while negotiating general treaties of peace, commerce and navigation by discussing the type of economic and personal privileges that Latin American states would grant to foreign residents and the conditions under which they would confer them (whether unilaterally, under reciprocity, or with preferential treatment for the newly independent nations).

At the same time, publicists from Latin America, for example, not only invoked international legal arguments to secure recognition for the international legal personality of their newly independent states and to gain sovereign autonomy from the very same powers that made their independence possible – namely, Britain and the United States – but also reinterpreted and changed existing legal doctrines governing recognition. This pattern was also remarkably similar to the one followed by Greek international lawyers like Nicolas Saripolos, both regarding the use of the classical synthesis to buttress Greek independence and deal with the Ottoman Empire and the migration to Europe's intellectual centres.[8] In Latin America, Argentinean lawyer Carlos Calvo, as we have seen, was the more prominent representative who attempted to exploit international law to promote the interests of the new American republics.

Since the Congress of Vienna, the international rules governing recognition had sanctioned the principle of legitimacy. The Spanish Chancellery was perfectly aware of this legal doctrine and used it in the diplomatic protests it presented to the European governments who were negotiating recognition and treaties with Spanish American 'rebel' governments, invoking the illegality of this course of action.[9] In order to push for recognition, the Latin American states challenged the principle of legitimacy.

[7] This was especially true in the case of Brazil, where '[i]ndependence . . . was won not on the field of battle but by diplomacy': A. Manchester, 'The recognition of Brazilian independence', *The Hispanic American Historical Review*, 31 (1951), 80–96, 80.

[8] N. Saripolos, 'La question gréco-turque, ses commencements, ses progrès, et son état actuel', *RDI*, 11 (1879), 119–43, 133–5; N. Saripolos, 'La question gréco-turque après l'acte final de la conférence de Berlin', *RDI*, 13 (1881), 231–45, 239–43; see also A. Rivier, 'Notice nécrologique sur M. Saripolos par M. Rivier', *Annuaire de l'Institut de droit international*, 10 (1888), 52, 55–6.

[9] W. S. Robertson, *France and Latin-American Independence* (Baltimore: Johns Hopkins Press, 1939), p. 560.

This challenge entailed a change in the international rules toward a conception of sovereignty based on a people's right to self-determination.[10] Recognition, in the writings of Carlos Calvo, also challenged the traditional interpretation of the doctrine of recognition itself.

Calvo embraced the distinction between internal and external sovereignty that positivist international lawyers had introduced, though he employed the distinction to support a shift towards a declaratory rather than a constitutive conception of recognition. Calvo followed the conventional view in affirming that sovereignty emerges as soon as a society gives itself a government, creating the internal sovereignty of the state. Internal sovereignty exists and is exercised *de plano* from the moment that the state is constituted, and therefore does not require sanction by other states. Calvo also accepted an idea of sovereignty that requires other states to recognize a nation in order for it to be included in the international community, thereby sanctioning its external sovereignty.[11] But Calvo inverted the consequences of this doctrinal distinction – the separation of a colony affects the external sovereignty of the metropole. As long as the struggle for independence continues, uninvolved states have to observe strict neutrality in their relations with the metropole and with the colonies fighting for independence. However, Calvo warned that uninvolved states have the right to grant recognition to colonies when there is a protracted war of independence or when it has become de facto impossible for the metropole to regain control over its colonies.[12]

I have sketched above Calvo's tactical appropriation of international law. It is also important to emphasize Calvo's professional presence in Europe and the local – Latin American – distinctiveness of his semi-peripheral legal consciousness. Carlos Calvo's career is a paradigmatic example of the professional patterns that nineteenth-century semi-peripheral lawyers followed. After pursuing studies in Buenos Aires and Paris, Calvo began a diplomatic career that put him in contact with the most prestigious intellectual milieus of mid-nineteenth-century Europe.[13]

[10] Self-determination was not a new concept. Its revival marked a return to the influence that the French revolution had exerted on pre-restoration international law. R. Redslob, 'Völkerrechtliche Ideen der französischen Revolution' in O. Mayer, *Festgabe für Otto Mayer zum siebzigsten Geburtstag, 29. März 1916* (Tübingen: Mohr, 1916), pp. 273–301.

[11] Calvo, *Le droit international*, p. 235. [12] *Ibid.*, p. 241.

[13] For an example of one diplomatic mission, in 1860 Calvo represented Paraguay in London with the main task of requesting reparations for the Paraguayan government in the Cansatt case. 'Calvo's success with the case opened the doors for him in the salons and intellectual circle of Europe': Obregón, 'Completing civilization', p. 96.

Calvo was remarkably successful.[14] Precisely at the time when international law became a professional activity, Calvo achieved wide impact by publishing treatises both in Spanish and French, some of which had various editions and translations.[15] In the prologue to the fifth edition of his treatise, Calvo notes the various translations and editions, commenting: 'Is it not the best proof of the usefulness of our work?'[16]

Calvo's success can be understood in the context of the transformations international law experienced during the course of the nineteenth century. I have argued above that international law both contracted and expanded its range of validity during that period. The geographical scope of international law shrank to govern exclusively the interactions between European, civilized and sovereign states – becoming the '*Droit publique de l'Europe*'.[17] While international lawyers began to articulate the idea of international law, expressing the juridical consciousness of civilized peoples, they saw themselves as embodying this consciousness in the form of an internationalist spirit and a profession defined by universality and inclusiveness.[18]

This double shift – both conceptual and professional – required someone like Calvo. As an Argentinean in Paris, he reminded Europeans of a parallel history of international law in the New World and reinstated the universality that international law had lost after the demise of naturalism. European international lawyers welcomed Calvo's inclusion of material relating to the Americas. For instance, in his book review of Calvo's *Derecho internacional*, Gustave Rolin-Jaequemyns notes: 'But what gives him special value, is the important and altogether new role that in the examination

14 Calvo was founding member of both the *Institut de Droit International*, established in 1873 in Ghent, and the Association for the Reform and Codification of the Law of Nations, later renamed the International Law Association.

15 In 1868, Calvo published *Derecho internacional teórico y práctico de Europa y América* (Paris: D'Amyot, 1868), which he published in French, with four editions between 1870 and 1896. See, Calvo, *Le droit international*. The fourth edition was translated into Chinese and Greek, and an abridged edition was translated to English. This is what Calvo maintains in the prologue to the fifth edition of *Le droit international*, p. xii. Map 5 shows only Calvo's translation to French because the other translations could not be found.

16 *Le droit international*, p. xii; Obregón has discussed this quote in 'Completing civilization', p. 91 n. 178.

17 See C. H. Alexandrowicz, 'Doctrinal aspects of the universality of the law of nations', *BYIL*, 37 (1961), 506–15, 506. On the distinction between a universal law of nations and a European public law, see Guggenheim, 'Jus publicum europeum'.

18 For an account of this emerging disciplinary sensibility, see Koskenniemi, *Gentle civilizer*, pp. 11–97.

of his questions, he gives to historical American precedent'.[19] A Latin American in Europe patently manifested European international law's universality and Latin America's civilized status as well as guaranteed the scientific impartiality of the international lawyers' doctrinal positions. Calvo himself was aware of the role that his foreignness served:

> My venerable colleague Professor Heffter, assured me, during the visit I paid to him in 1878, that the impartiality of my doctrines and the fact that I am a foreigner, bestowed my work, in the German high courts of justice, with an authority that the works of nationals often lacked.[20]

Latin Americans' singular history explains not only their elite's heavy reliance on the culture, tradition and values of 'Western civilization' to assert their own thoughts, but also their obsessive preoccupation with the recognition of their participation and contribution to the development of Western culture.[21]

International law was not immune from this general trend and shaped nineteenth-century Latin Americans' efforts to demonstrate the assimilation of the discourse of international law in ways that overemphasized the common religious substratum in order to assert membership in an international community of Christian nations.[22]

[19] G. Rolin-Jaequemyns, 'Derecho internacional teórico y práctico de Europa y América, por Carlos Calvo', *RDI*, 1 (1869), 294–6, 294.

[20] Calvo, 'Polémica', 635. The fact that Calvo mentions Heffter is remarkable. Heffter was renowned for maintaining that there was no single external public law (*äußeres Staatrecht*) because there was no law extending its scope to all states and peoples of the globe. According to Heffter, law only developed and achieved validity within determined circles. Specifically, a general legal consciousness manifested itself only within Christian Europe and in the states with European heritage. In the European realm, Heffter insisted, this law has acquired the name of European public law. A. Heffter and F. Geffcken, *Das europäische Völkerrecht der Gegenwart auf den bisherigen Grundlagen* (Berlin: H. W. Müller, 1882), pp. 1–2.

[21] L. Whitehead, *Latin America: a new interpretation* (New York: Palgrave Macmillan, 2006), pp. 1–18.

[22] For example, when Spain seized the Chincha Islands in Peru, Latin American authorities made diplomatic protests condemning the attack as not in accord with the practice of civilized nations. The Argentinean minister to Peru, D. F. Sarmiento, formulated his diplomatic protest using Christianity as a sign of civilization: 'The Republics of South America belong to the community of Christian nations which governs itself by international law; they exist by their own right, which they themselves have conquered, as proved by history, and secured by universal concurrence; whilst the people from whom they have served themselves can in no manner deny their existence, by urging the absence of Treaties or of explicit acknowledgement, after forty years renunciation of all pretension of dominion, and virtual approval of the Treaties of Ayacucho, which put an end to the war between the metropolis and its former colonies.' Don D. F.

However, the classical synthesis, as seen in the rules and principles of international law that Latin American appropriations brought about, did not simply reflect the legal order of the 'European Concert'. On the contrary, Latin Americans pushed to the forefront precepts that responded to the interests of their own countries. In the absence of this class of rules, they resorted to general principles of law to challenge the norms exclusively rooted in European state practice. What came to be known as the 'Calvo doctrine', for example, was an effort to argue – on the basis of classical international law's absolute sovereign autonomy and equality – that military as well as diplomatic interventions by European states in the domestic affairs of Latin American nations were unlawful. As shown above, Calvo reinterpreted the nature of the right to intervene as an exception to the principle of sovereign independence. Calvo claimed that the exception was only justified when exercised in Europe, for it followed 'a principle favourable to the development of civilisation'. In Latin America, on the contrary, intervention was unlawful since it was based on mere force.[23]

Western expansion through the forceful opening of weakened empires

Elites in Asia felt a similar pressure to appropriate international law when they confronted the reconfiguration of the nineteenth-century world system under European and American hegemony.[24] Although weakened, for different geopolitical reasons some Asian empires did not fall under direct European colonial rule. Yet they were not powerful enough to oppose the forced opening of their territories to Western commerce and influence. By the 1850s, Japan, China and Siam had signed unequal treaties with European powers and the United States that not only guaranteed freedom of trade and religion, unilateral most-favoured treatment, and reduction of tariffs, but also renounced any claim to subject foreign residents to

Sarmiento to Señor Ribeyro, Inclosure 1 in No. 7, Accounts and papers of the House of Commons, State Papers, vol. XXXII (1864), p. 15.

23 According to Calvo, affirming the principle of non-intervention gives foreigners recourse to the local tribunals where they have acquired domicile: Calvo, *Le droit international*, pp. 350–1.

24 For example, Auslin has shown a parallel between Japan, Burma and Siam, in their dealings with Western powers and the efforts to renegotiate unequal treaties: Auslin, *Negotiating with imperialism*, pp. 22–5.

their legal order and judicial system, thereby recognizing the exercise of consular jurisdiction in their territory.[25]

Japan

Japan saw its long-sustained policy of seclusion powerfully disrupted in 1853 with the arrival of an American expedition of ironclad steamers under the command of Commodore Matthew Perry, who proceeded to force the opening of Japanese ports to American trade.[26] After the conclusion of the US-Japan Treaty of Friendship of 1854, the Shogunate government felt pressured to rapidly acquire basic knowledge on the 'Western law of Nations' in order to handle the new relationship with the United States and European nations.[27]

Moreover, Japanese elites and government officials were in a different position than their Latin American or Greek counterparts. By the time international law became an essential knowledge to the Latin American or Greek nation formation projects, the elite and lettered people of these new republics had strong links of cultural dependency with Europe. They were ready to tackle the appropriation of European international legal thought because they had already been travelling to Europe for a long time and had also long been immersed in the Western legal tradition. The situation in Japan, or for that matter in China, was quite different not only because there was no significant economic or cultural exchange with Europe before the nineteenth century – Europe was in fact peripheral to the East Asian economic system – but also because the region had, under Chinese leadership, established a long-standing, stable and independent political order that governed relations between autonomous

[25] For a study of these treaties in general see Craven, 'What happened to unequal treaties?'; for an extended treatment in relation to China, see Fairbank, *Trade and diplomacy* and D. Wang, *China's unequal treaties*; regarding Japan, see Auslin, *Negotiating with imperialism*.

[26] Starting in the sixteenth century, Japan had contact with Portuguese, Spanish, English and Dutch envoys and merchants. In 1638, however, the regime adopted a policy of seclusion to eliminate the impact of Christian missionaries, as evidenced by the fact that only Dutch and Chinese merchants were exempted from the prohibition and were only allowed to engage in restricted trade. R. P. Anand, 'Family of "civilised" states and Japan: a story of humiliation, assimilation, defiance and confrontation', *Journal of the History of International Law*, 5 (2003), 1–75, 8.

[27] See Auslin, *Negotiating with imperialism*, p. 1 and *passim*. Thereafter, Japanese officials resisted US pressure to extend the scope of the 1854 treaty by delaying negotiations. The Western intervention in China sent a powerful message which by 1857 caused Japanese elites to change their stance and sign a new treaty. Other Western powers rapidly followed suit. Anand, 'Family of "civilised" states and Japan', 12–13.

political entities via hierarchical relations, namely under a tributary system.[28]

Consequently, European international law first had to be assimilated through direct importation. Japanese imperial authorities employed Western international lawyers to provide them with legal advice, teach international law to their young elites, and participate in the translation of classic international law textbooks. For example, between 1889 and 1892, the German-Swiss international lawyer Otfried Nippold was invited by the Japanese government to teach at the Society of German Sciences in Tokyo.[29] Moreover, the Japanese government employed an Italian, Alessandro Paternostro, to write an essay supporting Japan's full admission into the international legal community. Like the Japanese scholars we have seen, Paternostro highlighted the adoption of Western law as a sign of civilization.[30]

China and Korea and, to a lesser extent, Siam and Persia also acquired and translated US and European international law textbooks and hired foreign experts in international law.[31] For example, Gustave Rolin-Jaequemyns served as adviser to the Siamese government from 1892 to 1902. Searching for a successor to Rolin-Jaequemyns, Siamese officials did not trust European lawyers, because they could be co-opted by the French, and enrolled a series of American lawyers from Harvard, most prominently Francis B. Sayre.[32]

After direct importation, Asian states sought to train their own international lawyers. The Japanese government sent some of its officials to Europe where they studied international law and then served as legal

[28] On Western Europe as peripheral to China, see A. G. Frank, *ReOrient: global economy in the Asian Age* (Berkeley: University of California Press, 1998).

[29] O. Nippold, *Wanderungen durch Japan: Briefe und Tagebuchblätter* (Jena: Mauke, 1893). Miyasaki lists a number of Westerners who served as legal advisers to China, Japan and Korea: Miyasaki, 'History: Far East', p. 807.

[30] Paternostro's article includes three annexes, one summarizing Japanese work on codification, another on teaching and legal culture, including the curricula of law schools, a list of professional societies and a list of law books translated from French, English and German, and finally an annex describing the organization of the foreign office: A. Paternostro, 'La revision des traités avec le Japon au point de vue du droit international', *RDI*, 23 (1891), 176–200, 193–200.

[31] Fuji mentions the translation and publication of authors such as Hall, Westlake, Martens, Lawrence and von Liszt: Fuji, 'One hundred years', 29. See in general Map 5 showing the translation of Bluntschli (1856), Wheaton (1836), Martens (1882–3) and Calvo (1868).

[32] P. Oblas, 'Treaty revision and the role of the American foreign affairs adviser, 1909–1925', *Journal of the Siam Society*, 60 (1976), 171–86.

advisers in Japan's diplomatic missions or participated in the first international meetings of the 1890s (mainly in the first Hague Conference). After Commodore Perry forced the opening of Japanese ports, the Shogunate decided that a group of Japanese students had to learn the sciences and knowledge of the victor. The plan to send students to the US was dropped when the American civil war broke out. Instead, the Shogunate requested the Netherlands to receive a warship with a group of Japanese students. Among them, two studied international law. Between 1862 and 1865, Amane Nishi (Shusuke) (1829–1897) and Mamichi Tsuda (Shin'ichiro) (1829–1903), from the Bureau for the Inspection of Barbarian Books of the Shogunate, studied Western law under Simon Vissering at the University of Leiden.[33] Translating and publishing his handwritten notes on international law in 1868, and teaching international law after his return, Amane Nishi (Shusuke) became the first Japanese international law scholar.[34]

Some scholars have characterized the beginnings of international law in Japan as a period defined by the passive assimilation of Western legal thinking, which reflected the predominant ethos of the 'wholesale Westernization' of Japanese society.[35] As with studies on Latin American international law, studies on Japan assumed that Japanese international lawyers straightforwardly followed Western trends in international legal scholarship.[36] The story of nineteenth-century international law as the progressive defeat of naturalism by positivism is mirrored in the evolution of Japanese international law.

Many scholars think that the first generation of Japanese international lawyers adhered to natural law and made use of the analogy between natural law and Confucianism to render Western international

[33] 'Students studying in the Netherlands at the end of the Edo period', National Diet Library Japan, www.ndl.go.jp/nichiran/e/s2/s2_6.html.

[34] Miyasaki, 'History: Far East', p. 806; Fuji, 'One hundred years', 19.

[35] Early teaching and research of international law was, in the words of Onuma, 'practical, statism-oriented, Eurocentric and passive': Onuma, 'Japanese International Law', 23. Onuma argues that lawyers from nations that have entered the Eurocentric international society as 'late-comers' share a similar pragmatism, passivism and state-centrism in their understanding of international law: *ibid.*, 42. Along the same line, Yamamoto points out that Japan chose to 'accept and comply with the international legal order as it was', even if it had not taken part in its creation. Consequently, Japanese lawyers' approach was 'passive and conservative': S. Yamamoto, 'Japanese approaches and attitudes towards international law', *Japanese Annual of International Law*, 34 (1991), 115–24, 118.

[36] Jacobini, *Latin American writers*, pp. 38–76.

law understandable.[37] Nishi and Tsuda, the first Japanese who studied international law with Simon Vissering in Leiden, are deemed to have followed the natural law perspective of their master. Once back in Japan, Nishi taught 'universal law of nations' at the school of the Shogunate and published a translation of his notes of Vissering's lectures. Kinji Akashi suggests that most Japanese scholars have thought that the first generation of international lawyers adhered to natural law because of the influence Nishi's notes had on Japanese internationalists.[38] However, Japanese publicists imported European international legal thought due to a pragmatic need to achieve recognition from Western powers. They were not particularly inclined to examine international law's conceptual underpinnings. Rather, Japanese internationalists followed the general trend by moving to positivism during the second half of the century, focusing their attention on doctrinal and practical aspects.[39] For example, Akashi has argued that the distinction between naturalism and positivism was of only marginal importance to Japanese practitioners for whom the description of international law's substantive content was of much more relevance than the discussion about the theoretical foundations of the international legal order.[40]

By the 1890s, after the first generation of Japanese international lawyers had acquainted themselves with the international legal discourse and with European intellectual circles, their assimilation of international law became less subservient. Thus, Japanese publicists, who had translated Western international law treatises and written international law treatises in Japanese and for the local audience, began to publish monographs in European languages and to participate in the profession's European centres. For instance, Nagao Ariga studied in Tokyo and Berlin and upon his return to Japan taught international law, served as a legal adviser to the army during the War in China, participated in the First Hague

37 It is possible to draw this analogy because until the first half of the nineteenth century natural law was not completely out of fashion, particularly in the Western international law literature that was translated to Japanese. See Hirohiko Otsuka, 'Japan's early encounter with the concept of the "law of nations"', *Japanese Annual of International Law*, 13 (1969), 35–65, 45–6.

38 Akashi, 'Japanese "acceptance"', pp. 3–5. However, Akashi criticizes this conventional interpretation: *ibid.*, pp. 5–7, 18–19.

39 See Yamamoto, 'Japanese approaches', 118. Similarly, Fuji points out the influence exerted by the works of positivist authors such as Wheaton, Woolsey, Kent, Halleck and Bluntschli: Fuji, 'One hundred years', 20–2.

40 Akashi, 'Japanese "acceptance"', pp. 5–7, 18–19.

Conference as a technical expert, and published in French on the international legal aspects of the wars against China and Russia.[41]

In 1897, the Japanese government sent Sakuyé Takahashi to study international law in Europe. Takahashi provides an extraordinary example of intellectual agency in the appropriation of international law. During his European sojourn, Takahashi not only published pieces in English, French and German but also sought the involvement of European publicists in matters crucial to the interests of Japan. For instance, in Germany Takahashi published a collection of articles written by renowned European international lawyers on the Sino-Japanese War.[42] In Britain, Cambridge University Press published a book by Takahashi.[43] Takahashi managed to get T. E. Holland to write a preface and John Westlake to write an introduction for the book. Until 1899, the various editions of Holland's international law treatise had excluded Japan from the members of the 'family of civilized nations'.[44] In the third edition, for example, Holland affirmed that: 'within this charmed circle, according to the theory of international law, all States are equal. Without it, no State, be it as powerful and as civilised as China or Japan, can be regarded as a normal international person'.[45] After meeting Takahashi, Holland changed that passage in the 1900 edition to include Japan within the sphere of international law.[46] Conversely, as we will see, Westlake, one of the international lawyers most apologetic for British imperialism and the deployment of the standard of

41 Nagao Ariga, 'De la protection accordée aux chinois résidant au Japon pendant la guerre sino-japonaise', *RGDIP*, 2 (1895), 577–83; Ariga, *La guerre sino-japonaise*.

42 Many of the articles by Western authors were written under Takahashi's initiative: S. Takahashi (ed.), *Aeusserungen über völkerrechtlich bedeutsame Vorkommnisse aus dem chinesisch-japanischen Seekrieg und das darauf bezügliche Werk* ('*Cases on international law during the Chino-Japanese war*') (München: E. Reinhardt, 1900). The book included a selection of reviews of Takahashi's work in various European outlets.

43 Takahashi, *Cases on international law*. In 1908, Takahashi also published a study on the Russo-Japanese war, both in London and New York: S. Takahashi, *International law applied to the Russo-Japanese war: with the decisions of the Japanese prize courts* (London: Stevens and Sons, 1908) and S. Takahashi, *International law applied to the Russo-Japanese war: with the decisions of the Japanese prize courts* (New York: The Banks Law Pub. Co., 1908).

44 T. E. Holland, *The elements of jurisprudence*, 2nd edn (Oxford: Clarendon Press, 1882).

45 T. E. Holland, *The elements of jurisprudence*, 3rd edn (Oxford: Clarendon Press, 1886), p. 322.

46 'Within this charmed circle, to which Japan has also some time since fully established her claim to be admitted, all States, according to the theory of international law are equal. Outside of it no State, be it as powerful and as civilised as China as Persia, can be regarded as a normal international person': T. E. Holland, *The elements of jurisprudence*, 9th edn (Oxford: Clarendon Press, 1900), p. 373. See also Map 6 for a visual representation of the expansion of international law according to the definition of the international community in different editions of Holland's treatise.

civilization against Japan, uneasily came to terms with the very presence of a Japanese scholar – rather than a barbarian – in Cambridge.

As in Latin America, Japanese efforts to assimilate international law depended on a broader commitment to a modernizing ideology. This aspect distinguishes Japan from China, where the appropriation of international law experienced greater challenges as the modernization project slowed down. In Japan, the role of international law as a modernizing tool and as a marker of civilization became stronger during the Meiji Restoration.[47] The parallel between Japan and Latin America in their use of international law as part of the modernization project is clear in the following example.

In 1888, Japan concluded with Mexico its first treaty of amity, commerce and navigation under conditions of absolute equality. According to Auslin, Japan's foreign minister, Ōkuma Shigenobu hoped that the 1888 treaty between Mexico and Japan would serve as a precedent for future negotiations.[48] And in fact, Japan thereafter used this treaty as leverage to renegotiate unequal treaties with Western states. The negotiation and conclusion of this treaty was a remarkable episode in semi-peripheral diplomatic history. Ota Mishima's study shows that, even though absent actual commercial interactions between Mexico and Japan, both nations, under Meiji and the Porfiriato, faced similar challenges. With a treaty between these two nations, Mexico was looking for equilibrium in its international relations vis-à-vis the United States, whereas Japan was trying to get its sovereignty recognized by European states.[49]

Japan heavily relied on international law to pursue its policies, not simply as a consequence of the modernizing trend and the resultant Westernization of its legal institutions, but also because international law was appropriated in ways that made it seem useful for Japan in pursuing its own interests. International law served this purpose both in the context of the wars with China (1894–5) and then with Russia (1904–5) and at the end of the century while challenging the unequal treaties and justifying its own military expansionist and colonial policies. At the end of the century, Japan successfully renegotiated the unequal treaties it had

[47] Fuji, 'One hundred years', 19; Auslin, *Negotiating with imperialism*, p. 146 ff.

[48] Auslin, *Negotiating with imperialism*, p. 199.

[49] M. E. Ota Mishima, *México y Japón en el siglo XIX: la política exterior de México y la consolidación de la soberanía japonesa* (Tlatelolco, México: Secretaría de Relaciones Exteriores, 1976), p. 15; for an account of the negotiations, see *ibid.*, pp. 17–23.

concluded with core states. In 1894, Japan signed the first treaty under equality with Great Britain.[50] The unequal treaties signed with France, Germany, the United States and other European states were then also revised.[51]

Japan's success might be explained because of the military power it acquired, but also because, unlike its counterparts in China, Siam or Persia, whose governments relied more on foreign legal experts, Japan from very early on founded professional organizations, taught international law, and participated in international diplomatic events.[52]

China

China, in contrast, had the misfortune of being either too strong to pay any significant attention to Westerners' law of nations before the nineteenth century, or too weak afterwards to appropriate the discourse of international law quickly enough to use it successfully to contain Western intervention. Before the nineteenth century, relations with the West were extremely limited. The use of Western legal language to regulate those interactions was quite innocuous, so that there was never a serious need for China to internalize and assimilate Western international law.

Before the nineteenth century, international law was invoked by Christian missionaries who entered China during the last part of the sixteenth century and by the Dutch in their contacts with Qing officials between 1662 and 1690. In both cases, Chinese authorities refused attempts to validate the European law of nations and depart from their Sino-centred tributary system.[53] China first entered into a formal agreement with a foreign country on equal terms when China and Russia concluded the Treaty of Nerchinsk in 1689. China agreed, for example, to reciprocate ritual observances to maintain the prestige of each civilization.[54] Chinese authorities appointed two Jesuits as translators and advisers precisely in

[50] See Anglo-Japanese Treaty of Commerce and Navigation of July 1894. See also Anglo-Japanese Treaty of Alliance of 1902.

[51] Japan signed treaties under equality with: United States (22 November 1894); Russia (8 June 1895); Germany (4 April 1896); Belgium (22 June 1896); France (4 August 1896); Switzerland (10 November 1896); Spain (2 January 1897); Portugal (26 January 1897); Austria-Hungary (5 December 1897).

[52] Akashi, 'Japanese "acceptance"', pp. 3–6.

[53] Z. Li, 'International law in China: legal aspect of the Chinese perspective of world order', unpublished SJD dissertation, Toronto University (1995), pp. 120–1; Gong, *The standard of 'civilization'*, pp. 132–4.

[54] Gong, *The standard of 'civilization'*, p. 134.

order to conclude a treaty on the basis of equality and reciprocity. Their role was to ensure that the negotiations were carried out in accordance with the principles of international law.[55]

At the beginning of the nineteenth century, the situation changed dramatically. Immanuel Hsü, in his study on China's entrance into the family of nations, reconsiders the critique that modern Chinese scholars have frequently levelled against the Manchu government for its ignorance of international law in its early negotiations with the West. These scholars think that Chinese authorities were incompetent because they too easily signed away extraterritorial concessions, while being ridiculously obstinate about trivial formalities, which were ordinary diplomatic practices among Western states.[56] Hsü follows a different path, asking why Chinese authorities failed to use international legal arguments to assert China's sovereignty. On the one hand, Hsü stresses that the rules invoked to regulate the interactions between China and the Western powers were not part of general international law in the sense of conforming to the principles of sovereign autonomy and equality, but were contained in a series of unequal bilateral treaties that imposed daunting and exceptional limits on Chinese sovereignty. The general corpus of international law remained therefore unused in the regulation of Sino-Western interactions.[57] In this regard, Gong has proposed an alternative explanation of Chinese reluctance to give up the *kostow*, namely, the ritual by which foreign powers became a tributary of China. Rather than responding to an unreasonable and rigid formalism, China defended the *kostow* because recognizing foreign sovereigns as equals challenged its existing worldview.[58] On the other hand, Hsü and others have shown that Chinese authorities applied European international law without much success. It was not lack of legal knowledge on the part of Chinese officials, but the reality of power politics that explain Chinese disappointments.

In 1838, the Emperor appointed Lin Tse-hsü to lead the campaign to suppress opium trafficking and consumption in Canton. Since it was mostly

[55] T. Wang, 'International law in China', 227.

[56] I. Hsü, *China's entrance into the family of nations: the diplomatic phase, 1858–1880* (Cambridge, MA: Harvard University Press, 1960), p. 121.

[57] *Ibid.*, pp. 121–3.

[58] Gong, *The standard of 'civilization'*, pp. 130–3. Similarly, Liu contests the conventional suggestion that China's downfall is explained by its failure to abandon Sino-centric ways of thinking, especially its unwillingness to join free trade and to give up the tributary protocols and adopt modern European diplomacy: Liu, 'Legislating the universal', pp. 129–30.

English opium that was smuggled from India to China, Lin sought to find a justification to prohibit the opium trade in Western publicists' writings and consequently ordered the translation of a number of texts on the law of peoples. In particular, Lin requested the translation of passages from the English version of Vattel's *Le droit des gens* on the right to prohibit the entrance of foreign merchandise, to confiscate smuggled goods, and to wage war. In 1839, based on Vattel's writings, Lin declared opium to be contraband and wrote a letter to Queen Victoria requesting her to stop the opium trade. Using European international law proved futile when the First Opium War broke out, resulting in the Treaty of Nanking being concluded with Britain in 1842 after China's defeat. In exchange for a withdrawal of troops, Britain forced China not only to accept opium as legitimate merchandise, but also to open five ports to trade and residence of British merchants, to abolish the monopolistic trade system, to pay indemnity (compensating the loss of opium and British lives and covering debts owed to British merchants by Chinese merchants), to recognize extraterritoriality, to cede Hong Kong, and to fix tariffs. Britain obtained further concessions in a series of treaties that, as we have seen, came to be known as the treaty port system.[59]

There was one isolated experience of an advantageous use of international legal arguments in the 1860s that yielded a short-lived ascendance of the study of international law. The famous 1864 translation of the *Elements of international law* by Henry Wheaton (1785–1848) is commonly seen as a watershed in the introduction of international law in China. The usefulness of the translation was tested the same year when the Prussian minister to China seized Danish ships as a prize of war. Chinese officials successfully argued that the ships were on Chinese territorial waters.[60] After the use of the translation during the incident, China began to teach international law and some diplomats specialized in international law. In 1876, for example, Chien-Chung Ma (Jianzhong Ma) (1845–1900) travelled to France, becoming the first Chinese student who obtained a *baccalauréat* and then studying law at the École Libre des Sciences Politiques in Paris. In 1898, two professional societies dedicated to the study of international law (in order to revise unequal treaties) were established, only a year after the foundation of the Japanese society of international law and well before the establishment of the American society of international law in

[59] Li, 'International law in China', pp. 124–33; Hsü, *China's entrance*, pp. 138–45; Gong, *The standard of 'civilization'*, pp. 136–46; and D. Wang, *China's unequal treaties*, pp. 11–16.

[60] Li, 'International law in China', p. 129.

1906. However, the cumulative disappointments that Chinese authorities suffered when applying international law forestalled the development and study of a discipline they considered to be useless.[61]

Compared to Japan of the Meiji Restoration, Russia of Peter the Great, or Turkey under the influence of the Young Ottomans – where international law became part of the modernization process – China lagged behind. The erosion of the Qing Dynasty's internal rule, which made the modernizing project impossible to undertake, became also an obstacle to the appropriation of international legal thought. This explains why purposeful appropriation of international law came only after the Emperor was overthrown. Even after the founding of the Republic of China in 1912, international law was still barely taught.[62] For these reasons, there was considerable international legal activity during the nineteenth century, but no significant efforts by Chinese public servants to appropriate classical international law.[63]

Significant international legal scholarship appeared only in the 1920s when Chinese lawyers who had been studying abroad, first in Japan and then in Europe, returned to China after having completed their legal education.[64] For example, it was not until 1929 that China's first international law textbook was published by Keng-shen Chou (Gengsheng Zhou).[65] Educated in Edinburgh and Paris and teaching at Wuhan University, Zhou became the father of modern international law, not only because of his textbook and other writings, but also because he then

[61] T. Wang, 'International law in China', 236–7.

[62] Li, 'International law in China', p. 210.

[63] Cheng argues that from the Qing Dynasty to the Kuomintang only a handful of treaties were written and that the few lawyers that studied international law focused mainly on the unequal treaties, 'since they followed indiscriminately the theories expounded and rules made by the imperialist powers for the imperialist powers, and given the subservient attitude of the then Chinese government, they could do very little to advance the Chinese cause': T. Cheng, 'The People's Republic of China and international law', *Dalhousie Law Journal*, 8 (1984), 3–31, 8. Dong Wang, on the other hand, argues that during the period of the first Republic (1912–28) foreign relations were for the first time 'taken over by a foreign-trained elite': D. Wang, *China's unequal treaties*, p. 35. Unlike Cheng, Wang maintains that both the Kuomintang and the Communist Party condemned the unequal treaties while disputing how they should be abolished: *ibid.*, p. 87.

[64] Hungdah Chiu discusses China's delay in producing modern international lawyers: H. Chiu, 'The development of Chinese international law terms and the problems of translation into English' in J. A. Cohen and H. J. Berman (eds.), *Contemporary Chinese law: research problems and perspectives* (Cambridge, MA: Harvard University Press, 1970), pp. 139–57.

[65] Hsieh, 'The discipline of international law', p. 18.

became the mentor of the leading international lawyer of the People's Republic, Tieya Wang.[66] In spite of being part of the first generation of Chinese lawyers who became international legal scholars and practitioners, lawyers like Zhou and Wellington Koo did not share the classical legal consciousness. On the contrary, these lawyers, who were mainly active between the 1920s and 1940s, shared the modern legal consciousness that defined the disciplinary sensibilities of international lawyers at the beginning of the twentieth century.

Inclusion in the 'family of civilized nations' through re-admission

Faced with the pressures resulting from European and American ascendance and the nineteenth-century configuration of a world economic system that gravitated toward the West, Russian and Ottoman ruling elites decided to modernize their political systems. Unlike the previous examples, in which classical international law was appropriated to advance, negotiate and secure inclusion in the emerging international order, the Russian and Ottoman Empires had maintained long-standing commercial, cultural and political – military and diplomatic – interactions with European states, even before the modern law of nations emerged in the seventeenth century.

During different historical periods, rules and legal instruments have framed the relationship between the Russians and the Ottomans, as well as their relationship with the European powers.[67] On the one hand, the Russian and Ottoman empires have constantly been a factor in the European political order, not only during the earlier periods when they exercised their military might over Europe, but also during the course of the nineteenth century, when they were part of the system of power equilibrium and the concert of European states. For example, Russia participated in the Congress of Vienna, and the Ottoman Empire was included in the treaty of Paris of 1856. On the other hand, at some points in this long history, European, Russian and Ottoman powers recognized each other as equals.[68]

[66] *Ibid.*, p. 18 and R. St J. MacDonald, 'Introduction: Wang Tieya: persevering in adversity and shaping the future of public international law' in R. St J. MacDonald (ed.), *Essays in honour of Wang Tieya* (Dordrecht: Martinus Nijhoff, 1994), pp. 1–30, 5.

[67] Ago, 'Pluralism'.

[68] See K. H. Ziegler, 'The peace treaties of the Ottoman Empire with European Christian powers' in R. Lesaffer, *Peace treaties and international law in European history: from the late Middle Ages to World War One* (Cambridge University Press, 2004), pp. 338–64.

It seems counterintuitive to think that elites of these two non-European empires appropriated European classical international law in order to acquire membership in the international community, considering that the Russian and Ottoman empires had already been bound to Europe for centuries, through a series of treaties and the law of nations. However, as a consequence of the rise of positivism in European international law, the previous history of legal interactions between European, Russian and Ottoman powers was erased and Russian and Ottoman membership in the international community became contested.

I have argued, following Alexandrowicz, that the shift from naturalism to positivism redefined the types of interactions governed by international law. According to the natural law paradigm, polities across the globe were governed by the law of peoples simply as a result of their existence and interactions. Positivism, conversely, required polities to acquire legal personality as states in order to be governed by international law. States, furthermore, had to be linked through commercial, cultural, religious or political ties, in order to belong to the 'family of civilized nations' governed by law.[69] The changes brought about by positivism imposed on Russian and Ottoman lawyers (particularly for the latter as subjects of a non-Christian power) the burden of showing communal bonds between their respective states and the international community of civilized states.

Facing uncertainty about their membership in the European family of nations, and realizing the perils of a possible exclusion, Russian and Ottoman officials sought to assimilate classical international law with an eye towards securing re-entry. In addition to these transformations within the domain of legal doctrine, nineteenth-century European commercial expansion, economic growth, technical breakthroughs and military power put both the Russian and Ottoman empires under serious strain, threatening not only their borders and spheres of influence but also their domestic and long-established social and political forms of organization.

[69] This argument does not assume that naturalism was entirely superseded by positivism. To the contrary, both perspectives coexisted in the work of both early and late nineteenth-century European international lawyers. Lorimer, for example, believed that civilized states are governed by positive international law, whereas non-civilized states are governed by natural law. Only moral rules of good conduct but no positive legal obligations applied outside the 'family of civilized nations': Lorimer, *The institutes of the law of nations*, pp. 101–3. Moreover, authors of the European peripheries were slower to follow the turn to positivism, remaining attached longer to naturalism. See e.g. M. Torres Campos, *Elementos de derecho internacional público* (Madrid: Librería de F. Fé, 1890), pp. 58–9.

Russian and Ottoman ruling elites pushed forward vast projects of modernization, and both experienced similar opposition from traditionalist segments of the elite. The distinctive outcomes of these two cases, as compared to the ideal types discussed above, resulted from the fact that these empires were still powerful enough to participate militarily and politically in the European concert. It was the responsibility of international lawyers to translate the position of power enjoyed by the Russian and Ottoman empires into international law, thus ensuring their legal participation in the European concert.

At the same time, the adoption of the standard of civilization as a yardstick for the recognition of statehood presented Russian and Ottoman elites with an opportunity to justify not only the modernization and Westernization of their societies and political institutions, but also an expansionist policy. The Russian Empire, in particular, invoked its own civilized status to justify its tutelage over the conquered sovereigns in central Asia. In his study on Anglo-Russian relations in Persia, Firuz Kazemzadeh recounts how diplomats justified Russia's military expansion in central Asia. In 1864, Prince A. M. Gorchakov, the Chancellor under Nicholas I, sent a dispatch to Russian diplomats justifying expansion as an obligation of the more civilized states, a dispatch that 'became a landmark in the history of Russian diplomacy'.[70]

The Ottoman Empire

There has been much discussion over when the Ottoman Empire entered the European concert or the 'family of civilized nations', based on a literal interpretation of the text of the treaty of Paris of 1856, the intention of the European and Turkish signatories, or alternatively on a surviving natural law substratum.[71] This discussion misses the point, for it ignores the

[70] F. Kazemzadeh, *Russia and Britain in Persia, 1864–1914: a study in imperialism* (New Haven: Yale University Press, 1968), p. 8. Kazemzadeh quotes Gorchakov's dispatch: 'The position of Russia in Central Asia is that of all civilised States which are brought into contact with half savage, nomad populations, possessing no fixed social organisation. In such cases it always happens that the more civilised State is forced, in the interests of the security of its frontier and its commercial relations, to exercise a certain ascendancy over those whom their turbulent and unsettled character make most undesirable neighbors . . .' *Ibid.*

[71] See e.g. Nussbaum, *A concise history*, pp. 190–1; L. Oppenheim and H. Lauterpacht, *International law, a treatise*, 8th edn, 1 vol. (London: Longmans, 1955), p. 49; T. Toyoda, 'L'aspect universaliste du droit international européen du 19ème siècle et le statut

indeterminacy of the nineteenth-century doctrine and practice of recognition as well as the old legal rapports between European powers, Russia and Turkey.[72] The second half of the nineteenth century marked a greater involvement of Ottoman officials with international legal issues, including old grievances with Russia, Austria, Britain and France over the control of the Black Sea and the Straits and the rights to free navigation. However, Ottoman rulers, unlike Russia or Japan, failed to form professional international lawyers. Instead, Ottomans relied on diplomats with some legal training and a Western outlook, such as Etienne Carathéodory, an ethnic Greek, and Gabriel Noradounghian (1852–1936), an ethnic Armenian. Because of their diplomatic functions, both wrote about international legal matters close to their professional practice. Noradounghian published a collection of treaties and a compilation of other legal documents from the Ottoman Empire's international relations.[73] Carathéodory wrote about the legal status of international rivers and freedom of navigation.[74] It was not until well into the twentieth century that international law started off as a discipline and that the discourse of international law was imported, following the reforms passed by the Young Ottomans first and by the Young Turks thereafter. Thus, as in China, by the time a Turkish international legal profession emerged in the first decades of the twentieth century, the discourse had shifted from classical to modern international law.

Russia

It might appear as utterly misguided to include the Russian Empire and publicists central to the development of international law such as Friedrich Martens within the semi-periphery of international law.[75] Russia certainly exerted power as a member of the Holy Alliance and its expansionism placed it in overt conflict with Britain over Central Asia and Persia. Friedrich Martens, on the other hand, was a crucial figure in the

juridique de la Turquie avant 1856', *Journal of the History of International Law*, 8 (2006), 19–37.

72 See J. C. Hurewitz, 'Ottoman diplomacy and the European state system', *Middle East Journal*, 15 (1961), 141–52.

73 See e.g. G. Noradounghian, *Recueil d'actes internationaux de l'Empire Ottoman* (Paris: F. Pichon, 1897).

74 E. Carathéodory, *Du droit international concernant les grands cours d'eau: étude théorique et pratique sur la liberté de la navigation fluviale* (Leipzig: Brockhaus, 1861).

75 For a discussion of Russian international law in general, see W. Butler, *Russia and the law of nations in historical perspective* (London: Wildy, Simmonds & Hill, 2009).

development of humanitarian international law; a figure still remembered today when lawyers invoke the clause bearing his name, the 'Martens clause'. Today we remember that, pending the codification of the law of war, the Martens clause recognized a supplementary or residual protection based on the 'usages established between civilized nations'.[76] But we have forgotten that, using the distinction between civilized and uncivilized warfare, Martens revealed his semi-peripheral legal consciousness. Proclaiming Russia's commitment to civilized warfare was itself a marker of civilization.

Russia was not at the forefront of the nineteenth-century expansion of European international law. I have suggested that classical international law expanded as a consequence of the emergence of a modern world economy centred in Western Europe and the United States. Polities that were not at the centre of the world economic system, but had enough resources, appropriated classical legal thought to improve their standing within the emerging international order as well as to deal with Western encroachments on their territories. Russians had good reasons to be anxious. Lauri Mälksoo has argued that in spite of Russian jurists' efforts to internalize European international law, Western European authors questioned Russia's standing as a civilized nation. In consequence: '[m]any Russians felt that the Western alliance against the country during the Crimean war (1853–6) or the Balkan wars of the 1870s were not the "usual" clashes between European great powers – they were alliances specifically against the influence of Russia and its dangerous "otherness"'.[77]

To the extent that the world economic system did not consolidate around a division of labour and trade relations that favoured Russian interests, nineteenth-century Russia was semi-peripheral. Moreover, although Russia and the West shared a Christian heritage, Russia had followed its own path, marked by the Byzantine tradition and a feudal sociopolitical organization that led to the formation of a patrimonial empire. Therefore, as Mälksoo has suggested, when in the eighteenth century Russia broke out of her isolation and entered the European state system, Russian internationalists were intellectually dependent on Europe, thinking about themselves as 'translators and transferors of Western European international law scholarship'.[78]

[76] T. Meron, 'The Martens clause, principles of humanity, and dictates of public conscience', *AJIL*, 94 (2000), 78–89, 79.

[77] Mälksoo, 'The history of international legal theory in Russia', 219.

[78] *Ibid.*, 213. Moreover, Mälksoo argues that between Western and Russian international legal scholarship there has been not only a linguistic but also a mental divide. As a

Consequently, while neither downplaying Russia's participation in the European Concert, nor overlooking the professional recognition achieved by some Russian international lawyers, one might nevertheless interpret Russia's approach and use of international law as distinctively semi-peripheral. Russia used international law as a symbol of civilization in at least three different contexts: domestically, to support the modernization project; internationally (vis-à-vis Western powers) to secure international relations based on sovereign equality; and also internationally, to secure the unequal privileges classical international law bestowed on civilized states for the expansion in central Asia.

Domestically, nineteenth-century Russia had been engaged in a vast project of modernization since the reign of Peter the Great at the beginning of the eighteenth century. Modernization brought Western sciences to Russia, including law in general and international law in particular.[79] Specifically, under the reign of Alexander II (1855–1881), Russia supported the study of international law.[80] From then on, European international law textbooks were translated, and modern international law was taught in the newly founded universities, mostly by foreign professors.[81]

International law acquired an important place among Russian liberal elites, for it allowed them to openly support the principle of law within an autocratic society.[82] But as in other parts of the semi-periphery, in which elites were divided between modernizers and traditionalists, Russian elites were divided between Slavophiles and Westernizers. Most Russian international lawyers, as in other semi-peripheral locations, were Westernizers who advocated Russia to open itself to Western culture and science, and opposed Slavophiles, who resisted Westernization, urging Russia to follow its own path.[83] It was not until the mid-nineteenth century, particularly after the defeat in the Crimean War (1853–6), that a

result, Russian jurists appear to be under the illusion of Russia's intellectual self-sufficiency. The flipside effect of the mental and linguistic divide is Russian scholars' overemphasis of the contribution of Russia to the development of international law: *ibid.*, 215.

79 T. Långström, *Transformation in Russia and international law* (Leiden: M. Nijhoff, 2003), pp. 36–7.

80 See P. Holquist, 'The Russian Empire as a "civilised nation": international law as principle and practice in imperial Russia, 1874–1898', National Council for Eurasian and East European Research (2004), available at www.ucis.pitt.edu/nceeer/2004_818-06g_Holquist.pdf.

81 Långström, *Transformation in Russia*, p. 41. 82 Holquist, 'The Russian Empire', p. 7.

83 Långström, *Transformation in Russia*, p. 42; E. Myles, '"Humanity", "civilisation" and the "international community" in the late imperial Russian mirror: three ideas "topical for our days"', *Journal of the History of International Law*, 4 (2002), 310–34, 313–14.

consensus in favour of Westernization emerged. Once again, the introduction of the rule of law, individual rights, and Western laws, institutions and legal thinking in general were crucial not only for the modernization project, but also in supporting Russia's assertion of civilized status.[84] Martens, for instance, like Latin American and Ottoman modernizers, deployed the civilized/barbarian distinction into the domestic context. As Mälksoo has noted: 'It was Russia herself who had to be gently civilised in the hands of Martens and other Baltic German/Russian international law scholars – Westernisers'.[85]

Internationally, in ways similar to the experiences of other nations seeking entry into the international community, Russia also pointed to its behaviour vis-à-vis foreign nations to prove its civilized status. International lawyers guided Russia in order to behave in a civilized manner, waging wars humanely or pushing for breakthroughs in the development or codification of international law, demonstrating in the Hague Conferences more enthusiasm than the Europeans. International lawyers were also crucial in making Russia's civilized behaviour known among Europeans through their writings and through their direct participation in the transnational profession. Martens was the most prominent example.

Friedrich Fromholz Martens was born in 1845 in Pernov (Pärnu/Pernau), a town on the gulf of Riga in the province of Livonia.[86] Pustogarov has ascertained the Estonian origin of Martens, contradicting some German authors who affirm that he was a Baltic German.[87] Martens only adopted a Russian forename later on, when marrying and converting to the Orthodox faith. Even though he became known as Fedor Fedorovich Martens, according to Pustogarov, he continued calling himself Friedrich von Martens in German and Frederic de Martens in French.[88] The use of Western and Russian versions of his name point to Martens' commitment to both Russia's Westernization and imperial idea. Mälksoo has shown that Martens regarded the principle of nationality as unstable and dangerous; instead he believed that the state must respect the rights of citizens regardless of their national origin and the language they spoke.[89]

[84] Myles, 'Late imperial Russian mirror', 313–14.

[85] Mälksoo, 'The history of international legal theory in Russia', 220.

[86] V. V. Pustogarov, *Our Martens: F. F. Martens, international lawyer and architect of peace*, William Elliott Butler ed. trans. (The Hague: Kluwer Law International, 2000), p. 7.

[87] *Ibid.*, p. 13. [88] *Ibid.*, pp. 9–11.

[89] Lauri Mälksoo, 'The science of international law and the concept of politics. The arguments and lives of the international law professors at the University of Dorpat/Iur'ev/Tartu 1855–1985', *British Yearbook of International Law* 76 (2005) 383, 389.

Although born under extremely modest circumstances, and in spite of having been orphaned at an early age, Martens received a good education at a German school in St Petersburg and was admitted to the Law Faculty of St Petersburg University in 1863.[90] Upon graduation, Martens was offered to remain at the University to prepare for a professorship. When Martens suggested choosing the chair of criminal law, the Dean replied: '"No, remain at the chair of international law. Then we will have our Martens", alluding to the two noted European writers on international law... who bore this surname'.[91] Martens finished his magister, went abroad attending lectures in Vienna, Heidelberg (by Johann Caspar Bluntschli) and Leipzig, received his doctoral degree in 1873 and became professor in 1876.[92] Martens went on to become, among others, member of the *Institut de Droit International*, and Russian delegate to a number of conferences, including the First and Second Hague Conferences. At the time of his death in 1909, Martens had become immensely influential.[93]

In spite of his professional achievements, I suggest interpreting Martens as a classical jurist of the semi-periphery. Martens repeated the conventional view maintaining that international law is limited to peoples having achieved the same degree of civilization.[94] Martens' identification of civilization with European civilization was also conventional.[95] Moreover, similar to other semi-peripheral jurists we have seen, Martens affirmed that because of Russia's own history as well as the introduction of reforms that led to modernization and Westernization, Russia developed social and political institutions akin to those in Europe. Russia, in consequence,

90 Pustogarov, *Our Martens*, pp. 7, 14.

91 *Ibid.*, p. 19. 92 *Ibid.*, pp. 19, 20, 26.

93 See for instance the obituary written by a famous British jurist: T. E. Holland, 'Frederic de Martens', *Journal of the Society of Comparative Legislation*, 10 (1909), 10–12.

94 Martens, *Traité de droit*, p. iii. 'The geographical and economic differences and the ones that define the diverse degrees of civilization of peoples, have an influence on their domestic development and on their law. International law cannot become a reality except among peoples who have achieved much the same degree of civil and political development, for it is only among them that the notion of law is identical': *ibid.*, p. 20.
Martens later affirms that no civilized state can find all the elements of its life and fulfilment within its territory, which is why contemporary nations have established relations with one another: *ibid.*, p. 28.

95 'Contemporary international law is the result of civilized life and of the knowledge about the law among European nations. As history demonstrates, the essential conditions of the international juridical order... are first encountered in Europe and, up to the present, they are far from existing among all states of the globe. Therefore, the effect of international law is only understood among the nations that have recognized the fundamental principles of European civilization, and that are worthy to be called civilized peoples': *ibid.*, p. 238.

should be considered a member of the international community and a sovereign under international law.

What is distinctive in Martens is the way in which he pleads Russia's inclusion in the international community not just because of modernization but also because of religion. Russia and Europe were bound together by the Christian tradition, which was equivalent, in Martens' eyes, to Western civilization: 'I have the firm conviction that international relations and the principles of law that regulate them draw all of their importance and all of their force from the community of interests that unite civilized or Christian nations'.[96] It was also distinctive how Martens used the distinction between civilized and uncivilized peoples in order to justify Russian expansionism.

No different than other classical jurists, Martens insisted that nations lying outside the community of shared purposes, namely, the non-European entities that are deemed to lack mutual links of solidarity or interest and thus do not invite reciprocal relations, are excluded from positive international law. Contacts between sovereign states and uncivilized and savage peoples were for Martens de facto interactions subject to natural law.[97] Martens claimed that 'the social and political conditions under which Muslim, heathen or savage peoples live, render impossible the application of international law with these barbarous or half civilized nations'.[98] In contrast, Russia, according to Martens, was civilized.[99] Supporting Russia's expansionist policy in the Balkans and Central Asia, Martens disputed the inclusion of Asian states and Turkey in the international community of civilized peoples.[100] Martens viewed the absence of reciprocity that the capitulations stipulated in the relationship between European powers and Turkey, Persia, Japan or China as demonstrating their exclusion from the international community. Because these nations did not offer the guarantees necessary for the security of the interests and rights of foreigners, and did not implement essential transformations of the law and political and social regimes, Martens concluded that these nations should not enjoy the rights of civilized nations.[101]

96 *Ibid.*, pp. ii–iii. 97 *Ibid.*, p. 239. 98 *Ibid.*, pp. 238–9.

99 Holquist, 'The Russian Empire', pp. 4–6.

100 See F. F. Martens, *Russie et l'Angleterre dans l'Asie centrale* (Gand: I. S. Van Doosselaere, 1879); F. F. Martens, *Das Consularwesen und die Consularjurisdiction im Orient*, H. Skerst trans. (Berlin: Weidmannsche buchhandlung, 1874).

101 Martens, *Traité de droit*, pp. 240–1. It is quite interesting that Martens indicates that when this moment of a similar degree of 'instruction and civilisation' is reached, international law will no longer be exclusively based on Christian principles, and will

As long as the international community was composed only of peoples belonging to the European civilization, new states had to appropriate the fundamental elements of Western culture for the international community to progress.[102] Russia was a case in point in Martens' argument. Although Russia had engaged in commercial relations with England and Holland, signed treaties, and sent and received diplomatic missions from European states since at least the thirteenth century, Russia had not done enough to gain membership into the international community. Martens insisted that until the eighteenth century, Russia's internal social and political conditions made it impossible for a relationship with Western sovereigns to emerge on the basis of equality and reciprocity.

Martens wanted to persuade his readers (though without much discussion) that since the reign of Peter the Great and the consolidation of modernization during the reign of Catherine II, a change in domestic affairs had brought Russia into the international community of civilized nations. Martens' brief justification for including Russia within the international community might have made perfect sense to him: Martens' own professional success and recognition in diplomatic circles confirmed Russia's centrality in the European concert of nations. Martens, for example, was the author of the programme and a central figure in the First Hague Conference of 1899, which marked the beginning of the modern rules of warfare.[103] Tsar Nicholas II's initiative to advance humanitarian law and Martens' role in it might be seen as an illustration of Russia's commitment to Westernization. Contrary to what one might expect, Russia's determination to become a leading force in the advancement of humanitarian law and thus civilization did not contradict but rather endorsed Russia's expansionism, embodying a mission to civilize other nations. Similarly to the Japanese jurists who pointed to Japan's behaviour in warfare as a sign of Japan's civilized status, Martens also viewed Russia's active role in the development of humanitarian international law as a sign of Russia's place among civilized nations.

be obligatory beyond Christian nations. However, Martens warns that at that point, it will be necessary that peoples and societies under the rule of international law ensure 'reasonable conditions of human existence' in accordance with 'the secular civilisation of the European nations': *ibid.*

102 *Ibid.*, pp. 270–1.

103 Daniel Marc Segesser, '"Unlawful warfare is uncivilised": the international debate on the punishment of war crimes, 1872–1918', *European Review of History*, 14 (2007), 215–34; Myles, 'Late imperial Russian mirror', 318–23.

The expansion of international law as circulation

Martens became an important figure in professional circles. He sat on various arbitration tribunals, including the Anglo-Venezuelan arbitration of 1899, his treatises were translated and widely read, and he participated in professional debates that reached the public in the form of journalistic pieces, such as a piece on the tension between Russia and England over Central Asia.[104] Martens' participation in a professional dialogue of increasing global reach is a further indication of the process through which international law became universal.

Although trade relations had existed between some European and non-European nations as well as a considerable number of international legal regimes had governed their interactions well before the nineteenth century, during this century international relations intensified significantly.[105] During the nineteenth century, Western economic, political and military expansion was followed by the proliferation of bilateral treaties and the expansion of classical international law. I describe the expansion of international law as expansion by appropriation – rather than expansion by inclusion or imposition – because semi-peripheral jurists appropriated classical international law to support the inclusion of their polities in the family of nations. Moreover, I describe the process of international law's expansion by appropriation as process of circulation of people – diplomats, missionaries, armed forces personnel, law professors – carrying legal ideas and rules – in treaties, treatises, commentaries – to be used to both justify and resist the construction of a world economic and political system centred in the West.

Map 3 offers a visual representation of the nineteenth-century expansion of the international law profession, including lawyers from both centre and periphery. Let us briefly look at two examples illustrating the circulation of people and ideas within a global sphere of international legal practice. First, the translation of international law textbooks shows the appropriation and circulation of ideas. Second, an emerging transnational professional dialogue shows the transnational circulation of lawyers and scholars who notwithstanding unequal power relations between centre and periphery were reciprocally influenced.

Translation of textbooks

The patterns of translation of nineteenth-century international law treatises offer a material indication of the flow of international legal ideas.[106]

104 Martens, *Russie et l'Angleterre.* 105 See Map 2. 106 See Map 5.

It is unsurprising that following the unequal distribution of power and prestige ideas flowed from Europe or the United States to the rest of the world. However, this pattern also shows the efforts of semi-peripheral states to acquire international legal knowledge. Translating and publishing foreign textbooks was one of the necessary steps in the appropriation of classical international law.

In 1868, for example, Johann Caspar Bluntschli (1808–1881), the widely read and quoted Swiss international lawyer, professionally active in Germany, founding member of the *Institut de Droit International*, published an influential international law treatise.[107] Unsurprisingly, in 1870 Bluntschli's treatise was translated and published in France.[108] Only a year later, a Spanish translation was published, not in Spain but in Mexico, an indication that acquiring international legal knowledge was more important for Latin American states trying to secure independence, than for the decaying empire.[109] As one would expect, Japan under Meiji restoration was another place where Bluntschli's treatise was rapidly translated and published.[110] In the course of only a few years, the treatise was published also in Greek, Russian and Turkish.[111] In China, W. A. P. Martin, the American missionary who had translated Wheaton's textbook, published the French edition of Bluntschli's treatise first in English and then in Chinese. Martin's edition was then translated into Korean.[112]

The translation of Bluntschli's treatise shows a pattern of how ideas travelled from core to periphery that mirrors prevalent international power relations.[113] However, in this pattern we may also see some margin

[107] J. C. Bluntschli, *Das moderne Völkerrecht der civilisirten Staten als Rechtsbuch dargestellt* (Nördlingen: Beck, 1868). On Bluntschli see B. Baker, 'The method behind Bluntschli's "modern" international law', *Journal of the History of International Law*, 4 (2002), 249–92.

[108] J. C. Bluntschli, *Le droit international codifié*, C. Lardy, É. Laboulaye trans. (Paris: Guillaumin, 1870).

[109] J. C. Bluntschli, *El derecho internacional codificado*, José Díaz Covarrubias trans. (Mexico: Impr. J. Batiza, 1871).

[110] J. C. Bluntschli, *Kokuhō hanron*, Hiroyuki Katō trans. (Tōkyōfu: Kondō Keizō, 1876).

[111] J. C. Bluntschli, *Ho diethnes kodix* (Athenai, 1874); J. C. Bluntschli, *Sovremennoe mezhdunarodnoe pravo tsivilizovannykh gosudarstv, izlozhennoe v vidie kodeksa* (Moskva: Indrikh, 1876); J. C. Bluntschli, *Hukuk-ı beyneddüvel-i kanunu* (İstanbul: Vakit Gazetesi Matbaası, 1879).

[112] J. C. Bluntschli, *Bluntschli's International law*, C. Lardy, W. A. P. Martin trans. (Beijing: Tung Wên College Press, 1880); J. C. Bluntschli, *Gong fa hui tong*, W. A. P. Martin trans. (Beijing: Tong wen guan, 1884); J. C. Bluntschli, *Kongpop hoet'ong*, 1896 Chaeju chongnija p'an, W. A. P. Martin trans. (Hansōng: Hakbu P'yōnjipkuk, 1896).

[113] See Map 5 showing the translation of Bluntschli's treatise as a visual representation of the expansion of international law.

for agency. First, it is worth remembering that flows in the opposite direction, from the semi-periphery to the Western centres, were in principle not necessary. Participating in the discipline's transnational discussion, semi-peripheral international lawyers wrote directly in one of the main European languages. The writings of semi-peripheral international lawyers explored above were mostly published in Europe in English, French or German. At the same time, semi-peripheral authors published textbooks in their respective countries and in their own languages. Rather than getting involved in the discipline's transnational debates, these works presented the general field of international law to their local audiences. Takahashi, for example, in addition to the work that we have seen published in English, French and German, wrote a textbook in Japanese.[114] There was no need to translate the local semi-peripheral textbook back into the languages of the core.

Second, the degree of agency involved in publishing foreign books as well as in the practice of translation is not insignificant. Bluntschli, for example, was not involved in the translation of his treatise. In his diary, as Stefan Kroll has noted, Bluntschli expressed surprise and satisfaction for the visit that W. A. P. Martin paid him in 1881, bringing to Heidelberg 'a well printed' copy of 'my international law' in 'Chinese language and writing'.[115] Bluntschli's diary presents a picture of an eminent European international lawyer who at the end of his life sees with some surprise his work reaching unexpected places. The arrival of a Japanese translation by a former Japanese student as well as the personal visit of the attaché from the Chinese legation in Berlin, were events Bluntschli considered worth registering in his diary.[116]

These entries in Bluntschli's diary as well as the global circulation of his textbook suggest that appropriating international law, and more specifically translating and publishing foreign texts, was an enterprise led from the semi-periphery. Moreover, translating Western treatises, especially into non-European languages like Chinese, allowed and required the translator to create neologisms, find isomorphic terms and even invent new terminology.[117] For example, as Dong Wang has shown, the term 'unequal treaty', to describe the treaties that China concluded with

[114] S. Takahashi, *Heiji kokusaihōron* (Tōkyō: Nihon Daigaku, 1907).

[115] S. Kroll, *Normgenese durch Re-Interpretation: China und das europäische Völkerrecht im 19. und 20. Jahrhundert* (Baden-Baden: Nomos, 2012), p. 1; J. C. Bluntschli and R. Seyerlen, *Denkwürdiges aus meinem Leben* (Nördlingen: Beck, 1884), p. 488.

[116] Bluntschli and Seyerlen, *Denkwürdiges*, p. 489.

[117] See Kroll, *Normgenese durch Re-Interpretation.*

Western states at the end of the nineteenth century, was a term popularized by Chinese lawyers and diplomats during the first decades of the twentieth century.[118] Stefan Kroll, Rune Svarverud, Lydia Liu and others have studied the process of reception, translation and reinterpretation of international law in China.[119] These authors have shown how the process of translation of Western international law created a new language that had a great impact in China, but translation left also an imprint on the increasingly globalized discipline of international law.

Lydia Liu's path-breaking study on the reception of international law in nineteenth-century China conceives the translator as a diplomat who negotiates the outcome – the translated text – as a mode of exchange in the diplomatic and military intercourse between Western powers and China. Liu focuses particularly on the translation of Wheaton's treatise by W. A. P. Martin.[120]

In the course of the publication of the different editions of Wheaton's textbook, it is possible to distinguish a parallel development. There is a correlation between the translation of the textbook in the semi-periphery and the new states the textbook considers as members of the family of nations. For instance, in the first edition of the treatise published in 1836, Wheaton circumscribes international law to the nations that are civilized and Christian.[121] Wheaton considers the law of nations not as natural law applied to all states, but as law applicable only between certain states. There is in consequence no universal law of nations.[122] In the sixth edition

118 Wang, *China's unequal treaties*, pp. 63–80.

119 See e.g. R. Svarverud, *International law as world order in Late Imperial China: translation, reception and discourse, 1847–1911* (Leiden: Brill, 2007).

120 See Liu, 'Legislating the universal' and L. Liu, *The clash of empires: the invention of China in modern world making* (Cambridge: Harvard University Press, 2004), ch. 4, 'Translating international law'.

121 'The law of nations, or international law, as understood among civilised, Christian nations, may be defined as constituting of those rules of conduct which reason deduced, as consonant to justice, from the nature of the society existing among independent nations; with such definitions and modifications as may be established by general consent': H. Wheaton, *Elements of international law with a sketch of the history of the science* (Philadelphia: Carey, Lea & Blanchard, 1836), p. 46. For a similar trend in Holland, Oppenheim and Westlake, see Map 6.

122 'The ordinary *jus gentium* is only a particular law, applicable to a distinct set or family of nations, varying at different times with the change in religion, manners of government, and other institutions, among every class of nations. Hence the international law of the civilised, Christian nations of Europe and America, is one thing; and that which governs the intercourse of the Mohammedan nations of the East with each other, and with Christians, is another and a very different thing': *ibid.*, pp. 44–5.

of 1855, however, the sharp division is softened. The passage negating the universality of international law is replaced in 1855 by a paragraph that recognizes exceptions to the restriction of international law's scope of validity to Western nations.[123]

In 1855, on the other hand, Wheaton affirms that the intercourse between Christian and non-Christian states brings into being a law of nations that is analogous to the European international law based on the progress of civilization founded on Christianity.[124] As examples of the application of the law of nations to this class of international relations, Wheaton enumerates the recognition and extension of the rights of legation in places like Persia, Egypt or the States of Barbary, the independence and integrity of the Ottoman Empire as well as its participation in the European balance of power and the diplomatic transactions between the Chinese Empire and Christian nations, whereby the former was 'compelled to abandon its inveterate anti-commercial and anti-social principles'.[125]

In 1866, the abovementioned paragraph recounting the diplomatic intercourse between China and the Christian states of Europe and America is accompanied with a long footnote in which Richard Dana, the editor of the eighth edition, updates the text listing the treaties signed between Western and non-Western states, and making particular reference to the treaties that the United States had signed with states such as the Ottoman Empire, Japan, China, Siam, Tunis, Persia and Borneo. At the end of this enumeration, Dana inserts in the treatise an interesting comment of his own:

> The most remarkable proof of the advance of Western civilisation in the East, is the adoption of this work of Mr. Wheaton, by the Chinese government, as a text-book for its officials, in International Law, and its translation into that language, in 1864, under imperial auspices.... Already this work has been quoted

[123] 'Is there a uniform law of nations? There certainly is not the same one for all the nations and states of the world. The public law, with slight exceptions, has always been, and still is, limited to the civilised and Christian people of Europe or to those of European origin': H. Wheaton and W. B. Lawrence, *Elements of international law*, 6th edn (Boston: Little, Brown, 1855), p. 16.

[124] *Ibid.*, p. 20. 'The more recent intercourse between the Christian nations in Europe and America and the Mohammedan and Pagan nations of Asia and Africa indicates a disposition, on the part of the latter, to renounce their peculiar international usages and adopt those of Christendom': *ibid.*, p. 21.

[125] *Ibid.*, pp. 21–2.

and relied upon by the Chinese Government, in its diplomatic correspondence with ministers of Western Powers resident at Peking.[126]

Lydia Liu has noted the circularity of Dana's footnote. Universality and translation depend on each other: 'Wheaton's original text calls for translation because it possesses an inherent universal value, but it takes the existence of foreign translations to substantiate its universal claim. To aspire to the condition of the universal, the text demands universal recognition and demands being translated.'[127] The translation to Chinese has remained in the profession's imaginary as proof of Wheaton's universality and the universality of Western international law.[128]

Western expansion into new areas of the world like China was achieved through violence, from war to gunboat diplomacy, but also through negotiating treaties and negotiating the knowledge underpinning those treaties. The differences between the 1836 and 1866 editions of Wheaton's treatise reflected the progressive weakening of the standard of civilization after the renegotiation of unequal treaties binding a number of semi-peripheral states. But the treatise itself had to determine and sanction the inclusion of specific states in the family of nations. And this determination was not irrelevant, for treatises were – as Wheaton himself observed – a relevant source of nineteenth-century international law.[129] The semi-periphery, as Dana's footnote suggests, could influence the delimitation

126 H. Wheaton, R. H. Dana, *Elements of international law*, 8th edn (London: S. Low, Son and Co., 1866), p. 19.

127 Liu, 'Legislating the universal', p. 158.

128 For example, Andrew D. White (1832–1918), an American diplomat who was involved in the creation of the permanent court of arbitration at the first Hague Peace Conference and in convincing the philanthropist Andrew Carnegie to fund the construction of the Peace Palace in The Hague, recalled Wheaton when envisioning the building that would house the court. In a letter to Carnegie, White writes: 'I would have it a noble building, worthy of the donor, of the civilised world to which he gives it . . . the statue of Grotius should hold a central place . . . flanked on either side by those of his principal predecessors and successors in the evolution of international law . . . such as . . . our own Wheaton – whose book has been used at Oxford and was translated even into Chinese'. A. D. White to Carnegie, 5 Aug. 1902, Carnegie Papers, quoted in Davis, Calvin DeArmond, *The United States and the Second Hague Peace Conference: American diplomacy and international organisation, 1899–1914* (Durham, NC: Duke University Press, 1974), p. 94.

129 Among the sources of international law, Wheaton lists the 'text-writers of authority, showing what is the approved usage of nations, or the general opinion respecting their mutual conduct'. Wheaton affirms that 'generally impartial in their judgement', international law writers 'are witnesses of the sentiments and usages of civilised nations': Wheaton and Dana, *Elements*, p. 14.

of the international society. In the example of Wheaton's textbook, semi-peripheral influence was achieved through translation. Meeting and talking to professionals at the core was another way semi-peripheral lawyers shaped international legal ideas.

Transnational professional dialogue

Transnational professional dialogue was established either through direct contact or by publishing books and articles in the discipline's main journals. The number of articles published by semi-peripheral authors in European journals as well as the number of reviews of their writings by prominent European lawyers is quite remarkable, if compared to contemporary international law. However, the influence that exchanges between lawyers from core and semi-peripheral had on the discipline in general is difficult to demonstrate. Let me focus on the renowned English international lawyer and Whewell professor of international law at Cambridge University, John Westlake (1828–1913) and offer two examples of possible semi-peripheral influences over Westlake's ideas, involving an indirect influence through writings and a direct influence through professional contact.

In 1887, Amancio Alcorta, an Argentinean lawyer, politician and intellectual, published in Paris his international law treatise. In the standard introductory section about the historical development of international law, Alcorta's treatise includes a reference to international law in Mexico and Peru. In between the Greek and Roman periods, Alcorta inserts the Azteca and Inca Empire and compares the Inca to the Roman Empire. Alcorta affirms that politically autonomous entities coexisted in pre-Colombian America. Based on this fact Alcorta justified the civilized status and membership of Latin American republics in the international community.[130]

Recalling pre-Colombian coexistence between sovereigns was a rhetorical strategy invoked by Latin American intellectuals, regardless of the fact that after three centuries of colonial rule, independence from Spain had been achieved largely as a project of the creole elite in detriment of indigenous peoples. However, we may see this idea echoed by John Westlake. Discussing the treaties concluded with 'uncivilised tribes' Westlake

[130] A. Alcorta, *Cours de droit international public*, E. Lehr trans. (Paris: L. Larose et Forcel, 1887), vol. 1, pp. 202–13.

presents the following hypothetical: 'Let us suppose that officers or private subjects of a European state ... advance into a region where they find no native government capable of controlling white men or under which white civilisation can exist, and where also no state has yet acquired the sovereignty under the rules which are internationally recognized between white men'.[131] What happens when white men conclude treaties with the 'chiefs or authorities of uncivilised peoples?' – Westlake asks.[132] Natives in such 'rudimentary condition ... take no rights under international law' – Westlake responds.[133]

Westlake affirms that these are the principles that European states have applied to deal with native inhabitants of the Americas north of Mexico. Westlake, however, declares that: 'with Mexico and Peru we have nothing to do. Those countries had attained a degree of advancement ranking them rather as states than as uncivilised tribes'.[134] One can speculate about the origin and intentions of Westlake's declaration considering Mexico and Peru as states. It is the case that Westlake's inclusion of these states under the civilized world was functional to the British policy of informal imperialism in Latin America. But it is also interesting that Westlake's own argument about the inclusion of Latin American states under international law followed an argument typical of Latin American scholarship.

Semi-peripheral lawyers also sought to directly influence international law at the core, paying visits to or studying under renowned European international lawyers. Sakuyé Takahashi, who arrived at Cambridge University to write about the Japanese position in the Chino-Japanese war, offers a good example. Takahashi, as we have seen above, not only asked T. E. Holland to write a preface, but also asked John Westlake to write an introduction to his book on the Chino-Japanese war, published in 1899 by Cambridge University Press.[135] Westlake and Takahashi may have inaugurated the tradition of European professors bestowing approval – by way

131 J. Westlake, *Chapters on the principles of international law* (Cambridge University Press, 1894), p. 143.

132 *Ibid.*

133 The treaties in which natives cede sovereignty are not legitimate, because: 'a stream cannot rise higher than its source, and the right to establish the full system of civilised government, which in the cases is the essence of sovereignty, cannot be based on the consent of those who at the utmost know but a few of the needs which such a government is intended to meet': *ibid.*, p. 144.

134 *Ibid.*, p. 146.

135 Takahashi, *Cases on international law.*

of an introduction or preface – to the writings of semi-peripheral international lawyers. Westlake, at the time an eminent authority, had not long ago, in 1894, counted Japan among semi-civilized nations.[136] Having met Takahashi, Westlake seems to have happily fulfilled the request.[137] We may imagine Westlake to have been first surprised by the sight of an envoy of a semi-civilized nation strolling along the alleys of Cambridge. We may also imagine Westlake to have been surprised by the envoy's civilization. We may picture him changing his perception about Japan's place in the international legal order while getting to know Takahashi. What we definitely know is that Westlake's introduction no longer considers Japan among semi-civilized nations: 'Japan presents a rare and interesting example of the passage of a state from the oriental to the European class'.[138] Moreover, Westlake's new textbook published in 1904, continues to consider states like 'Morrocco, Turkey, Muscat, Persia, Siam and China' to be only partially admitted to the international society. These states are subject to consular jurisdiction because their 'civilisation . . . differs from that of the Christian world'.[139] On the other hand, Westlake affirms in 1904 that 'Japan has recently been raised from this class of states to the full community of international law. The consular jurisdiction there having been given up in pursuance of treaties with the European and American powers concluded with that empire, and which came into force in 1899'.[140]

Finally, it is interesting to note that core international lawyers were not indifferent about the English endorsement of Takahashi's work and

[136] 'Our international society exercises the right of admitting outside states to parts of its international law without necessarily admitting them to the whole of it. Thus a large part of the relations between the European and American states on the one hand, and China and Japan on the other hand, is conducted on the footing of ordinary international law; but the former enjoy in the latter a consular jurisdiction, substituted for the rules of jurisdiction belonging to ordinary international law': Westlake, *Chapters on the principles*, p. 82.

[137] 'This book, of my friend Professor Takahashi . . . is a valuable monument of the history of the Far East, and the details with which it is enriched are the best testimony to the care with which Japan entered on a line of operations, naval and judicial, quite novel to her': Takahashi, *Cases on international law*, p. xvi.

[138] 'By virtue of treaties already concluded with the leading Christian states of Europe and America she will shortly be freed from the institution of consular jurisdiction, and in her recent war with China she displayed both the disposition and in the main the ability to observe western rules concerning war and neutrality.' *Ibid.*

[139] J. Westlake, *International law: Part I Peace* (Cambridge: University Press, 1904), p. 40.

[140] *Ibid.*, p. 41. See also Map 6 for a visual representation of the expansion of international law according to the definition of the international community in different editions of Westlake's treatise.

more importantly about the role that this endorsement may have had in Takahashi's reliance on English scholarship and probably the impact that this reliance may have in the global spread of international legal thinking. Antoine Pillet (1857–1926), a French scholar, for example, published a sympathetic review of Takahashi's book. While positive in relation to the book's central argument, Pillet disapproves of the influence that Holland and Westlake have exercised over Takahashi. 'They are English, they represent the English doctrine' – Pillet protests, pointing out that, developed in a nation too confident of its superiority, the English doctrine treats neutral states unjustly. Depending too much on English sources, Pillet believes that Takahashi has lost the authority that a 'sage eclecticism' could have offered. By more eclecticism, Pillet means giving more consideration to the continental doctrine of maritime international law, which is better suited than the English to protect the interests of Japan.[141]

The meaning of universality in public international law

Conventional international legal scholarship claims that international law is European and that this legal order achieved universality when the international society of European states expanded globally. International lawyers consider to be European both the international legal order that globalized during the nineteenth century and the international legal order that attained universality at the end of the century, not just because its conceptual outlook developed out of the European legal tradition, but also because European states, their lawyers and their diplomats were the primary historical actors. International law therefore was globalized either when Western states recognized non-European sovereigns as members of the international community, or when Western states used international law to justify formal colonial rule or informal imperialism in Africa, Asia or Latin America. Either way, this conventional history of international law in the nineteenth century covers only the ideas and doctrines developed by European and North American international lawyers and the rules of international law devised by European states to govern the foreign relations with other Western states.

The belief in the exclusively European nature of international law limits the scope of analysis and prevents an understanding of the global character of the historical processes through which international law became

141 A. Pillet, 'Cases on international law during the Chino-Japanese war (*Cas de droit international pendant la guerre sino-japonaise*)', *RGDIP*, 6 (1899), 335–6.

universal. How did international legal rules, doctrines and ideas expand their range of validity, why did they gain traction outside Europe and to what extent did international law change in the process of expansion?

The second part of this book has strived to answer these questions, offering a global history of the emergence of an international legal order of universal character, suggesting that globalization did not follow international law's geographical expansion through inclusion of new states or through Western imposition. This history shows that international law became universal when, in a process that was both global and multidimensional, non-European lawyers appropriated European international legal thought and established, along with Western international lawyers, a global profession that articulated a transnational legal discourse.

In the previous chapters I have argued that, by the dawn of the nineteenth century, a significant number of international legal regimes had governed, under some degree of formal equality, the interaction between some European and non-European sovereigns. During the nineteenth century, European publicists had shifted their conceptual understanding of international law to positivism. A series of new legal doctrines emerged from this theoretical shift supporting a change toward unequal treatment in the international regimes governing relations with non-Western sovereigns. For example, according to a constitutive (as opposed to a declaratory) doctrine of recognition, international personality – which granted the privilege of equal treatment – depended on a state complying with the 'European standard of civilization'. Semi-peripheral international lawyers contested the unfavourable change in the rules of international law by engaging with the doctrines and debates that justified the new rules.

This explanation of the process through which international law became universal, a story emphasizing non-Western appropriations of the European international legal tradition and the constitution of a transnational legal discourse, invites us to rethink the meaning of 'universality' as a term describing the transformations that the international legal order underwent during the nineteenth century. International lawyers have typically used the term 'universality' to describe the final stage in the progressive expansion of international law's geographical range of validity. This study, however, suggests that, during the nineteenth century, international law underwent transformations more significant than a mere geographical expansion. I propose to use the term 'universality' with three additional implications: to indicate changes in international law's conceptual outlook, to describe the global aspects of the professionalization of international law, and to illustrate the transformations in the nature of the international legal discourse itself.

First, regarding the conceptual change, international law's space of validity, which had been theoretically reduced to intra-Western relations after the shift from naturalism to positivism, regained universality when semi-peripheral lawyers reinterpreted the doctrines of recognition and the standard of civilization, so that they became procedural, rather than substantive, limitations to the inclusion of non-Western states. I have shown that semi-peripheral international lawyers did this by disentangling the association between the ideas of the distinctiveness of European/Western statehood, the standard of civilization, and international legal personality. Their criticisms were therefore not directed at a standard of civilization, but rather at the malleability of this standard and the possibility – at least theoretically – of non-Western sovereigns internalizing it to support their international personality.

Second, semi-peripheral lawyers' appropriation of European international legal thought happened at a time when the practice of international law became specialized and turned into a distinctive profession forming a transnational community. During this period, professional activities undertaken by international lawyers became transnationally organized. As legal advisers serving their own foreign offices or foreign governments, international lawyers circulated globally, giving counsel, joining diplomatic negotiations, and becoming members of arbitration tribunals. As producers of ideas, international legal scholars published works that were translated into many languages and discussed around the world. As professionals, the first associations of international lawyers founded inside and outside Europe reflected a global constituency at the same time that the student bodies of European universities, where international law was taught, became increasingly cosmopolitan. The participation of semi-peripheral jurists and diplomats in the transnational professional community that emerged out of these events made it possible for this community to acquire a global character.

By the second half of the nineteenth century, semi-peripheral lawyers had become professional international law experts, negotiating, signing and invoking treaties, and insisting on compliance with these treaties. They had also discussed and contested established doctrinal positions, challenging extraterritoriality in Japan or China, or, in the case of Latin America, criticizing the doctrines supporting diplomatic intervention.

Yet it is not the mere participation of non-Europeans in the creation of international legal norms and concepts that makes the use, internalization and appropriation of international law interesting, but rather the ways in which these lawyers played with the discourse of international law, at times endorsing it while at other times being surprisingly critical – a strategic stance that I contend should be recovered by semi-peripheral internationalists today.

Third, one might believe that international law became universal only after having been articulated globally (by a transnationally constituted profession) and with some degree of inclusiveness (after semi-peripheral lawyers reinterpreted legal doctrines limiting the scope of the international community). If so, this international law would be qualitatively different from the law that Western powers unilaterally fashioned and imposed, which legitimized Western exercise of jurisdictional powers overseas and resolved disputes between Western states, particularly controversies emerging from conflicting colonial claims over territories overseas. This law became universal, because it not only enabled the Western powers to intervene politically and economically around the world, but also regulated and to some extent limited the mutual interaction between independent political organizations on a global scale.

During the course of the nineteenth century, semi-peripheral appropriations of international legal thought and the global circulation of rules, lawyers and legal ideas transformed existing international legal regimes into a universal international law. 'Universality', as a consequence, describes not only international law's geographic expansion, but also doctrinal changes, the global professionalization of international lawyers, and the transformation of the nature and functions of the international legal discourse. These are the central arguments I have put forward in Part II of the book.

PART III · THE FALL OF CLASSICAL THOUGHT AND THE TURN TO MODERN INTERNATIONAL LAW

During the nineteenth century, international lawyers understood sovereignty to be a 'gift of civilization'.[1] A gift non-Western states had to possess to protect themselves from intrusions by Western powers. During the nineteenth century, as we have seen in previous chapters, semi-peripheral states were admitted and began to participate in the international community. Did the rules of international law governing the interaction between Western and non-Western states change? What did it mean for semi-peripheral states to acquire sovereignty? Chapter 5 shows that during the first decades of the twentieth century, semi-peripheral lawyers realized that sovereignty, so longed-for during the nineteenth century, conferred, under classical international law, much less autonomy and equality than they had anticipated. Moreover, at the turn of the century, the specific challenges faced by semi-peripheral states in their interaction with Western powers shifted, so that classical international law exhausted its power and stopped being useful. Part III shows that, from the perspective of the semi-periphery, there were particular reasons explaining the shift from classical to modern international law.

Rather than seeking more sovereignty, the new generation of semi-peripheral lawyers that emerged at the beginning of the twentieth century recognized that an international legal order based on absolute sovereignty as law's sole principle, created in practice an order based on the will of the most powerful states. Semi-peripheral scholars had in consequence good reasons for joining their colleagues at the core in the critique of the centrality given by classical international law to the principle of absolute sovereignty. Semi-peripheral international lawyers joined the European

[1] Koskenniemi, *Gentle civilizer*, pp. 98–178.

intellectual trend that since the beginning of the twentieth century and most forcefully during the interwar years found absolute sovereignty to have become anachronistic. The new modern legal thought that emerged at the turn of the century no longer conceived sovereignty as the basis of the international order. Were the modern notions that came to replace classical sovereignty the notions that semi-peripherals had in mind when shifting to the modern legal discourse after realizing the shortcomings of classical international law? Chapter 6 answers this question showing that modern international law did not fundamentally change the rules and doctrines of the classical order that were most detrimental to the semi-periphery. What is more, it included new legal grounds to intervene in the semi-periphery.

5 Sovereignty beyond the West: the end of classical international law

During the first decades of the twentieth century and in particular during the interwar period, international law experienced a fundamental transformation. It progressively developed into a full-fledged legal order, including international tribunals, permanent interstate organizations and a greater number of rules limiting a state's autonomous behaviour. While this process was underway, international lawyers renewed their legal thinking. The old classical legal thought – based on the principle of absolute sovereignty, the standard of civilization and legal positivism – gave way to a modern legal sensibility that criticized absolute sovereignty, foregrounded the interest of the international community and supported anti-formalist legal doctrines. Most scholars have understood that this break in the intellectual history, a break from classical to modern international law, came as a consequence of the sobering lessons left by the First World War.

This chapter offers, from the perspective of the semi-periphery, an alternative historical explanation of the rise of modern international law. It argues that, at the turn of the century, the specific challenges faced by semi-peripheral states in their interaction with Western powers shifted, so that classical international law exhausted its power and stopped being useful. Before, as we have seen in the second part of the book, semi-peripheral states that had not fallen under colonial rule strived for their relations with Western states to be conducted according to the principles of classical international law. Their international lawyers appropriated the discourse of sovereign autonomy and equality to contest the validity of international legal rules and doctrines justifying Western power's unequal treatment of non-European polities. A semi-peripheral version of classical international law emerged in the nineteenth century when non-Western jurists appropriated legal positivism and the principle of absolute sovereignty and internalized the standard of civilization. I have suggested that this semi-peripheral legal consciousness was crucial in universalizing international law by carving out a space in the legal discourse for non-Western polities.

In consequence, at the beginning of the twentieth century, a greater number of semi-peripheral states, such as Brazil, China, Japan or Persia, became regular participants in the world's first international conferences. Some, like the new independent states resulting from the dismemberment of the Spanish, Portuguese and Ottoman empires, were formally recognized as members of the international community. With different grades of success, other states subjected to unequal treaties revised them, or abrogated them altogether.

Once semi-peripheral states were admitted, once they began to participate in the international community, did the rules of international law governing the interaction between Western and non-Western states change? What did it mean for semi-peripheral states to acquire sovereignty? Moreover, what transformations did the discipline of international law undergo when semi-peripheral jurists attended professional meetings, when they appeared in their own right, representing their states in intergovernmental conferences? As you might expect, this relationship was not easy. Sovereignty, so much longed for during the nineteenth century, conferred much less autonomy and equality than semi-peripherals had anticipated. An initial welcoming attitude turned sour as soon as semi-peripherals supported doctrines considered unacceptable by Western jurists – absolute sovereign equality, for example, or rules such as no use of force to collect public debt or equality between nations of different races. Understanding the antagonism between core and semi-peripheral states, the professional controversy between Western and non-Western international lawyers as well as the ways in which divergences were resolved or accommodated, is crucial to understanding the turn from classical to modern international law.

Let me offer an account of three international events that illustrate this antagonism and accommodation – that is, events that illustrate the articulation of classical legal ideas by semi-peripheral jurists, their failure to obtain the results they had expected, and the consequent shift to the language of modern international law: first, the European blockade of Venezuelan ports of 1902 and its aftermath; second, the proposal, presented at the Second Hague Peace Conference of 1907, to create a permanent international court with the great powers given the right to appoint more judges than the smaller powers; and, third, the

Japanese attempt, during the Paris Peace Conference of 1919, to include in the Covenant of the League of Nations a clause recognizing racial equality.

The limits of sovereign autonomy: Luis Drago and the Venezuelan blockade of 1902

The New York Times edition of 8 November 1903 included the following report:

> Prof. Pierantoni, before the Venezuelan Arbitration Tribunal today, continuing his argument for Italy, declared that the objections to the employment of force were purely sentimental, and sentiment ought to be left to women. The blockade had excellent results, as it forced Venezuela to recognize her responsibility for damages resulting from the civil war.[1]

In December 1902, Great Britain, Germany and Italy adopted coercive measures, imposing a blockade to force the settlement of a series of pecuniary claims against Venezuela. The Venezuelan fleet was seized or disabled, two Venezuelan gunboats were sunk and Puerto Cabello bombarded.[2] Whereas a long list of unsettled disputes in addition to Venezuelan president Cipriano Castro's erratic and defiant attitude were immediate causes explaining the show of force by Anglo-German-Italian powers on Venezuelan shores, the incident itself was nothing but ordinary.[3] Like most Latin American nations, Venezuela obtained independence at the beginning of the nineteenth century. Venezuela, as the other new republics, struggled throughout the century to gain political stability and national unity against the divisive power of regional caudillos, that is, charismatic strongmen holding control over armed followers in exchange for patronage, lying in wait to take over government. Like

[1] *The New York Times*, 8 November 1903, p. 4.

[2] See M. Hood, *Gunboat diplomacy, 1895–1905: great power pressure in Venezuela*, 2nd edn (London; Boston: Allen & Unwin, 1983) and D. G. Munro, *Intervention and dollar diplomacy in the Caribbean, 1900–1921* (Westport: Greenwood Press, 1980), especially ch. 3, 'The genesis of the Roosevelt corollary', pp. 65–111.

[3] See, e.g., Hood, *Gunboat diplomacy*, which points out that: 'for the two great powers Britain and Germany, the whole affair was of little importance except in so far as it affected their relations with the United States. At one time it seemed as if the whole blockade had hardly been worthwhile, for the claims were small in pecuniary amount': p. 186. See also Platt: 'coercion of Venezuela . . . was no more than a further example of a species common throughout the nineteenth century – i.e. the legitimate coercion of a State . . . ' D. C. M. Platt, 'The allied coercion of Venezuela, 1902–3 – a reassessment', *Inter-American Economic Affairs*, 15 (1961), 3–28, 4.

many semi-peripheral nations, Venezuela, a single-commodity exporter relying heavily on foreign capital, interacted with the international economy in a position of dependence. Like semi-peripheral economies in Latin America or Asia, Venezuela was exposed to price fluctuations and diminishing terms of exchange of export commodities, to capital repatriation, to uneven flows and shortages of capital, as well as subjected to commercial rivalries between Western powers.[4]

Political instability, the penetration of Western capital and presence of foreign populations in semi-peripheral countries proved to be a combination of factors prone to elicit conflict between semi-peripheral and Western states. Classical international law had developed a legal regime to regulate these types of interactions. Thus, the blockade of Venezuela was neither an exceptional international incident, nor an incident in blunt violation of international law. For example, in 1900, only two years before the Venezuelan affair, a coalition of Western powers had intervened in China to put an end to the Boxer uprising. Allied Western military forces marched into Beijing to protect foreign residents and to force the Chinese government to pay compensation for damages. Moreover, during the nineteenth century, European powers had commonly intervened in non-European states, from Mexico to Turkey, from China to Greece.[5] In fact, classical international law conferred upon great powers ample prerogatives to secure their global commercial interests as well as the interests of their nationals abroad. As I argue below, there was an actual international regime including rules governing the interposition of pecuniary claims and protection of nationals abroad through various means, ranging from consular protection to diplomatic intervention and the use of force.

Domestic and international politics played out in the Venezuelan affair against the backdrop of the legal regime governing international claims. Between 1892 and 1902, Venezuela had endured a wave of revolutionary rebellions and civil wars. At the end of this period, with an economy on the brink of collapse and public finances under great strain, Venezuela

[4] See in general Cardoso and Faletto, *Dependency and development*.

[5] On the legal regime governing these interventions see E. Borchard, *The diplomatic protection of citizens abroad; or, the law of international claims* (New York: The Banks Law Pub. Co., 1922). Based on the political reality of a state intervening to safeguard its interest in an alien territory, some international lawyers systematized the regime of military occupation in time of peace. See e.g. L. Jones, 'Military occupation of alien territory in time of peace', *Transactions of the Grotius Society*, 9 (1923), 149–63.

was barely serving its foreign public debt. Moreover, as a result of civil disturbances, foreign residents had sustained personal injury or damage to their property. Foreign residents and bondholders sought diplomatic protection from their governments in order to secure payment and compensation from Venezuela.[6]

Western states, above all, Great Britain, Germany and the United States, had been negotiating with Venezuela to secure the continuous payment of foreign debt and to solve particular controversies with foreign residents as well as foreign banks, railway, mining and shipping companies. Although Venezuela achieved some stability after Cipriano Castro seized power, negotiations with Western powers deteriorated when Castro repudiated some loans and acts of previous governments. Facing a new challenge to its power by insurgents supported from British territory, the Castro government in particular refused to settle any British pecuniary demand until resolution of the incident.[7]

While negotiations continued with the United States and other European powers, the Castro government hardened its positions vis-à-vis Great Britain, Germany and Italy, refusing to settle any pecuniary claims held by their nationals.[8] On 7 December, British and German authorities issued an ultimatum; Italy joined afterwards. Once Castro refused to meet the demands (even if willing, his government did not have enough resources to pay), the three European powers imposed a blockade. As soon as the blockade began, Venezuela agreed to submit the dispute to arbitration, appointing the US minister as representative to negotiate with

[6] However, Platt, and others argue that the Venezuelan blockade was not imposed on behalf of bondholders but followed denial of rights of aliens as guaranteed by international law. See Platt, 'The allied coercion of Venezuela'. As I discuss below, the Venezuelan incident gave rise to the Drago doctrine, excluding forcible collection of public debt. Even if public debt was not at the centre of the Venezuelan intervention, Latin American politicians thought it was a fundamental threat to the sovereignty of their nations and thus they supported this doctrine and pushed for its codification at the Second Hague Conference.

[7] The British steamship *Ban Righ* (although then flying the Colombian flag) had given support to Venezuelan insurgents and had launched raids, organized from the ports of British colony Trinidad, into the coast of Venezuela: M. Low, A. Maurice 'Venezuela and the powers', *The American Monthly Review of Reviews*, 27 (1903), 39–43, 42. See also Hood, *Gunboat diplomacy*, pp. 179–81.

[8] States holding claims against Venezuela included United States, Mexico, Spain, France, Belgium, the Netherlands and Sweden and Norway. See *The Venezuelan arbitration before the Hague tribunal 1903*, vol. no. 119 *[United States] 58th Congress 3d session Senate Document* (Washington: Government Printing Office, 1905), p. 11.

the blockading powers. An agreement on the settlement of claims was only reached after long negotiations, for the demand of the blockading powers for preferential treatment in the settlement of their claims over the claims of non-blockading states proved to be a difficult obstacle. The question of preferential treatment was finally submitted to the Permanent Court of Arbitration at The Hague, which decided in favour of the blockading powers.[9]

Castro's defiance proved misguided.[10] Thinking that the Monroe doctrine would protect Venezuela from European intervention, Castro's calculus proved incorrect. According to the Monroe doctrine, the United States would oppose any attempt by European powers to colonize or interfere with the independence of any state in the Americas. However, the Anglo-German coercive action moved carefully along the borderlines of the Monroe doctrine, avoiding any indication of an armed intervention within Venezuelan territory and enforcing instead a strict naval blockade. Moreover, the Venezuelan affair, specifically the decision by the Permanent Court of Arbitration granting preferential treatment to the blockading powers, triggered a reformulation of the Monroe doctrine. To prevent the intervention of European states to protect the rights of their nationals in Latin America, the Roosevelt corollary to the Monroe doctrine recognized the responsibility of the United States for the conduct of Latin American states toward European nationals. Accordingly, Roosevelt's corollary reserved for the United States the right to intervene and re-establish order in the states of Latin America that have infringed the right of European nationals.[11] The way in which the Roosevelt corollary rendered a right of intervention compatible with the Monroe doctrine shows that Castro equally miscalculated the scope of sovereign autonomy international law bestowed on semi-peripheral states.

[9] See Permanent Court of Arbitration, *The Venezuelan arbitration before the Hague tribunal 1903*. The court did not decide on the legality of the use of force. However, the remarks by the Italian lawyer Pierantoni quoted in *The New York Times* show that semi-peripheral jurists and commentators had good reasons to regard the decision recognizing preferential treatment in favour of the blockading powers as having validated the use of force to collect pecuniary claims.

[10] Hood provides a description of how Castro's self-aggrandizement, parochialism, and ignorance in international affairs contributed to the escalation of the conflict: see *Gunboat diplomacy*, pp. 170–1 and *passim*. The conflict also escalated because of British minister Haggard's own antipathy towards Venezuela: *ibid.*, 182–3.

[11] See F. Rippy, 'Antecedents of the Roosevelt corollary of the Monroe doctrine', *The Pacific Historical Review*, 9 (1940), 267–79.

A right of intervention in the law of international claims

As a matter of law, rather than 'sentiment', Pierantoni was correct. Under classical international law there was nothing extraordinary in the Venezuelan blockade. Western powers exercised a right. Venezuela was forced to recognize its responsibility. For not only had Western powers routinely intervened diplomatically as well as coercively to pursue claims based on the recovery of public debt and claims based on other injuries suffered by their nationals in a non-Western country, but also a number of Western jurists had affirmed the validity of diplomatic and coercive intervention.[12]

A right to coercively intervene in another state pursuing an international claim was the most extreme, but only one of the elements in a comprehensive regime governing the protection of foreign nationals and the recovery of pecuniary claims. Contrary to what one would expect, considering that since the seventeenth century international law had become primarily an interstate legal order in which each state has exclusive jurisdiction over its territory, classical international law included also a regime in which, based on the principle of nationality, states exercised extraterritorial jurisdiction over nationals residing abroad.[13] When Western informal imperialism became more pervasive, as the semi-periphery received a larger number of Western nationals as well as a greater amount of Western capital, the importance of a legal regime governing international claims increased.

According to this regime, a state may claim jurisdiction over acts occurring in a territory over which another state has territorial authority by virtue of the nature of the subjects involved, that is, when a foreign resident is involved. In addition to the common scenario in which a state protects the interests of its own nationals residing abroad, in Turkey, China or Morocco for example, that is, in states subjected to treaties establishing extraterritorial jurisdiction, some Western states extended their protection to other Western nationals of non-treaty powers, that is, foreign residents of states that had not concluded unequal treaties.[14]

12 According to the US author Amos Hershey, international lawyers supporting this position included Hall, Phillimore and Rivier: A. Hershey, 'The Calvo and Drago doctrines', *AJIL*, 1 (1907), 26–45, 37. Interestingly, Hershey believes that a majority of authors was opposed to the forceful collection of debts, including three lawyers from the semi-periphery: Calvo, Martens and Kebedgy.

13 See generally Borchard, *The diplomatic protection*.

14 Borchard, *The diplomatic protection*, pp. 467–8.

Moreover, as we have seen in Chapter 3, some unequal treaties instituted a protégé system, according to which Western states extended their protection even further covering certain classes of native residents.

The particular rights foreign residents and companies enjoyed in a country overseas depended on the treaties binding both the host state and the state to which foreign residents belong. However, a legal regime with similar rules emerged as a product of the most favoured nation clause. Even in the absence of such treaties, nineteenth-century state practice guaranteed Western nationals abroad a rather high baseline of protection, including not only rights to life and property, but also protection from unjust arrest, detention or ill-treatment by local officials, disproportionate sentencing by local tribunals, and personal losses in civil disturbances without adequate excuse by the local government.[15]

In addition to substantive rights and obligations, the regime of international claims included procedural rules. These rules were crucial to determine the regime's impact on semi-peripheral states, because they established the procedure to secure redress in case of violation of rights. In this regard, the general rule prescribing domestic judicial remedies to have been exhausted before seeking diplomatic protection did not apply to: 'countries of imperfect civilisation, or to cases in which prior proceeding show gross perversion of justice'.[16]

It is important to note that this was not just a special regime of consular protection and extraterritorial jurisdiction, to the extent that it conferred rights and obligations to states in their mutual relations: this was a regime, part of general public international law. Classical international law rendered states internationally liable for domestic acts in violation of the rights of foreign residents. States became directly responsible for the violation of foreigners' rights by governmental agents, or indirectly responsible when having failed to provide adequate protection to foreigners. In fact, the series of interventions by Western states in the semi-periphery, at the end of the nineteenth and beginning of

[15] Hershey, for example, maintains that as a matter of right in international law, aliens can only demand protection of life and property, and access to local courts. Other rights and privileges will depend on convention and the principle of reciprocity: Hershey, 'Calvo and Drago', 35. See generally Borchard, *The diplomatic protection*; Platt, 'The allied coercion of Venezuela', 11 and D. Anzilotti, 'La responsabilité internationale des etats a raison des dommages soufferts par des étrangers', *RGDIP* 13 (1906), 5–28, 285–309.

[16] F. Wharton, *A digest of the international law of the United States, taken from documents issued by presidents and secretaries of state, and from decisions of federal courts and opinions of attorneys-general* (Washington: Government Printing Office, 1886), p. 695.

the twentieth century, were taken by Western jurists as an expression of state practice consolidating a regime of international responsibility for the protection of foreign residents.[17] Linking the infringement by a state of the rights foreign residents enjoyed within its territory with the international responsibility of the host state, made available, to the state exercising protection, all the remedies international law considered in the case of a breach of an international obligation.

Under classical international law, remedies included the threat and use of coercion. Displays of force were at the base of a great power's gunboat diplomacy. Most commonly, American, British, French or German warships appeared in front of the main ports of a nation facing default or civil unrest and the show of force persuaded local authorities to settle or pay pecuniary demands, or to adopt measures preventing episodes of violence against foreign nationals.[18] Actual use of coercion to redress a violation of an international legal obligation included direct military interposition (euphemism for intervention) to protect nationals residing abroad as well as military reprisals. Military interpositions to protect foreign residents adopted the form of police actions to suppress riots and restore order.[19] Reprisals included embargoes, blockade of ports, bombardment of coastal towns, punitive expeditions, and military occupation of alien territory, typically involving the seizure of the local custom office in order to take direct control of the satisfaction of pecuniary claims.[20]

[17] Anzilotti is a good example of a renowned positivist, who thus gives privilege to state practice and identifies a regime governing the protection of nationals abroad: Anzilotti, 'La responsabilité internationale'.

[18] 'War-vessels have therefore on occasion been stationed for extended periods of time in the waters of the Mediterranean, around Turkey, and in the waters near Haiti and the Dominican republic': Borchard, *The diplomatic protection*, p. 446. Again: 'Practically all the great powers have at different times resorted to a display of force to give moral support to a request for the protection of nationals in foreign countries or for the redress of injuries inflicted upon nationals': *ibid.*, p. 447. Other examples include German threats, in 1897, to bombard Port-au-Prince to secure release of imprisoned German nationals. Moreover, Venezuela was not a unique case of joint action by Western powers, since similar interventions happened in Buenos Aires, China and Mexico.

[19] Borchard, *The diplomatic protection*, p. 449.

[20] For example, in 1895 British forces occupied the port of Corinto in Nicaragua and controlled its Custom House. In 1901, France seized the Custom House at Mitylene, in the island of Lesbos to force Turkey to pay her claims. In 1923, after the killing of an Italian general in Greek territory, Italian forces bombarded and occupied Corfu to secure indemnity. Italy defended its action in front of the League's Commission of Ambassadors, invoking a number of precedents in which: 'Powers have seized the territory of other Powers pending the fulfillment of demands for reparation.' Jones,

Although the blockade of Venezuela was in conformity to classical international law, and although the act of force itself was comparatively minor, the Venezuelan affair was met with unprecedented opposition. This time, Latin American jurists mounted a legal challenge to limit the scope of the right of intervention. In 1902 such a challenge was possible. By then, an earlier generation of semi-peripheral jurists had appropriated the Western international legal tradition and argued for the recognition of international legal personality to non-European polities. On the basis of the intellectual foundations laid down by their predecessors, early twentieth century semi-peripheral lawyers could simply assume that their states belonged to the international community and work out, through deduction and analogy, the legal consequences of such membership – namely to define the meaning of semi-peripheral sovereignty.

Limiting the scope of intervention: no use of force to collect public debt

A few weeks after the blockade, Luis Drago (1859–1921), Secretary of Foreign Affairs of Argentina, sent a diplomatic note to the Argentinean minister to the United States, in which, affirming the sovereignty of debtor states, he challenged the legality of the forcible collection of public debt.[21]

At the time he drafted the note, Drago was a prominent local politician, rather than the renowned international legal scholar and diplomat he became later, when the ideas expressed in the note came to represent the possibility for weaker states to resist the force of great powers by means of law – when these ideas became known as the Drago doctrine. In fact, the diplomatic note was the first articulation of the Drago doctrine. Although the note entailed mostly a restatement of semi-peripheral jurists' prevailing views about international law as applied to the Venezuelan affair, Drago succeeded in conveying a message that was both straightforward and in accordance rather than in opposition to classical international

'Military occupation', 158. Llewellyn Jones refers to these cases as examples of pacific military occupation: *ibid.*, 156–8.

[21] L. M. Drago, 'Letter of Dr. Luis Drago, Minister of Foreign Relations of the Argentine Republic, to Mr. Mérou, Argentine Minister to the United States, December 29, 1902' in A. Alvarez, *The Monroe doctrine, its importance in the international life of the states of the New World* (New York: Oxford University Press, 1924), 187–92. Evidently the note was well received by classical semi-peripheral international lawyers such as Martens: see F. F. Martens, *Par la justice vers la paix. Annexe: doctrine de Drago, ou note diplomatique du gouvernement argentin du 29 décembre 1902* (Paris: H. Charles-Lavauzelle, 1906).

law: Venezuela is a sovereign state. The autonomy of the government of Venezuela is an essential attribute deriving from its sovereignty. Issuing public debt is a sovereign act. In consequence, coercive collection of public debt violates the sovereign autonomy of Venezuela.[22]

Drago was remarkably successful in making his ideas widely known and discussed in diplomatic and international law circles. The note sparked off considerable controversy when, only a few months after it had been dispatched, Carlos Calvo translated it into French and passed it to his colleges at the *Institut de France* and the *Institut de droit international*. Responses, some of them fairly critical, by jurists like Westlake, Holland and Fiore were published in the *Revue de droit international et de législation comparée*.[23] Drago himself defended and reformulated his position in an article published both in French and English, in the *Revue générale de droit international public* and the *American Journal of International law*, the most prestigious journals of respectively France and the United States.[24] Moreover, what had become a professional controversy among international lawyers turned into a debate of diplomatic significance. As an Argentinean diplomatic delegate, and with the support of other Latin Americans, Drago submitted his doctrine to consideration and defended its crystallization into conventional international law, first at the 1906 Pan-American Conference in Rio, and then, and most importantly, at the 1907 Second Peace Conference in The Hague.

Taking stock of these professional and diplomatic debates, Drago's ideas gained strength. Drago went beyond the initial formulations of the doctrine, which affirmed that since states are sovereign entities enjoying absolute autonomy and equality, coercive collection of public debt was an illegal intervention under international law. Now, illegality became rather the end result of a more complex legal argumentation. Well aware of the legality of the use of force between states as a remedy under classical international law, Drago neither disputed the use of force in general, nor contested the use of coercion to protect foreign residents whose rights

[22] As we have seen, it was Carlos Calvo at the end of the nineteenth century who had inaugurated this general doctrinal move – i.e. deducing from the principle of sovereignty the argument against all forms of intervention pursuing private pecuniary claims. As Hershey pointed out, the Drago doctrine was much narrower than the Calvo doctrine: Hershey, 'Calvo and Drago', 31 and *passim*.

[23] *RDI*, 2me série, 5 (1903), 597 ff.

[24] L. M. Drago, 'Les emprunts d'état et leurs rapports avec la politique internationale', *RGDIP*, 14 (1907), 251–87 and L. M. Drago, 'State loans in their relation to international policy', *AJIL*, 1 (1907), 692–726.

have been infringed in particular.[25] It was clear to Drago that foreign residents enjoy rights whose infringement gives rise to state responsibility, diplomatic protection and eventually the use of force. Out of the wealth of claims a state can bring against another state, Drago only excluded one type of pecuniary claims, those resulting from the contractual relation between a foreign private lender and a sovereign state. Specifically, he excluded the claim of a state to forcefully collect bonds of public debt subscribed between their nationals and a foreign state.[26]

When a state borrows money emitting a bond, a state acts not in its private capacity but as a sovereign. In Drago's words: '[bonds] are issued by virtue of the sovereign power of the state, as is its currency, they are authorized by legislation and do not present any of the general characteristics of the contracts of private law, since there is no person specified in whose favour the obligations are incurred, payment being promised always to the bearer without discrimination'.[27] Important consequences derive from the fact that states act as sovereigns when issuing public debt. According to Drago, a state determines not only the public nature of the contractual relation, but also the remedies lenders have in case payment is suspended: 'interruption in the payments occurs in virtue of the sovereign authority of the states, manifested *jure imperii*'.[28]

In contractual relations regulated by private law, when justice is denied to a foreign claimant, disputes can be resolved either by a local tribunal, or through diplomatic intervention. In contrast, Drago argues that in the case of public debt:

> there is no tribunal competent to bring action against the debtor state, but it is impossible even hypothetically to conceive of such a tribunal. The same would be true of an attempt to bring to judgment a nation that had declared the forcible circulation of its paper currency. The sovereignty of the claimant state thus finds itself face to face with the debtor sovereignty without prescribed process and by virtue of facts that by their nature correspond to the exercise of the essential faculties of independence and self-government.[29]

The absence of a competent tribunal, Drago clarifies, means that no court has jurisdiction over these controversies without consent given by a state.

[25] Drago explicitly recognized the legality of war when dignity, integrity or security of the state is at stake: Drago, 'State loans', 701.

[26] Among pecuniary claims, Drago's diplomatic note 'deliberately excluded this class of relations and claims for whose adequate appreciation', it said, 'the laws of the respective countries would have to be consulted': *ibid.*, 693–5.

[27] *Ibid.*, 695. [28] *Ibid.*, 695. [29] *Ibid.*, 697.

It means also that even when competence is given to a court, the state does not authorize the use of force to execute the court's judgment.[30] And the lender knows this. Drago affirms:

> The lender knows that he is entering into a contract with a sovereign entity, and it is an inherent qualification of all sovereignty that no proceedings for the execution of a judgment may be instituted or carried out against it, since this manner of collection would compromise its very existence and cause the independence and freedom of action of the respective government to disappear.[31]

Lenders are well aware of the risks they incur when acquiring public debt; actually, they assume greater risks to obtain an interest premium when investing in unstable countries.[32] When payment is suspended – Drago argues – foreign investors sustain a loss no different from shareholders' losses in a corporation going bankrupt, the difference being that the state does not disappear; sooner or later, states regain solvency and lenders will obtain payment.[33] Thus, a government suspending in good faith payment of its public debt falls into insolvency, rather than giving rise to a legitimate cause for the use of coercion.

Arguing in this way Drago does not depart from classical international legal thinking. In fact, Drago was a typical classical jurist in that his doctrine did not challenge the use of force in general and did not have universal scope but it was meant to apply only to Latin America.[34] Drago also did not challenge classical international law's prevailing Darwinist assumptions: 'The European nations which have reached the summit of civilisation in the slow process of elaboration of the centuries have in consequence no right to attack the youthful nations of America, because the latter have not in a short time attained their degree of development

[30] Drago thinks that proceedings to achieve execution entail a new judgment. Thus summary proceedings cannot be directly executed against a sovereign; it is a privilege inherent in the nature of its functions to assess the legitimacy of the claims. Drago defended this idea as an answer to Westlake's criticism: *ibid.*, 700.

[31] Drago, 'Letter', p. 188.

[32] 'The rule of *caveat emptor*... seems to be becoming more and more deeply rooted in the public intelligence': Drago, 'State loans', 703.

[33] Moreover, it would be impossible to render operational a rule recognizing intervention. Drago points out that bonds change hands by simple transmission and the foreign debt of a country can be divided among various nations. It is therefore impossible to determine who is entitled to exercise diplomatic protection and preferential treatment: *ibid.*, 701.

[34] 'We should not have spoken if the country constrained by force to settle its accounts had been Tunis or Turkey': *ibid.*, 709.

and culture. The adult does not ill-treat the infant because he had not the discretion and the manners of maturity . . . '[35]

Drago's legal argumentation was also an authentic example of the semi-peripheral version of classical international law. Drago redefines the problem of non-payment of public debt within the general international law regime based on sovereign equality and autonomy, and away from the legal regime governing remedies as well as from the international regime governing relations with 'semi-civilized' states, regimes that as we have seen are based on inequality. That is, if a state acting in bad faith fails to pay its public debt, international responsibility and remedies will ensue, including the use of coercion. If a government fails to serve its public debt in good faith, default must be treated as a case of insolvency, thus solutions to the impasse have to respect the equality and autonomy of the debtor state.[36] Given that a state can voluntarily limit its own sovereignty, a solution might be reached by settling the dispute through arbitration, or by directly agreeing on a mode of payment in a treaty. Drago in consequence did not oppose arbitration.

That Drago was not against arbitration disproves one of the strongest criticisms he faced after defending his doctrine at the Second Hague Conference. French lawyer Albert de Lapradelle (1871–1955) thought that Drago's position, upholding sovereign autonomy in a peace conference, was 'shocking'.[37] Lapradelle affirmed: 'Drago made a mistake in presenting before a commission of arbitration a theory restricting instead of extending arbitration.'[38] Lapradelle was dismayed, I would argue, because he could only see in Drago an excessive defence of sovereign autonomy, which imposes a great obstacle for the legal institutionalization of the international community. At a time when sovereignty became a problem for modern Western jurists at the core like Lapradelle, a tension between national sovereignty and the international community was not apparent

35 *Ibid.*, 708.

36 'Among the fundamental principles of public international law . . . is that all states whatever be the force at their disposal, are entities in law, perfectly equal one to another, and mutually entitled by virtue thereof to the same consideration and respect. The acknowledgement of the debt, the payment of it, can and must be made by the nation without diminution of its rights as a sovereign entity but the summary and immediate collection at a given moment, by means of force, would occasion nothing less than the ruin of the weakest nations . . . by the mighty powers of the earth': Drago, 'Letter', p. 188.

37 A. G. de Lapradelle and E. C. Stowell, 'Latin America at the Hague Conference', *The Yale Law Journal*, 17 (1908), 270–80, 273.

38 *Ibid.*, 274.

to semi-peripheral jurists. Drago saw no contradiction because recognizing weaker states' sovereign autonomy decreases the chances of the use of force by stronger states. Thus at the Peace Conference Drago endorsed compulsory arbitration with a reservation, excluding 'public or national debt arising from government loans'.[39]

So far the story about the Venezuelan blockade suggests that having internalized classical international law, semi-peripheral jurists put classical legal thinking into use when facing concrete international problems. Although remaining within the frame given by classical international law, Drago's doctrine was not well received by Western legal scholars and diplomats. As we will see below, neither at the Pan-American Conference nor at The Hague did Drago manage to convert his doctrine into treaty law.[40] Actually, the Venezuelan blockade did not only elicit the Drago doctrine, but, as already mentioned, also Roosevelt's corollary to the Monroe doctrine, according to which the United States proclaimed, vis-à-vis European nations, a special responsibility to police and chasten Latin American states' misbehaviour.[41] Moreover, as mentioned above, the Venezuelan controversy was finally submitted to The Hague Court of Arbitration, which recognized preferential treatment to the blockading powers.[42]

[39] International Peace Conference, *The proceedings of the Hague Peace conferences: translation of the official texts*, prepared in the Division of International law of the Carnegie Endowment for International Peace, under the supervision of James Brown Scott et al. (repr. Buffalo, NY: W. S. Hein, 2000), p. 251. Drago explicitly endorsed arbitration, even in the case of controversies generated by pecuniary claims only when the source of the claim is not under dispute: 'As far as we South Americans are concerned, we find in that list a point which is of the highest importance: submission to obligatory arbitration of pecuniary claims when the principle of indemnification has been accepted by the parties. Very recently we have found out to what extremes this sort of claims may be carried, and how they are reduced, once they have been subjected to the study of an impartial jurisdiction': *ibid.*, p. 54.

[40] From the perspective of law in the books, the principle of non-intervention was only recognized at the Seventh Pan-American Conference held in 1933 at Montevideo. However, the United States issued a reservation qualifying the obligation to respect the principle. The United States unequivocally adhered to the principles of non-intervention in the Declaration of Principles of Inter-American Solidarity and Cooperation, adopted in December 1936 at the Inter-American Conference for the Maintenance of Peace at Buenos Aires.

[41] Drago also defended the doctrine of no forcible collection of public debt in the context of the Monroe doctrine and the fact that Western powers always targeted weaker states with colonial interests, in violation of the Monroe doctrine.

[42] The court did not decide over the legality of the use of force, and actually did not recognize per se preferential treatment to the states that enforced the blockade. Because the non-blockading creditors consented to the preference given to blockading

The Venezuelan controversy, Drago's doctrine and the ensuing professional and diplomatic debates over the legality of the coercive collection of public debt, reveal the uncertain limits of sovereignty, when the sovereign in question was a newly recognized semi-peripheral state. The beginning of the twentieth century was a period of transition, for not only was the scope of autonomy of semi-peripheral states to be determined, but also the broad extraterritorial rights that Western powers exercised in the non-Western world throughout the nineteenth century had yet to be limited. This story illustrates the nature and limits of sovereign autonomy in semi-peripheral states. Let us explore now another episode, one illustrating the nature and limits of the principle of sovereign equality, a principle that generated controversy when semi-peripheral jurists demanded international rules and institutions to govern relations between great powers and small states, based on equality between Western and non-Western states.

The limits of sovereign equality: Ruy Barbosa at the Second Hague Conference of 1907

At the Second Hague Conference of 1907, the great powers submitted a proposal to establish a permanent international court, according to which great powers would have a larger representation in the court than smaller states.[43] Ruy Barbosa (1849–1923) became best known for opposing any method for selecting judges or determining the composition of the court that did not respect the absolute equality between great powers and small states. This is the much-celebrated story of Ruy Barbosa at The Hague: with elegance and eloquence Ruy Barbosa, a renowned Brazilian politician, writer and jurist, stood up in front of the great powers of the West and defended the sovereignty of small states.[44]

powers, the court's decision was perceived as endorsing the legality of the use of force to pursue pecuniary claims.

43 The Hague Peace Conferences were convened in 1899 and 1907 to limit armaments, to further regulate warfare and to institutionalize the peaceful settlement of disputes. The First Hague Conference adopted a number of conventions that developed and codified international humanitarian law; it also established the Permanent Court of Arbitration. The Second Hague Conference was convened, among others goals, to expand the original Hague Conventions and to establish a world court.

44 On Barbosa see R. Magalhães Júnior, *Rui, o homen e o mito* (Rio de Janeiro: Civilização Brasileira, 1979), which includes a biographical sketch critical of Barbosa's prominence in Brazilian political history.

In Brazil, Barbosa's firm stance captivated popular imagination. Earning the nickname 'eagle of the Hague', Barbosa became a heroic, even mythical, figure.[45] But also international lawyers from Latin America and beyond have long invoked Barbosa's defence of equality as a foundational landmark in their struggle to bring law to govern interstate relations.[46] Surely, the Brazilian government, Barbosa himself, as well as Latin American commentators, were all eager to produce a sympathetic account of the participation and contribution of Latin America at the Hague Conference. For it was the first time all Latin American Republics had been invited to and attended an international conference in Europe.

Similar to Luis Drago, Barbosa appealed to the absolute character of sovereignty in classical international law to defend the equality between states. In its simplicity, Barbosa's position was well suited to become a great story of heroic resistance:

> [S]overeignty is the prime and elemental right of constituted and independent states. Therefore sovereignty signifies equality. In theory, as in practice sovereignty is absolute. It knows no grades. The juridical administration of law is a branch of sovereignty. If there must be among States a common organ of justice, all the States must have of necessity an equivalent representation.[47]

Barbosa's defence of equality, as in the case of Drago, was not well received.[48] But regardless of how much controversy it sparked, Barbosa's

[45] Back in Brazil, Barbosa was greeted by a prestigious writer and politician, Coelho Neto, as the 'eagle of the Hague' (in Portuguese, the expression 'eagle' is referred to smart and tough characters). A march, *Saudação à Águia* was composed and, since then, Barbosa's deed has reached Brazilian pop-culture status, having been represented in carnival. Barbosa is not the only international lawyer revered in his country. Korean envoys travelled at great pains to the The Hague to participate at the Second Hague Conference, but found out that because of the veto of Japan they would not be allowed to participate in the conference and could not enter or meet other delegates in the conference hall. One of them, Ji Yun, was found dead in his hotel room; Koreans assumed that he committed suicide as a protest and, ever since, have treated him as a national hero. See S. Murase, 'The presence of Asia at the 1907 Hague Conference' in Daudet, *Topicality*, pp. 88–101.

[46] See the Brazilian Antonio Cançado Trindade, 'The presence and participation' and the Indian R. P. Anand, 'Sovereign equality of states in international law', *RdC*, 197 (1986-II), 9–228, 71–5.

[47] Ruy Barbosa, *The equality of sovereign states* (The Hague, 1907) (originally published by *The Independent*). This quote, in a different translation, can be found in *The proceedings of the Hague*, p. 150.

[48] For example *The London Times* reported:

> The last speech of the most industrious and eloquent first Brazilian delegate, M. Ruy de Barbosa, was described by one of the leading Continental members of the Conference as a 'fierce [*farouche*] exposition' of the extreme conception of the

was neither an isolated heroic deed nor a blunt and naïve invocation of an abstract legal principle. It was neither isolated nor exceptional, since, as I have argued above, and as the example of Drago has shown, Barbosa's principled defence of equality belonged to a particular way of thinking about international law. Invoking the principle of sovereignty and deducing from it concrete legal consequences, was not only part of a distinctively semi-peripheral understanding of classical international law, but also part of a positivist mode of advancing legal arguments. Moreover, Barbosa was not alone. Other Latin American and Asian delegates to the Hague Conference, who shared the classical legal sensibility, supported Barbosa's defence of equality.

A permanent international court

During the four months that the Conference lasted, Barbosa had many opportunities to defend the principle of legal equality. I focus on his defence of equality in the debates around the establishment of a permanent international court, since it was in relation to this initiative that Barbosa's position drew most attention and criticism. In these debates Barbosa opposed any formula – regarding the jurisdiction of the court, its composition and the procedure to select its judges – entailing a distinction between great powers and small states. The United States, on the other hand, believed its initiative to create a permanent international court to be one of the most important goals the Conference should achieve, and thus pushed for different solutions to overcome the impasse caused by Barbosa.

The Conference opened with a plenary meeting on 15 June 1907, organizing its work in commissions, subcommissions and committees of examination.[49] Discussions of plans to prevent warfare and to improve

> equality of States and Governments. The excessive prolongation of the labours of the Conference . . . was mainly due to the determination of the United States delegates to see the Court of Arbitral Justice through at all costs, and to the equal obstinacy of the South American States in their resolution to prevent the adoption of the project unless it recognized the equality of all Governments in regard to the nomination of Judges.

'The Second Peace Conference. Its results and lessons', *The London Times*, 21 October 1907, p. 3.

[49] According to the conference procedure, general topics would be debated in the commissions, while subcommissions would hear and discuss the proposals presented by the Russian delegation, which had the presidency of the Conference. A committee of examination would be appointed to study a particular issue and report on the

the peaceful settlement of disputes, including arbitration and the project to create a permanent court were assigned to the First Subcommission.

In its first meeting, on 25 June, the First Subcommission began its work by revising the convention on pacific settlement of international disputes, concluded in 1899 at the First Hague Peace Conference. As soon as the subcommission had reached the discussion of arbitration and the permanent court 'an avalanche of projects were presented, mostly dealing with recovery of public debt'.[50] Therefore, it was not until the ninth meeting, on 1 August, that Russia and the United States presented their individual projects to revamp the 1899 Permanent Court of Arbitration, which thus far had merely operated as a list from which states could pick an arbitrator to submit their controversies.

James Brown Scott (1866–1943) delivered a detailed exposition of the American proposal to create a court that would function as a real and permanent judicial institution. Right from the start, Scott juggled to present a proposal in favour of a court that would respect both the independence and equality of states. First, he swiftly clarified that a court sits as a judicial tribunal to give a judgment. Since judges examine a case, establish the facts and apply the law – Scott explained – a judgment is only possible in relation to 'strictly judicial questions', excluding in consequence questions of special national interest as well as questions of a political nature. Second, he explained that the court could not have original jurisdiction, but that jurisdiction must be expressly conferred upon it, either by a general treaty of arbitration or a specific treaty (cases in which the court would possess obligatory jurisdiction), or by the agreement of nations to submit to the court a specific controversy (a case in which the court would have facultative jurisdiction).[51] Having cleared the way to make national sovereignty and the court's international jurisdiction compatible, Scott pauses to prepare the audience for what would become the most polemic aspect of the proposal:

> It is probable that the views already presented will meet with general acceptance, but the main question still remains, How is the Permanent Court composed of judges, to be constituted? No attempt is made to disguise the difficulties of this

propositions submitted by other delegations. Reports by the committees would be discussed and amended by the subcommissions, their recommendations would then pass to the commissions and finally to the conference's plenary to adopt a final agreement. The first commission was divided into two subcommissions.

[50] D. Myers, 'The origin of the Hague arbitral courts', *AJIL*, 10 (1916), 270–311, 279.

[51] International Peace Conference, *The proceedings of the Hague*, 319.

question; for if it were an easy task, we would not be engaged in discussing it in this year of grace 1907.[52]

It is obvious – Scott continued – that to be international, the court should be represented by all nations. But then, he immediately affirmed: 'It is equally obvious that a court composed of a single representative from each independent and sovereign nation would be unwieldy.' While insisting that every state is equal and thus any distinction between large and small states is not proper to international law, Scott also cautioned that if each state would be allowed to sit in court, according to an 'abstract right' to equality, the court itself would lose its judicial character and become a panel, exactly like the court created in 1899.[53]

Scott was at pains to show that there is an alternative method to select a smaller number of judges without violating the sovereign equality of states. 'Fortunately, another principle exists' – he announced, solving the riddle. There is a standpoint that does not give into the relative strength and weakness of nations. This standpoint, which is 'independent of the question of power', is the standpoint of material interests. While the interest in justice is abstract, it manifests itself in concrete relationships. The greater the frequency of interactions, the greater the concrete interests and the occurrence of conflicts to be resolved by courts. Thus, Scott concluded: the population of different nations becomes an indicator of degrees of interest and a method to determine the composition of the court.[54]

Scott's exposition was well received by the German and British delegates. In contrast, Martens, the renowned jurist and member of the Russian delegation, presented his own project retaining the 'principle of the absolute freedom of states' to choose arbitrators, thus defending the idea of a court based on a list of arbitrators.[55] Other semi-peripheral international lawyers followed suit. Affirming the importance of the principles involved in the constitution of the court, the Mexican and Serbian representatives reserved their definite vote for a later discussion on the substance of the American proposal. The Serbian delegate, Milovan Milovanovich (Milovanović) (1863–1912), explicitly conditioned his support of the initiative to the respect of the principle of absolute equality in the election of judges. Then, delegates from Haiti, Venezuela, Brazil and

[52] *Ibid.*, 321. [53] *Ibid.*, 321–2. [54] *Ibid.*, 322. [55] *Ibid.*, 325–9.

Bulgaria followed with similar declarations pointing at the problems that choosing the method to select of judges will cause.[56]

After these initial expressions of criticism it became clear that the American project had to be revised before its discussion in the Committee of Examination B, which was established by the First Commission to study the different proposals to institute a permanent court. Germany, the United States and Great Britain jointly presented a new project. Scott was again the most articulate exponent of the proposal and again he juggled to show that it did not violate the principle of sovereign equality. This time, Scott distinguished between the sovereign right of states and the conditions, imposed by international law, under which the right is exercised. Accordingly, in the new Anglo-German-American proposal, each state would appoint a judge, thus respecting the equality of representation of all states. However, regulating the exercise of this right, judges would rotate, serving for periods that would be longer or shorter, depending on a ranking of states.[57] The ranking would consider a variety of indicators, such as the state's population, industry and commerce, system of law and language.[58]

At the third meeting of the Committee of Examination B, Barbosa attacked the new project. He first presented an alternative proposal based on the right of each state to designate a judge and the right of states engaged in a dispute to elect the judges to whom they submit the settlement of a controversy. Then he deployed against the newly proposed method to elect judges to the court his critique based on sovereign equality, affirming that the Anglo-German-American project was based on the 'the principle of rotation, that is to say, the principle of inequality of the States in the Arbitral Court'. Given that inequality is a new principle

[56] *Ibid.*, 336–7. See Leger for Haiti, *ibid.*, 338–9, and statements by representatives from Venezuela, *ibid.*, 341, Brazil, *ibid.*, 342 and Bulgaria, *ibid.*, 347–8, which I discuss below. The Persian delegate expressed his intention to vote in favour of the American proposal, *ibid.*, 349, though later while sitting in the committee he withdrew his support.

[57] Scott first describes the problem: 'If each country were to appoint one judge, and if these judges so appointed should be entitled to sit at one and the same time, the problem would be simple . . . Each State – be it large or small . . . should possess the right to appoint, and should actually appoint, a judge of its own choice for the full period contemplated by the Convention, namely, twelve years.' *Ibid.*, 609.

[58] *Ibid.*, 610. Germany, the United Sates, Austria-Hungary, France, Great Britain, Japan and Russia would serve for the full period; Spain, Netherlands and Turkey for ten years; some Latin American states, China and other small European states four years; Persia, and other small states for one year. See full table in *ibid.*, 612–13.

that changes the principle of equality, under which the 1899 court was founded, and given that the Commission did not foresee any transformation in the principle underlying the organization of the court, Barbosa argued that the Committee of Examination lacked competence and that the discussion should be referred back to the Commission.

Notwithstanding Barbosa's opposition, the debate continued in the Committee. However, as Barbosa defended his position, the tide turned against the new project when other semi-peripheral delegates joined him with similar types of criticism. For instance, in the fourth meeting of the Committee, Samad Khan Momtas-es-Saltaneh (Momtaz os-Saltaneh) (1869–1955) from Iran, who had thus far supported the American plan declared: 'The Persian delegation has sincerely concurred in any proposition tending to develop the principle of arbitration . . . Unfortunately, the various propositions that have been submitted to us have not sufficiently taken into account the principle of the juridical equality of States.'[59]

The fact that the views held by Barbosa were supported for the most part by semi-peripheral delegates suggests that he was the most prominent but not the only supporter of sovereign equality. Interventions in the Committee by delegates from Bulgaria, China, Persia and Mexico indicate that Barbosa's views were part of a shared position.

Absolute equality: a demand within classical international law

The defence of sovereign equality by semi-peripheral states, I would argue, was not a position determined exclusively by the analogous interests of these governments. It also expressed the semi-peripheral version of classical international law. As a legal consciousness, it was more complex than the idealistic appeal to a legal principle.

The Committee did not adopt Barbosa's request to defer the discussion of the Anglo-German-American plan until the problem of defining its underlying principle had been resolved, and continued discussing other aspects of the new project. In the fifth meeting, however, Barbosa interrupted the debate with another intervention in which he straightforwardly maintained that all states that have been admitted to the international community enjoy the same sovereign rights, regardless

[59] *Ibid.*, 634. Momtas resents that Persia was relegated to the fourth rank, for in the past Persia was 'one of the greatest civilizations' and today: 'The Persian nation, so calm and worthy in its claims, has shown that it is a friend of progress and that it likewise desires to enter into the ways of western civilisation'. *Ibid.*, 634.

of their power, size or origin.[60] According to classical legal thought, sovereignty was both absolute and an attribute of civilization. Barbosa's intervention reflected the modes of argumentation that semi-peripheral jurists had developed to appropriate the markers of civilization and consequently support the acquisition of sovereignty.

During the second half of the nineteenth century, as we have seen in the second part of the book, semi-peripheral jurists supported the claim to sovereignty by showing their states' progress and civilization. Having achieved recognition as members of the international community, however, semi-peripheral lawyers assumed progress had been achieved and turned to defend the civilized status of their states, devoting most of their efforts to support specific rules deriving from this status. Barbosa, therefore, took progress for granted, remonstrating with Western unawareness of Latin American accomplishments: 'If Europe and the United States itself were better acquainted with our continent, no attempt would be made to inflict this grave injustice upon nations with a future before them and already remarkable because of the progress they have achieved.'[61] Barbosa insisted that Latin American nations were not tributary states, that they inherited something from every European civilization, that in fact they were not removed from its intellectual centres, and that they had thus surpassed many of the states ranked above in the classification proposed by the Americans.

Barbosa was not the only one following this mode of thinking. For example, when expressing his support to the permanent court, the Bulgarian delegate Ivan Karandjouloff framed his reservations to the American proposal in the language of civilizational progress. Karandjouloff explained that although a young nation at the beginning of her 'renaissance', Bulgaria felt the financial burden it would take to maintain an army, and thus strived instead for the 'advent of an era of equity and of justice between the nations'. For it is not by force that Bulgaria 'endeavours to reconquer her place among the civilised nations'. On the contrary, not only are Bulgarians 'peaceful, hardworking and devoted to science and justice', but also they judge their governments by the progress they make to develop schools and courts. Karandjouloff insists:

> The progress made ... especially as regards the development of the courts of justice, has already been recognized by the great European Powers which ... have recently renounced to the privileges of capitulations, in favour of the European

60 *Ibid.*, 645 ff. 61 *Ibid.*, 646.

residents in the countries of the Orient. Thus rewarded by that love of impartiality and justice, my country naturally hopes to be treated with the same impartiality, beyond her boundaries.[62]

On the other hand, the very same participation at the Second Hague Conference was invoked to indicate sovereign status, to signal membership in the family of civilized nations. Thus, Barbosa was ready to make the most out of the presence of new semi-peripheral states.[63] Moreover, participation of semi-peripheral lawyers in international life was taken as a further sign of their states' civilized status. For example, facing the criticism his opposition had stirred up in public opinion, and, in particular, facing the attacks levelled against Brazil and other non-Western states for frustrating the conference's goals, Barbosa was ready to invoke Brazil's international legal tradition.[64] That a controversy as prominent as the *Alabama* case, in addition to other controversies involving Western powers, were decided by panels including Brazilian arbitrators – Barbosa mused – shows how ridiculous it was to think that the great powers would never accept a court constituted by judges from nations like Brazil.[65]

At the fifth meeting, the Mexican, Rumanian and Greek delegates joined Barbosa in declaring that they would refrain from taking part in the debate until the principles according to which the court would be composed were fully discussed.[66] By the seventh meeting it became clear that the Anglo-German-American project had not gathered enough support.[67] To overcome the deadlock the committee appointed a preparatory subcommittee to reach an agreement on the composition of the Court. At the eighth meeting, held on 8 September, the President of the Committee of Examination announced that the Anglo-German-American project had not been supported and that the system of rotation of judges had been defeated.

62 *Ibid.*, 347–8.

63 '[I]f States excluded from the First Peace Conference have been invited to the Second, it is not with a view to having them solemnly sign an act derogatory of their sovereignty by reducing them to a scale of classification which the more powerful nations would like to have recognized': *ibid.*, 620.

64 '[I]n view of the fact that the great Powers are not at all disposed to put over them, as their judges, the most corrupt and the most backward States of Asia and of South America.' *Ibid.*, 150.

65 *Ibid.*,151–2.

66 See respectively statements by Esteva (Mexico), *ibid.*, 653 and 660, Beldiman (Rumania) and Streit (Greece), *ibid.*, 660.

67 Semi-peripheral delegates were not the only ones to oppose; they were also joined by Belgium: *ibid.*, 705.

Without delay, the American ambassador Choate pleaded for an alternative proposal, which was as well quickly defeated. To avoid a complete diplomatic blunder, the British representative, Edward Fry, proposed a diluted *vœu*, a recommendation for signatory states to adopt the project, and a recommendation to put the convention into force as soon as agreement had been reached in relation to the selection of judges. The committee decided to leave aside the draft articles regarding the composition of the court and the selection of judges and to put the whole project as well as Fry's *vœu* to a vote. The majority of the committee approved the project and the *vœu* and designated Scott as reporter to the First Commission.[68]

Debate in the First Commission gave a final opportunity to representatives from semi-peripheral states, especially the ones that were not represented in the committee, to voice their views about the creation of a permanent court. Supporting the *vœu*, they adopted a conciliatory position, although without missing the occasion to express their firm opposition to the principle of inequality. The Chinese delegate Lou Tseng-tsiang, for example, approved the *vœu* proposing an additional declaration: 'we may no more . . . disregard the sovereign and independent rights and the equality of States which form the fundamental principles of international arbitral justice . . . the new court . . . shall have as its basis this same principle of equality'.[69] In turn, Barbosa had the final opportunity to defend the principle of sovereign equality, explain his fierce opposition to the projects discussed in the committee and to respond to the critiques his opposition had generated. The speech, translated and published in various venues, became the Hague Conference's most compelling and celebrated defence of sovereign equality.[70]

Barbosa as well as Drago became symbols of the struggle of small states resisting by means of law the imperialist demands of great powers. In spite of apparent heroisms, both jurists articulated well-known positions within the language of classical international law. Both appealed to the sovereignty of small states, Barbosa defending the equality between great

[68] Even though the vote included Fry's amendment and the court project as a whole, thus excluding the articles about the composition of the court, Greece, Peru, Brazil, Rumania and Belgium cast negative votes: *ibid.*, 705.

[69] *Ibid.*, 161. See similar declarations by Uruguay, *ibid.*, 156, Guatemala, *ibid.*, 159, Norway (although Western), *ibid.*, 160, Iran, *ibid.*, 161, Rumania, *ibid.*, 178, Siam, *ibid.*, 180 and Chile, *ibid.*, 180.

[70] *Ibid.*, 147–56. The speech was translated and published in *The Independent*, and then reprinted as 'The equality of sovereign states', also published in French and Portuguese.

powers and small states, and Drago standing for the autonomy of weaker countries. Though by the 1900s neither Barbosa's Brazil, nor Drago's Argentina were exactly small or particularly weak, these were relatively new independent republics still struggling to obtain political stability, economic progress and national unity. At the turn of the century, semi-peripheral states in general faced serious challenges in their international relations.

The comparatively weak position semi-peripheral states occupied vis-à-vis states at the core explains both the use of international law by semi-peripheral states to resist the incursions of greater powers as well as the opposition doctrines, such as those of Drago and Barbosa, generated on the part of Western governments and their international lawyers. However, one might also see the same pattern – of adverse reactions in front of the use of classical international law – replicated in the case of a powerful non-Western state as Japan. During the second half of the nineteenth century, Japanese jurists successfully appropriated classical international law. But Japan, at the beginning of the twentieth century, was in a unique position. Japan had not only effectively modernized, but also had become a strong military power. Let me now briefly consider a general overview of the period of the history of international law in which Japan, as the only non-Western state having achieved great power status, appealed to the language of classical international law to pursue its interests, particularly to demand equality as well as a special role in Asia.

Japan between the revision of unequal treaties in the 1890s and the Paris Peace Conference of 1919

Japan was the only non-Western great power attending the Paris Peace Conference of 1919. By then, after the Meiji restoration, Japan had not only modernized but also become a strong military power. Japan had defeated China (1894–95) and Russia (1904–5), annexed Taiwan (1895) and Korea (1910), overrunning, after the First World War, Germany's colonies in the Pacific Islands and the lease it held over the province of Shandong in China. In fact, at the Paris Peace Conference Japan was accorded the status of great power.[71]

[71] In consequence, Japan appointed two representatives in the committee. See T. Burkman, *Japan and the League of Nations: Empire and world order, 1914–1938* (Honolulu: University of Hawaii Press, 2008).

On the backdrop of Japan's modernization in general, the second part of the book sketched a correlation between the abrogation of unequal treaties – as a sign of Japan's entry into the international legal regime of equality – and the appropriation of the language of classical international law by a generation of Japanese elites who, having studied international law in the West, made their way into the professional and diplomatic circles at the centre, publishing their scholarship in Western languages, engaging in disciplinary debates, and participating in professional organizations. Japan was the most successful example of a non-Western polity internalizing the standard of civilization, that is, internalizing and manipulating the doctrine determining the applicability of the international law regime of equality to non-Western states.

Throughout the last three decades of the nineteenth century, Japan struggled to renegotiate the unequal treaties it had concluded with Western states, signing the first treaty under equality with Great Britain in 1894.[72] Having successfully revised the treaties signed with France, Germany and the United States, having also attended the First Hague Peace Conference of 1899, Japan's admission into the international community of civilized nations, was not only apparent to Japanese elites, but also recognized by the most renowned international law scholars at the core.[73]

While Drago and Barbosa, that is, while international lawyers belonging to relatively weaker semi-peripheral states, unambiguously thought that non-Western states' admission into the international community implied recognition of sovereign status within an international regime based on the equality between states, to Japanese eyes things looked much more complex. The position of Japanese jurists and politicians was as much imbued by their country's newly acquired condition of great power status as marked by Japan's nineteenth-century traumatic opening to the West, through imposition of inequality and extraterritoriality. By way of their own historical experience dealing with European international law, Japanese jurists learned that equality and inequality coexisted in nineteenth-century international law. Therefore one would only expect that the generation of Japanese jurists and diplomats who succeeded in

[72] See Anglo-Japanese Treaty of Commerce and Navigation of July 1894. See also Anglo-Japanese Treaty of Alliance of 1902.

[73] Among late nineteenth-century treatises recognizing Japan's admission into the international community see Wheaton's *Elements of international law* and Westlake's *Chapters on the principles of international law*.

revising Japan's unequal treaties, pursued thereafter a legal and diplomatic strategy favouring both equality and inequality.

On the one hand, on the basis of Japan's full insertion into the international legal regime founded on equality, Japanese lawyers deduced particular legal arguments. For example, as described below, appealing to sovereign equality, they offered international legal support for taxing property held by foreigners under perpetual leases, or demanded, at the Paris Peace Conference of 1919, a rule recognizing equality between races. At the same time, Japanese jurists and diplomats sought the privileges classical international law conferred on great powers over 'less civilized peoples'. They mostly supported Japan's imperialistic expansion in Asia, providing legal legitimacy as well as a concrete regime, based on inequality, to govern Japan's interactions with polities like Korea, Taiwan and the Shandong province in mainland China.[74]

Paradoxically, Japanese international lawyers were more effective in pursuing legal arguments and doctrines entailing inequality than in defending legal arguments presupposing equality. Even though the sovereignty of Japan was beyond dispute, in a number of episodes, Japanese lawyers and diplomats failed to put forward demands of equality against other states. For example, as explained below, Japan lost the house tax case submitted to the Permanent Court of Arbitration (1905). Japan also failed to pass a racial equality clause at the Paris Peace Conference (1919) and did not achieve parity in the limitation of naval forces at the Washington Conference (1921). On the other hand, Japanese lawyers and diplomats faced much less opposition from Western counterparts when they justified unequal treatment vis-à-vis Korea or China, on the basis of Japan's sovereign and civilized status. For example, Japan signed unequal treaties with China (1895, after the first Sino-Japanese war, opening ports and recognizing Korean autonomy from China) and Korea (1905, establishing a protectorate), participated in the coalition intervening in China following the Boxer uprising (1900), and during the negotiations ahead of the Second Peace Conference (1907) blocked the participation of Korea and Ethiopia.[75]

Between the beginning of the twentieth century and its retreat from the League, Japan followed a stance inspired by classical international law. It is therefore misleading to understand Japan's international behaviour

[74] Japan had signed treaties with Korea: 26 February 1876 and with China: 31 October 1874; 18 April 1885; and 30 March 1895.

[75] In fact, Korea was invited to the Second Hague Conference before falling under Japanese rule.

during that period as opposing international law. The more poignant question is to determine what happened later, by the time of the Mukden (or Manchurian, or 18 September) incident of 1931 and the invasion of Manchuria, when Japan unambiguously embarked on an imperialistic adventure. This turn can be equally seen within rather than in opposition to the conventional international law of the time. Although the incident was justified as an act in self-defence, Japan, like other Western powers, progressively shifted towards a legal justification of regional hegemony based on the doctrine of a sphere of influence (like the Monroe doctrine); in the case of Japan this turn definitely came about during the Sino-Japanese War (1937–45) and then the Second World War (1941–5) (the Pacific War, or Greater East Asian War).

Taxing perpetual leases: the limits of Japanese sovereignty

Under the unequal treaties, Japan opened to foreign commerce a number of ports. Foreign citizens were permitted to reside in specially designated areas of these cities. While Japan retained property over these areas, foreign residents had: 'the right, therein to lease land, purchase houses and to erect dwelling and warehouses'. In accordance with the treaties and under consultation between Japanese authorities and foreign consuls, special settlements for foreign residents were built in the treaty ports. Land in the settlements was 'held under governmental leases in perpetuity . . . subject to a fixed rate of rent'. As the land remained property of the state, the 'leases were exempted from taxation of all kinds'.[76]

The revision of unequal treaties meant the abolition of extraterritoriality. That is, foreign residents started to be subjected to Japanese law and judicial institutions.[77] Though the perpetual leases continued, they had to be incorporated into Japanese jurisdiction. According to Article 18 of the Anglo-Japanese treaty of 1894: 'The several foreign Settlements in Japan shall be incorporated with the respective Japanese Commune, and shall thenceforth form part of the general municipal system of Japan'.[78]

Appealing to the absolute sovereign autonomy recognized in the revised treaties, the Japanese government argued it could tax the properties

[76] See Japan, *The case presented by the imperial Japanese government to the Tribunal of Arbitration constituted under section 1 of the protocol concluded at Tokio, August 28, 1902, between Japan and Germany, France and Great Britain* (1904).

[77] Treaty of Commerce and Navigation between Britain and Japan, 16 July 1894. Article 18: 'It is, however, understood that the Consular authorities mentioned in the same are in all cases to be replaced by the Japanese authorities': 180 Consol. T.S., p. 265.

[78] *Ibid.*

leased by foreign residents. According to Japan, the exemption from taxes established in the revised treaties extended only to the land, and not to the buildings constructed on such land. In 1902, when the governments of Germany, France and Great Britain defended the absolute character of tax exemptions, Japan offered to submit the dispute to the Permanent Court of Arbitration.

After the revision of the unequal treaties, the perception of the Meiji government towards international law had improved considerably. Indeed, during the years preceding this controversy Japan submitted various disputes to arbitration. Japanese elites, therefore, welcomed the government's decision to send the house tax case to the recently created court of arbitration, both as a sign of Japan's commitment to international law and as a safe form of resolving the dispute, this in light of their conviction about the strength of the Japanese position.[79]

Japanese officials argued that the fiscal immunity foreigners enjoyed derived from the regime of extraterritoriality established by unequal treaties. Accordingly, all land, including the buildings erected on the land, had been exempted from all taxes and charges. The abrogation of unequal treaties abolished extraterritoriality and thus fiscal immunity. Given that, under Japanese law, foreigners could not own land, the Japanese government leased land for them to use in perpetuity. Japan acknowledged that foreigners' annual payment represented both rent and taxes over the land. Because buildings, being property of the lessees, had no fiscal immunity, Japan argued that it could tax buildings owned by foreigners.[80] The court decided otherwise:

> The provisions of the Treaties . . . exempt not only the land held in virtue of the leases in perpetuity granted by or on behalf of the Government of Japan, but they exempt the land and buildings of every description constructed or which may hereafter be constructed on such land, from all imposts, taxes, charges, contributions, or conditions whatsoever, other than those expressly stipulated in the leases in question.[81]

Japanese lawyers and politicians were massively disappointed. Hisashi Owada has suggested that the adverse decision reached by the court

[79] See H. Owada, 'Japan, international law and the international community' in N. Andō (ed.), *Japan and international law: past, present and future* (The Hague: Kluwer Law International, 1999), pp. 347–78, 355–6.

[80] See Japan, *The case presented by the imperial Japanese government*, Part V, pp. 156–95.

[81] Award of the Tribunal. Japan House Tax. Germany, France and Great Britain v. Japan. The Hague, 22 May 1905. See www.pcacpa.org/upload/files/Japanese%20House%20Tax%20English%20Sentence.pdf.

marked a turning point in the Japanese attitude towards international law. Before, during the period Japan set to revise unequal treaties, the government 'adopted a policy of strict adherence to the precepts of Western international law'.[82] After the setback, Japanese reverted to their initial suspicion about Western international law – suspicion that international law works against the interests of Japan and that the West generally bears some inherent prejudice against Japan. Moreover, Japanese stopped believing that international law could represent 'a body of principles based on natural justice which the East could share in common with the West' and turned to see international law as a set of technical tools to be manipulated.[83] Owada in fact believes that once Japanese lost conviction in international law, when they began to manipulate the law to serve the interests of the state, the gates were opened for Japan's repudiation of international law and for Japan's political realignment; both transformations led to the Second World War: 'a sad page of history both for Japan and for the world'.[84]

Most contemporary Japanese scholars share this interpretation about the history of international law in Japan.[85] A first period of 'exposure and absorption' of international law in the nineteenth century was followed by a period of 'adherence and application' of rules, guiding Japan towards becoming a member of the international community. A third period of 'repudiation and realignment' led Japan into war.[86] Within this periodization, the conventional view has the decades preceding the Great East Asian War witnessing Japan's departure from the international legal tradition, departure letting Japan slide down on an imperialistic path culminating with the war crimes committed during the Great East Asian War, a traumatic adventure from which Japan recovered only after being defeated.[87]

There is, however, the paradox I mentioned earlier. As Japanese failed in their pursuit of equality, diplomats and politicians had international law on their side when crafting legal arguments or using legal rules to justify Japan's imperialist adventure. This insight is not meant to exonerate

82 Owada, 'Japan, international law', p. 356. 83 *Ibid.* 84 *Ibid.*, pp. 357–8.

85 But this trend is not unique to legal scholars. Thomas Burkman, whose study departs from this interpretation, explains that the interwar period is usually depicted as a 'history of incremental imperialism and intensifying militarism' and the account continues after 1945 as a reaction to and recovery from that war: Burkman, *Japan and the League of Nations*, p. xi.

86 Owada, 'Japan, international law', p. 356.

87 For the idea of pre-World War departure from international law, see Onuma, 'Japanese international law', 39–40.

historical agents from their moral and political responsibilities. It only reinstates this dark period of Japanese history within, rather than outside international law.[88] And as such, it explains from the Japanese perspective, as argued below, the context and reasons for the shift from classical to modern international law. The Japanese House Tax Case marked a turning point because it showed the limits of sovereignty, when the sovereign autonomy Japan had recently acquired was invoked against the great powers at the Western centres. But Japan had still to experience the limits of sovereign equality to definitely turn away from classical international law.

Paris Peace Conference of 1919: no racial equality in the League of Nations

Japan did not consider the creation of a permanent international institution, the League of Nations, as one of the central goals to be achieved by the Conference. Rather, Japan attended the Paris Peace Conference eager to assert its newly acquired status, not only as one of the five great powers, but also as the only non-Western great power. The recognition of its special power position in East Asia was therefore one of Japan's priorities. Japan considered, as a fundamental element of its plan for a post-war peace settlement, to displace German influence in East Asia, acquiring German colonies in the Pacific islands as well as the German lease and economic rights in Shandong Province. At the same time, however, Japan came to the Peace Conference ready to assert its status vis-à-vis the Western powers. Japan's proposal to include in the Covenant of the League of Nations a clause recognizing the principle of racial equality became, for Japanese elites and the general public, a symbol of Japan's aspirations to be recognized by the West as equal.[89]

Japanese eagerness in asserting its status as a great power did not contradict international law. Japan, in fact, came to the Conference with policy priorities informed by classical international law: securing, on the one

[88] Some Japanese scholars have noticed that international law included a vertical and a horizontal concept, criticizing Japan for endorsing only the former, thus adopting the standard of civilization only to be recognized as an equal member and then to redeploy it against other Asian countries: S. Yamauchi, 'Civilization and international law in Japan during the Meiji Era (1868–1912)', *Hitotsubashi Journal of Law and Politics*, 24 (1996), 1–25, 24–5.

[89] This is the central line of interpretation proposed by N. Shimazu, *Japan, race, and equality: the racial equality proposal of 1919* (London/New York: Routledge, 1998).

hand, a hegemonic position in East Asia, was consistent with the regime of inequality governing the relations with polities whose civilized status was not recognized. Reassuring equal treatment vis-à-vis Western powers, by way of declaring equality between races in a clause in the League's Covenant, on the other hand, entailed participation in the regime of equality reserved to civilized nations.

At the Paris Peace Conference Japan's racial equality proposal was defeated. With the proposal rejected, Japan realized that in 1919 the world was still dominated by Western great powers.[90] Although the fate of the racial equality proposal is primarily part of the history of international relations in general, and Japan's diplomatic history in particular, this episode is also relevant from the point of view of the history of international law.[91] First, it shows how Japan conveyed its foreign policy interests through the language of classical international law, specifically by way of demanding sovereign equality between states: 'The equality of nations being a basic principle of the League of Nations, the High Contracting Parties agree to accord, as soon as possible, to all alien nationals of States members of the League, equal and just treatment in every respect, making no distinction, either in law or fact, on account of their race or nationality'.[92] This was the proposal submitted by Japanese delegate Nobuaki Makino (1861–1949) to the League of Nations Commission, the commission in charge of discussing the draft of the statute of the Covenant of the League.[93]

Unlike the other great powers, Japan did not reach the Conference with a draft version of a League of Nations. Moreover, according to Naoko Shimazu, the Japanese government had not fully realized that accepting Wilson's Fourteen Points as the basis for the armistice implied also accepting the League.[94] But by the time the Japanese delegation arrived in Paris, the wave in favour of the League seemed irreversible and the draft that would serve as the basis for deliberation had already been hatched out of several drafts and compromises between the US and Britain. When the

90 Shimazu, *Japan, race, and equality.*

91 There is no need to explore this episode in great detail, since there are excellent monographs covering both Japan's participation in the League and the controversy on the racial equality proposal. See especially Shimazu, *Japan, race, and equality*, and Burkman, *Japan and the League of Nations.*

92 D. Miller, *The drafting of the Covenant* (New York: G. P. Putnam's Sons, 1928), vol. 2, p. 324.

93 The Japanese proposal was submitted as an additional clause to Article 21 on religious freedom.

94 Shimazu, *Japan, race, and equality*, pp. 16–17.

Japanese delegation decided to change its initial aloofness and support the League, they sought to secure the Japanese foreign policy goals regarding German colonies and Shandong. In relation to the Covenant itself, they pursued the introduction of the racial equality clause as a revision that would safeguard Japan's equal standing at the League, a revision that would render the League acceptable to Japanese public opinion.[95] Submitting the draft article, Makino declared: 'The future States members of the League, comprising all kinds of races, constitute a great family of nations'. Should the League work as a world organization protecting its members against aggression by a third power – Makino explained – members should be prepared to take arms against the aggressor or to enforce common obligations. If citizens should assume this sacrifice for the common cause: 'each national would like to feel and in fact demand that he should be placed on an equal footing with people he undertakes to defend even with his life'.[96]

Second, and more importantly, the defeat of the racial equality proposal is relevant because it marked a watershed in Japanese attitudes towards international law. Although supported by a number of semi-peripheral states, such as Brazil, China and Rumania, Makino's proposal was met with strong opposition from the British delegate. The proposal was defeated and Article 21 dropped altogether.[97] On 11 April, at the final meeting of the Commission, Japan presented a second amendment, this time, in the form of a declaration to be included in the Covenant's Preamble: 'by the endorsement of the principle of the equality of Nations and the just treatment of their nationals'.[98]

The British delegate Cecil opposed again the Japanese proposition, arguing that the racial question encroaches on the sovereignty of League members. Japanese delegate Sutemi Chinda (1857–1929) replied, pointing out that the purpose of the declaration was nothing but recognizing that 'all members of the League should be treated with equality and justice', and that the League should 'be founded upon justice'. Chinda asked the Commission to put the amendment to a vote, warning that should the amendment be rejected, it would be difficult for Japan to be part of the League, considering the concerns that the Japanese public had manifested.[99] This

[95] Burkman argues that Japan initially did not support the League because the Covenant would include provisions on disarmament and sanctions: Burkman, *Japan and the League of Nations*, p. 66. For a description of the shift from distance to cautious support see *ibid.*, pp. 60–8.

[96] Miller, *The drafting*, pp. 324–5. [97] *Ibid.*, p. 269.

[98] *Ibid.*, p. 389. [99] *Ibid.*, pp. 389–90.

time, the Japanese proposal gathered support from semi-peripheral as well as European delegates.[100] Out of seventeen votes, the amendment obtained a majority of eleven votes. Wilson, however, rejected the amendment because it had not received unanimous approval.[101]

A number of scholars have studied the reasons behind Japan's proposal and explained the causes for the defeat of the racial equality clause at the Paris Conference. Among them, Naoko Shimazu's research is particularly illuminating. Shimazu explores how five explanatory factors played out differently for the three main actors in this story: Japan, the United States and Great Britain. According to Shimazu, the racial equality proposal can be interpreted: as an attempt at solving the migration problems faced by Japanese nationals in the United States and in the British dominions; as a demand for a universal principle of equality; as a way of securing Japan's status of great power; as motivated by domestic politics; and as a bargaining strategy to achieve other ends, mainly the lease and rights over Shandong. Shimazu argues that the idea of demanding at the Conference the recognition of racial equality originated in the domestic political context as a compromise to gather support in favour of the League while appeasing sceptics as well as Japanese public opinion in general. Bringing to the negotiation table a demand for racial equality, however, was not intended as recognizing a universal principle. The proposal was rather limited to recognizing the status achieved by Japan. Although the immigration problem and the treatment of Japanese nationals abroad was of great concern, Shimazu suggests that Japanese diplomats did not attach practical consequences to the racial equality proposal, they rather sought to secure Japan's status as a great power, within a group formed exclusively by Western states.[102]

The repercussions of the defeat of the proposal, in consequence, were mainly felt in Japan. Specifically, Shimazu argues that the defeat of the

[100] The Italian delegate Orlando as well as French delegates Bourgeois and Larnaude supported the amendment: Miller, *ibid.*, p. 390. Veniselos, the Greek delegate, who previously opposed the racial equality clause, gave his support now, arguing that it was clear that the amendment did not involve any state obligation in respect to immigration, but reflected the principle of equality of nations. Delegates from Czechoslovakia, China and Poland expressed their support: *ibid.*, p. 391.

[101] *Ibid.*, p. 392.

[102] The British delegation, on the contrary, interpreted the proposal as inspired by the problem of immigration and thus left it to the jurisdiction of the Dominions, and that is why the Australian premier, Huges had the capacity to block and defeat the proposal, defending his 'white Australia' policy. Shimazu, *Japan, race, and equality*, p. 164 and *passim*.

racial equality proposal fuelled interwar Japan with a general sense of disillusionment towards the West. Japanese elites felt that the international system emerging from the Conference was unjust. It perpetuated the status quo and showed Western powers' unwillingness to recognize Japan's equality.[103] Moreover, by the 1930s, the disillusion of the 1920s turned into disengagement. When the United States failed to ratify Versailles, when Britain refused to renew the Anglo-Japanese treaty of alliance, when the Washington Conference imposed unequal restrictions on Japan's naval power, Japan felt pushed away from the internationalist project, in the direction of a pan-Asian foreign policy.

From the point of view of the history of international law, the rejection of the racial equality proposal was followed by Japanese mistrust regarding Western powers' willingness to extend equality beyond the West. This suggests an explanation why Japanese jurists stopped conceptualizing international law in universal terms. Mistrust towards the West marked Japanese international lawyers' progressive but definite shift in favour of a pan-Asian legal order, that is, in the direction of modern international law.

The 'arrogance' of the newcomers

The previous stories about the Venezuelan blockade, the defence of equality at The Hague and the setbacks Japan confronted when demanding sovereign autonomy and equality illustrate a fundamental change in the legal terrain on which semi-peripheral states conducted their international affairs. Now, more and more semi-peripheral polities used international law from within. But these stories, as I have already anticipated, also show that Western states and their jurists met semi-peripheral demands for formal autonomy and equality with strong resistance. The disciplinary debate that followed was extremely important. At stake was the definition of modern sovereignty. What was the scope of sovereign rights and privileges, when sovereignty was held by a non-Western state?

On the one hand, the debut of a number of semi-peripheral states as formal participants in the international society was infused with high expectations. Semi-peripheral jurists strived to translate the formal sovereignty their states had acquired into concrete rules of international law, rules governing their interaction with Western states as well as rules

103 *Ibid.*, p. 171.

pertaining to the design of international organizations. On the other hand, for Western jurists at the core it was far from clear that admission of states in the international community, through revision of unequal treaties or participation in multilateral international conferences, meant absolute sovereign autonomy and equality for semi-peripheral states.

In each of the examples described so far, the two tendencies – semi-peripheral jurists demanding sovereign autonomy and equality, jurists at the core redefining sovereignty to re-accommodate intervention and unequal treatment – came together. Let us focus on one example, the proposal to create a permanent international court at the Second Hague Conference, an example illustrating the encounter between the conflicting positions of core and semi-periphery as well as the accommodation of conflicting views by way of redefining sovereignty and international law in general.[104]

The Second Hague Conference: modern sovereignty

'The form is nothing; the substance is everything . . . '[105]

The Second Hague Peace Conference of 1907 was a crucial milestone in the development of international law – at least this is the image most contemporary commentators cast on the conference.[106] They remember the Conference as a stepping-stone in the universalization of international law, the development of international adjudication and the codification of the laws of war. The Hague Conference is understood to fit in a larger historical trajectory culminating in the international legal order of today, a trajectory marked by the rhetoric of heroic lawyers fighting against the power politics of self-interested states.[107] However, this celebratory assessment of the historical significance of the Hague Conference contrasts sharply with the unfavourable impressions participants and commentators had at the time of its conclusion.

A majority of liberal internationalist lawyers were disillusioned by how little the Conference achieved. None of the most ambitious proposals, the

[104] At the Hague Conference Drago's doctrine was also defeated.

[105] J. B. Scott, *The Hague peace conferences of 1899 and 1907; a series of lectures delivered before the Johns Hopkins University in the year 1908* (Baltimore: The Johns Hopkins Press, 1909), p. 750.

[106] See in general, Daudet, *Topicality*. An exception is G. Simpson, *Great powers and outlaw states: unequal sovereigns in the international legal order* (Cambridge University Press, 2004).

[107] E.g. A. Eyffinger, 'A highly critical moment: role and record of the 1907 Hague Peace Conference', *Netherlands International Law Review*, 54 (2007), 197–228.

ones carrying the most publicity, such as a general convention on compulsory arbitration, an agreement limiting armaments, or the establishment of a permanent international tribunal, gathered sufficient support from participant states. In fact, none of these proposals was adopted by the Conference. Most liberal internationalists, however, sought to temper dissatisfaction by putting matters in perspective and thus finding a distinctive point of view from which to judge the work of the Conference in positive terms.[108] They thought it was only natural that pursuing a goal as ambitious as 'universal peace' would generate extreme expectations in some quarters as well as unwarranted suspicion in others.[109] Rejecting both the naïve idealism of the peace movement and the pessimistic realism of the statesman, international lawyers found a juridical middle ground to dispel criticism as political.[110]

For international lawyers like James Brown Scott from the United States, Albert de Lapradelle from France, Walther Schücking (1875–1935) from Germany or Max Huber (1874–1960) from Switzerland, The Hague was a sign of a new internationalist spirit, of a 'society of states that organizes itself under law'; its relevance, therefore, did not depend on putting an end to war or on adopting a particular convention, but rested on its contribution to the foundation of an international community constituted by law.[111] As soon as progressive international lawyers had placed goals and expectations within the right frame, they could also put aside the perils

108 J. B. Scott, 'The work of the Second Hague Peace Conference', *AJIL*, 2 (1908), 1–28.

109 A. de Lapradelle and N. Politis, 'La deuxième conference de la paix,' *RGDIP*, 16 (1909), 385–437, 388.

110 See e.g. M. Huber, *Die Gleichheit der Staaten*, offprint from *Juristische Festgabe des Auslandes zu Josef Kohlers 60. Geburtstag*, ed. F. Berolzheimer (Stuttgart: Enke, 1909), 87, 88–118, considering several of the critiques levelled against the conference: that it achieved too little; that inconclusive negotiations created more international friction; that its meagre results proved the utopian character of the effort.

111 For instance, Schücking argued that the Hague Conferences changed the nature of the international world, from anarchy to a world federation. The Hague provided the 'community of states' with the 'common organs for the fulfillment of the ends of the association': W. Schücking, *The international union of the Hague conferences,work of the Hague*, Charles G. Fenwick, trans. (Oxford: The Clarendon Press, 1918), vol. 1, p. 79. See also Scott's pompous statement: 'The form is nothing; the substance is everything, and the uniformity produced by international conference and decision differs so little from the uniformity resulting from a federation as to be negligible. An internal conference meeting at regular stated intervals, in which nations large and small meet on a plane of equality to discuss question of universal importance and to legislate *ad referendum*, offers the advantages. Public opinion determines the destiny of a nation; international opinion, stronger than any combination of nations, draws the world more closely together than a mere political union.' Scott, *Hague peace conferences*, p. 750.

of idealist and realist politics and underscore the distinctively juridical problems that afflicted the Conference.

These liberal international lawyers engaged in a juridical debate in which the old law of sovereign independence was set up against a new law of solidarity and interdependence.[112] Quite remarkably, they did not lay the blame on conservative international lawyers blocking the internationalist agenda when giving precedence to narrow state interests.[113] Rather, they pointed at the participation of semi-peripheral delegates; in particular, the staunch defence of sovereign autonomy and equality by Luis Drago and Ruy Barbosa was discussed and highlighted as contributing to The Hague's problems.

At the same time, conservative publicists, who were candid detractors of both the ideas inspiring the Conference as well as the results obtained in it, disputed the exaggerated notion of sovereignty held by semi-peripheral jurists, blaming them for the perils of The Hague. Actually, most vehement attacks against semi-peripheral international lawyers came from Anglo-American publicists, who openly opposed the Hague Conference and the direction international law would have taken had the Conference succeeded. Conservative international lawyers were far from supporting an international legal order based on solidarity and interdependence, nevertheless, conservative and liberal jurists found a common ground in the critique of semi-peripherals' understanding of sovereignty.

A new debate: the sovereign equality of semi-peripheral states

[I]t was Brazil, at the head of the South American states, which prevented the acceptance of the scheme for a new and permanently effective Court of Arbitral Justice... obstinacy of the South American states in their resolution to prevent the adoption of the project unless it recognized the equality of all governments in regard to the nomination of judges.[114]

[112] This is in striking contrast to contemporary observers, who see in the Hague a conflict between *raison d'état* and the humanism of law: see e.g. Eyffinger, 'A highly critical moment', 200.

[113] That is, unlike contemporary observers, jurists and commentators contemporaneous to the Conference did not think that its problems originated from the fact that the humanist ideas put forward by international lawyers were not ripe enough for the scepticism and realism of big power politics.

[114] 'The Second Peace Conference: its results and lessons', *The London Times*, 21 October 1907, p. 3.

The distinction between liberal and conservative international lawyers is conventionally understood as based on the difference between giving priority to the legal organization of the international community versus giving precedence to the rights of sovereign states. That these two groups lined up together in opposition to the 'obstinacy' of Barbosa and Drago, in opposition to semi-peripheral jurists' interpretation of sovereignty, illustrates that the Hague Conference stands as a landmark in a different story.

This controversy was of a new type. A unique type of tension emerged during the Conference and its aftermath, a tension underlying both a conflict between legal ideas or sensibilities – classical versus modern – and a conflict between groups of international lawyers belonging to different cultural or geopolitical regions – core and periphery. For the first time, instead of finding themselves divided along doctrinal lines delineated by different schools of thought, divided along lines based on the self-interested positions of their respective states, or divided according to their own political – liberal or conservative – preferences, international lawyers came to The Hague to find themselves disagreeing along geopolitical or cultural lines.

On the one hand, semi-peripheral delegates and commentators pursued a strategy in favour of equality, following the classical legal language of sovereignty. Delegates and commentators from the core, on the other hand, strived to deepen the international legal structure and institutionalize the international sphere, in the case of liberal jurists, or tried to secure legal inequality, in the case of conservative publicists. While pursuing this agenda, international lawyers at the core shifted toward a modern legal sensibility. For the first time, scholars and commentators lined up theoretical and geopolitical divisions in ways that have become familiar ever since: ideas supported by semi-peripheral authors are 'old', too formalistic in their attachment to the principle of sovereignty, whereas ideas advanced by Western authors at the centre are 'modern', attuned with the imperatives of time and closer to the real nature (anarchic) and needs (interdependence) of the international community.

For example, when Walther Schücking, a renowned German exponent of liberal internationalism, discussed the Prize Court Convention adopted in The Hague and argued that it has not limited the sovereignty of contracting states, he affirmed:

> The Japanese delegate, Tsudzuki, was therefore entirely wrong when he stated at the Second Hague Conference that the Convention was of a character to 'impose

a serious limitation upon the sovereign rights of states . . . ' Here appears again the old idea of sovereignty which opposed every legal obligation upon the will of the state. Fried [another German scholar] says . . . that many of the delegates at the Hague had not yet come into touch with the modern concept of sovereignty.[115]

Equality versus inequality

Conservative classical legal scholars from the core opposed the demand for legal equality by small states, for they thought it not enough for states to pass the test of civilization to enjoy legal equality.[116] Thomas Joseph Lawrence (1849–1919), for instance, loosened up the standard to confer international legal personality, that is, the standard determining to whom international law applies. Lawrence argued that, although having grown up in Christian Europe, international law is not confined to Christian states only. It applies to non-Christian states that are civilized and have thus adopted the 'European international code'.[117] However, recognizing a greater number of sovereign states does not mean that all of them will be considered equal. The great powers of Europe and the United States – Lawrence cautions – have 'obtained such a predominant position as to render untenable the proposition that there is no distinction between them and other sovereign states'.[118] Great powers do not possess more rights in ordinary matters, but collectively they possess a 'regulative authority and are deemed to speak for the whole body' of states in Europe and the Americas.[119]

Classical legal scholars from the Anglo-American world like the English T. J. Lawrence and John Westlake or the American Frederick Hicks resisted Barbosa because they opposed any attempt to transform the

[115] Schücking, *The international union*, 123–4.

[116] Earlier classical international lawyers, such as Lorimer, supported both the standard of civilization and inequality: Lorimer, *The institutes of the law of nations*, pp. 170–2. It was later on, when the standard became more porous, that inequality became an issue vis-à-vis non-Western sovereigns.

[117] T. J. Lawrence, *The principles of international law* (Boston: D. C. Heath, 1895), pp. 4–5.

[118] *Ibid.*, p. 65.

[119] *Ibid.*, pp. 66–7. See also Lawrence's essay 'The primacy of great powers', where he claims that 'the old doctrine of the absolute equality before International Law of all sovereign states is no longer applicable'. It is noted merely that the stronger states have influence proportionate to their strength, but that custom has given them what can hardly be distinguished from a legal right to settle certain questions as they please, the smaller states being obliged to acquiesce in their decisions: T. J. Lawrence, *Essays on some disputed questions in modern international law* (Cambridge: Deighton, Bell, 1885), p. 208 and quote, p. 227.

nineteenth-century international legal order. They opposed the turn to modern international law itself. In Barbosa's defence of equality, these lawyers saw the epitome of the idealism and populism inspiring the Second Hague Conference, the idealism and populism they opposed. For example, a few months after the Conference, John Westlake published a review deploring the fact that the Conference abandoned traditional diplomatic means in favour of popular demands.[120] Unlike liberal jurists, like Schücking, who saw states coming together to The Hague as inaugurating a new era in which the internationalist spirit acquired institutional form in a world federation, Westlake criticized The Hague's surrender to democratic populism, when the Conference, marking its 'popular affinity, if not its popular origin', adopted 'the forms of a legislature' and put projects to a vote.[121] Westlake was sceptical not just because of the use of the domestic analogy, to bring more law and democratic principles to the international sphere, he was also sceptical of this new cry for peace: 'To bring [international] action under some responsibility is the object of a great cry which goes up from modern Europe, a cry based on no new spiritual vision, but wrung from suffering and fear... We have now learnt the passionate tension which unites people in different countries in a cry for peace, while as yet few have considered whether they are prepared to renounce for themselves the desires which make for war.'[122]

Westlake's critique of the Conference was not just confined within a theoretical plane. It was not only poised against a departure from an order bestowing special privileges on the great powers, but it was also directed against the practical consequences of introducing democratic and 'populist' principles into international law. For Westlake, the Conference provided a good example of a path international law should not follow. The inability to pass any of its most ambitious projects was only predictable: none of them had been 'mooted even in scientific assemblies'; putting them to a vote proved moreover impractical.[123] The conference became a 'parody of a parliament' – Westlake affirms – because delegates were not ready to accept any outcome obtained by voting: 'Speeches and votes gave a parliamentary air... For the purpose of announcing the result of a division the votes of all States were treated as equal. For the purpose of carrying any matter a stage further they were treated as unequal.'[124]

[120] J. Westlake, 'The Hague Conferences'. [121] *Ibid.*, p. 534. [122] *Ibid.*, pp. 532–3.
[123] *Ibid.*, p. 534. [124] *Ibid.*, p. 534, 'parody', *ibid.*, p. 535.

Subordinating international politics to voting was for Westlake unrealistic, but not the only reason why voting should be avoided. The equality of the vote of each state was an additional peril associated with the democratic principle, which had given high and false expectations to the states that were newcomers to the Second Hague Conference:

> The equality of votes flattered the small States, of which, not to mention that strength must always tell, the opinion of international doctrines is diminished in value by their inexperience of the situations to which they have to be applied. But that pleasure must have vanished when they found that delegations of the larger States were prevented by the force of things from admitting them to a real equality.[125]

Given that to Westlake semi-peripheral states were unimportant and their international lawyers inexperienced, the Conference's mistake seems to have been the leeway, given by continental and American representatives to delegates from small states, to indulge in idealistic legalism. Westlake mocks Barbosa's intervention at the Conference, quoting a newspaper account describing his last speech as a 'fierce' exposition of equality. Westlake sarcastically remarks: 'Perhaps it might have been less fierce if the conception had not been pampered'.[126]

The stakes of the debate were clear for Westlake as well as for Barbosa. The fundamental question was neither about voting, nor about the method to select judges, but about the principle under which the international legal order should be organized. It was about the clash between the principles of equality and inequality. Barbosa, in turn, saw in inequality a recipe for instability:

> Under the preoccupation of removing war, we are tending to shake the most solid basis of peace by attacking the equality of right that stops ambition and prides of peoples . . . The Powers would then no longer be formidable only by the weight of their armies and their fleets. They would also have a superiority of right in the international magistracy, by arrogating unto themselves a privileged position in the institutions to which we pretend to entrust the meting out of justice to the nations.[127]

In contrast, pointing at the Conference's shortcomings, Westlake voiced personal attacks against Barbosa, a practice that had become quite

125 *Ibid.*, p. 537. 126 *Ibid.*

127 International Peace Conference, *The proceedings of the Hague* (fifth meeting subcommission, 27 August), p. 645.

common since he came to personify the defence of sovereign equality.[128] Westlake probably thought that in a review of the Second Hague Conference there was no need to defend the principle of inequality underlying classical international law, for he had extensively done so in his celebrated manual. Like Westlake, Lawrence supported inequality in his hornbook. In a monograph on the Hague Conferences, Lawrence characterized small states as followers of a 'cult of equality'.[129]

It was an American scholar, Frederick Charles Hicks (1875–1956) who, in an article published in the *American Journal of International Law* in 1908, explicitly supported inequality in the context of the Hague Conference. Hicks, then a librarian at the Naval War College who later became a law librarian and law professor at Yale, stated: 'the doctrine of equality was untrue in its origin, was preserved in international law by a verbal consent which is not followed by performance'.[130] Hicks starts his article by affirming that the Conference 'accomplished many valuable results and failed in much it attempted' because the method of organization it adopted recognized equal weight to the vote of all states.[131] Without being sanguine about the Conference, Hicks openly recognizes the division between two parties, one in favour and the other against equality, and sets out to show that, although seen as a fundamental principle of international law, equality has been based on a political theory long discarded by political scientists.[132] Hicks concludes that equality is no

[128] According to Simpson, after Barbosa's interventions at the Conference, international lawyers characterized sovereign equality as an obstacle to international institutions: Simpson, *Great powers*, p. 135.

[129] Lawrence criticizes the reservation (as to the selection of judges) that small states attached to the signature of the convention establishing an International Prize Court: 'The fetish of absolute equality forbids its worshippers to accept any plan for the grading of states in the matter of the appointment of judges. But the devotees of this particular cult are not of much importance in maritime affairs. If the worst came to the worst and they declined to ratify the Convention, the rest of the world would get on very well without them': Lawrence, *Essays on some disputed questions*, p. 148.

[130] F. Hicks, 'The equality of states and the Hague conferences', *AJIL*, 2 (1908), 530–61, 535.

[131] *Ibid.*, 530.

[132] *Ibid.*, 531–2. According to Hicks, liberty did not precede but was a result of political organization. In the absence of international organizations, states have no rights but powers. Thus there is no need to premise the rights of states to be equal: *ibid.*, 534. Hicks criticizes the use of the domestic analogy to justify the so-called law between states, on the basis of the right enjoyed by citizens. Moreover, liberal jurists assuming the domestic analogy, such as Oppenheim, define equality as an attribute of the international personality of states, which they obtain by consent given by other states through recognition. In this regard, Hicks affirms that as a matter of fact strong states have not treated weak states as sovereigns, begging the whole question of equality.

longer suitable to modern conditions, because it has ceased to protect small states from intervention by great powers and if allowed to become operative, it would give too much power to weak states.[133]

Conservative Anglo-American scholars explicitly defending inequality were a minority, though an important minority, given that the great European powers, Britain above all, that proposed the system of rotation of judges saw the opposition by small states both as a threat to the privileges bestowed to them by classical international law and as a source of future problems.[134] A majority of Western international lawyers in both Europe and the United Sates, even during the classical period but more so during the course of the transition towards modern international law, endorsed the principle of equality. A different debate about equality ensued between these Western liberal jurists and semi-peripheral international lawyers.

Equality in a new international law

Western jurists, who defended The Hague and the creation of a permanent court, belonged to a group very different from the conservative publicists of the classical period. Throughout the last decades of the nineteenth century, a new figure was emerging in European diplomatic circles, a professional international lawyer with a liberal internationalist sensibility.[135] The professional international lawyer carried on with the traditional liberal internationalist agenda, supporting the extension of the rule of law at the international plane. Classical international law had therefore to shift away from the hierarchical, 'aristocratic' system instituted by the Vienna Congress, according to which great powers had, for example, a special right to intervene in the affairs of other sovereigns, to re-establish the balance of power, or to protect the principle of legitimacy. Accordingly, liberal-oriented international lawyers defended the equality of all members of the international community. However, the scope of validity of sovereign equality was clearly limited within Western statehood. Western liberal jurists shared with their conservative counterparts the

[133] Hicks, 'The equality of states', 536–7.

[134] See e.g. the British Bluebook about the Conference: 'The claim of many smaller states to equality as regards not only their independence, but their share in all international institutions . . . is one which may produce great difficulties, and may perhaps drive the greater Powers to act in many cases by themselves': Miscellaneous, No. 1 (1908), p. 21.

[135] That is, a professional international lawyer, in contradistinction to the natural law oriented publicist and to the diplomat. See Koskenniemi, *Gentle civilizer*, especially ch. 1.

use of the doctrine 'the standard of civilization' to justify exclusion of non-Western polities from the realm of equality. That is, the liberalism of these international lawyers coexisted well with inequality outside the sphere of international law, outside the international community.[136]

Although liberal and conservative international lawyers at the core were together making the standard of civilization real, thus giving legitimacy to colonialism and informal empire, the debate between semi-peripheral jurists defending equality and Western jurists with liberal sensibilities was of a different kind. Rather than opposing sovereign equality by way of recognizing inequality between sovereigns, Western jurists with liberal sensibilities sought to redefine equality, making this principle compatible with a more robust international legal order, an order including permanent international institutions. While arguing in favour of the institutional development of international law, Western liberal jurists began to see a problem in the centrality classical international law conferred on the principle of sovereignty. Sovereignty had become a 'dogma', an obstacle to the creation of international organizations, tribunals and stronger rules limiting the autonomy of states. Liberal-oriented jurists at the core thought that the main problem with the principle of sovereignty lay in its absolute character. Absolute sovereignty made it more difficult for states to limit their independence or to transfer some of their powers to international institutions. There was, however, an additional and different problem, triggered by the recognition of non-Western states as members of the international community.

When, during the course of the second half of the nineteenth century, non-Western sovereigns irrupted into the international sphere appropriating the standard of civilization, the configuration of the international legal landscape changed. Until then, the international legal order had governed relations between sovereigns, big and small, Catholic and Lutheran.[137] But now, it would govern relations between radically diverse

[136] For example, Holland believed that: '"The family of nations" is an aggregate of States which as the result of their historical antecedents have inherited a common civilisation, and are at a similar level of moral and political opinion. The term may be said to include the Christian nations of Europe and their offshoots in America, with the addition of the Ottoman Empire, which was declared by the treaty of Paris of 1856 to be admitted to the "*concert Européen*". Within this charmed circle, according to the theory of International law, all States are equal. Without it, no State, be it as powerful and as civilised as China or Japan, can be regarded as a normal international person.' Holland, *The elements of jurisprudence*, 2nd edn, p. 295.

[137] Historically, however, this is not entirely true, but it was the underlying assumption under positivism.

sovereigns, different in their social, economic and political organization, in their culture and religion, in their power resources. As argued above, conservative publicists were willing to recycle the old idea of *Jus Publicum Europaeum* for the purpose of reasserting the principle of inequality vis-à-vis newcomers. To liberal-minded jurists, who were pushing for more law to govern interstate relations, moving back to classical international law was not an option; though, at the same time, they were not willing to extend classical international law's absolute sovereignty to newcomers.

While rethinking the concept of sovereignty, developing weaker or relative notions of sovereign autonomy and equality to make them compatible with a stronger international legal order, liberal jurists deployed these new notions to answer the question about the nature and scope of the rights non-Western newcomers would enjoy. On the one hand, American international lawyers, who were at centre of the Conference's effort to create a permanent tribunal, supported a pragmatic understanding of international law under which the principle of sovereign equality could be regulated to adapt to political circumstances. Continental lawyers, on the other hand, redefined equality under narrower or relative terms, to meet the perceived needs of an interdependent international community.

Formalism versus pragmatism

James Brown Scott, as explained above, one of the most prominent American international lawyers behind the plan to create a permanent international court, firmly defended the idea that the projected court did not infringe upon the principle of sovereign equality. If each state had the right to appoint a judge, and since the law can regulate the conditions under which a right is exercised, judges from different states would sit for longer or shorter periods without undermining the sovereign equality of states. At the Conference, Scott defended the system of rotation of judges underscoring the need to think about his proposal in pragmatic terms:

> We do not believe that any one principle should be pushed to its logical extreme without due regard to other interests. The theorist and logician might be content to rise and fall in the defence of a principle adopted by him. The practical man – the man of affairs, the statesman – must many a time modify, indeed sacrifice, a principle, however just, to meet a present and pressing need.[138]

[138] International Peace Conference, *The proceedings of the Hague*, p. 610. Obviously, Barbosa remained unconvinced:

Scott seems to address Barbosa and those international lawyers who defend formal rights, and to suggest to them to move beyond formalism because international law has developed in a new direction. In a review of the Conference, Scott played down the fact that none of the most ambitious projects were passed.[139] Instead, Scott sees the Hague Conference within a larger trajectory, in which international law as interstate law has evolved into a law emanating from the people and its interests.[140] Scott draws a parallel between the evolution of the common law and international law. In both, law has evolved from usage, to custom, to statute. Only complex societies have given rise to a complex system of law; in complex societies the natural progress of customs becomes insufficient and has to be guided and supplemented by a legislature enacting statutes. Scott believes that the international world has become a complex society in need of a complex legal system. With nations growing and coming into closer contact, customary law has given its place to a more complex code or has been developed to meet new needs. Scott saw this process occurring in a series of international conferences and congresses leading up to the Hague Conference. At first, these were meetings between rulers and nations dealing with specific controversies; the Hague Conference, in contrast, established a system of law and expressed the hopes and interests of not only states, but scholars, the peace movement, the public opinion.

> The conditions of exercise respect the equality of right only when they are *equal* for all those possessing that right. On the other hand, inequality in the exercise implies inequality in the right itself, for the value of a right can be measured only by the juridical possibility of exercising it . . . The proposition contains two distincts rights: the right to appoint and the right to sit. In the right of appointing we would indeed be equals. But in the right of sitting in the court we would be absolutely unequals. And it is this inequality which violates the equality of Sates.

Ibid., 628 (italics and mistakes in the original).

139 'Deeply interested in the success of these projects, the great public felt that their failure necessarily involved the failure of the conference . . . But we should not in our disappointment, and perhaps bitterness of soul, overlook positive and beneficent progress, and if we could not take the advanced position outlined by the friends of peace, we should nevertheless rejoice that many a mile-stone has been passed.' Scott, 'The work of the Second Hague,' 1.

140 '[E]nlightened people of all countries take a deep and abiding interest in international law . . . From the cell of the cloister international law passed into the study of the philosopher, the jurist, and the scholar; from the study it entered the cabinets of Europe . . . from the cabinet to courts of justice . . . and finally, from the court-room international law has made its way to the people, who, in last resort, dominate court and cabinet, and enlist in their service scholar as well as priest.' *Ibid.*, 2.

If the Hague Conference marked a step forward in the development of an international society, if international law is no longer imposed on people, if it no longer reflects simply the will of states, but if international law springs out of the needs of the people, Scott could confidently assert that the limits to independence imposed by the international legal order on states are based on the solidarity of interests between peoples, rather than on the interest of powerful states.[141] The system of rotating judges, in consequence, limits a small state's exercise of the right to equality, but it does so based on the needs and the nature of the international community. If the international community is not perfectly homogeneous, its institutions cannot mirror absolute equality. Thus, in Scott's view, the method he proposed to select judges did not reflect power equations, but a state's different levels of international interaction and commerce, its experience and legal traditions.

As mentioned above, towards the end of the Conference, Barbosa opposed any attempt to deduce legal consequences out of political or economic differences between the members of the international community.[142] As the Conference was progressing, Barbosa's rhetoric became sharper and more passionate, though his defence of equality as well as his mode of arguing remained unchanged. For Barbosa operated within the classical legal sensibility, according to which it was natural to assume first the absolute character of sovereignty and then to work out from the principle a series of doctrinal manifestations. In fact, by the time of the Second Hague Conference, rather than inducing a rule from state practice, semi-peripheral classical international lawyers had deduced from sovereignty the principle of absolute equality. For instance,

[141] *Ibid.*, 4.

[142] In Barbosa's words:

> Between States even as between individuals, there are of course diversities of culture, of honesty, of wealth and of strength, but will this fact create any differences whatever as regards their essential rights? Political rights are the same for men anywhere . . . Lord Kelvin or Mr. John Morley [British delegates to the Conference] have the same vote in electing the august and sovereign Parliament of Great Britain as the ordinary workmen dulled by work and misery. But is the intellectual and moral capacity of this laboring man, who has been degraded by suffering and distress, equal to that of the statesman or of the scholar? The fact is that sovereignty is the elementary right par excellence of organised and independent States. Now sovereignty means equality. In principle and in practice sovereignty is absolute.

International Peace Conference, *The proceedings of the Hague*, p. 150.

facing divergent behaviour, especially the intervention of great powers in small states, Russian jurist Martens affirmed the principled nature of equality: 'If their equality is not always respected in practice, this does not disrupt at all the force of the principle.'[143]

At the turn of the century, on the basis of the classical legal discourse, semi-peripheral authors argued in favour of absolute equality, in direct opposition to those Western authors who recognized special rights in great powers. Greek international lawyers Michel Kebedgy and Georgios Streit, for example, examined the legality of the privileged position great powers claimed to hold in the international society.[144]

Streit argued that legal scholars who affirmed great powers' special prerogatives did not simply base their proposition on the power and political weight of big states, but asserted the juridical hegemony of big powers in accordance with the aristocratic organization of European international society. If great powers would find legal justification to impose their will on small states, intervene in their domestic affairs or assume tutelage over their external relations, it was clear for Streit that international law would recognize a juridical distinction between great powers and small states, vindicating the juridical inequality between them.[145] In a clear display of classical legal thinking, Streit firmly opposed this proposition: in essence states are sovereign and independent. From this it necessarily follows that they are legally equal. Juridical equality is absolute, that is, it may be neither restricted nor subjected to gradation, unless states consent to the imposition of limits on their own sovereign powers. So far – Streit insists – no small state has ever recognized or tolerated restricting its autonomy vis-à-vis great powers.[146]

Regardless of this well-established semi-peripheral legal discourse backing legal equality, the press of the time as well as conservative publicists

143 Martens, *Traité*, vol. 1, p. 381. See also similar remarks by Berghom, the Russian delegate to the Second Hague Conference, arguing that interventions had been lacking legal justification: International Peace Conference, *The proceedings of the Hague*, p. 289. Note that this way of defending the normative strength of a legal principle in front of conflicting state practice is not a relic from the past. Remember the ICJ decision in the Nicaragua case.

144 'Sovereignty is the fundamental attribute which the juridical conscience of peoples and the science of internal law recognize in the different moral persons forming the society of nations, the persons we call states': Kebedgy, 'Principes du droit', 84.

145 Streit, 'Les grandes puissances', 13.

146 *Ibid.*, 14. Streit criticizes Scottish lawyer James Lorimer and others who defend inequality as mistaking juridical, social and factual equality: *ibid.*, 15–16.

portrayed Barbosa's position as intransigent and unreasonable.[147] Liberal internationalists, on the other hand, realized the shortcomings of a principled defence of equality. They saw in Barbosa a sign of the exhaustion of classical international law. His inability to produce a wider range of arguments to defend his position and to engage in a discussion about how to create a stronger international legal order, was, for liberal jurists, Barbosa's main weakness. While classical international lawyers insisted on defending equality deploying deductive legal reasoning, liberal jurists' central predicament was to find new ways to rethink the meaning of absolute sovereignty and reconstruct a relative concept of equality, without retreating into the principle of inequality supported by conservative classical international lawyers.

Absolute versus relative equality

Liberal internationalist jurists at the core were well aware of the need to reconceptualize equality in view of the argumentative dead end in which Barbosa put himself. Max Huber, one of the Swiss delegates at the Second Hague Conference, who would later become not only a central figure in the sociological approach to international law but also a judge at the Permanent Court of International Justice (PCIJ), published after the Conference an article on state equality.[148] Although sovereign equality had been widely invoked during the Hague Conference, Max Huber argued that negotiations did not provide relevant material to determine the meaning of equality: 'States other than the great powers, which invoked state equality, have neither given reasons for the necessity of legal equality nor discussed its meaning. They started out assuming this proposition to be at the basis of international law and to stand as a matter of principle beyond discussion.'[149] Huber was prepared to pronounce state equality part of positive international law without giving too much weight to sovereignty, since its specific meaning and place within the legal system remained to be determined.

First, Huber limits the scope of application of equality to legal relations between states. As a strictly juridical concept, equality neither

[147] See the previous comments by Westlake and Lawrence and the newspaper article 'The Second Peace Conference: its results and lessons', *The London Times*, 21 October 1907, p. 3.

[148] Huber, *Die Gleichheit*. [149] *Ibid.*, p. 95.

levels actual interactions between states, nor evens out the influence states exert to determine the content of international rules. Legal equality rather means equality in terms of the rights states possess and obligations they assume under international law.[150] Therefore, equality between states would be infringed if great powers would possess special rights based on their particular position.

Second, Huber, however, introduces a distinction between absolute and relative equality to probe if differences in a state's rights and obligations are always in tension with the principle of equality. In the most developed democracies – Huber argues – equality is only relative, given that equality can be limited, that is, given that differential treatment can be established by a rule of general nature. Although the doctrine of relative equality had not been crystallized into positive international law, with the exception of the differential contribution of states to finance international organizations, Huber asks if the system of rotation of judges proposed during the Hague Conference would infringe on the relative equality of states.

Huber recounts the unsuccessful attempts, by smaller states and great powers attending the Conference, to find a general criterion on the basis of which to rank states.[151] As long as states run into insurmountable contradictions when searching for a rule of general character, it will be impossible to create different rights and obligations for great powers and small states without breaching relative equality. But Huber was not willing to accept the principle of inequality to justify the proposed method to select judges.

Huber recognizes that a deeper, fully developed international legal order would have to include stronger international organizations and to limit the equality of states. Although identifying a contradiction between the interest of sovereign states and the international community, Huber manages the contradiction by shifting the problem to a different plane. Namely, instead of asking if rules establishing differential treatment would breach equality, Huber turns to explore the type of legal propositions that could be inferred from the principle of equality, specifically in relation to the participation of states in international organizations.

[150] *Ibid.*, p. 106.

[151] In fact – Huber argues – these attempts were riddled by contradictions. When a general criterion was accepted for the prize court and rejected for the international court, no general yardstick could be found: *ibid.*, p. 107.

There is no mandatory rule of international law demanding equal participation of states – Huber argues – since states other than great powers, as they are free to become vassal-states, can freely subject themselves to differential treatment. Whereas a classical international lawyer would have stopped the analysis here, Huber assumes the will theory, that is, a state's sovereign autonomy, to open room for a variety of possible valid legal propositions. The issue therefore becomes for Huber to find out which of these alternative rules better represents the essence of contemporary international law.[152]

The soundness of a rule ranking the participation of states in international organizations will depend on the type of interactions states establish with international organizations.[153] In the case of an international tribunal, the exercise of the judicial function depends on the consent given by the states to the tribunal. As states negotiate and conclude general agreements, formally exercising the same amount of influence over the outcome, they also come as formally equal parties when submitting a controversy to an arbitration court and selecting the judges to sit in court. Accordingly, if a permanent international court is created, Huber thinks that there is no reason to refuse formal equality between all participant states. That is, if states are ranked and allowed to exercise different degrees of influence, it would amount to recognizing the political overweight of great powers. Would this ranking of states be in harmony with existing international law? – asks Huber.

To answer this question, Huber distinguishes between interstate relations constituting a community (*Gemeinschaft*) or a commonwealth (*Gemeinwesen*). In a community, the association as a whole has no independent will from the associated members. The community can be individual-regulated or social-regulated (*sozialrechtlich*): individual, when the association is limited to a concrete legal relationship (*Rechtverhältnis*); or social,

[152] 'Which organisation conforms to the essence of present-day international law?' *Ibid.*, p. 108.

[153] Huber identifies a whole range of legally irrelevant administrative matters in which the division of tasks between states is unproblematic. When it comes to the legally relevant functions of international organizations, Huber distinguishes between legislating, issuing binding decrees and judicial decisions. The first two involve agreements that will only be binding regarding consenting states. Given that ranking the consent of states has been out of question, Huber argues that in multilateral conferences it does not make sense to give more votes to great powers, because small states would then not ratify the agreements reached by the conference: *ibid.*, pp. 109–10. Huber does not take into account the Anglo-American conservative publicists explored above who in fact criticized the Conference's voting method.

when a legal relationship develops between multiple states, a legal relation under which individual interactions are subjected. A commonwealth, in turn, has a common will, which is different from the sum of wills of its individual members.[154]

There is no doubt – Huber affirms – that the community of states is not a commonwealth, unless one recognizes that the community of great powers has a dominion over the other states. Thus, a permanent court, as an institution of the international community, can only be founded on the principles under which the interstate community is based. In this regard, Huber thinks that, from antiquity up to the sixteenth century, international legal relations had not been permanent enough to confirm a legal community (*Rechtsgemeinschaft*). Interstate relations were simply contractual, giving rise to an individual-regulated community, in which the law merely ordered the free will of individual subjects based on their absolute freedom and therefore absolute equality.

Inequality and differentiation between states can only be possible in the second type of community, that is, in a social-regulated community (*sozialrechtliche Gemeinschaft*), where concrete legal relations are based on the status states possess within the international community. Huber declares international law to have reached this phase of development. Therefore, international law no longer appears just in concrete individually circumscribed legal relationships, but so far as all states of the society (*Kulturkreis*) authoritatively recognize the existence of legal propositions governing their reciprocal interactions, international law grows out of common conviction.

It is only at this point, after a very long analysis, that Huber finishes setting the stage to tackle the central problem faced by the Second Hague Conference: the problem of equality and inequality of newly admitted states. The international community – Huber argues – may establish concrete legal relations with states that have been so far outside its realm, which will be treated as individual-regulated relations, that is, under international law in its original contractual phase, under equality.[155] Once legal relations have been established, newcomers can be included in the interstate community, in which case a specific status can be attached to the admitted state, a status that can be different from the one enjoyed by states already belonging to the community. Huber believes that at the time of international law's contractual phase, all states stood next to each

[154] Huber, *Die Gleichheit*, p. 112.

[155] Huber mentions the original treaties concluded with China and Japan: *ibid.*, p. 114.

other as equals. By the same token, he argues that before their admission into the interstate community, individual states relate as equals to the community: 'though doubtfully they enter the interstate community as equals'.[156]

The turn to modern international law in the semi-periphery

The way in which Scott, Huber and other Western liberal jurists answered semi-peripheral's principled defence of equality is crucial to understand. Conventional histories of international law consider that the idea of an interdependent international community becoming the new basis of international law, the idea that limiting the sovereign autonomy of states and legitimizing the transfer of some state competences to the international sphere, contributed to the founding of a more robust international legal order. Sovereignty, however, did not disappear. Rather, sovereignty became a claim in the name of the interests of states and the reality of power, which in the production of legal arguments had to be mediated against opposite claims representing the interest of the international community and the reality of interdependence.[157]

The debate that followed the failure of the Second Hague Conference exemplifies this transformation in legal thinking. It suggests that jurists with liberal sensibilities at the core advocated for a stronger international legal order mediating the contradictions between the interests of sovereign states and the international community from the standpoint of core states. They advocated limitations to sovereignty not only justifying the creation of permanent international organizations, but also limiting the autonomy and equality of semi-peripheral states. We will see, for example, that they reinterpreted interventions in the semi-periphery as interventions on behalf of the interests of the international community, or they redefined the legal regime governing semi-sovereign polities, as in the case of the mandate system, as a regime that in the name of the international community established the tutelage of Western over non-Western peoples.

When jurists began advancing legal arguments that mediated between rules, doctrines and principles reflecting the interest of state sovereignty

156 *Ibid.*, p. 115.

157 See D. Kennedy, *International legal structures* (Baden-Baden: Nomos, 1987) and M. Koskenniemi, *From apology to utopia: the structure of international legal argument* (Helsinki: Finnish Lawyers' Pub. Co., 1989).

and the international community, it became more difficult – for the classical lawyer both at core and semi-periphery – to argue for equality or inequality in the language of absolute rights. This transformation in the way legal arguments were framed produced a break in the intellectual history of international law, inaugurating the transition from classical to modern international law. But, as we will see in the next chapters, this break in the intellectual history did not come with a fundamental change in the actual rules governing international relations between states at the core and peripheries of the world. Unequal treatment, armed interventions in peripheral states and the exclusion of non-Western polities from membership in the international community, continued to mark the life of international law in the periphery.

This paradox in the rise of modern international law – namely a transformation in legal thinking that did not change the rules applicable in relation to the world's peripheries – presented semi-peripheral lawyers with a challenge. Of course we know that conceptually there is no paradox here, for the diversity of rules and legal arguments that lawyers can produce articulating the classical or modern discourse of international law is, if not unlimited, very wide indeed.[158] Semi-peripheral lawyers, as we saw in the second part of the book, mastered the classical legal discourse, producing legal arguments regarding non-intervention or the abrogation of unequal treaties that opposed the rules of international law advanced by core jurists. Modern international law, as we will see in Part IV, was no different. The challenge that semi-peripherals faced was about finding ways to support in the new language of modern international law apparently classical rules and doctrines like those defended by Barbosa, Drago and Makino, rules and doctrines securing semi-peripheral autonomy and equality.

Chilean international lawyer Alejandro Alvarez (1868–1960) offers a good example of semi-peripheral departure from classical legal thinking while supporting rules defending semi-peripheral autonomy and equality. Alvarez, as we will see, explicitly rejected the position adopted by a prominent classical predecessor like Drago, declaring that the Drago doctrine, 'examined from the purely doctrinal standpoint, was too absolute'.[159] At the same time Alvarez favoured and participated in the codification of a

[158] See Kennedy, *International legal structures* and Koskenniemi, *From apology to utopia.*

[159] A. Alvarez, 'Latin America and international law', *AJIL*, 3 (1909), 269–353, 335 footnote 85.

rule of non-intervention. Why did Alvarez reject Drago?[160] Liberal lawyers like Scott and Huber, accommodating inequality while advocating a stronger international legal order, broke The Hague's stalemate between core and semi-peripheral jurists – both defending absolute equality and inequality based on the classical discourse of international law. This resolution of the stalemate, as we will see in the next chapter, became the dominant view, especially after the First World War, after classical international law was blamed for its inability to limit sovereignty and militarism, its inability to secure international peace. Alvarez and other semi-peripherals benefited from this trend at the core, adopting and further developing the modern discourse, as they benefited from the defeat experienced by classical semi-peripherals at The Hague and beyond, thus becoming the first generation of modern semi-peripherals.

[160] A more detailed explanation is offered in the last chapter of the book.

6 Modern international law: good news for the semi-periphery?

'. . . for a new epoch, a new law.'[1]

Albert de Lapradelle, as we will see, announced at the turn of the century the advent of a new epoch, which inaugurated a new law. Alvarez and the new generation of semi-peripheral lawyers that emerged during the first decades of the twentieth century followed suit, abandoning classical international law and adopting the emerging modern legal discourse. The modern sensibility no longer saw the international order as centred around states and sovereignty, but around legal subjects and the international community. Georges Scelle (1878–1961), one of the most prominent members of the sociological school in interwar France, for instance, pronounced the end of interstate relations as the most important political phenomenon: 'From now on *internationalism* is the essential fact'.[2] Universal solidarity, the social fact identified by Scelle as underlying an emerging internationalist spirit, rendered fundamental classical notions like 'states', 'sovereignty' and 'legal personality' obsolete.[3]

As a discourse that proclaimed the limitation of sovereignty in the name of the interests of the international community, was the rise of modern international law a welcomed development for the semi-periphery? We may think that a legal order based on the fact of solidarity rather than on the egoistic interest of states would limit the powers of Western states in order to recognize the political existence and autonomy of semi-peripheral polities. We may also assume that efforts to prevent another

[1] A. de Lapradelle, 'La question chinoise' (Part 1), *RGDIP*, 8 (1901), 272–340, 339.

[2] G. Scelle, *Précis de droit des gens; principes et systématique* (Paris: Librairie du Recueil Sirey, 1932), p. viii (italics in the original).

[3] *Ibid.*, pp. viii–ix.

World War would extend beyond Europe including the prevention of collective violence in the struggle for non-Western peoples' independence. In fact, as we will see, semi-peripheral aspirations remained unanswered after the rise of modern international law. Were ideals overruled by the realpolitik of Western states? This seems to be the conventional way to explain the failures of modern international law: the failure, for example, to extend self-determination beyond the West at the Paris Peace Conference of 1919. Without the interference of international politics, it appears that the modern discourse of international law would have changed the rules foreclosing semi-peripheral aspirations. This chapter shows the opposite. It presents a short genealogy of French international law scholarship to show that modern international law as articulated by core jurists did not change many of the classical international law rules and doctrines, like a right of intervention, that were most detrimental to the semi-periphery. In fact, under the modern discourse a rule sanctioning intervention acquired renewed strength. There were now good reasons for core states to intervene in the peripheries in the name and in the interest of the international community.

This finding is neither novel nor surprising. Antony Anghie has shown how the modern discourse reproduced in new forms international law's old dynamic of assimilation and differentiation through which the non-Western world has been dominated. When the old, positivist and formalist nineteenth-century classical notion of sovereignty as absolute was replaced by a modern, more pragmatic and anti-formalist notion of sovereignty as legal personality, international law could break into the sovereign's domestic realm. Inside Western sovereigns, modern international law discovered the real legal subject, individuals with human rights to be protected. Inside non-Western legal persons, international law found primitive societies to modernize and Western residents to protect.[4]

This chapter follows Anghie's lead. It looks at the impact that the modern discourse had on the rules and doctrines that were most relevant to the semi-periphery. The chapter argues that in relation to these rules and doctrines there was a stark continuity between classical and modern international law. In relation to the classical standard of civilization, for example, modern international law did not change it as a criterion for inclusion into the international community and for recognizing statehood. In relation to new rules and doctrines, modern international law,

[4] Anghie, *Imperialism*, pp. 134–5.

as articulated by European lawyers, did not improve the situation of semi-peripheral states. Foregrounding the legal status of individuals and the interests of the international community, the scope for military interventions in the non-Western world was widened. If the modern discourse of international law, as this chapter suggests, did not improve the rules and doctrines relevant to the semi-periphery, why did semi-peripheral lawyers endorse the modern discourse? Why did semi-peripherals become modern international lawyers?

Power imbalances in the world system certainly contributed to the flow of intellectual influences from core to periphery. Semi-peripherals became modern jurists following a trend dictated from Europe.[5] The change came also as a natural substitution of an older generation of lawyers. The first generation of classical semi-peripheral lawyers was replaced during the first decade of the twentieth century by a younger generation of lawyers.[6] The Second Hague Conference also marks this generational divide. Martens, who attended the Conference quite ill and weak, died in 1909. Calvo had died the year before. Those who took the lead at The Hague, Barbosa and Drago were at the peak of their careers in 1907. But those who were critical of the classical semi-peripherals were part of a younger generation, including Alejandro Alvarez and Vi Kyuin Wellington Koo, who though not powerful enough in 1907 became important professional figures during the interwar and post-war periods, both for example becoming ICJ judges.

In addition to structural constraints and a generational change, there are two other reasons explaining the rise of the modern trend in the semi-periphery, which reveal the margins for semi-peripheral resistance. First, as showed in the previous chapter, towards the beginning of the twentieth century the use of classical international law in the defence of semi-peripheral autonomy and equality failed notoriously. Seen from the periphery, when the classical discourse exhausted its power to protect autonomy and equality, good reasons emerged to pursue these same objectives in the modern language of international law. Second, framing arguments in the modern language was not a self-defeating choice. The modern discourse of international law, as any legal discourse, was indeterminate enough to allow for the articulation of a wide range of

[5] Even conservative jurists like Schmitt shifted towards a modern legal consciousness. When defending the old privileges classical international law had given to European states, he did not recall abolute sovereignty but proposed a *Großraum lehre*: see C. Schmitt, 'Raum und Großraum im Völkerrecht' in Schmitt, *Staat, Großraum, Nomos*, pp. 234–68.

[6] Compare the dates of birth and death of the international lawyers included in Map 3 and in Map 4.

arguments supporting a wide range of rules and doctrines. This chapter explores the articulation of modern international law by core lawyers in ways that limited the autonomy and equality of semi-peripheral polities. The fourth and last part of the book explores the semi-peripheral articulation of the modern discourse, articulations which were intended not just to appropriate the discourse but to support new rules of international law. It is this aspect that makes semi-peripheral articulation of the modern discourse relevant to a global history of international law. Whereas at the beginning of the century rules relevant to the peripheries were still the rules that under classical international law limited semi-peripheral autonomy and equality, at end of the interwar period, international law abandoned the standard of civilization, adopted a formal doctrine of recognition, narrowed the scope of intervention and arguably had developed a right to self-determination waiting for the political context to change in order to make its realization possible.

The European affair and the rules for the semi-periphery

Conventionally, the sobering lessons left by the First World War have been understood to mark the fall of classical international law.[7] Jurists of the interwar period singled out the principle of sovereign autonomy as the main factor responsible for classical international law's inability to secure peaceful relations between states. Given that nineteenth-century international law was based on the principle of sovereign autonomy, it could only recognize the existence of valid legal norms when states had bestowed their consent. Modern jurists believed that as long as international law allowed states to subordinate the interest of the international community to their own self-interest, states would be reluctant to give consent to legal rules regulating or limiting their autonomy. In fact, because international rules had to be based on the will of states, classical international law included only a small number of rules. International law granted too much autonomy to states, which therefore would not be willing to give up the right to wage war to resolve disputes.

[7] See for example, O. Nippold, *Die Gestaltung des Völkerrechts nach dem Weltkriege* (Zürich: Orell Füssli, 1917) and Scelle, *Précis de droit*, p. viii. In fact, the story is much more complicated. Koskenniemi, for instance, traces a different disciplinary break back to the foundation of professional organizations in the 1870s: see *Gentle civilizer*. Kennedy, in 'History of an illusion', suggests that it was the modern international lawyer who produced the image of a formalist past, in order to justify the institutional development of international law.

The post-war reconstruction of the international order in Paris and Geneva, on the other hand, is conventionally understood to mark the rise of modern international law. The answer to the shortcomings of the classical international order was a fully fledged international law consisting of permanent tribunals, permanent interstate organizations and a greater number of rules limiting the scope for sovereigns' individualistic behaviour, first and foremost, a rule proscribing war. Moreover, international lawyers believed that the reconstruction of international law had to confront a deeper problem at the root of the crisis in the intellectual and doctrinal foundations of the classical order. A reconstruction had to confront the centrality bestowed by classical international lawyers to state sovereignty.

We know that the critique of classical international law had been developing since the turn of the century and that it crystallized in the aftermath of the Great War.[8] We also know well the general thrust of the critique. Modern international lawyers in Europe believed that classical international law, centred on absolute sovereignty and legal positivism was incapable of adapting to an international reality marked by a new sense of solidarity reflecting deeper levels of interdependence between nations.[9] We also understand that the critique translated into new international rules, doctrines and institutions that limited sovereignty in favour of a more robust international community. Respectively, for example, the Briand-Kellogg Pact prohibited war as a method to resolve international disputes; the doctrine of abuse of right limited the scope of action of states by circumscribing the exercise of sovereign rights to purposes defined in light of the interest of the international community; and the PCIJ,

[8] Oliver Diggelmann has examined the emergence of the sociological approach as part of the transition from classical to modern international law, arguing that the transition began before the First World War, but once hopes for peace were shattered by the war, the modern sociological trend consolidated during the interwar years: O. Diggelmann, *Anfänge der Völkerrechtssoziologie: die Völkerrechtskonzeptionen von Max Huber und Georges Scelle im Vergleich* (Zürich: Sculthess, 2000), pp. 13, 21–3. That the transition had begun before the war was also acknowledged by interwar jurists. Walther Schücking, for example, saw a progression from a period of disorganization, when states obtained autonomy at the cost of the unity of the international, into a period in which international organization has been regained. Schücking laments German opposition to compulsory arbitration at the Second Hague Conference. Though celebrated in Germany, Schücking condemns this 'reactionary attitude' that forestalled a development in international law: Walther Schücking, *Die Organisation der Welt* (Tübingen: J. C. B. Mohr, P. Siebeck, 1908), pp. 605–6.

[9] Both Huber and Scelle, the prominent Swiss and French lawyers mentioned above, played active roles in the development of a sociological approach to international law. See Diggelmann, *Anfänge der Völkerrechtssoziologie*.

although with no compulsory jurisdiction, inaugurated the first permanent tribunal. However, we do not know much about the modern critique of classical international law and the search for new foundations in relation to the rules, doctrines and institutions regulating interactions with the peripheries, like the rules behind colonialism, self-determination of non-Western peoples as well as rules regulating interventions and war in the semi-periphery.

In 1894, on the inaugural issue of the *Revue générale de droit international public*, Antoine Pillet, then a private international lawyer from Grenoble, who would later be called to Paris to occupy the chair in the history of international treaties,[10] cautions about the problems confronted by a science that has not yet defined its constitutive elements, domain and object.[11] Pillet sets out to define the elements, domain and object of the science of international law, and he does so foreshadowing the central tenets of what became the modern French sociological approach. Pillet's main departure from classical law was substituting 'men' for 'states' as the subject on which every notion of law is founded.[12]

There is no doubt that the international society exists – Pillet declares. For men find themselves naturally connected not only to a national society, but also to an international society and as well as to the great association to which all humans belong.[13] All three associations, Pillet thinks, are constituted by individuals. Occupying a place between national law and the common law of humanity, international law is the law of the international society.[14] The international society in turn finds its basis in an undeniable social fact. This social fact – Pillet explains – does not emerge from the interaction between sovereigns, but from the interaction between peoples. It is the individual who establishes the social relations at the base of the international society.

[10] See J. P. Niboyet, 'Antoine Pillet (1857–1926)' in *Mélanges Antoine Pillet* (Paris: Sirey, 1929), vol. 1, pp. 3–15.

[11] A. Pillet, 'Le droit international public, ses éléments constitutifs, son domaine, son objet', 1 *RGDIP* (1894), 1–32.

[12] *Ibid.*, 2.

[13] 'Men, where one finds the personality at the basis of any conception of law, appears to us, if we consider its situation, as naturally bound by three societies, national, international and the largest association formed around members of the human race.' *Ibid.*, 2.

[14] Pillet warns, however, that international law, the law of the international society, should not be confused with the law common to all humanity: *ibid.*, 14. While international law rules are imperative and obligatory, the enforceability of the law of humanity, deriving from shared principles of human nature and considerations of human dignity, is contested: *ibid.*, 20.

Pillet here foreshadows nothing but the typical modern trope substituting 'men' for 'states' as the basis of society and the law. But Pillet's man is no ordinary individual. Pillet believes this to be a man with

> no other limits than those imposed by his own powers, beset with needs of very different order, hardworking without stop to increase the amount of wealth concentrated on his head, motivated at the end by the still unfulfilled desire of progress which is a characteristic feature of his nature, this individual is inevitably inclined to look in all places for the goods he ambitions.[15]

It is this man – Pillet concludes – who establishes international commercial relations, who establishes stable interactions between peoples.[16]

Unlike classical jurists who conditioned the existence of a society between nations to cultural similarities between peoples, embodied in a standard of civilization, Pillet's argument depends neither on cultural similarities, nor on commonalities based on similar legal institutions. Commerce – Pillet argues – establishes a community of functions, the only real community between states. All states have the same obligations regarding their subjects. To the extent that individuals are engaged in international commerce, their sovereigns will find themselves bounded by analogous obligations. International commerce – concludes Pillet – is the social phenomenon that draws different nations into an international community.[17]

So far, we see nothing particularly detrimental to the semi-periphery and nothing intrinsically imperialistic about this new approach. Unless we make explicit what is implicit in Pillet's argument, namely that the unbounded and ambitious man finding untapped resources around the world is actually a Frenchman, a man of the Western core, we would think that the international society may well be formed by any individual engaged in international commerce from any nation across the globe. In other words, is there a criterion to determine participation in commerce similar to the classical criterion for membership in the family of nations, that is, the classical standard of civilization?

Pillet considers the conventional delimitation of international law, as a European or Christian law of peoples, too narrow. Pillet finds equally insufficient a delimitation based on the idea that for law to be common and regularly followed it requires peoples to have achieved an equal degree of civilization.[18] Understood as a sharp distinction determining inclusion and exclusion in the family of nations, modern international lawyers in

[15] *Ibid.*, 3. [16] *Ibid.* [17] *Ibid.* [18] *Ibid.*, 24.

the core, seem to have left the classical standard of civilization behind. In light of the incorporation of the American continent, the progress made by Japan jumping quickly through the stages of civilization and the progressive development of the international society, a very measured Pillet asks if all peoples should be now considered members of the same family and international law: 'we think not, and we wish to get out of the analysis we have undertaken a fair assessment of this grave matter'.[19] Then, a less cautious Pillet reverts to social facts to analyse this question. 'In fact the law of peoples developed between Christian nations and until today it only applies fully and with complete reciprocity between them.' Nations do not always treat each other under perfect equal footing. 'In fact' – Pillet continues – 'the degree of civilization of each nation is the measure of its rights.'[20]

Pillet does not hesitate when affirming that a civilized state, a big power, may only consent to regard a small community as equal in rights, if its inhabitants have achieved a higher level of social culture. But what a small community will never obtain – Pillet warns – is equal treatment if 'still half in the darkness of barbarism, whatever remains the importance of its resources or the number of its people'.[21] Drawing the line between inclusion and exclusion according to the degree of civilization, Pillet, as a precursor of the modern legal discourse as articulated in the core, suggests that the dissolution of the standard of civilization was not part of the modern project. The dissolution of the standard was rather attempted by semi-peripherals articulating the modern discourse. Core jurists instead reinserted the old standard into the new discourse. Pillet, for example, affirms that if the international community is a community of functions and if international law enables the exercise of these functions, international law will only apply between states with sufficient understanding and capacity to exercise with regularity their functions.[22] European states, in consequence, exercise broad consular privileges in Oriental countries because the latter cannot guarantee public order in their territories. Thus, Pillet concludes contending that in all its effects, with full equality, reciprocity and with respect for the freedom of each nation, international law only applies between nations conscious of their social duties and well organized to be able to fulfil them, that is, between nations that have achieved a higher degree of civilization.[23]

[19] *Ibid.* [20] *Ibid.*, 24. [21] *Ibid.*, 25. [22] *Ibid.* [23] *Ibid.*, 26.

A critique of sovereignty with imperialistic overtones: Politis

The modern approach foreshadowed by Pillet at the turn of the century acquired renewed force during the first decades of the twentieth century, when classical legal thought, especially the centrality it bestowed to sovereignty, came to be seen as a major obstacle to the development of a stronger international legal order. Thus, a critique of sovereignty took centre stage. In 1925, Nicolas Politis (1872–1942) delivered the Hague Lectures on the limitation of sovereignty and the theory of abuse of right.[24] Widely read and quoted, the Hague Lectures proposed a redefinition of sovereign autonomy, which suited well the modern internationalist project, for Politis argued that states pursuing goals that are in conflict with the goals of international law would see their sovereign prerogatives limited. Certainly most interwar lawyers had in mind the limitation of the sovereign prerogative to wage war.

However, Western interventions in the semi-periphery also figured prominently in the mind of Politis and other French lawyers as examples of the limitation of absolute sovereign prerogatives. But as we will see, it was the limitation of the sovereign autonomy of semi-peripheral states that the critique of sovereignty justified. This is not what Alejandro Alvarez and other semi-peripheral international lawyers had in mind when advocating a new modern international law. Taking a closer look at Politis' argument will help to reveal the imperialistic overtones in the articulation of the modern discourse by lawyers from the core.

Although a Greek national, I interpret the work of Nicolas Politis as part of modern legal thought at the core. A renowned Greek lawyer and diplomat, Politis served at different periods of his career as professor at the University of Paris, Greek Minister of Foreign Affairs and President of the Assembly of the League of Nations.[25] But it is not because of the professional success achieved in Europe that I regard Politis as an exponent of modern thought at the core. For semi-peripheral states, the whole point

[24] N. Politis, 'Le problème des limitations de la souveraineté et la théorie de l'abus des droits dans les rapports internationaux', *RdC*, 6 (1925-I), 1–121.

[25] Politis was born in Corfu, pursuing, as many of his generation, higher education in Paris. After his doctoral studies in law at the University of Paris, Politis obtained a teaching position at Aix-en-Provence and thereafter a chair at Poitiers. Politis had a very successful career publishing mostly in French and in Paris many important works such as *Les nouvelles tendances du droit international* in 1927. Politis also assumed important professional undertakings such as the preparation of the statute of the League together with Léon Bourgeois. See biographical note by Georges Scelle, *Annuaire de l'Institut de Droit International*, 43 II (1950), 492–5.

of producing international lawyers was to have someone voicing the particular non-Western viewpoint in Europe. Let us remember, for example, Carlos Calvo in nineteenth-century Paris. It is the specific version of the modern reconstruction of international law Politis exposed that placed him closer to the French school than to the modern version pursued by other semi-peripheral lawyers.

The lectures at *The Hague Academy of International Law* transformed Politis into one of the most visible and outspoken interwar advocates for the renewal of international law.[26] Politis opened the 1925 lectures declaring that international law had finally arrived at a veritable turning point. After three centuries dominated by the idea that international law is exclusively a law between states, international legal thought was ready to do away with the 'dogma of sovereignty', which imposes 'a formidable obstacle to the pacific organisation of the world'.[27]

Conceived solely as a law between states, international law ignored individuals as legal subjects. Reaffirming one of the central tenets of the modern discourse, Politis explains that if individuals were only considered by international law as subjects of a state, only states would be treated as moral and sovereign persons.[28] Like Pillet and Scelle, Politis believed that mistakenly assuming states to be the real subjects of the law, treating them as persons, international law had been left in a very weak position. For, under this mistaken assumption, states could only be subjected to the 'empire of law', if by their 'free and uncontrollable' consent, they agree to recognize international law as obligatory.[29]

But the state – Politis contends – is not an end but a means, it is pure abstraction. The international community as a collective of states is a greater abstraction: 'it is an immense sum of fictions'.[30] Politis invites to look behind 'vain legal fictions' and find solid ground on which to root modern law in 'the dominant fact of our epoch', namely in the 'solidarity of human relations'.[31] Quoting Léon Duguit, Politis declares membership in the French sociological school affirming that, like all law, international law consists of imperatives addressed to individuals, based on the solidarity existing between them.[32] In fact, as we will see, Politis conceives his argument as following a line of French legal thinking that

[26] The impact of Politis' introduction of the private law doctrine of abuse of right into international law has been long-lasting: see e.g. R. Neuhaus, *Das Rechtsmissbrauchsverbot im heutigen Völkerrecht: eine Untersuchung zur Entwicklung und Anwendbarkeit eines Begriffes*, (Berlin: Duncker & Humblot, 1984), pp. 25–6.

[27] Politis, 'Le problème des limitations', 5, 16. [28] *Ibid.*, 5.

[29] *Ibid.* [30] *Ibid.*, 6. [31] *Ibid.* [32] *Ibid.*, 9.

Antoine Pillet had started and that others like Jules Basdevant, Albert de Lapradelle and Georges Scelle continued.[33] Politis' own contribution was to channel this tradition into a specific critique of sovereignty.

Politis strongly denounces sovereignty as a 'vicious terminology', which should be 'completely and definitively eliminated from juridical language'.[34] Actually, the final triumph of the new conception of international law – Politis announces – is based on the incurable ruin of sovereignty, the central principle of the classical doctrine.[35] According to Politis, sovereignty gives rise to a dilemma between the autonomy of states and their subjection to law. But there are two additional problems. As a legal term, sovereignty infuses the international lawyer with nationalist sentiments. Somewhat unconsciously, lawyers distance themselves from the international perspective that – Politis reminds – should constantly be coveted to realize the oeuvre of science.[36] Even worse are the practical problems. Sovereignty provides apparent justification for the arbitrary pretentions of governments, their 'intransigence', their 'ambition' – and most interestingly for the reasons referred to below – for 'imperialism', 'wars and conquests'.[37]

Sovereignty – Politis argues – should be replaced by the concept of freedom.[38] Freedom, unlike sovereignty is neither omnipotent nor absolute. Ultimately, saying that a nation is sovereign means that it enjoys the greater freedom conceivable within existing law. Modern social phenomena have connected individuals in multiple and complex relations of interdependence. Since neither the individual nor the state exists in absolute isolation, freedom is no longer a negative concept circumscribing an unregulated realm of activity, but a positive concept carrying forward the imperatives of solidarity.[39]

This is the conventional Politis one remembers as a prominent representative of the French interwar sociological school. More intriguing are the concrete limitations to state sovereignty that Politis identifies and the examples he offers as articulation of the new idea of law based on solidarity and interdependence. Sovereignty as freedom means that states encounter a realm of action regulated by law as well as a realm that has not yet been formally limited, the 'reserved domain'.[40] In relation

[33] *Ibid.*, 7. [34] *Ibid.*, 19–20. [35] *Ibid.*, 10–11. [36] *Ibid.*, 19–20.
[37] *Ibid.*, 20. [38] *Ibid.*, 21. [39] *Ibid.*, 22 and *passim*.
[40] The reserved domain carves for the state an autonomous space comprising domestic matters that stay outside the purview of international law. But Politis maintains that the line dividing the reserved domestic domain from the international sphere is not

to the former, Politis discusses the specific limitations international law imposes on sovereignty and, in relation to the latter, the reserved domain, Politis suggests limitations based on the doctrine of abuse of rights.

Limitations to sovereignty – Politis believes – follow from solidarity, which derives from the social necessities of international life.[41] In the search for the reconstruction of international law and examples of the limitation of sovereignty, Politis looks into the past, into nineteenth-century international law, and offers examples in six different areas. Three of them are particularly relevant for the semi-periphery: the prohibition of commercial isolation, the example being the opening of Japan and China; the imposition of international financial controls in the wake of the Venezuelan blockade; and the extension of international state responsibility in relation to injuries suffered by foreign residents.[42]

The examples chosen by Politis are not simply important for the semi-periphery, these were appalling experiences of imperialism, which we have already explored in the second part of the book, including the legal arguments produced by classical semi-peripheral jurists opposing the opening of Japan and China, the Venezuelan blockade and the protection of nationals abroad. Politis' choosing could not be more telling, for it conveys a desire to protect and legitimate Western capital expansion through military enforcement of international law, enabling international communication and commerce as well as the circulation of commodities, people and capital.

'Japan was forced to open its doors in 1853' – Politis affirmed, sounding like a classical lawyer.[43] Politis, however, did not justify the opening of Japan based on the standard of civilization, but based on the freedom of communication and equitable treatment in commerce. Nations are required not to subtract themselves from international intercourse.[44] Whereas for Pillet participating in international trade was one of the

fixed, but depends on 'international relations and the successive advances of international law': N. Politis, *Les nouvelles tendances du droit international* (Paris: Hachette, 1927), p. 7.

41 Based on these social necessities, Politis indentifies two basic rules, which precede any treaty, for treaties give only concrete formulation to international law's rule of solidarity and economic interdependence: Politis, 'Le problème des limitations', 26, 29–30.

42 *Ibid.*, 32–42. The other areas are not irrelevant to the semi-periphery: freedom of communication and transit, minority regimes and the use of force and the law of war. I am not looking at these in particular because Politis does not include specific examples involving the limitation of sovereignty of semi-peripheral states.

43 *Ibid.*, 34. 44 *Ibid.*

markers of civilization, for Politis there is a minimum level of relations that every nation has to maintain with the international community regardless of civilization, a level that expands according to the development of international law.[45]

The example of nineteenth-century Japan is invoked by Politis in order to describe the Chinese question in the twentieth century as a battle between the general interest of the international community and the particular interest of a sovereign. In this battle, general interest of the international community should prevail, by 'persuasion and force', over the particular interest of selfish states: 'a nation that possesses natural resources exceeding its needs, which does not allow the rest of humanity to take its part, fails its social duty; it violates the juridical principle of freedom of commerce derived from the economic interdependence of peoples'.[46] The articulation of the modern discourse by Politis is full of imperialist overtones. Modern international law limits China's egoistic behaviour. Western states have a right to extract resources not exploited by non-Western nations.

Moreover, as a consequence of the modern limitations on sovereignty, Western states have also a right to protect their capital and nationals abroad. For a long time – Politis explains – financial obligations of nations in relation to foreigners fell under the domain of their uncontrollable freedom. For a long time, servicing debt was not a legal, but a moral obligation. A state under default could neither be brought in front of a judge, nor incur international responsibility – Politis affirms quoting the Drago doctrine.[47] Politis explicitly refutes Drago. The Drago doctrine was never fully admitted in practice, Politis points out, reminding that the interventions to force payment were not only frequent, but also evolved into an international rule according to which payment of public debt is a legal obligation and non-performance involves international responsibility of the debtor state. A state that fails to pay can be lawfully intervened. Public opinion – Politis notes – found the Venezuelan intervention of 1902 absolutely normal. The Porter Convention adopted at the Second Hague Conference of 1907 is brought up by Politis as the final rebuttal to Drago. It recognized the legality of intervention if the

[45] *Ibid.*, 34.

[46] 'Participation in international trade is currently one of the conditions of existence of a civilised state': A. Pillet, 'Recherches sur les droits fondamentaux des états dans l'ordre des rapports internationaux et sur la solution des conflits qu'ils font naître' (Part 1) *RGDIP*, 5 (1898), 66–89, 80; Politis, 'Le problème des limitations', 34–5.

[47] Politis, 'Le problème des limitations', 35.

debtor nation refuses to accept arbitration or if it ignores an arbitral award.[48]

Politis not only defended the legality of interventions like the Venezuelan blockade, but also favoured a deeper limit to the financial sovereignty of debtor states. To secure payment, creditor nations should have control over the domestic public finances of debtor states.[49] Politis sees the imposition of financial controls as part of a larger trend limiting sovereignty when it conflicts with international obligations. Under modern law, states have become internationally responsible for their legislative acts and judicial decisions breaching international law obligation as well as for a denial of justice. 'In this sense, it is unquestionable and undisputed that international law is superior to domestic law.'[50] This trend, expanding international responsibility of states for behaviour within their territories – Politis notes – has transformed the legal treatment of foreign residents. In the past, a state's international duty in relation to foreign residents was to afford them the same treatment given to nationals. This is no longer allowed – Politis affirms. The measure of responsibility cannot be other than the one determined by international law itself.[51] Five years later, in strong opposition to semi-peripheral international lawyers, as we will see, Politis defended this view at the Third Hague Conference on codification.

Interdependence and social duties as new grounds for intervention: Lapradelle and Basdevant

We still remember, as one of the greatest achievements of the interwar period, the proscription of war as a means to solve interstate disputes. Politis in fact pointed out that modern sovereignty has imposed limits on the freedom of states to have recourse to war as well as on the freedom of states to choose the means through which warfare is carried out.[52] However, it is quite remarkable that we have generally forgotten the extent to which limitations to sovereignty, such as those advanced by Politis and other modern jurists, widened the bases for the use of force in the form of armed interventions in the semi-periphery. There is no contradiction for the modern jurist situated at the centre of the world system. Interventions are not war, but enforcement of international obligations in relation to violations of the new rights enjoyed by individuals and new social duties imposed on states resulting from interdependence. This was particularly

[48] *Ibid.*, 36. [49] *Ibid.*, 37. [50] *Ibid.*, 38. [51] *Ibid.*, 39. [52] *Ibid.*, 33–4.

clear in French scholarship. In his discussion of the interventions in China and Venezuela, Politis draws from the work of Albert de Lapradelle and Jules Basdevant.

In the immediate aftermath of the allied intervention in China to quell the Boxer rebellion of 1900, Albert de Lapradelle writes a series of articles about the 'Chinese question'.[53] Lapradelle, a renowned French jurist cofounder of the *Institut des Hautes Etudes Internationales*, sees the difference between old and new international law as rooted in the distinction between an international society of independent states and one based on interdependence, between a law that requires restraint from intervention and a law that allows action, between a law based on the separation of states and a law based on international assistance.[54] The dichotomy between old and new, inaction and action is unsurprisingly replicated in order to mark the difference between China and Europe: 'Western civilisation, which is movement and progress, runs up against the Oriental civilisation, too contemplative for not being sluggish, too fatalistic for not being dull.'[55]

Those who are optimistic about China and pessimistic about the West – Lapradelle warns – those who deny the reality of the Chinese question are wrong. They believe that China is a peaceful culture and Europe is driven by moral, economic and military ambitions. For them Christianity and militarism are the causes of the problem. Although there are certainly crimes here and there – Lapradelle recognizes – and although Spaniards have brought missionaries as the British have brought opium, the Chinese question is real. For, in the modern interdependent world, it is not enough to achieve peace for one people isolated from others. Having renounced offensive wars is good but not sufficient to realize the ends of international law – an overly dramatic Lapradelle concludes: 'humanity requires more'.[56] The imagery chosen by Lapradelle to press forward his point is quite indicative of the modern jurist's dispositions towards the semi-peripheral world.

The overall picture offered by Lapradelle seems politically progressive. There is no justice in withdrawing from the international community. Men are social beings; they have duties of solidarity vis-à-vis other men. Lapradelle explains the nature of these duties by comparing a selfish man to a bandit. 'The peaceful man who locks himself, closed doors, selfish is not comparable to the bandit.' Although the violation of another's dwelling in the fury of looting is different from the selfish man, the

[53] A. de Lapradelle, 'La question chinoise'. [54] *Ibid.*, 340.
[55] *Ibid.*, 277. [56] *Ibid.*, 327.

latter – Lapradelle cautions – 'does not fulfil his duty, he is not within the limits of his right, or if it appears so, it is a mistake'. Foreshadowing Politis' doctrine of abuse of rights, Lapradelle closes the argument about the selfish man quoting the old legal maxim: '*Summus jus, summa injuria*'.[57] But Lapradelle's allegory does not end here. The selfish and the bandit are personified by two prominent non-Western nations: 'The Turk, throughout history, is the bandit . . . The Chinese is the peaceful man . . . the first is a criminal the second is guilty.'[58]

We know from Politis that the modern allegory of interdependence and social duty was not only articulated to prevent another European war, but also deployed to justify Western imperialism. If isolation of a nation breaches an international social duty, if China has the hands full of wealth and does not want to open them up, if they have treasures that exceed their needs, has China a right to deprive humanity from the resources that nature has arranged for her? – Lapradelle asks.[59] The answer is obvious: if China refuses a pacific penetration and if Europe attempts to conquer China, both would exceed the legitimate exercise of their rights. 'Finding the way to open the door without forcing it, that is the Chinese question.'[60]

As a modern jurist, Lapradelle believes that the Chinese question, opening the door without forcing it, represents a different problem than determining membership in the family of civilized nations in accordance to classical international law. Rather than uncivilized, in Lapradelle's rendering, China is like a dinosaur that needs to be awakened and get back to the task of economic and social renovation.[61] After a long description of the resources and riches that China cannot develop and threatens to withhold from the rest of the world, Lapradelle throws another impossible metaphor about China having means, while Europe has vision.[62] These new metaphors are no longer about opening the door, but about the consequences once the door has been gently opened. That men should reciprocally be able to trade commodities is the economic axiom of modern times and derives from the principle of fraternal solidarity. If this is a social truth – concludes Lapradelle – it is also a juridical truth.[63] Lapradelle is candid about the implications of his argument. At first,

[57] *Ibid.* [58] *Ibid.*, 327. [59] *Ibid.* [60] *Ibid.*, 329.

[61] In fact, Lapradelle compares China to a 'plesiosaur': *ibid.*

[62] *Ibid.*, 329–30. 'Like the blind and the paralytic, China has the legs and Europe the eyes, one has resources the other the means for action. The same way that a blind [person] has no right to refuse its legs to a paralytic that offers himself to guide his path, China has not right to refuse access to its riches to Europe . . . ': *ibid.*, 333.

[63] *Ibid.*, 335.

Lapradelle recognizes his thesis to seem subversive. It seems contrary to both peace and independence between states. However, this would only be so for classical jurists who compare and confuse the state with men. The classical jurist sees an opposition between sovereignty and independence, that is, the power of the state and the power of men. In light of this confusion, classical lawyers believe not only that states have sovereignty, but also that they have independence as a fundamental international right. Lapradelle believes that this confusion explains why under classical international law states are only subjected to negative duties. It also explains why international law becomes an order requiring only non-interference and abstention.[64] Lapradelle, however, announces the end of classical international law: 'for a new epoch, a new law.'[65]

The new law is no longer a simple defence against war and conquest, but organizes economic and social relations, as the progress of science facilitates interaction between peoples.[66] In the new context, nations no longer think about power, but commerce, not about retreating into their borders but about developing the sphere of their trade and the scope of their customers. In the name of interdependence, the new law of people facilitates trade, and, in the name of social duties, it lowers the barriers classical sovereignty had erected between states. It is not difficult to anticipate that a more proactive international law may facilitate European imperialism. In fact Lapradelle believed that the modern conqueror no longer absorbs the defeated, but dismembers its sovereignty. Thus, 'colonial policy blossoms again in the protectorate, the lease, the mandate, the condominium . . . '.[67]

The demise of the 'dogma of sovereignty' means that when humanity requires it, the prohibition against intervention should not be an excuse for inaction.[68] Lapradelle understands this change in the rules of international law to reflect a deeper transformation brought about by the progression from individualism to solidarity. When the 'negative philosophy' that discovered the individual and individual conscience is replaced by the new philosophy based on solidarity, not only society and social conscience were discovered, but also social work, from the family, to the nation, to international assistance.[69] Thus, states no longer have merely a duty not to harm other states, but have a social duty to assist men to realize in humanity the rights that belong to them. Among these rights, Lapradelle includes the right to commerce, freedom of movement, freedom

[64] *Ibid.*, 335–7. [65] *Ibid.*, 339. [66] *Ibid.*, 338. [67] *Ibid.* [68] *Ibid.*, 339.
[69] *Ibid.*, 339, quoting Leon Bourgeois and Émile Durkheim.

of thought and right to life.[70] International law no longer draws its principles and goals from the respect of sovereignty but from the defence of the rights of men. The new public law that has placed the will of men at the basis of government requires a new law of peoples that places the protection of humanity as the programme and the end of international law.[71]

For those like Pillet, Politis and Lapradelle, namely for modern jurists situated at the Western core, the transformation of a classical international law, based on absolute sovereignty, into a modern law of people, recognizing that international social duties limited state sovereignty, was a welcome development. But for those situated in the semi-peripheries of the world, the weakening of sovereignty under modern grounds presented new challenges and dangers. Lapradelle, for example, in subsequent instalments of his article about the Chinese question, understood the series of forceful interventions through which China was opened, as an exercise of the duty to protect humanity.[72] Moreover, in the aftermath of the Venezuelan blockade of 1902, Jules Basdevant reaffirmed the connection between modern international law and the new grounds for intervention. Before concluding this chapter, let me briefly examine Basdevant's discussion of the Venezuelan incident.

In the previous chapter we saw Luis Drago articulating the classical principle of absolute sovereignty and failing in his denunciation of the illegality of the Venezuelan blockade. Basdevant's justification of the Venezuelan blockade under modern basis suggests that at the beginning of the twentieth century Drago's defence of absolute sovereignty to condemn interventions in the semi-periphery was simply too anachronistic to be successful. Moreover, the modern justifications for intervention by Basdevant and other core jurists suggest that semi-peripheral engagements with modern international law could not simply be based on a plain appropriation of the modern discourse. As we will see in the last part of the book, semi-peripherals had not only to speak the modern language, but also confront the rules and doctrines supported by core jurists articulating modern ideas. Semi-peripherals had to confront the modern rules that were most detrimental to their polities by proposing alternative rules: for example, introducing a formal definition of statehood (to dissolve the standard of civilization) and the principle of non-intervention (to render interventions to protect foreign interests unlawful).

[70] *Ibid.* [71] *Ibid.*

[72] A. de Lapradelle, 'La question chinoise' (Part 2), 9 (1902), 49–115; (Part 3), 9 (1902), 367–405; (Part 4), 10 (1903), 742–99.

In 1904, Jules Basdevant (1877–1968), a professor in Rennes, who later became professor in Paris and judge and president of the ICJ, publishes in the *Revue* a defence of the legality of the intervention in Venezuela.[73] Basdevant argued that the use of force by the powers intervening in Venezuela was justified. Like every modern international lawyer, Basdevant believes that the ultimate end of international law is to create a good international order and that a good order presupposes peace. States should therefore not use force to solve conflicts, unless the attempts to reach a peaceful resolution fail.[74] In typical sociological parlance, Basdevant couches his argument in the language of social facts and functions. But we also see in Basdevant that the modern discourse based on facts and functions could fit well within a less internationalist and more conservative approach. Basdevant's starting point is the needs of individuals and state independence, rather than social needs and state interdependence. To the extent that individuals pursue their destiny within political organizations, within 'so-called states', Basdevant argues that the law will recognize independence to states acting within their domain. Each state has in principle no right to substitute another state against its will.[75] The independence of states, namely the right not to be substituted by another state, however, is not absolute, and the Venezuelan blockade is a case in point.

Invoking sovereignty, Venezuela looked at the complaints by foreign residents as a domestic problem. The European powers, on the other hand, sought diplomatic negotiations, invoking the right to protect their nationals abroad.[76] Seen in this light, Basdevant understands the controversy as a conflict between two equally valid claims. Venezuela's attempt to exclude diplomatic negotiations, however, seemed to Basdevant as an unwarranted demand.[77] The reasons given by Basdevant are entirely modern. The ultimate goal of the state is to serve individuals. Thus, the rights that states have to pursue their interests are different from the rights of individuals to protect their interests. The rights of states are nothing but the powers given to them to achieve their functions. Thus the right of a state to enact and enforce the law within its territory, that is, its jurisdictional rights, are only means to assure order and the development

73 J. Basdevant, 'L'action coercitive anglo-germano-italienne contre le Vénézuéla, 1902–1903', *RGDIP*, 11 (1904), 362–458. The article was also published as a monograph, J. Basdevant, *L'action coercitive anglo-germano-italienne contre le Vénézuéla, 1902–1903* (Paris: A. Pédone, 1904).

74 *Ibid.*, p. 11.

75 'The state determines itself, it has the faculty of self-determination': *ibid.*, p. 12.

76 *Ibid.*, p. 24. 77 *Ibid.*, p. 25.

of civilization. Sovereignty and independence are not metaphysical prerogatives, but prerogatives recognized to satisfy the interests of the individual.[78] The right of a state to independence in consequence exists only for practical reasons. This right can be removed if the state invokes independence undermining its ends. When this link between states and individuals breaks, that is, the link between the prerogatives recognized to states to fulfil their functions and the protection of the interests of the individual, the state whose independence is afforded by international law may be substituted, a 'vigilant' state substituted for the 'negligent' state.[79]

The Venezuelan blockade was thus a legitimate recourse to force diplomatic negotiations in order to prevent the substitution or actually replace a negligent state. 'In our opinion – Basdevant concludes – the three powers [Britain, Germany and Italy] were entitled to use diplomatic channels to put pressure on Venezuela, to ignore the exclusive character of its jurisdiction, because the disorder they brought to the international order was less serious than that resulting from the constant negligence of Venezuela in the fulfilment of its judicial function.'[80]

Let me finally take up the question in the title of this chapter. Was the modern discourse of international law good news for the semi-periphery? Posed in abstract, this question makes little sense, for the actual impact of a legal discourse will depend on the position, politics and standpoint of those who use it in order to support concrete rules. Between the last decade of the nineteenth century and the first decades of the twentieth century, the modes of understanding the nature and meaning of international law changed. But the power dynamics between centre and periphery did not change. What this chapter suggests is that, as articulated by core jurists, the modern discourse continued to perpetuate exclusion and inequality. Let me conclude, quoting again Basdevant in order to illustrate the continuities and changes in the shift from classical to modern international law, as conceived by core jurists:

> . . . if state functions are not performed by a state, they can be legitimately fulfilled by another, if the local state does not deliver justice or does it wrongly, the state where nationals are harmed is substituted to accomplish this function: there is

[78] *Ibid.*, pp. 25–6.

[79] *Ibid.*, p. 26. Similarly, Lapradelle and Politis argued that in the context of recovering public debt (the central hypothesis behind Drago's doctrine), interventions are lawful when the debtor state abuses its autonomy and inflicts unjustified injury to creditors: A. de Lapradelle and N. Politis, *Recueil des arbitrages internationaux* (Paris: A. Pédone, 1923), vol. II, p. 548.

[80] Basdevant, *L'action coercitive*, p. 30.

not, nowadays, other possible legal explanation of the regime of capitulations. This substitution of a vigilant state for a negligent state, is lawful, because it is the best way to provide individuals with the services they expect from the state; and this [substitution] may be present in various forms including diplomatic channels, employed to assert pecuniary claims against the state responsible for certain acts [against foreign individuals] committed during a civil war.[81]

We see here strong continuities in the rules perpetuating unequal treatment – in capitulations and the forceful intervention to secure compensation for injuries to foreign residents. And we see change in how these rules sanctioning inequality were justified. This passage illustrates also the challenge faced by semi-peripheral lawyers. How can rules sanctioning autonomy and equality be justified in modern terms? The next and final part of the book shows some of the answers and strategies devised by interwar semi-peripherals.

81 *Ibid.*, p. 26.

PART IV · MODERN INTERNATIONAL LAW

During the interwar years, international lawyers from semi-peripheral polities that had been formally recognized as sovereigns – like Latin American states – articulated the modern legal discourse in order to support rules of international law that could realize their aspirations for substantive autonomy and equality. As we will see, they partially succeeded, transforming basic international law rules and doctrines sustaining inequality into rules and doctrines recognizing formal and equal participation in the international community. Semi-peripherals, for example, contributed to the substitution of the standard of civilization – as a doctrine determining membership in the international community – with a formal definition of statehood.

On the other hand, politicians, lawyers and activists from semi-peripheral polities under colonial or mandate rule or under protectorates, continued the struggle for independence and self-government. During the interwar period, politicians, lawyers and rebels tried out several courses of action, ranging from peaceful negotiations to violent resistance. In view of the arresting differences in power between Western and non-Western nations, we tend to think that the struggle for independence was halted by force. But similarly to colonial rule itself – founded by force and gaining legitimacy and stability through violent repression as well as in part through international law – the struggle for independence was also advanced through a mix of peaceful and violent means. In both violent and non-violent resistance, international legal arguments were used to gain legitimacy.

The war of the Rif (1921–6), for example, is mostly remembered for the spectacular defeats Riffian rebels inflicted upon the Spanish military. Abd-el-Krim (1883–1963), the leader of the Rif nation, was not only skilled in guerrilla warfare, but also in putting together a diplomatic offensive that appealed to a global audience sympathetic to the anti-imperialist struggle. This offensive showcased Riffian heroic victories as well as the atrocities committed by the Spaniards. As we will see, it also included a wide range of international legal arguments: a general justification for independence, particular arguments against the treaties establishing the French and Spanish protectorates in Morocco as well as specific arguments to internationalize the conflict by involving the League of Nations and the Red Cross.

This combination of peaceful and violent resistance accompanied with international law arguments was common across the semi-periphery, not only among nationalist organizations, but also among other transnational movements, like Pan-African organizations. Marcus Garvey's Universal Negro Improvement Association (UNIA), for example, relied on general arguments in favour of self-determination for the black race. Nationalist organizations, like India's Home Rule League, the Korean 'March First Movement', the Syro-Palestinian Congress, and other nationalist parties from Armenia to Egypt, on the other hand, resorted to concrete arguments specific to each struggle. Appealing both to the League as well as to the Western enemies of their respective rulers, nationalist parties criticized the treaties legitimizing colonial or mandate rule, pointed at the abuses committed by the colonial or mandate power and devised ways to combine these and other arguments in a general plea for self-government. When violence erupted, as happened during the Syrian revolt of 1925, arguments justifying violent struggle followed as well. Violence was not a continuation of political struggle by other means. Rather, violent and non-violent modes of resistance coexisted, both including international legal justifications. On some occasions, the preference for one strategy over the other reflected the different interests of, as well as resources available to, elite and popular agents. In the Syrian mandate, for example, rebels and rebel leaders fighting the French were mostly of rural Druze extraction, while members of the Syrian political movement in exile, the Syro-Palestinian Congress, were mostly part of the Syrian elite. Although discrepancies and animosity between the two groups were not unusual, the latter group included a defence of violent resistance in their diplomatic offensive at the League of Nations.[1]

[1] For example, diplomatic undertakings by Shakib Arslan, envoy of the Syro-Palestinian Congress in Geneva, were met with indignation by Druze rebel leader Sultan al-Atrash, who objected to Arslan's moderate stance during the revolt, although, after being

At other times the same group resorted to violent and non-violent means of resistance. During the Riffian rebellion, Abd-el-Krim both fought the Spanish with armed force and addressed the League of Nations. In other places of the semi-periphery, it was not the struggle for national self-determination that connected those resorting to force with those invoking international legal arguments, but a commitment to a broader anti-imperialist ideology. In Latin America, as we will see, while international lawyers and diplomats were fighting to pass a rule prohibiting interventions at the 1928 Pan-American Conference of Habana, the Nicaraguan rebel leader Sandino was fighting American occupation. When, in the South West African mandate, South African forces repressed the Bondelswart tribe, bombarding both rebels and civilians, Garvey's UNIA not only condemned the massacre, but the envoys it had sent to the Third Assembly of the League of Nations, were in contact with Louis-Dantès Bellegarde (1877–1966), the Haitian delegate who drafted a resolution passed by the League's Assembly, demanding South Africa to 'make every effort to relieve the suffering of victims, particularly the women and the children' and requesting the Permanent Mandates Commission (PMC) to address South Africa's brutal repression of the Bondelswarts.[2]

Self-determination coalesced as a *lege lata* international right only in 1960. Semi-peripherals used peaceful and violent means in order to obtain self-government and invoked legal arguments sustaining both strategies almost half a century before the rise of a *lege lata* right. We will explore first the legal arguments supporting the struggle for self-government through non-violent means. Chapter 7 examines the arguments used by semi-peripherals to support the recognition of self-determination at the Paris Peace Conference and then at the League of Nations. These attempts worked for some, but not for all semi-peripheral polities. Chapter 8 explores how semi-peripherals sought to obtain self-government circumventing self-determination, that is, it studies the arguments developed to request admission to the League based on statehood and the arguments regarding the regulation of armed repression in order to make easier acquiring statehood by force. The last chapter of the book argues that the semi-peripheral engagements with modern international law culminated in the Montevideo Convention of 1933, when, in the pan-American

defeated, rebels also moderated their demands. M. Provence, *The great Syrian revolt and the rise of Arab nationalism* (Austin: University of Texas Press, 2005), p. 144.

2 *Records of the Third Assembly. Plenary meetings* (Geneva: 1922), p. 143.

context, Latin American states changed through regional codification some of the basic rules of international law determining membership in the international community as well as regulating the use of force against semi-peripheral states, that is, the definition of statehood and non-intervention.

7 Petitioning the international: a 'pre-history' of self-determination

Peoples struggling for self-government have always resorted to a mix of violent and non-violent means to achieve their goals. While the resort to collective violence has remained relatively constant, have ideals invoked and arguments made in support of political autonomy changed over time? Since decolonization, since the 1960s, a claim to self-determination according to international law has been a central strategy for those fighting for independence. What ideas and principles were invoked by peoples demanding political autonomy before the emergence of a right to self-determination? Was international law of any use to those fighting against foreign rule before decolonization?

Answers to these questions will certainly depend on what we mean by self-determination – one of international law's most riddled concepts. If peoples have a right to self-determination, how does international law define a people? And what rights should people enjoy under self-determination, a right to independence from foreign rule, or a right to secession from existing states? While defining the nature and scope of this right is difficult, identifying the historical origins of self-determination seems much less controversial. Conventionally, self-determination is understood to have been born as a political ideal. After the First World War, self-determination became a political principle to organize the post-war international order. Only after the Second World War did it become a principle included in the 1945 Charter of the United Nations. And only in the 1960s, after the General Assembly resolutions on decolonization and the general human rights conventions, did self-determination finally emerge as a right.[1]

[1] Cassese, for example, maintains that '. . . the UN Charter marks an important turning-point; it signals the maturing of the political postulate of self-determination

In this linear progression, self-determination transitioned from politics to law. In this sense, the legal history of self-determination before 1945 and 1960 would be 'pre-history'. Exploring the 'pre-history' of self-determination, this chapter finds the conventional linear narrative unconvincing. In support of the demand for self-government, during the first three decades of the twentieth century and in particular during the inter-war period, lawyers, politicians and activists from the semi-periphery articulated claims that were legal rather than political. In this process, semi-peripherals appropriated the modern international law discourse and tried to change international law rules and doctrines. Removing the obstacles that classical international law had erected – namely the standard of civilization as the doctrine on the basis of which sovereignty was denied outside the West – semi-peripherals made possible the emergence of a right to self-determination.

At the Paris Peace Conference of 1919, this strategy failed. This defeat was political. It failed because great powers ignored semi-peripheral claims to self-determination. But as a matter of law, in the sense of disciplinary debates in the intellectual history of international law, semi-peripherals succeeded in dissolving the standard of civilization. After the political defeat suffered in 1919, semi-peripheral lawyers dropped explicit references to self-determination and continued the struggle for self-government making use of the emerging doctrine of statehood. In part through requests for admission to the League – some polities like Ethiopia being admitted and many others like Armenia, Azerbaijan and the Six Nations of the Iroquois being rejected – statehood evolved into a formal rather than substantive criterion to determine membership into the international community.

Rather than a linear progression, the brief story recounted in this chapter points at ebbs and flows. In the semi-peripheral petitions of 1919, self-determination was born as an international right. Also in 1919, self-determination was politically defeated. During the 1920s, self-determination and statehood coexisted as alternative argumentative avenues, the first more apt for polities fighting for independence without having secured territorial control, the second more appropriate for polities that had secured some territorial control. During the interwar, invoking self-determination remained mostly an argumentative strategy,

into a legal standard of behaviour'. See e.g. A. Cassese, *Self-determination of peoples: a legal reappraisal* (Cambridge University Press, 1995), p. 43 and see in general pp. 11–33.

while a standard based on statehood became established law, in the procedure to decide on the admission of new members to the League (as we will see in Chapter 8) and in the Montevideo Convention of 1933 (as we will see in Chapter 9). Once statehood was conceptualized in formal terms as government, people and territory, the way was paved for semi-peripheral polities to demand or obtain by force territorial control and thus acquire self-determination. Given these transformations in the doctrinal structure of international law – from civilization to statehood – when political conditions changed, after the second post-war, self-determination could re-emerge as an international right. This was semi-peripherals' remarkable feat. Looking back at the interwar period we may learn about semi-peripheral uses of international law, about a professional style of resistance that seems to have been forgotten and might be fruitfully remembered today.

Petitioning at the Peace Conference, Paris, 1919

In New York, on 20 July 1922, the executive officers of the UNIA, the black organization founded by Marcus Garvey (1887–1940) – the famous Jamaican activist and intellectual – drafted a petition and decided to send a delegation to the Third Assembly of the League of Nations. On behalf of the 'four hundred million black people of Africa and the world', Garvey's organization requested the League to transfer to the black race the former German colonies of East Africa and Southwest Africa.[2]

This was not the first time black intellectuals had sought a broader constituency in the search for new strategies to improve the condition of black people and channel aspirations for self-government. Since the turn of the century, a pan-African movement emerged under the leadership of W. E. B. Du Bois (1868–1963), the well-known American black scholar and cofounder of the National Association for the Advancement of Coloured People (NAACP). A first pan-African congress was organized in 1900 in London and then a second in Paris in 1919. Throughout the addresses and declarations adopted after each of these meetings, an elite group

[2] Universal Negro Improvement Association (UNIA), 'Petition of the Universal Negro Improvement Association League to the League of Nations, The Hague', LoN Archive, 1/22354/21159 and in R. Hill (ed.), *The Marcus Garvey and Universal Negro Improvement Association papers* (Berkeley: University of California Press, 1983), vol. IV, pp. 735–40.

of the African diaspora united around a discourse of racial identity and solidarity.[3]

The UNIA petition of 1922 was not an isolated attempt to reach out to the international world to channel aspirations for self-government. During the first decades of the century the black transnational intelligentsia turned decisively towards the international sphere to pursue their objectives. In 1919, at the end of the First World War, W. E. B. Du Bois himself as well as Eliézer Cadet (1897–?), a young Haitian envoy of Garvey's UNIA, arrived in Paris at the time leaders and activists from around the world were gathering to negotiate the terms of the peace settlement. Both Du Bois and Cadet were eager to defend the interests of the black race, hoping to be heard by the great powers as they were laying down the foundations of the post-war international order.

Eliézer Cadet had gained prominence within Garvey's circles after writing a letter to UNIA's newspaper – the *Negro World* – condemning the American intervention in Haiti. Cadet was thus enlisted to serve as an interpreter to the delegation to be sent to Paris. But in addition to speaking French, Cadet proved useful to the UNIA because of his Haitian nationality. When the American government denied passports to the envoys appointed by the UNIA, he became the only member who could travel to Paris. Cadet thus became the UNIA High Commissioner to the Peace Conference.[4] To Paris Cadet brought the 'nine point declaration', the resolution adopted in 1922 by the UNIA that, in clear allusion to Wilson's fourteen points, demanded self-determination and equality for the black race: '1. The right of self-determination will be applied to Africans and to every European colony where the African race predominates . . . 9. The return to the natives of Germany's African colonies, which will be governed by Negroes educated in the Eastern and Western countries'.[5]

Du Bois, on the other hand, believed that the natives of Africa should have the right to participate in government as fast as their development permitted. With Du Bois and other members of the pan-African movement in Paris, a Pan-African Congress was organized in February 1919. The Congress passed a resolution demanding that 'the natives of Africa and

[3] See M. Kaapanda, 'The pan-African movement' (unpublished paper). My understanding of the connection between the pan-African movement and international law relies on Mekondjo Kaapanda's work.

[4] C. Grant, *Negro with a hat. The rise and fall of Marcus Garvey* (Oxford University Press, 2008), pp. 173, 175.

[5] R. Hill, *The Marcus Garvey and Universal Negro Improvement Association papers* (Berkeley: University of California Press, 2011), vol. XI, p. 191.

the Peoples of African descent' be governed according to nine principles. Principle number eight stated:

> *Civilised Negroes:* Wherever persons of African descent are civilised and able to meet the tests of surrounding culture, they shall be accorded the same rights as their fellow citizens; they shall not be denied on account of race or color a voice in their own government, justice before the courts and economic and social equality according to ability and desert.[6]

The pleas by Cadet and Du Bois contained the central elements that every discussion about the admission of non-Western polities had to include at the beginning of the twentieth century: self-determination and the standard of civilization. In 1918, Woodrow Wilson (1856–1924) had declared his 'Fourteen Points' proposal for ending the war. Wilson's speech to Congress set out the basis for a peace treaty and the foundation of a permanent international organization. Although not explicitly mentioned in the speech, self-determination rose to become one of the principles guiding the post-war settlement.[7] As the principle of self-determination attained centrality, politicians and activists from non-Western polities subjected to formal or informal colonialism harnessed the principle to demand political independence for their nations. During the first decades of the twentieth century, however, every international legal argument in favour of sovereignty for non-Western states had also to confront the standard of civilization, the nineteenth-century legal doctrine according to which the distinction between formal sovereignty and formal or informal colonial rule was justified.

The allied powers gathered in Paris with ambitious goals. Negotiating the terms of the peace settlement with Germany and creating a permanent League of Nations, they sought nothing less than to transform the pre-war international order and classical international law. For once, classical sovereignty would not be the same if winners would no longer be entitled to rip unjust territorial and monetary compensations from losers, if collective security would be provided by the League, rather than through the balance of power, if the practice of secret diplomacy would be eradicated.[8]

[6] 'Resolutions passed at the 1919 Pan-African Congress' in R. Hill (ed.), *The Marcus Garvey and Universal Negro Improvement Association papers: Africa for the Africans June 1921–December 1922* (Berkeley: University of California Press, 1995), vol. IX, p. 5.

[7] E. Manela, *Wilsonian moment: self-determination and the international origins of anticolonial nationalism* (Oxford University Press, 2007), pp. 24, 25 ff.

[8] M. MacMillan, *Paris 1919: six months that changed the world* (New York: Random House, 2002).

The allied powers, however, had no plans to relinquish the standard of civilization. The standard was not part of the classical international law that had to be reconstructed to secure peace. The future of the German colonies and the territories of the Ottoman Empire that had fallen under the allied powers' control or influence was part of the negotiations in Paris. But the future of European colonialism was not part of the Paris agenda. In fact, the Peace Conference invoked the idea of a standard of civilization and the idea of Western civilizing mission to establish the League's Mandate System.[9] Wilson's project to renew the international order neither included the end of colonialism, nor the end of unequal treatment. Moreover, there was no effort in Paris to revise the open door policy in China, or the United State's corollary to the Monroe doctrine, namely the policy of intervention in Latin America. While the practice of concluding secret treaties had to be renounced, since secret diplomacy became inconsistent with Wilson's ideal of open and fair international relations, there was nothing in the Wilsonian ideal about the abrogation of unequal treaties, about Western powers giving up, for example, extraterritorial rights and consular jurisdiction in China.

Wilson's idealism did not reach outside the West. Although discouraging, leaders of the non-Western world were not discouraged. During the year between Wilson's 'Fourteen Points' speech and the inauguration of the Peace Conference, semi-peripheral lawyers' and politicians' activism was formidable. Demands for political independence framed in both the language of self-determination and the standard of civilization proliferated. In addition to black activists, diplomatic representatives from states subjected to informal colonial domination, that is, unequal treatment, like China, the Ottoman Empire and Persia, as well as delegations from territories under colonial rule, tried hard to have a say at the Peace Conference. Members of nationalist parties from Egypt to India and Korea, organizations of Chinese students abroad, all converged in Paris. Also citizens representing a wide variety of organizations from polities that did not make it to Paris, from Syria to Transjordan and Togoland, sent countless cables and letters to the authorities of the allied powers meeting in Paris, especially to the United States and to the French Prime Minister, Georges Clemenceau (1841–1929) as Secretariat of the Conference.[10]

[9] See Anghie, *Imperialism*, pp. 115–195; B. Rajagopal, *International law from below development, social movements, and Third World resistance* (Cambridge University Press), pp. 50–72; and Q. Wright, *Mandates under the League of Nations* (University of Chicago Press, 1930).

[10] For a list of authenticated and unauthenticated documents presented at the Conference, see Hoover War Library, *A catalogue of Paris Peace Conference delegation propaganda in the*

This chapter explores some of these petitions, memoranda, manifestos and telegrams drafted by non-Western politicians, intellectuals, activists and citizens in 1919 and during the interwar period. These documents are interesting in their own right. They show that the international peace conference in Paris and then the inauguration of the League, a permanent international organization in Geneva, opened new opportunities for using the language of international law and mobilizing in favour of equality and self-government. These documents suggest that during the interwar period, the language of international law was not only articulated to sustain new modes of Western domination outside the West, recognizing Western states' civilizing mission in the League's Mandate system, or, as we have seen in the previous chapter, widening the basis for intervention under humanitarian grounds. Semi-peripheral petitions and memoranda also show new modes of resistance through international law. How did semi-peripheral lawyers and activists frame their demands for self-governance in the language of international law? What are the stories behind these examples of international legal mobilization?

Exploring these questions, there might be a more ambitious goal in sight. Although we know little about these stories of resistance, their outcome is well known. Decolonization did not occur until well into the second post-war period. The League never intervened decisively against Western violence waged in European colonies, mandates or protectorates. Semi-peripheral mobilization through the language of international law was not successful. These stories show that interwar international law secured Western domination rather than non-Western resistance. To the extent that attempts by semi-peripherals to use international law in their plight for political autonomy failed, there is a story to tell about international law's involvement in imperialism, but this would be not a significant story for the intellectual history of international law.

I suggest the opposite. Interwar petitioning was a relevant event in the history of international law. The stories that follow show that non-Western petitioners appropriated the modern language of international law to pursue their quest for equality and self-governance, defending new rules of international law. This appropriation was significant. The main rules and doctrines of late nineteenth-century classical international law and early twentieth-century modern international law were not beneficial

Hoover War Library (Stanford University Press, 1926). For examples of the countless documents addressed to Clemenceau, see the letters, petitions and memoranda examined below by delegates from Egypt, Korea and the pan-African movement.

to those struggling for equality and self-governance. Semi-peripheral lawyers conversant with modern legal thinking changed international law rules, transforming modern international law into a discourse on the basis of which their goals could be justified. Moreover, once petitioners became well versed in the modern discourse, they outdid Western lawyers who thus appeared to be defending conservative positions to justify special, egoistic or absolute rights in favour of the core and against the peripheries of the world.

Specifically, interwar letters, petitions and memoranda by semi-peripheral lawyers and activists show a general shift in the structure of international law from the standard of civilization to statehood in the conceptualization of the requisites for self-governance and the recognition of sovereignty. These documents also suggest that the modern shift from sovereignty to internationalism was harnessed by semi-peripherals to narrow the basis for European sovereignty in mandates, protectorates or colonies and to expand the basis for international and League involvement. These accomplishments in the intellectual history of international law do not disavow responsibility for the failure to produce actual change in the non-Western world. But in terms of the transformation of rules and doctrines the change was remarkable. We may not have to be fully aware of this change because we tend to think about modern international law as it looked towards the end of the interwar period and furthermore after its reconstruction following the Second World War: with self-determination and without the standard of civilization. These stories about petitioning explain in part how we got there. They explain the transformations in the conceptual structure of international law, transformations that were necessary in order to produce, though much later, change in the form of decolonization.

The reconstruction of international law in the semi-periphery

Before turning to the exploration of semi-peripheral petitions and memoranda, let us explore briefly modern international legal thinking as it stood at the beginning of the interwar period. The previous chapter already examined the modern legal discourse as articulated by Western, specifically French lawyers before the Great War, arguing that it opened new justifications for Western intervention in the semi-periphery. The exploration of the modern discourse here focuses briefly on the rhetoric of reconstruction of international law after the war by core and semi-peripheral jurists. In order to obtain sovereign autonomy and equality for their polities, semi-peripherals' jurists invoked modern legal ideas about solidarity, interdependence and the limitation of sovereignty, as well as articulating anti-formalist legal arguments based on the doctrine of change of circumstances and necessity.

In 1919, the winners of the war laid down the foundations for a new international order. However, as we have seen in the third part of the book, since the turn of the century, international legal scholars had already been thinking about the inadequacies of classical international law to sustain a more robust international order. In France, since the end of the nineteenth century and all through the interwar period, a 'sociological school' emerged – including a lineage from Antoine Pillet, to Albert de Lapradelle, Nicolas Politis and Georges Scelle, among others – believing that international solidarity, grown from the fact of interstate interdependence, required a stronger international law. Moreover, after the setback experienced at the Second Hague Conference of 1907, when the proposal to create the first permanent international court was defeated because it was seen as infringing upon states' sovereign equality, lawyers like James Brown Scott and Max Huber blamed and criticized classical international law for the defeat.

After the Great War, legal scholars seized the opportunity opened by the creation of the first permanent international organization and later the first permanent international court, the League of Nations and the PCIJ, to pronounce the beginning of a new era and reconstruct international legal thought. In addition to French jurists, Hersch Lauterpacht, one of the most prominent scholars in Britain, for example, revised and critiqued central doctrines of classical international law, such as the doctrine of the non-justiciability of political disputes, which because of the belief in the absolute nature of sovereignty, denied the possibility of resolving controversies by international courts.[11] Others, like the same Huber, examined the sociological underpinnings of the law to justify international obligations beyond or against state consent.[12] Interwar international lawyers reworked the central elements of classical international law. International legal thought experienced profound changes, including a critique of absolute sovereignty, a critique of legal positivism and the idea that international law was not just the law regulating the conduct

[11] H. Lauterpacht, *The function of law in the international community* (Cambridge University Press, 1933).

[12] M. Huber, *Die soziologischen Grundlagen des Völkerrechts* (Berlin-Grunewald: W. Rothschild, 1928). On Huber, see O. Spiermann, *International legal argument in the Permanent Court of International Justice* (Cambridge University Press, 2010), pp. 186–7.

between states, but the law establishing an order for the international community.

During the interwar years a legal consciousness or sensibility emerged that, in contradistinction to classical international law, may be described as modern international law. The international legal order that came into being during the interwar period was believed to be more internationalist than the classical order based on absolute sovereignty. This modern legal order was thought to guarantee international peace by limiting the absolute sovereignty of states. The League of Nations, founded after the peace negotiations in Paris, marked international law's 'move to institutions' – the organization of the international community not just through laws, but including permanent international institutions.[13] The League became the central actor responsible for the coordination and cooperation between sovereigns on matters of common interest.

Modern efforts to limit classical sovereignty, as we have seen in the previous chapter, were dangerous for the semi-periphery. Limiting sovereignty, in order to carve out a space for permanent international organizations to operate, and in order to reduce the incidence of war (proscribing it as a means to solve interstate disputes), was not accompanied by limitations to the powers Western sovereigns could wield in the peripheries of the world. Sovereignty was not limited in order to limit interventions to protect nationals abroad, or in order to limit armed repression of uprisings in mandates, protectorates or colonies. In Paris, the demands for self-determination fell on deaf ears. After Paris, Western sovereigns continued to exercise absolute sovereignty in overseas territories subjected to formal colonial rule and continued to exercise special consular privileges and intervene in territories subjected to informal colonialism. Though, as we will see, states that obtained territories under mandates saw their powers limited by League supervision through the PMC.

In relation to the new established mandates, the League marked a radical departure from the classical paradigm. The League inaugurated the international involvement in the administration of territories not recognized as sovereign states. After Paris, it was still to be seen how the PMC would define the duties of the mandatory power, duties emanating from the mandate as a 'sacred trust of civilization'. But it soon became clear that the mandatory power would use overwhelming force to ensure – in the words of Article 22 of the League's Covenant – the 'well-being and development' of 'peoples not yet able to stand by themselves under

[13] D. Kennedy, 'The move to institutions', *Cardozo Law Review*, 8 (1986), 841–987.

the strenuous conditions of the modern world'.[14] Rebellions, not only in colonies and protectorates but also in the mandates, were quashed by military force, including the aerial bombardment of rebels and their villages. More importantly, repression of uprisings, as we will see by examining the 1922 Bondelswarts uprising in the South West African mandate and the 1925 rebellion in the Syrian mandate, were sanctioned under modern international law. For those subjected to foreign rule, the limitations imposed by modern international law on sovereignty were mostly irrelevant. Sovereignty itself remained a most cherished and distant aspiration for many semi-peripheral peoples.

Semi-peripheral politicians and activists who gathered in Paris hoped that the shift from a 'familiy of nations' to an international community governed by law and administered by a permanent international organization would change the fate of the non-Western world. Hopes dissipated rapidly. Not only because of the disappointment experienced in Paris, after most semi-peripheral delegations were not listened to, after the aspirations for self-determination remained unanswered; but because the international community under modern international law turned out to be no more inclusive than classical international law's family of civilized nations. If during the nineteenth century there was room to appropriate and internalize the standard of civilization, this strategy reached its limits by the end of the century. At the beginning of the twentieth century, from the point of view of core states, the standard appeared not only doctrinally strong, but also actively invoked to limit the scope of self-determination, justifying the continuity of Western colonialism as well as the League's mandates system. Rather than recognizing independence to the former colonies of the powers defeated in the Great War, the League transferred these territories as mandates.

The interwar reconstruction of the international legal order did not put an end to the conflict of interests between great powers at the centre and small polities at the peripheries of the world system. Modern international law, no different than classical international law, became an instrument to express singular interests in the general language of law. And modern international law offered again a terrain on which divergent interests clashed. Jurists from the core, as we have seen, believed that an international community formed by interdependent states required a stronger international law limiting state sovereignty. They also believed that the international community and modern international law was

[14] Article 22, Covenant of the League of Nations.

restricted to the 'civilized West'. Semi-peripheral lawyers, on the other hand, also believed that the reconstruction of international law should create a stronger legal order, but they thought that a stronger legal order should primarily protect the rights of smaller states. They also believed that the modern reconstruction of international law should give rise to a more inclusive international community.

Similar to the nineteenth century, semi-peripheral elites of the turn of the century and the interwar years understood that international law could provide avenues to resist power and intrusions from core states. As before, some members of the elites in the semi-periphery became international lawyers. They pursued doctoral studies in Europe and the United States, became members of professional organizations, published books and wrote in the discipline's main journals. Similar to their classical predecessors, modern semi-peripherals appropriated international legal thought and then reinterpreted rules and doctrines to protect the autonomy and inclusion of semi-peripheral polities. However, while professional interventions of classical semi-peripherals remained mostly within the limits of the discipline of international law (as we have seen, changing legal thought in order to change international rules), modern jurists tried to change international law rules directly. They not only produced academic writing to influence the discourse of international law, but also argued for semi-peripheral autonomy and equality, based on their own doctrines and legal interpretations, directly in front of the League of Nations, that is, using the new channels opened by the establishment of a permanent international organization.

Taking part in professional debates and academic writing, semi-peripherals participated in the articulation of the modern discourse of international law. There was a semi-peripheral version of the critique of sovereignty that in the hands of Japanese scholar Sakutaro Tachi (1874–1943) for example, and in contrast to Politis' writings we examined before, demanded the limitation of the extraterritorial powers of states, while preserving states' domestic powers and independence from foreign intervention.[15] Semi-peripherals challenged also classical international law's universality. Not only Latin Americans, as we will see, proposed the

[15] S. Tachi, *La souveraineté et l'indépendance de l'état et les questions intérieures en droit international* (Paris: Les Éditions internationals, 1930). Tachi argues that the state is sovereign only in the sense that it holds a supreme power to command within the domestic domain, even in matters concerning international law. The sovereignty of states, outside the territory, is therefore limited by the fact of the existence of other states: pp. 11–12, 111 and *passim*.

existence of an American international law based on a distinctively continental juridical consciousness. Other semi-peripherals like the Egyptian jurist Abdel-Razzak al-Sanhuri (1895–1971), mainly known as a private law scholar and drafter of the Egyptian Civil Code, proposed the foundation of an Oriental League of Nations based not on sovereign consent of its potential members, but on the doctrine of necessity.[16]

However, the most interesting dimension of semi-peripheral use and practice of international law during the first decades of the twentieth century was not the appropriation of international legal thought, but the ways in which this appropriation was channelled towards producing international legal arguments to defend concrete rules and doctrines securing semi-peripheral interests, efforts that in turn transformed international legal thought and the basic elements of modern international law. These efforts adopted various forms. Peoples fighting to acquire sovereignty, for instance, drafted petitions, documents and memoranda. This chapter examines a number of these petitions by a wide range of groups like Armenian, Azerbaijani, Egyptian, Ethiopian, Indian, Korean and Syrian nationalist parties as well as the pan-African movement. It also looks briefly into another class of documents, namely memoranda produced by states which had been formally recognized as sovereign, like China, the Ottoman Empire and Persia, but that continued, at the time of the Peace Conference, to be treated unequally and thus sought to abrogate unequal treaties.

Petitioning for self-government: from Paris to Geneva, from civilization to statehood

In 1919, nationalist parties of a number of peoples fighting for political independence not only elected representatives to attend the Paris Peace Conference, they also drafted documents exposing and justifying their claims. Without direct access to the negotiations, nationalist activists were conscious of the importance of publishing the pamphlets, memoranda and manifestos they had written for the conference. These publications became the main channel for their demands to be heard, for only a few non-Western delegations seeking political independence were admitted to the Peace Conference. However, even delegations admitted to the negotiations published their memoranda. Representing a nation

[16] A. al-Sanhuri, *Le califat, son évolution vers une société des nations orientales* (Paris: P. Geuthner, 1926).

that had been under alien Ottoman, Russian and Persian rule and had not fallen under direct Western occupation, the Armenian delegates Boghos Nubar Pasha (1851–1930) and Avetis Aharonian (1866–1948), respectively a rich and cultivated member of the diaspora and a tough poet from the Caucasus, for example, were admitted to the negotiations.[17] Armenian memoranda were published and authenticated by the conference.[18] Ottomans, although as a losing power being expected to simply accept the terms of the peace settlement rather than participate in the negotiations, published a number of memoranda.[19] Other semi-peripheral states that had been recognized as members, though not full members of the international community, and had for example participated in the Hague Conferences, were also invited to Paris. Enjoying formal recognition, they did not struggle for independence but equality. Brazil, for instance, demanded equal rights for small states.[20] And both Persia and China attempted to abrogate unequal treaties. China also tried to recover the Shandong province, under Japanese occupation.[21]

Among those delegations that were neither allowed to travel to Paris, nor allowed to participate in the negotiations, the Wafd Party, the nationalist liberal party of Egypt, for example, drafted in 1919 a memorandum to be presented at the Paris Peace Conference entitled 'The Egyptian National Claims'.[22] Signed by Saad Zaghloul and other members of the delegation

17 MacMillan, *Paris 1919*, p. 377.

18 See *A catalogue of Paris Peace Conference delegation propaganda*, p. 7 and A. Aharonian and B. Nubar, *The Armenian question before the Peace Conference* (New York: Press Bureau, the Armenian National Union of America, 1919).

19 C. Aydin, *The politics of anti-Westernism in Asia: visions of world order in pan-Islamic and pan-Asian thought* (New York: Columbia University Press, 2007); Conférence intergouvernementale, *Observations présentées par la délégation Ottomane à la Conférence de la Paix* (Versailles, 1920).

20 M. Streeter, *Epitácio Pessôa, Brazil the makers of the modern world, the peace conferences of 1919–23 and their aftermath* (London: Haus Publishing, 2010).

21 M. ol-Memalek, *Claims of Persia before the Conference of the Preliminaries of Peace at Paris*, (Paris Peace Conference, 1919); Chinese delegation to the Peace Conference, *The claim of China: submitting for abrogation by the Peace conference the treaties and notes made and exchanged by and between China and Japan on May 25, 1915* (Paris: Impr. de Vaugirard, 1919); Chinese delegation to the Peace Conference, *Questions for readjustment submitted by China to the Peace conference* (Paris: Impr. de Vaugirard, 1919); Chinese National Welfare Society in America, *The Shantung question, a statement of China's claim together with important documents submitted to the Peace conference in Paris* (San Francisco: Chinese National Welfare Society in America, 1919).

22 Paris Peace Conference, Egyptian Delegation, *The Egyptian national claims: a memorandum presented to the Peace Conference by the Egyptian delegation charged with the defence of Egyptian independence* (Paris: Imprimerie artistique Lux, 1919).

the Wafd had appointed to attend the peace negotiations, the memorandum defended Egypt's claim to self-determination. Similar documents were drafted by other nationalist organizations that sent delegates to Paris, such as delegations from Azerbaijan, India's Home Rule League and the Korean 'March First Movement', as well as by organizations belonging to the pan-African movement, as mentioned above, the NAACP and UNIA. How did these documents frame the claim for self-determination?

'We have a civilization' (rather than: 'we have met the standard of civilization')

In 1919, semi-peripheral lawyers and activists grafted the principle of self-determination into nineteenth-century classical international law. Classical international law had the standard of civilization as the central doctrine determining membership in the international community. Like their predecessors, that is, like the first generation of semi-peripheral international lawyers who internalized the standard of civilization, Egyptian, Indian and Korean as well as pan-African activists, supported the demand for sovereignty, showing that their peoples were civilized. The Korean petition to the Peace Conference, signed by the nationalist leader John Kiusic S. Kimm (Kim Kyu-shik, 1881–1950) and sent to Clemenceau, for example, begins with the following sentence: 'The Korean people forms today a homogeneous nation, having their own civilisation and culture, and having constituted one of the historical states in the Far East for more than four thousand and two hundred years. During those forty two centuries Korea has always enjoyed national independence.'[23]

An accompanying mémoire adds that the Korean people has a national language and civilization that was more developed than that of Japan before it left barbarism.[24] We can see similar statements by other semi-peripherals affirming the civilized nature of their polities.[25] These documents, however, did not exactly articulate the idea of civilization in the way nineteenth-century semi-peripheral international lawyers internalized the standard. If nineteenth-century lawyers looked for the markers of civilization to argue that these had been internalized and that in

23 Conférence de la paix, *Pétition présentée par la délégation Coréenne* (Paris, 1919), p. 1.

24 *Ibid.*

25 E.g. Egyptian Delegation, *The Egyptian national claims*, p. 4 and *Observations délégation Ottomane*.

consequence equality in the interaction with Western states should follow, demanding for instance the revision of unequal treaties, their modern successors simply asserted 'having civilization', or invoked ancient civilizational roots in order to argue in favour of the recognition of sovereignty.

The pamphlet entitled 'Self-determination for India', published by the India Home Rule League of America offers a good example. The drafter, Lala Lajpat Rai (1865–1928), a lawyer and renowned figure in the Indian independence movement, welcomed the formation of a League of Nations for maintaining peace and fostering the development of different nationalities based on the principle of self-determination.[26] The peoples of India – Lala Lajpat Rai declared – constitute nationalities, for they share: 'the same blood, the same language, the same civilisation, literature, customs, and traditions'. They are thus entitled to self-determination.[27] Lajpat Rai, like classical international lawyers, shows India as a civilized people. But, unlike the classical predecessors, Lajpat Rai neither constructs a Western standard to be internalized: 'India is not an infant nation, not a primitive people, but the eldest brother in the family of man, noted for her philosophy and for being the home of religions that console half of mankind'; nor, in typical nineteenth-century fashion, does he demonstrate that the standard has been met by distinguishing between a civilized and an uncivilized people, and by pointing out at the lower civilization of a foreign or domestic barbarian. Instead, Lajpat Rai considers also the demands of other non-Western peoples as legitimate. Lajpat Rai argues in favour of self-determination and an international regional regime analogous to the Monroe doctrine to obtain protection from European imperialism, a legal shelter from colonialism, not just for India, but also for Africa as well as Asia.[28]

This strategy was certainly fraught with problems. The standard of civilization, as the outcome of the Peace Conference showed, continued to be defined by Western powers and in Western terms. As the twentieth century progressed, it was thus sensible for semi-peripherals to use less frequently the idea of civilization. What is more, they began to invert the

[26] India Home Rule League of America, *Self-determination for India* (New York: India Home Rule League of America, Paris Peace Conference, 1919), p. 5. In 1917, Lajpat Rai established the 'India Home Rule League of America' in New York to support the Home Rule movement back home in India and started a monthly journal, *Young India*. Stepping up his campaign for mobilizing the support of the progressive opinion in the United States and Britain, Lajpat Rai wrote this pamphlet.

[27] *Ibid.*, p. 8. [28] *Ibid.*, p. 7.

order of the peoples classically allocated along the civilized/uncivilized divide. As we will see, semi-peripherals argued that imperialistic violence and the denial of justice and equality made Western powers uncivilized. The problem of civilization was especially burdensome to those who could not invoke ancient roots, for those who in European eyes had no ancient civilization. This problem was particularly challenging for the pan-African movement.

The 'Address to the Nations of the World' adopted by the first Pan-African Conference held in London in 1900, shows how intricate the balancing act was for black activists trying both to meet classical international law's standard of civilization and to fulfil aspirations for self-government. The address, on the one hand, concedes that 'the darker races are today the least advanced in culture according to European standards'.[29] On the other hand, it notes that 'this has not always been the case in the past'. If there was in the past a disparity of civilizations, the address famously observes that the problem of the new century 'is the problem of the colour-line, the question as to how far differences of race . . . will hereafter be made the basis of denying to over half of the world the right of sharing . . . the opportunities and privileges of modern civilisation'. The answer is clear. The modern world is changing, peoples of different races are 'being brought so near together' that contact is inevitable. If opportunities for 'education and self-development' are given to dark men – the address affirms – beneficial effects and human progress will be felt by the world.[30]

Yet again, the address does not challenge but calls for an enlightened European colonialism: 'Let the German Empire and the French Republic . . . remember that the true worth of colonies lies in their prosperity and progress, and that justice, impartial alike to black and white, is the first element of prosperity.' It also demands 'rights of responsible government' within the British order, rather than the end of British rule. However, if the future of black people is marred with exploitation because of prejudice and injustice, the address on the other hand cautions about fatal results: 'the high ideals of justice, freedom and culture', which years of 'Christian civilisation have held before Europe', will be threatened. With this admonition, the address concludes by demanding that the Congo

29 'Address to the nations of the world' in J. Ayodele Langley (ed.), *Ideologies of liberation in Black Africa, 1856–1970: documents on modern African political thought from colonial times to the present* (London: R. Collings, 1979), pp. 738–40.

30 *Ibid.*

Free State 'become a great central Negro State of the world'. Moreover, it demands the great powers to respect the 'integrity and independence of the first Negro States of Abyssinia, Liberia, Haiti . . . '[31]

The pan-African movement's ambivalent attitude towards African independence, European colonialism and the Western civilizing mission might be explained, as Mekondjo Kaapanda suggests, through Du Bois' concept of 'double consciousness'; that is, the difficulty that the pan-African movement confronted when constructing a vision for African statehood through the lenses of the Western conqueror, specifically, in our case, through European international law.[32] Pan-African petitions and documents by other semi-peripherals show how non-Western lawyers and activists worked through the problem of 'double consciousness' producing a variety of strategies to achieve their goals. Depending on questions of strategy, the content of petitions and other documents changed in relation to audience and possibilities of success. Independently of the question of ambivalence regarding African sovereignty, it would have been impractical for the pan-African 'Address to the Nations' of 1900 to circumvent the standard of civilization: in 1900, before unequal treaties in the semi-periphery were abolished (with the sole exception of Japan that managed to revise treaty relations with Britain only a few years before, in 1894). Before the declarations on self-determination by Wilson and Lenin were uttered. Before the Great War and before the Bolshevik revolution, the future of a post-war order recognizing self-determination was unthinkable. The standard of civilization was a central part of international law and political discourse. In fact, only later did the Great War and its aftermath massively transform the attitudes of non-Western elites towards the West.[33]

For example, during the war Du Bois wrote about European imperialism as one of its causes. After the war and in preparation for the Peace Conference, Du Bois wrote in 1918 to Wilson and Clemenceau laying out his vision for black peoples in Africa and the black diaspora. Unlike the 1900 pan-African declaration, these letters as well as other documents drafted ahead of Paris, reflected a much more ambiguous stance in relation to the standard of civilization and a stronger position regarding peoples' self-determination. In 1915, Du Bois published an article on the position of Africa in relation to the war. If European imperialism

[31] *Ibid.* [32] Kaapanda, 'Pan-African movement'.

[33] See e.g. M. Adas, 'Contested hegemony: the Great War and the Afro-Asian assault on the civilizing mission ideology', *Journal of World History*, 15 (2004), 31–63.

counted among the causes explaining the war, peace can only be secured by extending the 'principle of home rule' to 'groups, nations, and races'.[34] In the 1918 letter to Wilson, Du Bois simply takes Wilson's word on self-determination: 'The ideals of the peace Congress have to do with the rights of distinctive peoples'.[35] Du Bois points out to Wilson that recognizing the principle of the consent of the governed to peoples around the world without resolving the question of the black people in America, would not only be incoherent, but also expose America to embarrassment:

> It would be unworthy of the noblest traditions of our country and the grand ideals which Your Excellency has so often expressed, for men to consider for an instant, that the question could embarrass the activity of the American Delegates . . . The world is wondering to-day how America is going to avoid at least an indictment of inconsistency and perhaps a suspicion of insincerity . . . The international peace Congress that is to decide whether or not peoples shall have the right to dispose of themselves will find in its midst delegates from a nation which champions the principles of the 'consent of the governed' . . . that nation . . . includes in itself more than twelve million souls whose consent to be governed is never asked.[36]

In the letter to Clemenceau, Du Bois invites the French statesman to consider during the negotiations 'the establishing of a great Independent State in Africa, to be settled and governed by Negroes'. In this letter, it is not just the German colonies in Africa that should be given to the black race, but also an 'Independent Negro Central African State', including the Belgian Congo, Uganda, French Equatorial Africa and the Portuguese Angola and Mozambique.[37]

Once in Paris, in spite of counting on a long list of contacts, Du Bois failed to secure admission to the peace negotiations and instead, with the help of Blaise Diagne, a French deputy from Senegal, the organization of a Pan-African Congress was authorized by the allied powers only with reluctance and under strict conditions not to steer the demand for self-government.[38] Thus, the memorandum written ahead of the congress as well as the resolution of the Pan-African Congress passed in Paris reverts to more modest demands and to the distinction between civilized and uncivilized negroes. If Du Bois had demanded self-determination before the war,

[34] W. E. B. Du Bois, 'The African roots of war', *Atlantic Monthly*, 115 (1915), 707–14.

[35] W. E. B. Du Bois, 'Letter from W. E. B. Du Bois to President Woodrow Wilson, ca. November 1918', *W. E. B. Du Bois Papers* (MS 312). Special Collections and University Archives, University of Massachusetts Amherst Libraries, p. 4.

[36] *Ibid.*, pp. 1–2.

[37] W. E. B. Du Bois, 'Letter from W. E. B. Du Bois to Premier of France (1918)', *Du Bois Papers*.

[38] Grant, *Negro with a hat*, p. 179 and MacMillan, *Paris 1919*, pp. 104–5.

the memorandum demands 'political rights for the civilised'.[39] And the 1919 Resolution of the Pan-African congress, quoted before, demanded that 'for strengthening the forces of civilisation', immediate steps be taken to 'develop' black peoples. These steps included that allied powers establish a 'code of laws for the international protection of the natives of Africa', and that the League establish a Permanent Bureau in charge of overseeing the welfare of natives.[40]

Change of circumstances: a new international order after the Great War

The shifting back and forth, including and excluding self-determination, in the petitions of the pan-African movement illustrates the disadvantages of arguments based on civilization and the need to find alternative routes to justify self-government. Drafters of some of the petitions sent to Paris did not spend much ink on showing that their polities had met the standard of civilization, rather they quickly assumed that the preconditions of sovereignty had been satisfied. They emphasized the high ideals on the basis of which the allied powers had fought and won the Great War. Then, they noticed the dissonance between these high ideals and the denial of sovereignty for those peoples who had been assured or implicitly promised self-government because of having joined the allied powers in the war effort and its sacrifices.

The memorandum prepared by the Armenian delegation to the Peace Conference, for example, affirmed that after the Great War and centuries of oppression, the Armenian Nation 'finds itself torn up and bleeding', but ready and determined to 'attain the realization of its national ideal through the victory of the Associated Powers, which have inscribed on their banners the principles of Right, Justice and of the rights of peoples to dispose their own destiny'.[41]

The high ideals for which the war had been fought would be subverted if, after the war, allied forces refused independence to peoples living under colonial rule. The abovementioned 1922 petition by Marcus Garvey's UNIA, for example, demanded 'racial political liberty' for the black race, because of the 'splendid service' it had delivered to the allied forces during the First World War. The black race deserves a government of its

[39] W. E. B. Du Bois, 'Memorandum to M. Diagne and others on a Pan-African Congress to be held in Paris in February, 1919', *Crisis*, 17 (1919), 224–5, 224.

[40] 'Resolutions passed at the 1919 Pan-African Congress', *Marcus Garvey papers*, p. 5.

[41] Aharonian and Nubar, *The Armenian question*, p. 3.

own, the petition argues, recalling the promises given during the Great War: 'all peoples who contributed to the war would be considered at its conclusion'.[42] Similarly, the Armenian petition, where the human costs of the war had been enormous, invoked war sacrifices as a basis for a right to independence:

> Armenia has won her right to independence by her voluntary and spontaneous participation in the war on the three fronts of the Caucasus, of Syria and of France, and by the sacrifice of hundreds of thousands of men, women and children who fell victims for her fidelity to the Entete cause. On the fields of battle, through massacre and deportation, Armenia has proportionally paid in this war a heavier tribute to death than any other belligerent nation.[43]

But more important than any promise, semi-peripherals believed that the Great War itself changed the international order in general as well as the circumstances under which pre-war international arrangements had been established, rendering the old order obsolete. On grounds that the war had introduced new international ideals, the 'Egyptian National Claims', the Memorandum signed by Saad Zaghloul (1858?–1927) and other nationalist leaders, for example, critiques the protectorate the English had established during the war. Saad Zaghloul was a lawyer who, with studies in Cairo and Paris, served as Minister of Education and leader of the opposition in the legislative assembly before the war. After the war, Zaghloul sought authorization from the British High Commissioner to travel to London in order to discuss Egypt's post-war status. After British refusal, Zaghloul organized a *wafd*, or delegation to attend the Peace Conference, which later became the nationalist Wafd Party. When the British authorities denied the delegation permission to travel to Paris, Egyptian ministers in the protectorate resigned, riots broke out in Cairo and Zaghloul was arrested and interned in Malta.[44]

The Claim of the *wafd*, in a nod to the standard of civilization, like most petitions drafted to be presented at Paris, recalls Egypt's 'glorious history' and 'moral and material conditions'. But then the 'National Claims' turns to other types of arguments. It explains that the Egyptian requests made during the war to the English 'to recognise the independence of Egypt in return for her engagement to take part in the war on the side of Great Britain' were ignored. Egyptians – the 'National Claims'

42 UNIA, 'Petition to the League'. 43 Aharonian and Nubar, *The Armenian question*, p. 4.
44 A. Goldschmidt, *Biographical dictionary of modern Egypt* (Boulder, CO: Lynne Rienner, 2000), p. 234.

observes – were moreover shocked when Britain declared Egypt a protectorate under the excuse of the special circumstances brought by the war. Nevertheless, Egyptians felt reassured, for they knew that the allied forces were 'only fighting for the triumph of Right and the defence of oppressed nations'. When the United States got involved in the war, 'no one in Egypt' doubted American involvement responded to one sole aim: 'liberating the world'.[45]

Highlighting the values and ideals for which the war was fought allowed the drafters of the Egyptian memorandum to consider the standard of civilization as an anachronistic doctrine. 'The right to life and to liberty' can no longer be 'confined to certain continents or to certain latitudes'.[46] Egyptians – the memorandum warns – refuse to serve the 'appetites of Imperialists'. In a direct attack against the standard, the memorandum affirms that the new order 'cannot continue to distinguish between nations, some to be made free and others to be doomed to slavery, only because the Western mind has been pleased for long centuries to trace limits, both ethnic and geographic'. Doing so would be in 'absolute contradiction to the new spirit which the result of the war has happily consecrated'.[47] The 'National Claims' insists: 'all particular considerations of belief, of special customs, of mentality' should not be considered when determining the rights and privileges governing the relations between nations.[48] Because in fact, the memorandum concludes: 'each country has its own civilisation'.[49]

Change of circumstances, in its technical legal meaning was also present in some of the semi-peripheral petitions drafted for the Peace Conference. Change of circumstances, namely a doctrine allowing a treaty to become invalid after entering into force, because of a fundamental modification of the conditions under which the treaty had been negotiated and concluded, was a distinctively modern doctrine. Classical international legal thought, emphasizing absolute sovereignty, based the binding force of treaties on state consent. More specifically, on the principle of *pacta sunt servanda*, that recognizes consent as the main source of obligation. Change

[45] Egyptian Delegation, *The Egyptian national claims*, p. 3. [46] *Ibid.* [47] *Ibid.*, p. 4.

[48] Moreover, a challenge to the standard allowed the Egyptian drafters to turn the conventional argument upside down: 'We would not insult the Western peoples by supposing that because the greater part of the Egyptians practice a religion different to theirs, because our everyday life and our traditions are inspired by different ideas, they consider us from the point of view of political rights in an unfavourable light.' *Ibid.*, p. 6.

[49] *Ibid.*, p. 6. The memorandum turns then to support the claim to independence recounting Egypt's economic advances, cultural status ('moral state') and administrative organization. Unless Wilson's program is ignored, the memorandum argues that Egypt should enjoy full independence: *ibid*, pp. 6–10.

of circumstances, the principle of *rebus sic stantibus*, on the other hand, was among the doctrines modern legal scholars developed to attenuate the absolute character of classical sovereignty. In 1919, when semi-peripheral petitions began to make use of this doctrine, it was invoked by some peoples fighting for self-determination but more frequently by peoples whose formal sovereignty was recognized but who were subjected to inequality. Among the former, the Korean petition of 1919, for example, regarded the Japanese treaty of annexation of 1910, null and void, or abrogated by the Peace Conference: 'in virtue of the fundamental rules of international law and the *new justice* which is to redress the wrongs of nations'.[50] Among the latter, the claims brought to the peace negotiations by the Chinese, Ottoman and Persian delegations relied on the doctrine of change of circumstances to justify the abrogation of treaties concluded with core states before the war.[51]

The 'Claims of Persia', for example, requested the Peace Conference that treaties 'in contravention of Persia's independence be recognized null and void and that guarantees be given her to the future'.[52] Like other memoranda drafted in 1919, this document simply assumes the right of independence and integrity of Iran.[53] Then, it exposes violations of Iran's political, economic and juridical independence.[54] And it concludes with a call to put an end to these violations in the name of a 'new Era of Justice and Equality which is drawing in every country and which adumbrates the advent of the reign of Humanity and Justice and the aegis of the League of Nations . . . '[55] Also, Chinese delegates at the Paris Conference and then during the interwar years at the League, and Turkish delegates at the

50 Conférence de la paix, *Pétition délégation Coréenne*, p. 6 (emphasis in the original).

51 Chinese delegation, *The claim of China*; Chinese delegation, *Questions for readjustment*; Memalek, *Claims of Persia*; Conférence intergouvernementale, *Observations délégation Ottomane*.

52 Memalek, *Claims of Persia*, p. 1.

53 Rather than making use of the argument about meeting the standard, the Iranian claim advances two historical arguments. One is based on the historical roots of Persian civilization: 'the importance of Persia is a matter of universal knowledge, and the glorious part she has played during the past ages and centuries is not denied'. The claim notes that those who know about 'Eastern matters' recognize 'Persians to be an intelligent race, having always produced great scholars and thinkers'. The other argument is based on the treaties concluded with other powers recognizing Persian independence: *ibid.*

54 These violations, according to the Iranian claim, include, for example: consular jurisdiction for foreign residents; the British and Russian spheres of influence imposed on Iran by the Anglo-Russian treaty of 1907; and the restriction, imposed in the same treaty, on Iran's right to give concessions to other companies. *Ibid.*, pp. 3–5.

55 *Ibid.*, p. 5.

Lausanne Conference of 1922–3, invoked the *rebus sic stantibus* doctrine. In Lausanne, as Umut Özsu has shown, the Turkish delegation not only advanced the argument it had repeatedly claimed in order to abrogate capitulations, namely, it argued that as unilateral concessions, Turkey had the right to revoke capitulations at will; but also, Turkish diplomats argued that even if capitulations were to be understood as treaties, the circumstances under which they had been agreed had fundamentally changed after the war, rendering capitulatory privileges void.[56] In Lausanne the Turkish delegation succeeded in negotiating a peace treaty abrogating capitulatory privileges. China, on the other hand, failed in Paris and during the interwar years to renegotiate unequal treaties with core powers.

As we have seen in the second part of the book, treaties conferring a series of privileges, including consular jurisdiction, were concluded during the nineteenth century between Western states and China. Chinese diplomats, as we have seen, tried to renegotiate these treaties based on the internalization of the standard of civilization. Meanwhile, western international law scholars – as Hungdah Chiu has noted – paid no special attention to these treaties.[57] The examination of these treaties was mostly carried out by a new generation of Chinese international lawyers and diplomats who studied in Europe and the United States during the first decade of the twentieth century, like Wellington Koo, the most outspoken Chinese delegate in Paris who at Columbia University, under supervision of John Bassett Moore, wrote his doctoral dissertation on extraterritorial privileges.[58] Moreover, the term 'unequal treaties' as an expression used to describe and criticize treaties granting extraterritorial privileges to Western states and justify their abrogation, was only adopted during the 1920s by Chinese lawyers and politicians.[59] And *rebus sic stantibus* was one

56 U. Özsu, 'Ottoman Empire' in Fassbender and Peters, *Oxford Handbook*, pp. 429–48, 444–5.

57 *Ibid.*, p. 246.

58 W. Koo, *The status of aliens in China* (New York: Columbia University, 1912). In addition to Koo and Jin Zhu who studied at Columbia, among other Chinese students pursuing doctoral studies and focusing on unequal treaties, Min-chien Tyau studied at the University of London and Chung Sing Chan in Paris. See J. Zhu, *The tariff problem in China* (New York: Columbia University, 1916); M. Tyau, *The legal obligations arising out of treaty relations between China and other states* (Shanghai: Commercial Press, 1917); C. S. Chan, *Les concessions en Chine* (Paris: Les presses universitaires de France, 1925).

59 The discourse of 'unequal treaties', rather than relying on Western authors, developed in China out of its own experience with inequality: H. Chiu, 'Comparison of the nationalist and communist Chinese views of unequal treaties' in J. A. Cohen (ed.), *China's practice of international law: some case studies* (Cambridge: Harvard University Press, 1972),

of the specific arguments used by Chinese diplomats in Paris and then in Geneva in order to renegotiate unequal treaties.

In preparation for Paris, Chinese delegates drafted memoranda supporting China's main objectives to be obtained at the Peace Conference: recovering the Shandong province from Japan; and revising treaties concluded with Western powers.[60] In 1919, Chinese delegates no longer based their arguments on having met the classical standard of civilization.[61] The restitution of Shandong was argued in modern terms. The agreements by which Germany obtained a lease over Shandong, as well as the transfer of the German lease to Japan, were regarded as void because they were extracted by coercion. Specifically, the 1915 secret treaty between China and Japan, signed when China was a neutral party, was deemed annulled because of the fundamental change of circumstances arising from China's entry into the war. Moreover, restitution of Shandong was considered the only just alternative because 'occupation, does not give Japan title over territory and property'.[62]

A second memorandum dealing in general with the 'adjustment' of treaties concluded with Western states stated clearly that adjustment meant abrogation of treaty privileges.[63] In 1919, however, the discourse of 'unequal treaties' and the legal arguments against these treaties were still under development. Legal arguments continued to depend on the classical idea about the incompatibility between sovereignty and consular jurisdiction and only secondarily on the change of circumstances

p. 248; Kroll, *Normgenese durch Re-Interpretation*, p. 180. The term itself, according to Dong Wang, was first used by Sun Yat-sen, founder of the Chinese Nationalist Party (*Koumintang*), then by Mao and then adopted by both the Nationalist and communist parties: Wang, *China's unequal treaties*, p. 64.

60 'Memorandum, the claim of China for the direct restitution to herself of the leased territory of Kiaochow, the Tsingtao-China Railway and other German rights in the respect of Shantung Province' in *Chinese Social and Political Science Review*, 5 (1920), 15–115 and 'Chinese delegation, questions for adjustment, submitted by China to the Peace Conference' in *Chinese Social and Political Science Review*, 5 (1920), 116–61.

61 Similar to the petitions examined above in which 'having civilization' justified the claim to self-determination, the Chinese memorandum argued that the territories under Japanese occupation should be restituted to China, since its inhabitants are part of the Chinese race, speak and write the same language, have the same Confucian religion and meet every requirement of the principle of nationality. 'Shantung is the cradle of Chinese civilisation . . . the Holy Land for Chinese people': 'The claim of China', 26.

62 *Ibid.*, 25, 26, 29.

63 The memorandum demanded the renunciation of the spheres of influence, withdrawal of foreign troops, abolition of consular jurisdiction, relinquishment of leased territories, return of all foreign concessions to China: 'Questions for adjustment', 116.

brought by the new post-war international order.[64] As a doctrine supporting the abrogation of unequal treaties in China, *rebus sic stantibus* was first studied by Chinese international lawyers and then expressly invoked by Chinese diplomats in 1925, at the Sixth Assembly of the League of Nations. At the beginning of the twentieth century, a considerable number of Chinese students pursued doctoral studies in the West and focused on unequal treaties. Having studied at the University of London, Min-chien Tyau (1888–?), for example, argued for the revision of the obligations in the treaties concluded between China and Western powers, which 'bear inequitably upon China'. Tyau argued that 'having been contracted sixty or seventy years ago' these treaties 'are antiquated, and the doctrine of *rebus sic stantibus* may with good cause be appealed to. In short, the relations between China and other states need to be readjusted in harmony with its acknowledged status, the status of member in the family of nations'.[65] Chung Sing Chan, who studied in Paris, believed that concessions established in unequal treaties would disappear, since they emerged from a de facto situation, rather than from law, their existence depended on de facto circumstances that will change.[66]

It was at the Sixth Assembly of the League of Nations of 1925 that Chinese diplomats used uniquely modern legal arguments in order to demand the revision of unequal treaties. This time, substituting unequal treaties with treaties recognizing sovereign equality was not demanded in order to respect Chinese sovereignty, but demanded in order to secure the objectives for which the League was founded, in order to secure international peace and development. Change of circumstances was simply the way to achieve these objectives by justifying the abrogation of international obligations that were no longer compatible with the post-war order.[67] The Chinese delegate to the Assembly Chao-Hsin Chu maintained

64 For example, the memorandum speaks about a general readjustment in the international regime governing the relations between China and foreign governments, in order to recognize the new status that China achieved after the foundation of the Republic and in accordance to the principle of justice on which the post-war order should be based. At the same time the memorandum declares that 'it is hardly necessary to dwell on the incompatibility of consular jurisdiction with the exercise of the right of territorial sovereignty': 'Questions for adjustment', 134.

65 Tyau, *The legal obligations*, p. 3; note that in 1917, the expression 'unequal treaty' is not yet used by Tyau.

66 Chan, *Les concessions*, p. 132.

67 'It has been generally admitted that the treaties now in force between China and other Powers which were entered into in the old days are regarded as having become inapplicable and as not being in harmony with international conditions in respect of China's position in the family of nations': C. Chu, *Revision of unequal treaties. China appeals*

that unequal treaties 'negotiated in circumstances which hardly permitted the formulation, by full and free discussion, of principles which should permanently regulate normal intercourse between China and the foreign Powers', have been allowed to remain in force notwithstanding the privileges they have conferred on Western states are no longer warranted by current circumstances.[68] The end of these privileges, in particular restrictions on tariff autonomy, would finally put China into the path of economic progress.[69]

Chu proposes an 'amicable readjustment' bringing these treaties in line with modern international law, equity and present conditions in China, which would put an end to frictions and misunderstandings between foreign powers and China. Additionally, Chu asked the League to apply Article 19 of the Covenant, which allows the Assembly to advise the reconsideration of treaties, which have become inapplicable and international conditions which might endanger peace. 'Preventing war is to change inequality into equality' – Chu concludes.[70] Another world war passed before unequal treaties were renegotiated; although a treaty under equality with the Soviet Union was signed in 1924, the final abrogation of unequal treaties happened only during the Second World War.[71]

Destabilizing the civilized/uncivilized divide

The transformations of the international order that the First World War brought about, as we have seen, were invoked to justify the demand for

to the League of Nations. Official text of the speeches of Mr Chao-Hsin Chu, and press comments thereon (London: London Caledonian Press, 1926), p. 2.

68 *Ibid.*

69 The imposition of a maximum tariff of 5% not only for common goods but also for luxury products like fine cigars and champagne, strain public finances. Without treaty privileges 'foreign trade and commerce will be more rapidly and greatly developed to mutual advantage': *ibid.*, p. 4.

70 *Ibid.*, p. 3. LoN Article 19: 'The Assembly may from time to time advise the reconsideration by Members of the League of treaties which have become inapplicable and the consideration of international conditions whose continuance might endanger the peace of the world.'

71 Although Bolsheviks' promises to establish relations with China under equality and the conclusion of the Sino-Soviet treaty of 1924, Soviet diplomats, as Bruce Elleman has argued, resorted to secret diplomacy to maintain the unequal terms of the treaties concluded with Tsarist Russia: B. Elleman, *Wilson and China: a revised history of the Shandong question* (Armonk, NY: M. E. Sharpe, 2002), pp. 155–6. The end of formal inequality came only during the war when in 1942 the United States and Britain announced that they would renounce the privileges accorded in unequal treaties, concluding a treaty under equality in 1943: Chiu, 'Comparison', pp. 239–67, 239.

self-government. Semi-peripherals moreover highlighted the human disaster brought about by the war in order to directly challenge the validity of the standard of civilization. When the Great War irreparably damaged European prestige, when the monopoly over civilization had slipped away from the West, semi-peripherals were ready to critique Western powers' rule over the non-Western world and destabilize the standard of civilization. After the war, the concept of civilization and civilized nations was no longer self-evident.[72] Semi-peripheral petitions and memoranda drafted after 1919 began to question and blur the difference between the civilized and the uncivilized and its correspondence to Western and non-Western peoples. It was later on and in the context of European military violence waged against non-Western peoples fighting for independence that semi-peripherals explicitly discredited the standard by pointing out Western powers' savage behaviour.

In 1919, for example, in a draft version of the Egyptian National Claims, which, according to Erez Manela, circulated among diplomatic circles in Cairo, Zaghloul compared Egypt's ancient civilization with British rule in Egypt. British rule was 'at utter variance with justice, not to mention civilisation'.[73] Similarly, Lajpat Rai questioned the capacity of the British Empire to be India's trustee.[74] Moreover, the Egypt Association in Great Britain drafted a letter that circulated among diplomatic circles in London, denouncing British atrocities by including photographs of detained Egyptian notables.[75]

The Egyptian National Claims sent to Paris, on the other hand, destabilized the standard by contextualizing its application and showing that, rather than a legal doctrine, it was a cover for self-interest. In 1881 – the Memorandum explains – Colonel Ahmed Orabi initiated an insurrection against the pro-Western Khedive, Tewfik Pasha. The governments of France and Britain did not recognize the new government. Moreover, Britain bombarded Alexandria to protect foreign residents and punish Egyptians for the killing of Western residents during the Orabi uprising.

[72] L. Obregon, 'The civilised and the uncivilised' in B. Fassbender et al. (eds.), *The Oxford handbook of the history of international law* (Oxford University Press, 2012), pp. 919–39, 928.

[73] E. Manela, *Wilsonian moment: self-determination and the international origins of anticolonial nationalism* (Oxford University Press, 2007), p. 73.

[74] Lajpat Rai, among other arguments, affirmed that ancient Emperors of India were more liberal than modern Tzars and Kaisers: India Home Rule League, *Self-determination*, p. 10.

[75] 'Letter sent to certain leaders of public opinion about the Egyptian Question by H. Y. Awad, May 1st 1919', USNA, RG 256, 883.00/159.

The bombardment was followed by permanent occupation. Since occupation – the Claim notes – the British government had been changing the justifications for its rule over Egypt. 'First of all it was the restoration of the Khedive's authority, then the menace of the Dervishes, later the retaking of Sudan, and finally when all these pretexts were exhausted, it became the well-known fiction of civilising people insufficiently developed.'[76] Great Britain – the Memorandum concludes – is thus left with no other justification than its own 'desires and interests which are solely maintained by force'.[77]

This critique of the standard of civilization later became much stronger when semi-peripherals explicitly denounced the military tactics of Western forces combating non-Western insurgents fighting for independence as uncivilized. Syrian organizations, for example, protested the 'barbarian outrages' committed by the French in Damascus.[78] Moroccans condemned French bombardment of villages, the killing of women and children and the use of poison gas.[79] Similarly, Koreans denounced not Western but Japanese forces for atrocities committed against civilians.[80]

Pointing to uncivilized behaviour to disgrace states repressing insurgents served to weaken colonial or mandatory powers' claim to superior civilization, and thus arguably weakened the very same basis on which the mandates, colonies or protectorates rested. Some of these documents strove for an additional objective. Denouncing outrages supported the call for greater involvement by the international community. This strategy, as we will see with greater detail in the next chapter, was followed by semi-peripheral activists. For, example, members of the pan-African movement denouncing the military repression by South African forces against the Bondelswarts in the South West African mandate, called for involvement of the League's Assembly and PMC. Petitions from Syrian organizations condemning French atrocities in the Syrian mandate requested the PMC to appoint a special mission of enquiry. During the war of the Rif, rebels

[76] Egyptian Delegation, *The Egyptian national claims*, p. 13. [77] *Ibid.*

[78] 'Protest der Syrer Berlin, Heftiger Protest gegen die barbarischen Schandtaten der Franzosen in Syrien', *Die Welt des Islams*, 8 (1926), 133.

[79] 'To the International Court, by order of the Moroccan People'. In 1925 the petition was sent to the Permanent Court of International Justice. The court's registrar resent the petition to the League of Nations Secretary General. LoN Archive, 11/41616/12861.

[80] Among the many documents sent by the Korean nationalist movement, recounting Japanese outrages, repression and statements by prisoners, see 'Organizing Committee of the Independent Movement, The grievances of the Korean people and the bad government of Japan', 1920 LoN Archive 11/4515/302.

fighting Spanish and French forces in the Moroccan protectorate, called for the Red Cross to provide humanitarian protection to Riffians.

In May 1922, South African aeroplanes bombarded the Bondelswarts, a Khoekhoe people (called Hottentots by Europeans), part of the Nama group in South West Africa, present-day Namibia, killing rebels as well as women and children.[81] During the First World War, South Africa occupied the German colony of South West Africa. After the war, the League transferred the former German colony as a mandate to South Africa. Since the constitution of the mandate, relations between the mandatory power and local populations were fraught with tensions over a number of policies, including compulsory labour, wages, encroachment of new settlers and a special tax on dogs.[82] The causes and events leading to the military repression of May 1922 were highly disputed. Tensions seem to have been escalated when the Bondelswarts refused to pay the special dog tax after the mandatory power had increased it and when they refused to hand over Abraham Morris, a rebel leader who had re-entered the mandate without authorization and who was believed to be armed. What followed was not disputed. Gysbert Reitz Hofmeyr, the administrator of the mandate, organized an armed expedition to capture Morris, including 348 soldiers, four machine guns and two aeroplanes. When the Bondelswarts failed to comply with Hofmeyr's ultimatum, South African forces rounded up, attacked and quickly defeated the Bondelswarts rebels.[83]

South African military repression against the Bondelswarts made headlines only months before the Third Assembly of the League of Nations. The first page of the June edition of *The Negro World*, UNIA's newspaper edited by Marcus Garvey read: 'Christian Boers of South Africa use Airplanes to bomb Hottentots.'[84] In addition to publishing an editorial on the Bondelswarts affair, the UNIA sought to involve the League in order to condemn South Africa and to gather support for the request to transfer former German colonies in Africa to the black race.[85] The UNIA had sent a delegation to Geneva with the intention of attending the Assembly.

[81] PMC, *Minutes of the Third Session*, p. 123.

[82] See N. Crawford, *Argument and change in world politics: ethics, decolonization, and humanitarian intervention* (Cambridge University Press, 2012), p. 276.

[83] A. M. Davey, *The Bondelzwarts affair: a study of the repercussions, 1922–1959* (Pretoria: University of South Africa, 1961), pp. 5–8.

[84] M. Garvey, 'Christian Boers of South Africa use airplanes to bomb Hottentots', *The Negro World*, Saturday 17 June 1922, p. 1.

[85] 'Petition of the Universal Negro Improvement Association League to the League of Nations'.

Having failed to obtain admission to the League, the head of the UNIA delegation, G. O. Marke, sought contacts with diplomats friendly to the pan-African cause and thus willing to bring up the Bondelswarts affair before the League. Marke found an ally in Louis-Dantès Bellegarde, the Haitian representative to the Assembly. After studying law, working for a literary publication and serving as presidential adviser, in 1921 Bellegarde was appointed as Haitian representative to Paris and the League.[86] In Europe, Bellegarde participated in the pan-African movement. When the 1921 Second Pan-African Congress, meeting in London, Brussels and Paris, passed a resolution entitled 'Manifesto to the League of Nations', it was Bellegarde who, as the Haitian delegate to the League, was asked to present the resolution to the League of Nations.[87]

Bellegarde, in consequence, was well aware of his role as representative not just of Haiti, but of the aspiration of the black race and pan-Africanism. Bellegarde brought the Bondelswarts affair to the Assembly's attention, noting the 'modest position of the Republic of Haiti', which – Bellegarde continued – does not 'give me the right to take part on a discussion which touches on some of the most serious problems that require the world's attention. But I overcame my scruples' – Bellegarde declared, invoking the special position of smaller states as a guarantee of impartiality, a typically modern semi-peripheral argument: 'owing to its remoteness and because it has not been involved in any of the conflicts by which the League is or has been preoccupied, my country possesses . . . the detachment necessary to form a disinterested judgment . . . and therefore to express in this Assembly an absolutely impartial position'.[88]

Recounting some of the League's achievements, shortcomings and challenges, the speech delivered by Bellegarde seems to have been spirited and well received – judging from the interspersed laughter and applause noted in the proceedings.[89] Then, Bellegarde declared: 'Gentlemen, I had intended to conclude my speech with these remarks, but I must now draw

[86] P. Bellegarde-Smith, 'Dantes Bellegarde and pan-Africanism', *Phylon*, 12 (1981), 233–44, 234.

[87] J. Fauset, 'Impressions of the Second Pan-African Congress', *The Crisis*, 23 (1921), 12–18, 17.

[88] *Records of the Third Assembly*, p. 73.

[89] 'Has the League of Nations made any progress in the work of peace, for which it was created? . . . in two cases at least the League of Nations has preserved the peace of the world . . . In spite of its efforts, in spite of its services, the League of Nations, although respected by the majority of people, does not arise, or has ceased to arise, passionate enthusiasm among the peoples. In some cases indifference is carried to the point of skepticism and mockery.' *Ibid.*, p. 74.

your attention to an event of special gravity'.[90] Although the South African delegate had previously made reference to the Bondelswarts affair, Bellegarde warned: 'I do not think that your attention had been sufficiently drawn to the gravity of the facts.' Bellegarde offered an ironic description of the circumstances causing the affair: 'Taxation is the usual form in which civilisation makes its appearance to savages' – statement that again according to the proceedings was followed with laughter. The description of the affair itself, had a more sober tone: 'Although there was no act of rebellion and no attempts against life, an expedition was undertaken with all the materials of modern warfare – machine-guns, artillery, and aeroplanes.' Bellegarde then concluded with a rather dramatic statement: 'The natives who were practically unarmed were massacred . . . That women and children should have been massacred in the name of the League of Nations and under its protection is an abominable outrage which we cannot suffer.'[91] A 'loud and prolonged applause' followed, which might have contributed to the passing by the Assembly of a motion drafted by Bellegarde demanding South Africa to 'make every effort to relieve the suffering of the victims, particularly the women and the children . . . and ensure . . . the restoration of the economic life in the Bondelzwart district'. Bellegarde's motion also expressed satisfaction with the official statement by the South African delegate declaring that 'impartial inquiry will be made into all the facts of the Bondelzwarts Rebellion'. Finally, the motion expressed confidence that the 'Permanent Mandates Commission at its next session will consider this question and be able to report that satisfactory conditions have been established'.[92]

The Bondelswarts affair set up a precedent regarding supervision of mandate rule by the PMC when the mandatory power had been embroiled in the violent repression of native populations. Specifically, the Bondelswarts affair set a precedent in relation to how the PMC proceeded to fulfil its responsibility, receiving reports from the mandatory power, drafting a questionnaire to interrogate representatives of the mandatory power and writing a report to be submitted to the League's Council, but refusing to become itself a commission of inquiry and thus visiting mandate territories and refusing to hear directly parties other than the mandatory power, like the Anti-Slavery Society.[93]

After the Bondelswarts affair, it became common for semi-peripherals resisting foreign rule under mandate or protectorate, to point out

[90] *Ibid.*, p. 76. [91] *Ibid.* [92] *Records of the Third Assembly*, p. 143.
[93] PMC, *Minutes of the Third Session*, pp. 64–7.

Western brutality in order to secure international involvement. Petitions from Syrian organizations called the PMC to investigate French atrocities. During the war of the Rif, rebels fighting Spanish and French forces called the Red Cross to provide humanitarian protection to Riffians.

In June 1926, after the French bombardment of Damascus and after a special session of the Permanent Mandates Commission to discuss the Syrian uprising was held in Rome, the delegates of the Syro-Palestinian Congress in Geneva, Chekib Arslan (Shakib Arslan) (1869–1946) and Hsan el Djabri (Ihsan al-Jabiri) (1882–?), drafted a new report to the commission.[94] Following the Commission's advice, the report notes that Syrians have tried to reach an understanding with the French. But the French, the report complains, have ignored the commission's recommendations and have refused to consider Syrians' aspirations. These aspirations, which are based on 'the spirit of the Covenant of the League', have been shattered by French 'force and violence'.[95]

'Under the eyes of the League of Nations,' the French have inflicted 'a regime of terror' upon Syrians. Recalling the 'indescribable horrors' suffered by the Syrian people, the report requests the PMC to send a special mission of inquiry. The French horrors are evoked by reference to both word and image: 'The son of the Cadi of Damascus Alhalabi and many others were executed without any sentence and under a simple accusation . . . A photograph is attached . . . representing patriots decapitated and exposed on the street for seven days, after having suffered the most indescribable torture.'[96]

During the war of the Rif (1921–6), Riffian rebels resisted the Spanish protectorate by force, first fighting and defeating Spanish forces and then fighting and being defeated by both the Spanish and French military. In addition to waging guerrilla warfare, Rif rebels drafted documents which not only denounced an 'unjust war', but also accused Spain of 'barbarism'. In 1922, the leader of the Rif insurgent nation Abd-el-Krim, issued an address, notably entitled 'To the Civilised Nations':

> It is now high time that Europe, who, in this twentieth century claims that she stands to uphold the standard of civilisation and to uplift humanity, should carry this noble principle from the domain of precept into that of practice . . . The

[94] 'Communication datée de Genève le 7 juin 1926 et signée par L'Emir Chekib Arslan et Ihsan El Djarbi', C.P.M. 440.

[95] *Ibid.*, p. 1.

[96] *Ibid.*, p. 4: the report mentions that the photography is held in the Archives of the Secretariat. However, the picture is nowhere to be found.

Spaniards believe that they have been entrusted by Europe with the work of reformation and civilisation. But the Riffians ask: Does reformation consist in destruction of habitations by the use of forbidden weapons?[97]

Placing the Spaniards on the side of barbarism and the rebels on the side of humanity, the address affirms that the Rif 'is anxious to set up a system of government for herself'.[98] In fact, four years later, in 1926 Abd-el-Krim invokes the interest of humanity to request the intervention of the Red Cross to provide medical assistance.[99] Riffians never opposed 'European rights and reforms and civilisation'. What Riffians oppose is rule by Spaniards, who – Abd-el-Krim affirms – 'simply because they go by the name of Europeans, they claim to be civilised, while as a matter of fact, far from being reformers or protectors, they are only blind conquerors'.[100]

After the defeat of self-determination, statehood

The dissociation of the classical equation between civilization and sovereignty was an important step on the road towards the dissolution of the standard. The dissolution of the standard, in turn, was a crucial step towards the emergence of self-determination. But what was the meaning of Wilsonian self-determination? What was the scope of self-determination in 1919 when the standard of civilization had yet to be dissolved?

Self-determination, as conceived by Wilson, was neither the right peoples without sovereignty demanded in 1919, nor the continuation of the standard of civilization as the central doctrine on which inclusion in the international community depended. Erez Manela has convincingly argued that Wilson's position was much more complicated. There is 'little evidence', Manela suggests, that Wilson considered the impact of self-determination on colonial peoples. At the same time, Wilson 'did not exclude non-European peoples . . . as a matter of principle'.[101] Unlike Lenin's direct challenge to imperialism, Wilson's ideal combined both a principle of self-government, as originally affirmed in relation to the European situation requiring consent of the governed, as well as a belief

[97] Abd-el-Krim, 'To the civilised nations', 1922 LoN Archive, 11/23217/12861, p. 2.

[98] *Ibid.*, p. 3.

[99] D. Sasse, *Franzosen, Briten und Deutsche im Rifkrieg 1921–1926: Spekulanten und Sympathisanten, Deserteure und Hasardeure im Dienste Abdelkrims* (München: Oldenbourg, 2006), p. 82.

[100] Abd-el-Krim, 'To the civilised', pp. 2–3.

[101] Manela, *Wilsonian moment*, p. 25.

in the role Western states should have in assisting less developed peoples. Guiding peoples, in a gradual and orderly manner, through the steps towards modernization, was in fact the principle adopted by the League's mandate system. Combining these two facets, the Wilsonian principle was ambiguous enough to allow for the appropriation of self-determination by non-European peoples fighting for independence. Thus, if there was ambiguity and room for interpretation in Wilson's principle, it is not surprising that peoples claiming self-government in 1919, as we have seen, included a range of arguments that sometimes contradicted each other. The 1919 petitions included claims based on the deep historical roots of non-Western civilizations, claims based on war promises and on the subversion of the distinction between civilized and uncivilized, as well as claims based on the right to self-determination or political independence, pure and simple, that is, for example, 'because independence is a natural indefeasible right of nations'.[102]

However, there was a long road to travel for self-determination to become an autonomous right. In fact, self-determination has never become a right independent from other doctrinal considerations, such as the definition of a people, the prohibition of secession and the actual enjoyment of political independence.[103] During the interwar years, this last consideration was determining. Self-determination would lose much of its rhetorical or strategic appeal, if peoples which did not in fact enjoy independence could not effectively invoke self-determination against the power holding a colony, protectorate or mandate. And this is what actually happened.

When hopes for a future with political independence and equality were shattered by the Paris peace settlement, semi-peripheral lawyers and activists reassessed their strategies. Neither nationalist leaders, nor pan-African activists were allowed to attend the Peace Conference and present their demands. Eliézer Cadet, the envoy from the UNIA, could report on various adventures in Paris, but nothing beyond making some inroads into intellectual circles and meeting progressive journalists. Du Bois failed in his attempt to be received by Clemenceau and Wilson. The more renowned members of the nationalist movement in Egypt and India, Saad Zaghloul and Lala Lajpat Rai, were excluded from the delegations authorized by Britain to travel to Paris; while the Korean delegate Kim

102 Egyptian Delegation, *The Egyptian national claims*, p. 20.

103 See, in general, J. Fisch, *Das Selbstbestimmungsrecht der Völker oder die Domestizierung einer Illusion: Eine Geschichte* (München: C. H. Beck, 2010).

Kyu-shik, although making it to Paris, was not admitted to the negotiations.[104]

Without representation from peoples without sovereignty, like delegates from the former colonies and territories of Germany and the Ottoman Empire, the disappointing outcome reached at the Paris Peace Conference was not surprising. The German colonies in Africa were given as mandates to Belgium, Britain and South Africa. Moreover, Armenian independence was not recognized, as the former territories of the Ottoman Empire outside Turkey were also converted into mandates.[105] Chinese and Korean leaders were no less disappointed: China losing Shandong to Japan and Korea remaining under Japanese rule. Moreover, those who had hoped for a new order based on equality, like those in Latin America wary about the introduction of the Monroe doctrine into the Covenant of the League, were also disappointed.[106] States subjected to unequal treaties that participated in the treaty of Versailles and then sought to abrogate them at the League, like China and Persia, were equally disappointed.

In consequence, the combination of arguments in the petitions drafted after 1919 changed. On the one hand, peoples that had obtained or enjoyed some level of independence, like Armenia, Azerbaijan and Ethiopia, sought direct admission into the League. The new combination of arguments in the requests for admission had self-determination occupying a much more modest role. Instead, centre stage was given to the requirements of statehood. On the other hand, peoples that could not secure some level of factual independence continued petitioning the League of Nations. They continued combining a variety of arguments, but overall giving also more relevance to arguments based on statehood and admission to the League, than to arguments based on self-determination. Some additionally resorted to collective violence, making use of international legal arguments to make military resistance successful. Finally, during the interwar years, semi-peripheral lawyers and diplomats, in particular

104 Manela, *Wilsonian moment*, p. 207; H. Hu, *Le problème coréen* (Paris: A. Pédone, 1953).

105 The creation of an Armenian mandate in the hands of the United States also failed when the Treaty of Sèvres of 1920 was not ratified, and finally came under Turkish rule in the Treaty of Lausanne 1923, after the Armenian-Turkish war.

106 To gather support from the American public, Wilson pushed for the inclusion of the Monroe doctrine in the League's Covenant. Article 21: 'Nothing in this Covenant shall be deemed to affect the validity of international engagements, such as treaties of arbitration or regional understandings like the Monroe doctrine, for securing the maintenance of peace.'

Latin Americans, harnessed the modern discourse of international law to codify rules granting equality and to renegotiate unequal treaties.

The interwar reassessment of semi-peripheral legal strategies marked a trend in the intellectual history of international law. The standard of civilization and self-determination were gradually substituted by statehood. Peoples without independence, although defeated at the Peace Conference, continued their struggle using international legal arguments. Garvey's UNIA continued drafting petitions to be carried by special delegations arriving, now that the League was inaugurated, in Geneva. The UNIA petition of 1922, mentioned above, neither makes explicit reference to self-determination, nor mentions the standard of civilization. Instead we see the formal steps a recognized state would have followed to be heard at the League of Nations. A copy of the petition by the UNIA was enclosed in a letter to Eric Drummond (1876–1951), Secretary General of the League. With a colourful stamp and solemn language, Marcus Garvey informs him that a delegation has been appointed to present the petition to the impending Assembly of the League.[107] The form of the petition changed, but not the answer given by the League. Drummond's laconic reply explained that rules of procedure did not provide for hearing delegations other than those officially representing states members of the League. Rather condescendingly, Drummond notes that meetings are held in public and that seats to hear the debates can be reserved on application to the Secretariat.[108]

Regardless of the disenchanting reply, a UNIA delegation arrived in Geneva in September. The delegation was led by George Osborne Marke (1867–1929), a Sierra Leonean who, after studying in England and working as a government clerk in Sierra Leone, moved to the US and became UNIA's supreme deputy potentate. Upon arrival, Marke reserved seats and asked for an interview with Drummond. The Secretary General and Marke never met. Marke, however, managed to meet with the head of the Iranian delegation, Prince Mirza Reza Khan Arfa-ed-Dowleh (1854–1938), who agreed to submit the UNIA petition to the Assembly of the League. At the request of the Iranian delegation, copies of the petition circulated and the petition was mentioned in the League's official journal.[109]

107 LoN Archive, 1/22354/21159. 108 *Ibid.*

109 See Marke's request to submit UNIA's petition to the Assembly, LoN Archive 1/21159/21159. Rather than meeting with Drummond, Marke met with the League's director of the mandates section and the minorities section, William Rappard, who officially requested the petition be included in the League's Journal: see *ibid.*

Similarly, during the 1920s, the Syro-Palestinian Congress and the *Conseil Administratif du Liban* sent countless petitions to the League of Nations mentioning neither the standard of civilization, nor self-determination.[110] The Lebanese petition affirms that Lebanon has become in fact a sovereign state after the abolition of the Turkish suzerainty. The Syro-Palestinian Congress, on the other hand, like the UNIA, behaved like a sovereign entity, appointing a permanent delegate, Shakib Arslan, to represent the Syrian cause in front of the League. In 1922, a petition by the Syro-Palestinian Congress demanded, among other things: 'recognition of independence and sovereignty of Syria, Libya and Palestine; evacuation of foreign occupying armies; annulment of treaties against our rights; non-ratification of the Syrian Mandate and authorization to present a request for admission to the League'.[111]

[110] See e.g. 'Les droits du Liban après la guerre avec la disparition de la suzeraineté turque' in *Die Welt des Islams*, 8 (1926), 105–6; 'Pétition du Comité exécutif du Congrès syro-palestinein', LoN C.P.M. 368.

[111] Congrès Syrio-Palestinien (Genève 25 août–21 sept. 1921), *Appel adressé à la Assemblée générale de la Société des Nations* (Impr. Tribune de Genève, 1921).

8 Circumventing self-determination: League membership and armed resistance

The Syro-Palestinian petition of 1922 suggests that after demands for self-determination were defeated in Paris, admission to the League became an alternative strategy for demanding the recognition of sovereignty. This option became even more promising for semi-peripheral peoples that had acquired a modicum of political independence and territorial control. Thus, during the early years of the League, semi-peripheral states that had not been invited to join the League, like Ethiopia and Hedjaz, in addition to other polities formerly part of the Russian empire, such as Azerbaijan and the Ukraine, drafted requests for admission to the League of Nations. These documents as well as the procedure developed to deal with the requests for membership marked a clear departure from the standard of civilization. The trend initiated by the 1919 petitions, in which having civilization was combined with claims to self-determination, gave way to requests for admission to the League based on showing compliance with a standard of statehood and on committing to the observance of international obligations.

Not every polity requesting membership to the League was actually admitted. Actually, there is no reason to assume that the standard of statehood that emerged during the interwar was a priori or in practice more inclusive than the old standard of civilization. The doctrinal change benefited only polities able to show that they had acquired the elements of statehood – territory, people and government. Others were excluded. The decline of civilization as a substantive standard meant also that government and people became less important requisites to recognize statehood than the fact of having territory, namely exercising territorial control. Thus, for polities excluded because not able to meet the requirements of statehood, acquiring territory by force became the only alternative to meet the standard and claim sovereignty. The international regulation of violence between core states and semi-peripheral polities fighting over territorial control became in consequence crucial to the fate of peoples demanding self-determination.

Membership in the League of Nations

According to Article 1 of the Covenant of the League of Nations, 'any fully self-governing State, Dominion or Colony' may become a member, 'provided that it shall give effective guarantees of its sincere intention to observe its international obligations, and shall accept such regulations as may be prescribed by the League in regard to its military, naval and air forces and armaments'.[1] The vague wording of Article 1, requiring but not defining self-government, reflected the complexities of the question of membership. These complexities have been well illustrated by Alison Duxbury, in her study on the participation of states in international organizations.[2] The definition of membership, Duxbury argues, had been one of the difficult issues to discuss as soon as the idea of establishing a permanent international organization was considered during the war. It was the same problem that had been previously confronted at the Hague Conference of 1907. If universal membership were to be granted, Great Powers could be outnumbered by small states. Universal membership, even for activists in the peace movement, was out of question. For example, the British League of Nations Society, as Duxbury shows, limited membership to 'any civilised State' desiring to join the League.[3] Among American groups, the private study group lead by Theodore Marburg restricted membership to the Great Powers and some 'secondary powers'. While 'smaller states' could be admitted if they had 'settled conditions', 'backward nations including Balkan States and Turkey' should be absolutely kept out.[4]

The restrictive standard of membership supported by different study groups simply reflected the view most commonly held in the West regarding the limitation of self-determination to European peoples. When this

1 According to Article 1, the Assembly decided upon admission by a two-thirds vote, in which one state counted the same.

2 A. Duxbury, *The participation of states in international organisations: the role of human rights and democracy* (Cambridge University Press, 2011).

3 *Ibid.*, pp. 64–5.

4 T. Marburg, *Development of the League of Nations idea* (New York: Macmillan, 1932), vol. II, pp. 725–6; and also Duxbury.

idea came to fruition with the establishment of the Mandate system, the discussion about the rules of membership during the Paris Conference presupposed the exclusion of non-Western peoples who were not enjoying self-government. It is in the context of this prior exclusion that during the Paris negotiations the Commission of the League of Nations discussed several proposals that sought to define membership based on a principle of universality and according to criteria of self-government, democracy or independence.[5] 'Self-governing State, Dominion or Colony,' the formula adopted by the Commission and included in Article 1, was broad and ambiguous enough to embrace the conflicting positions taken by the great powers. It was also ambiguous enough to be appropriated by non-Western peoples, not just in support of their requests to enter the League, but also in the effort to define the general rules of statehood.

When the First Assembly of the League met at the end of 1920, sixteen requests for admission had been sent to Geneva. The Fifth Committee, entrusted by the First Assembly to study the admission of new members confronted the difficulty of giving practical meaning to the formula contained in Article 1. As in the Hague Conference, semi-peripheral states admitted to the League took advantage of the opportunity that an international forum offers to less powerful players. For example, the Chilean delegate Antonio Huneeus (1870–1951) became Chairman of the Fifth Committee, simply because it was thought practical to find someone without connections to the big powers to head the Committee.[6] The Argentinean delegate Honorio Pueyrredón (1876–1945), on the other hand, used the international stage to act as a big power, demanding universal membership, under the threat of withdrawing Argentina from the League. In general, delegates from other semi-peripheral states used every opportunity to defend the position of smaller states. Antonio Restrepo (1855–1933) from Colombia and Emir Zoka-ed-Dowleh from Iran, for example, were described by British participants as 'champions of the small states'.[7]

[5] See Duxbury, *The participation of states*, pp. 66–71. Interestingly, neutral states, mostly Latin American states, supported an inclusive standard for membership: G. Schwarzenberger, *The League of Nations and world order* (London: Constable, 1936), p. 44.

[6] '[T]here was considerable surprise ... and there seemed little reason for his election except that the country he represented was as far as possible to find one': O. Brett, R. Cecil and W. Phillimore, *The first Assembly; a study of the proceedings of the first Assembly of the League of Nations* (London: Macmillan, 1921), p. 197.

[7] Brett, *The first Assembly*, p. 207.

At its first meeting, the Fifth Committee adopted a general questionnaire and appointed three sub-committees to consider the different requests for admission. The questionnaire, adopted by the Committee contained the requirements states should meet to join the League:

> (1) Was the application in order? (2) Was the Government applying for admission recognized 'de jure' or 'de facto' and by which states? (3) Was the applicant a nation with a stable government and settled frontiers? What was its size and population? (4) Was it fully self-governing? (5) What had been its conduct with regard to (i) its international obligations; (ii) the prescriptions of the League as to armaments?[8]

Some have interpreted the questionnaire as spelling out a 'new standard of civilization' foreshadowing the definition of statehood in the Montevideo Convention of 1933.[9] As a criterion for membership and statehood, the questionnaire certainly entailed new grounds for exclusion, like the requirement regarding settled frontiers, which was frequently invoked to deny membership to polities formerly part of the Russian empire.[10] But the requirements listed in the questionnaire were different, more concrete and procedural, than the nineteenth-century standard of civilization, which before its appropriation by semi-peripherals, was infused with religious and cultural elements.[11]

Semi-peripherals, however, were well aware that discussing new criteria for membership could reopen the debate about the universality of international law and renew the threat of new grounds emerging to justify the exclusion of smaller states. In 1920, Honorio Pueyrredón, the Argentinean minister of foreign relations and delegate to the First Assembly took the

[8] LoN, *Records of the First Assembly. Meetings of the Committees* (Geneva, 1920), p. 159.

[9] Gong, *The standard of 'civilization'*, p. 26. However, in the next chapter I argue that the Montevideo definition is significantly different from the criterion reflected in the questionnaire. Montevideo does not include the requirement of full self-governance, an element crucial to exclude polities fighting for independence without securing actual territorial control.

[10] For example, the rapporteur appointed by the Fifth Committee to examine the applications by Azerbaijan and Ukraine did not favour their admission because 'frontiers did not appear either stable or clearly defined': LoN, *First Assembly Committees*, pp. 173–4.

[11] For example, if the standard of civilization, as interpreted by Western lawyers made reference to forms of punishment, the questionnaire talks about stable government. However, it is true that the questionnaire developed for admission of new states coexisted with the mandate system denying self-government. Thus, the idea here is that semi-peripherals made use of the questionnaire to circumvent the mandate system.

stand to voice dissent. At the fifth plenary meeting, Pueyrredón recalled the central principles of international law Argentina had defended before the war, namely: sovereign equality, compulsory arbitration, respect for decisions by arbitration courts and the proscription of force to secure the payment of sovereign debts, which as we have seen were the central elements of classical semi-peripheral thinking.[12] Pueyrredón, in fact, reiterated one of the major claims defended by semi-peripherals at the Second Hague Conference, namely respect for the principle of sovereign equality in international organizations. Pueyrredón thus demanded respect for sovereign equality, in terms both of admission to and participation in the League. All members of the Council should be 'voted by the Assembly in conformity with the principle of the equality of States'. Otherwise – Pueyrredón warned – the League would not be in harmony with the democratic regime.[13] To respect the equality of all states, Pueyrredón moreover believed that the League should be open to universal membership: 'The strength of the League lies in the incorporation of the greatest number of Members; the fewer the states outside it, the more numerous will be those submitted to its discipline and ready to carry out the duties which it imposes upon them.'[14]

Universality was invoked by Pueyrredón in the context of the exclusion of the states defeated in the war: 'the non-admission of certain countries might be the cause of dangerous antagonisms ... The League would appear ... to be an alliance formed to conclude the late war, and not, as it is in reality, a powerful organization to maintain peace.'[15] Although these interventions were interpreted by some contemporaries as a defence of German interests, Pueyrredón defended a principled position of general application.[16] For instance, Pueyrredón formulated at the Fifth Committee a proposal specifically connected to 'nations ... not permitted to become members of the League of Nations because they are not recognized as sovereign States'. Pueyrredón proposed that 'with the permission of the Council', these nations could 'appoint representatives to sit in the Assembly, but without right to vote'.[17] Had this proposal had support, it is worth remembering, the UNIA or Syrian delegations would have had the right

[12] LoN, *Records of the First Assembly. Plenary meetings* (Geneva, 1920), pp. 87–90 (fifth plenary meeting).
[13] *Ibid.*, p. 90. [14] *Ibid.* [15] *Ibid.*
[16] See e.g. W. Rappard, 'Germany at Geneva', *Foreign Affairs*, 4 (1926), 535–46, 537.
[17] LoN, *First Assembly Committees*, p. 211.

to take seat in the Assembly and Eric Drummond, the League's Secretary General, would not have been right telling it to seek seating among the general public.

At the thirteenth plenary meeting, Pueyrredón presented a general motion to amend the Covenant's rules to recognize universal membership: 'That all Sovereign States recognised by the community of Nations be admitted to join the League of Nations in such a manner that if they do not become Members of the League, this can only be the result of a voluntary decision on their part.'[18] The motion was not discussed and Pueyrredón announced at the next plenary session that Argentina would be withdrawing from the League.[19]

Pueyrredón's proposal was only and finally discussed the following year at the First Committee of the Second Assembly. Among others, delegates from Chile, Colombia, Finland and Iran defended the Argentinean amendment.[20] Strong opposition came from most delegates, including those from Belgium, Britain, France, Japan and Switzerland.[21] The French delegate Georges Noblemaire (1867–?), who believed that the amendment 'would destroy the very essence of the League', put forward a motion rejecting universal membership. Although the Colombian delegate, José Francisco Urrutia (1870–1950), proposed adjourning rather than rejecting the amendment, Noblemaire's motion was passed and a rapporteur was appointed.[22] At the following meeting, when the report was discussed, and regardless of the passing of the French motion, again a number of semi-peripheral delegates mostly from Latin America, unsuccessfully

[18] LoN, *First Assembly, Plenary meetings*, p. 261 (request at the Fifth Committee).

[19] *Ibid.*, pp. 276–8. The complete Argentinean proposal included 'admission of all sovereign States; admission of small States, but without the right of voting; the Council to be constituted by election on democratic lines; obligatory submission of disputes to the Courts of Arbitration and Justice': *ibid.*, 277. The letter concludes (*ibid.*): 'For the above reasons . . . the Argentine Delegation considers its mission at an end'.

[20] LoN, *Records of the Second Assembly. Meetings of the Committees* (Geneva, 1921), vol. I, pp. 5–7 and 13–17 and in particular see statement by Prince Arfa-ed-Dowleh, pp. 677–8 (plenary meetings).

[21] LoN, *Second Assembly, Committees*, pp. 5–7 and 13–17. The British delegate Arthur Balfour, for example, rejected the principle of universality on 'practical considerations'. Balfour used the example of the 'three great and striking absences' from the League: the United States, Germany and Russia. In the case of the former, there would be no use of the principle, for the US was opposed to joining. In the case of Germany, the exact moment at which it should enter the League 'raised difficult considerations'. Finally, in relation to Russia, Balfour concluded that 'it was extremely doubtful whether the majority of the Members of the League would regard the addition of Bolshevist Russia as an improvement to the League': *ibid.*, p. 6.

[22] *Ibid.*, pp. 9–11.

defended the amendment. However, they successfully pushed for adjourning rather than rejecting the Argentinean proposal.[23] The final report thus reads: 'The Committee is therefore, to its regret, compelled to declare that, ... the idea itself ... though in theory it meets with the full approval of the Committee, is, nevertheless, scarcely compatible with the actual conditions of the world, and cannot, therefore, be accepted.'[24]

The defeat of the Argentinean amendment was not surprising, considering what had happened thirteen years before at The Second Hague Conference, when Ruy Barbosa and others defended sovereign equality as a matter of principle. It is true that this time Pueyrredón's proposal was framed as both a matter of respecting sovereignty and upholding the interests of the international community.[25] But invoking sovereignty at the end of the war, at the time when the international legal discourse had been decisively shifting towards the modern paradigm, was not a popular strategy to follow.[26] Great powers' rejection of Pueyrredón's proposal could be anticipated. This time, however, neither Latin Americans, nor other semi-peripherals gave full support to a proposal based on sovereign equality.[27] Instead, as shown above, they successfully pushed for a

[23] For example, Alejandro Alvarez from Chile tried unsuccessfully to argue that it was not a problem for universal membership that some states would be recognized *de jure* or de facto only by some but not all states, since recognition by the League would itself suffice and would carry with it recognition by all members: *ibid.*, p. 15.

[24] *Ibid.*, p. 136.

[25] Pueyrredón affirmed: 'we are speaking on behalf of principles ... The tie which is to unite the Members of the new organization is a strictly legal and contractual one; it is the outcome of the necessity for the nations to live in close relationship ... duty which lies upon us to sacrifice ourselves in the interests of the general well-being in order to attain the ideal of justice which humanity so ardently desires'. LoN, *First Assembly, Plenary Meetings*, p. 90. We can see a similar combination of sovereign equality and the interests of the international community at the fourteenth plenary meeting, when defending the motion to amend the Covenant, with 'the noble aim of ensuring for humanity in the future the abolition of war, the rule of justice, and practical solidarity and equality between States': *ibid.*, p. 277.

[26] As we have seen, the critique of sovereignty was part of the modern discourse of international law that emerged at the turn of the century and consolidated after the war. This trend was also present among the groups formed to study the problem of war and peace. See, for instance, A. Zimmern, *The League of Nations and the rule of law, 1918–1935* (London: Macmillan, 1936), pp. 161–2. Among the American group, Theodore Marburg affirmed that 'the doctrine of absolute sovereignty set up to guard the State itself against interference by other States must ultimately give way before the conception of a society of nations': Marburg, *League*, pp. 58–9.

[27] For example, Pueyrredón's intervention was harshly criticized by the British delegates. 'This speech, so greatly in the realm of theory, so little, if at all, addressed to the immediate business of the Assembly or to the report on the work of the Council, was

permanent adjournment of universal membership. A deferral of the Argentine proposal allowed semi-peripherals to renew the effort to shape the emerging rules governing admission to the League.

Requesting admission at the First Assembly: independence, statehood and recognition

On 1 November 1920, Alimardan Topchubashev (1862–1934), head of the Azerbaidjan Peace Delegation at Paris, now in Geneva, submitted a request for admission to Secretary General Drummond. The request recalls the memorandum presented the year before by the delegation in Paris. Like most documents brought to the Peace Conference in 1919, the Azerbaijani memorandum appealed to 'great Wilsonian principles'. It demanded independence based on 'the rights of peoples to self-determination'. Moreover, 'wishing to place itself... beneath the high protection of the League', the memorandum also requested admission to the League.[28] The following year, in preparation for the First Assembly of the League of Nations, the Azerbaijani delegation followed up on the request for admission. The 1920 request, however, did not reiterate the appeal to the right to self-determination, instead it appealed to political independence based on statehood and recognition.

'Led by an ardent aspiration to independent life based on political, social and religious liberty', the request declares that the Azerbaijani people is 'anxious to become a Mohamedan State of Republican form, democratic in character from both the political and religious point of view, with equal universal suffrage for all elements of the population'.[29] The request declared repeatedly the Republic's adherence to democratic principles, including universal suffrage – 'the first time women have voted in a Mohamedan country' – and equality – 'with guarantees for the rights of minorities'.[30] The Azerbaijani Delegation, however, faced a serious obstacle. A few months before the presentation of the request, after the

followed by some brief but eminent practical remarks from Dr. Hagenrup of Norway': Brett, *The first Assembly*, p. 39. In Brazil, for example, if public opinion had been supportive of Barbosa's role at the Hague, it was now critical of Pueyrredón: O. Paiz, 8 December 1920, enclosed USNA, 500C001/157.

[28] Paris Peace Conference, *Claims of the peace delegation of the republic of Caucasian Azerbaidjan presented to the Peace conference in Paris* (Paris: Robinet-Houtain, 1919) and LoN, 'Admission of the Azerbaidjan Republic to the League', Document de l'Assemblée 20/48/68.

[29] LoN, 'Admission of the Azerbaidjan', p. 3. [30] *Ibid.*, p. 3.

invasion by Soviet forces, the Republic had lost absolute control of its territory. Thus, on the one hand, the request recalls the Azerbaijani people's struggle for independence against 'Red terror', assuring that it will rid itself of 'Russian Bolsheviks'. On the other hand, the request reminds one that in 1919 the independence of Azerbaijan had already been de facto recognized by the Supreme Council of the Allied Powers.[31] This combination of statehood, struggle against oppression to secure actual territorial control and de facto recognition was also at the centre of the requests for admission drafted by the other two Caucasian states recognized by the Council, Armenia and Georgia.[32]

But hopes that Azerbaijani, Armenian or Georgian peoples could repel foreign forces remained just a distant aspiration. And probably intuitions about the fate of their peoples were behind the sombre tone adopted by the drafters. Compared to the optimism of the memorandum of 1919, the Azerbaijani request for admission concludes with a technical appeal to legal formality. If expressing commitment to restricting sovereign autonomy in the name of international obligations, including limitations on armaments, was the most demanding requisite asked of states intending to join the League, the Azerbaijani request eagerly proclaimed commitment, at a point at which it may have been clear that international obligations would never come to life: 'The Delegation regards its duty to accept all obligations imposed by the Covenant . . . as well as all obligations of an international character.' Furthermore, the request affirmed that the Azerbaijani people would hope 'to be free from military service, and not be compelled to maintain an army. To achieve this, we placed all our hopes on the League of Nations, the supreme organization of morality and justice.'[33] One can only guess with difficulty whether the appeal to legal formality dressed a utopian faith in international law, or whether it concealed a sense of resignation. But we know that, dying in Parisian exile, Alimardan Topchubashev never returned to Baku.[34]

[31] *Ibid.*, p. 4. 'All classes rejoiced and blessed this first step towards entry into the great family of States': *ibid.* See also Republic of Azerbaidjan, 'Letter from the President of the Peace Delegation of the Republic of Azerbaidjan': Document de l'Assemblée 206, December 1920.

[32] See LoN, 'Request from Armenia for Admission to the League of Nations', Document de l'Assemblée 20/48/33.

[33] LoN, 'Admission of the Azerbaidjan', p. 4.

[34] F. Akhundov, 'Democratic Republic of Azerbaijan Leaders (1918–1920), Alimardan Topchubashev – Minister of Foreign Affairs (1862–1934)', *Azerbaijan International*, 6 (1998), 31–3, 31.

At the First Assembly, towards the end of the plenary meetings, the Chairman of the Fifth Committee, Antonio Huneeus, presented his report on the admission of new states. Huneeus recalls first the general principle under which the Committee worked: 'all free States, who give adequate guarantees of their sincere intention to fulfil their international engagements should be admitted to the League'. A principle, Huneeus reminds again, that was 'supported from the beginning by all the members of the Committee'. Recalling the general principle, Huneeus evaded the main problem faced by the Committee, namely determining if admission involved recognition by all members. Huneeus affirmed: 'we did not allow legal considerations to hamper us'.

Both the Committee and the First Assembly rejected the Azerbaijani, Armenian and Georgian requests.[35] Notwithstanding the Committee's rejection, Huneeus expressly affirmed that rejection should not prevent the taking of future applications into consideration. Huneeus also proposed to give new states that were not admitted 'the best welcome that we can, let us show them our sympathy, and give them access to the Technical Organizations, above all that of Labour'.[36] Similarly, the Iranian delegate Emir Zoka-ed-Dowleh, supporting universal membership, regretted that 'Armenia, Azerbaidjan, the Caucasus and the Ukraine' did not fulfil the requirements for admission and hoped that they would be admitted in the future. With this purpose, Zoka-ed-Dowleh demanded that all 'requests for admission of all States possessing defined frontiers and stable Governments, and inspired by democratic ideas, should be accepted'.[37]

When the Assembly discussed the requests by the Baltic states and Georgia, in relation to which the Committee had also suggested rejecting admission, granting instead participation in technical organizations, the Colombian delegate Restrepo expressed loud opposition to the report and proposed immediate admission.[38] Restrepo informed the Assembly that he was 'forced regretfully' to vote against Armenia, because under occupation it did not satisfy the requirements of statehood. Restrepo however contended that there was no legal reason to deny admission to the Baltic states and Georgia.[39] The Portuguese delegate refuted Restrepo's

[35] The report by the Fifth Committee did not recommend admission because of Azerbaidjan's lack of a stable government extending over the whole of its territory: LoN, *First Assembly, Plenary meetings*, p. 664. The Assembly rejected admission by twenty-eight votes and fourteen abstentions: *ibid.*, p. 625.

[36] *Ibid.*, pp. 561–2. [37] *Ibid.*, p. 567. [38] *Ibid.*, pp. 616–17.

[39] *Ibid.*, p. 616. Similarly, the Iranian delegate Zoka-ed-Dowleh complained that if Finland's request was accepted why would the Baltic and Caucasian states not be admitted: 'Why should we not always be guided by the same principle?' *Ibid.*, p. 624.

argument, maintaining that only states recognized *de jure* could be admitted, since the independent existence of states that have not been recognized is not protected by international law. Otherwise, the League would have to protect the integrity of non-recognized states, which is an obligation that 'the League could not assume'.[40] This exchange foreshadowed the controversy between Western and semi-peripheral states regarding the nature of recognition. In fact, Restrepo protested that requiring recognition amounts to creating a new requirement for membership.[41]

For most Western delegates, admission of new members posed an important problem arising from Article 10 of the Covenant, which imposed a collective obligation to preserve territorial integrity in front of an aggression. During the debate on the admission of Armenia, Robert Cecil (1864–1958), the renowned lawyer, politician, British League activist and at this time also representative of the dominion of South Africa, called for realism. Cecil cautioned that it is the collective obligation to preserve territorial integrity in front of an aggression that no one has real intention to carry out.[42] During the debate on the admission of the Baltic states the French delegate repeated the argument about not deceiving nations and not fostering false expectations regarding Europe's willingness to protect nations under aggression. Restrepo answered: 'Although the State I represent is a small one, I can declare that it is ready to come to the assistance of these small countries'.[43] Regardless of Restrepo's best efforts the requests from the Baltic states, from Estonia, Latvia and Lithuania as well as from the Ukraine and Georgia, were all rejected.[44]

The rejection of all Baltic and Caucasian states as well as Georgia and Ukraine was no success for the semi-periphery. However, throughout the discussions about admission, the rules governing membership were redrawn to require a formal standard including stable government, set boundaries and commitment to obligations imposed by international law.[45] Rather than making reference to the form of government, to the functioning of courts and the protection of foreign residents, or to other cultural and religious practices, delegates from Western sovereigns invoked the inability to defend small states with unstable boundaries. That considerations related to statehood displaced those which would

[40] *Ibid.*, p. 618. [41] *Ibid.*, p. 629. [42] *Ibid.*, p. 590. [43] *Ibid.*, p. 629.

[44] Ukraine, *ibid.*, p. 651; Liechtenstein, p. 652; Armenia, p. 613; Estonia, p. 627; Latvia, p. 630; Lithuania, p. 630; and Georgia, p. 633.

[45] For example, the Secretary General, in the 'Memorandum on the admission of Azerbaijan' considers 'whether the Government is in a position to undertake obligations and give the guarantees involved by membership of the League of Nations', LoN Document de l'Assemblée 20/48/108, 1920, p. 4.

previously have been required as part of the standard of civilization, could be regarded as a remarkable victory. But we can already suspect, after all the examples we have encountered so far, that this victory was neither absolute, nor available for every semi-peripheral polity. Though China and Ethiopia were members of the League at the time of the Japanese and Italian aggression, the League failed to make the collective security system work. Membership of polities that could not fit into the emerging standard of statehood, on the other hand, continued to be rejected. Let us briefly consider the requests for membership by Ethiopia and the Six Nations, which illustrate a definitive turn in the direction of statehood; at the same time it reminds us about the shortcomings of the semi-peripheral appropriations of modern international law.

Requesting admission after the First Assembly: Ethiopia and the Six Nations

After the First Assembly, the question of admission of new members was again discussed not only in relation to the German request, but also in relation to other semi-peripheral polities like Egypt and Iraq. Let us focus on the two applications for membership submitted to the League in 1923 by Ethiopia and by the Six Nations, a confederation of Haudenosaunee (or Iroquois) nations of North America. These two applications confirm the trend from civilization to statehood that we saw in the 1919 petitions and the 1920 requests for admission. These requests, however, also reveal the limitations that a standard of statehood requiring actual independence imposed on semi-peripheral polities. For the fortunes of these two applications anticipate the failures of the League as an avenue to secure sovereign autonomy for semi-peripheral peoples.

Ethiopian admission

On 1 August 1923, the Crown Prince of Ethiopia, Ras Tafari Mekonnen (1892–1975), the future Emperor Haile Selassie, sent a telegram from Addis Ababa to Geneva. The telegram solicited the impending Assembly to consider Ethiopia's admission to the League. Containing the basic formal requirements, the short request was technically impeccable: 'In conformity with Article I of the Covenant . . . I have the honour to solicit admission of the Empire of Ethiopia as a Member of the League of Nations . . . Ethiopia . . . is prepared to accept conditions contained in Article I of the Covenant, and to carry out all the obligations incumbent on Members.'[46] On 4 September, the Secretariat received a longer note confirming the telegram.[47]

This note was not only longer, but also a much more complex document. In addition to the familiar elements we have seen so far in the other requests for admission, the note contained rather unconventional allusions to Ethiopian peculiarities. Ethiopian statehood, on the one hand, was supported in a conventional manner by reference to the establishment of international relations regulated by law: 'we endeavoured to establish bonds of friendship: we built a railway, we adhered to the Brussels Convention, we joined the Universal Postal Union, and we signed treaties, which we have always observed, with the Powers which cooperated to found the League of Nations'.[48] The note also contained unconventional passages: 'The Holy Scriptures bear witness that, since the year 1500 after Solomon we have been contending with the heathen . . . for the true faith and the laws of God . . . With God's help we have baptized thousand of heathen, who have become our brothers, and only in the time of our Emperor Menelek II have we had peace'.[49]

It would be tempting to understand this second statement in the note as an anachronistic reference to a classical standard of civilization dependent on Christianity. Rose Parfitt, however, has highlighted the hybrid nature, both Ethiopian and European, of this document and generally of Ethiopian engagements with international law.[50] Thus, like the telegram, the note appropriated European international legal concepts. For example, in addition to the way in which Ethiopian statehood was affirmed, the note recalls the central advantages Ethiopia should gain from membership: 'We know that the League of Nations guarantees the independence and territorial integrity of all nations in the world'.[51]

In the same vein, the reference to Christianity served to point out that Ethiopia had settled boundaries.[52] But this reference also reflected a distinctive mode of affirming Ethiopian identity, in relation to Ethiopia's

[46] LoN Doc A.25.1923.VII. In fact, the telegram was quoted in the report of the Sixth Committee to the Assembly.

[47] LoN Doc A.55.1923.VII. Original copies in Amharic and French LoN Archive 28/30357/29888.

[48] *Ibid.* [49] *Ibid.*

[50] R. Parfitt, 'Empire des nègres blancs: the hybridity of international personality and the Abyssinia crisis of 1935–36', *Leiden Journal of International Law*, 24 (2011), 849–72.

[51] LoN Archive 28/30357/29888.

[52] The limits between Christians and non-Christians served to delimit Ethiopian territory: 'as may be seen from a map of our country', *ibid.*

position in the international context as well as in relation to domestic Ethiopian politics. In relation to the international context, Parfitt demonstrates that since at least the late nineteenth century the image of a 'Christian Island surrounded by an ocean of unbelievers', had been invoked by Emperor Menelek II to prevent the European scramble of Africa to reach Ethiopia.[53] More importantly, regarding the domestic context, Parfitt explains that at the time of the request of admission, the Ethiopian elite was divided between a conservative faction, which under Empress Zewditu supported Ethiopia's traditional isolation, and a faction of modernizers, the 'Young Ethiopians' who under the leadership of Tafari sought not just admission to the League, but also the abolition of slavery and the modernization of Ethiopia.[54] In fact, only a few months before the telegram was sent to Geneva, both factions confronted each other when Ethiopian elites were summoned to the capital to discuss a possible request for membership.

When conservative clergy and nobility pressed Tafari to explain the effects that membership would bring, Parfitt shows that Tafari translated the idea of the League with a specifically Ethiopian term conveying a religious fraternal association. When further pressed to explain if by entering this close association Ethiopia's ability to defend itself would be diminished, Tafari diffused this fear using the same Christian/non-Christian distinction present in the note. Instead of fearing an association with Christian nations, Tafari suggested that, historically surrounded by Muslims and Animists, Ethiopians have been seen as enemies precisely because of their Christian faith.[55] Finally, Parfitt argues that when invited to consider the threat that European Christian influence would pose to the authority of the Ethiopian Orthodox Church, Tafari countered this suspicion 'with a vision of Ethiopia as a member of a worldwide Christian civilization'.[56]

Tafari succeeded. Not only did he secure consent from the Empress to request admission, but also obtained admission to the League. The proceedings of the Seventh Plenary Meeting of the Fourth Assembly record the President announcing, 'As the Assembly has voted unanimously in favour of the admission of Abyssinia, I declare Abyssinia admitted to the League of Nations (*Unanimous and prolonged applause*)'.[57] Before the vote was taken at the League's Assembly, the rapporteur of the Sub-Committee appointed to study the request explained that the Sixth Committee had

[53] Parfitt, 'Empire des nègres blancs', 863, quoting a letter by Menelik II sent in 1891.
[54] *Ibid.*, 859. [55] *Ibid.*, 862. [56] *Ibid.*, 863. [57] *Ibid.*

drafted a declaration in relation to Ethiopia's international obligations regarding slavery and traffic in arms, which the Government of Abyssinia should sign in order to be admitted to the League. The Sixth Committee had devised a special and intricate formula to deal with the Ethiopian request. The Report by the Sub-Committee on the Abyssinian Request, although recommending admission, cautioned about the real extent of Abyssinian territorial control over its provinces as well as about its past fulfilment of international obligations. In light of this conclusion, the Report proposed, before recommending admission, that Abyssinia be required to sign a special declaration on the fulfilment of its international obligations in relation to slavery and the importation of arms and ammunitions. The Report was met with a strong protest by the Abyssinian delegation.[58] The discussion that ensued within the Committee reflected again the different positions held by delegates from the centre and semi-periphery.

Members of the Committee had a clear idea about the problem underlying the admission of Ethiopia. In the words of the French delegate Henry de Jouvenel (1876–1935), a renowned journalist who would later become High Commissioner of the Syrian mandate, the point was 'to know whether the Abyssinian Government intended to cooperate with the League in the abolition of slavery'.[59] Once again semi-peripherals defended a strict reading of the rules governing membership that excluded references to a substantive criterion. Delegates from China and Venezuela supported Abyssinian admission affirming that all conditions contained in Article 1 of the Covenant and the questionnaire formulated by the Committee to deal with admissions – recognition, self-governance, frontiers and fulfilment of international obligations – were satisfied and that admission should not depend on any additional requirement.[60] Moreover, they argued that demanding that Abyssinia sign a special declaration was superfluous, for all members should fulfil their international obligations.[61]

Delegates representing Western states, on the other hand, were ready to foreground the abolition of slavery as a condition for admission. The question, however, was to determine whether this requirement would be

58 'It is the duty of the Abyssinian delegation to protest against reservations of this nature, which, by giving rise to uncertainty, are calculated to cast unjustifiable suspicion upon the Abyssinian Government.' LoN, *Official Journal*, Special Supplement, 19 (1923), 17.

59 *Ibid.*, 14.

60 *Ibid.*, 14 (Venezuelan delegate) and 15 (Chinese delegate, Tcheu-Wei: 'the League is an association of Nations . . . should include all mankind').

61 *Ibid.*, 14.

understood only as spelling out one of the elements of the questionnaire, namely meeting international obligations, as semi-peripherals argued, or if slavery constituted a practice that in contradiction to the standard of civilization would condition or preclude admission to the League.

The latter position was defended by Joseph Cook (1860–1947) and E. F. L. Wood (1881–1959), the Australian and British delegates.[62] In addition to requesting an inquiry into the capacity of the Abyssinian government to enforce its rule, Cook, a former Australian prime minister, argued that although the League 'recognized different degrees of civilization', admitting Abyssinia might 'create an anomaly, as that country might ... examine and criticise countries whose civilization was more advanced than her own'.[63] Likewise, Wood, a conservative politician, called attention to the conflicting motives delegates appealed to when deciding on the Abyssinian question. On the one hand, membership would 'help Abyssinia to raise herself in the scale of civilisation ... more effectively'. On the other hand, Wood invited the Committee to consider 'very carefully' whether 'Abyssinia was in a position to make a worthy contribution to the League', for 'the wellbeing of the League depended on the level of public opinion in each of the Member States'.[64]

Other Western delegates opposed the statements by Cook and Wood. Octave Louwers (1878–1959), the Belgian representative, invoked his country's 'natural tendency to defend the cause of the small States'. Criticizing Cook's appeal to the 'state of civilization', Louwers, a lawyer, expert in the Belgian Congo and member of the Colonial Council of the Belgian Ministry of Foreign Affairs, pointed out that civilization was required neither by the Covenant nor by the Committee. Since civilization was not a requisite to grant admission, Louwers believed that there was no reason to require Ethiopia to sign a special declaration. But if the declaration simply spelled out Ethiopia's international obligations, 'the prestige of the ancient African Empire could not therefore be affected by the signature of the proposed undertakings'. On the contrary, Louwers affirmed that 'countries with advanced civilisation' had also been asked to accept a declaration of special undertakings, which in this particular case would

[62] Both were conservative politicians.

[63] *Ibid.*, 15. Later Cook admitted that his preoccupation was based on the fear that, if admitted, Abyssinia could 'question Australia as to the treatment of the natives in New Guinea, although those natives were in a much better position than the natives of Abyssinia': *ibid.*, 21.

[64] *Ibid.*, 15.

'help the Ethiopian Government, with its public opinion, in that effort towards civilisation which it is determined to make'.[65]

The remarks by the Belgian representative did not dispel the chauvinistic and racist assumptions behind the idea of more and less civilized nations. Louwers, however, did deprive the distinction of legal meaning when invoked with the purpose of determining admission to the League. In this respect there was a marked difference in opinions between the Australian and Belgian delegates. Cook defended the legal meaning of the standard. For instance, the French delegate de Jouvenel reproached Cook for retrieving the classical standard, arguing that 'it might be unwise and dangerous to make classifications which might re-open the way to prejudices of race, caste, colour and nationality'.[66] Cook answered maintaining that his was not a reference to creed or race, but that 'admission to the League of peoples in a backward state of civilisation was rather anomalous when similar admission was refused, and with good reasons, to mandated territories'.[67] Cook was right when he defended his position based on the 'clear distinction between different degrees of civilisation' instituted by the 'Covenant and indeed the Peace Treaty'. But the Australian delegate was only partially right, for 1923 was not 1919. In 1923, no other delegate was ready to defend the standard of civilization as a requirement of membership. Cook's words died in the air without echo. After Cook's intervention, Paul Hymans (1865–1941), the Belgian minister of foreign affairs and Chairman of the meeting closed the discussion and the Committee decided to recommend admission to the League if the Abyssinian delegation possessing full powers signed the declaration.[68] The declaration itself was modified to reflect that Abyssinia is 'fully self-governing' and that the declaration was required in order to assist Abyssinia to overcome the difficulties that in the past had been obstacles to fulfil its international

[65] *Ibid.*, 16.

[66] *Ibid.*, 20. Louwers was honest when declaring that the League had previously required special obligations to be fulfilled by a state requesting admission. Since the First Assembly, Robert Cecil (representing South Africa), proposed a motion according to which, in the event that Albania, the Baltic and Caucasian states would be admitted, they should 'enforce the principles of the Minority Treaties': *Records of the First Assembly. Plenary meetings*, pp. 568–9. For example, after the vote was taken and Finland admitted, the Finnish delegate declared commitment to change the law to protect minorities: *ibid.*, p. 585.

[67] LoN, *Official Journal*, Special Supplement, 19 (1923), 21: Cook was sanguine 'it was the Covenant and indeed the Peace Treaty which made the clear distinction between different degrees of civilisation'.

[68] *Ibid.*, 21.

obligations.[69] Then, the rapporteur announced: 'The Abyssinian delegation having received full powers to sign the declaration, I have the honour to inform you that the Sixth Committee is unanimously in favour of the admission of Abyssinia to the League of Nations'.[70]

In terms of how the rules governing membership were formed, the admission of Ethiopia was a victory for the semi-periphery. But the argument here is not that the idealism of international law prevailed over sovereign interests. The argument is rather that when interests of great powers conflicted, so that Ethiopia's admission was politically feasible, semi-peripheral delegates seized the opportunity to shape the rules of membership to their advantage. From the Ethiopian perspective, however, it was a victory that soon showed fundamental shortcomings. Although formally sovereign, although now admitted to the League of Nations, Ethiopia was not free from foreign intervention. The League's collective security mechanism failed to defend Ethiopia from Italian aggression. That modern international law did not narrow the bases for lawful interventions in the semi-periphery, was a lesson painfully realized from China to Latin America.

We will see in the next chapter how Latin Americans sought to harness a principle of non-intervention into the modern legal discourse, a story that culminated in the conclusion of the Montevideo Convention of 1933. The Italian invasion of Ethiopia in 1935 therefore occurred in a new international environment. Mussolini's Italy invoked modern legal justifications at a time when the bases for intervention were narrowing. The Italian aggression was in consequence mostly criticized, understood to be unlawful and met with economic sanctions by the League. However, there was neither collective military action by the League in order to rescue Ethiopia, nor an attempt to invoke the doctrine of non-recognition of territorial acquisition by force to challenge Italian occupation. For the Italo-Ethiopian war came at a moment when the 'spirit of Geneva' was exhausting its steam, about to collapse in front of the rising winds of war.

However, the rules governing membership that emerged between 1919 and 1923 were beneficial to the semi-periphery because the shift from civilization to statehood introduced requirements that were more formal and thus easier for semi-peripheral polities to meet. Arguably, the requirements of statehood were easier to fulfil than the more substantive and thus vaguer and easier to manipulate standard of civilization. But

[69] *Ibid.*, 34. [70] LoN, *Official Journal*, Special Supplement, 13 (1923), 125.

this advantage was not real for all semi-peripheral polities. Statehood as the emerging standard according to which membership and more importantly sovereignty would be recognized, imposed important limitations on polities seeking independence without having secured territorial control. On the one hand, let us remember that statehood not only came to replace the standard of civilization, but also came as an alternative strategy after the failure of self-determination. We have seen that after the setback of 1919, semi-peripheral petitions emphasized less a right to self-determination than the satisfaction of the conditions of statehood. Without a right to self-determination, polities struggling against foreign rule were left with few options other than resisting by force to regain territorial control. International law, in this case, was called into play by semi-peripherals, for example in the case of Syria and the Rif, to afford better rules to those resorting to armed force.

Paradoxically, statehood brought about new problems for peoples fighting for self-government who had now to gain territorial control. The pressure to exercise territorial control by states increased in order to prevent a legal claim based on statehood from those fighting for self-determination. This shortcoming was especially serious for indigenous peoples. The struggle for autonomy by the Haudenosaunee Confederacy, also known as the Iroquois Six Nations of the Grand River, nowadays in Ontario Canada, offers an unfortunate example.

The exclusion of the Six Nations

In September 1923, the Chief of the Six Nations, Deskaheh (1872–1925) arrived in Geneva with the intention of involving the League in the resolution of the conflict between the Six Nations and the Canadian dominion.[71] The Six Nations had enjoyed relative independence from the British colony, independence that had been recognized by a series of treaties, most importantly by the treaty of Haldimand concluded in 1784 between the British Crown and the Six Nations.[72] After the First War, at

[71] In 1917, Deskaheh, whose original name was Levi General, acquired that name when becoming hereditary chief of the Cayuga, one of the Six Nations. See B. Johansen and B. Pritzker, 'Deskaheh' in *Encyclopedia of American Indian History* (Santa Barbara, CA: ABC-CLIO, 2007), pp. 712–13.

[72] In the Haldimand treaty of 1784, Iroquois loyalists who supported the King during the American Revolution obtained from the British Crown land along the Grand River: J. Rostowski, 'The Redman's appeal for justice: Deskaheh and the League of Nations' in Christian F. Feest (ed.), *Indians and Europe: an interdisciplinary collection of essays* (Aachen: Edition Herodot, 1987), pp. 435–53, 437.

the time Canada was experiencing greater levels of autonomy and was admitted to the League of Nations as a British dominion, the Canadian government increased its presence in native territories. If Canada aspired to consolidate its new status, it seemed only sensible for its authorities to assert statehood by exercising actual control over indigenous territories and refusing to recognize traditional indigenous governance.[73]

Attempts to exercise jurisdiction by the Canadian Department of Indian Affairs were strongly opposed by Deskaheh who enlisted an American lawyer, George Decker, to obtain legal counsel.[74] Deskaheh began his defence of independence in 1921, travelling to London to petition the British Government.[75] After British refusal to mediate between the Six Nations and the Canadian dominion, Deskaheh sought the good offices of the Government of the Netherlands. In 1922 Deskaheh and Decker travelled to Washington where they met the Dutch chargé d'affaires.[76] The Six Nations diplomatic mission had a promising start. As we have seen, in the case of Marcus Garvey and other semi-peripheral petitions, like petitions from peoples under Mandates, unless a League member supported the petitioners asking the Secretariat to circulate or publish the petitions, the League's Secretariat strictly policed access, shelving any petitions from peoples not recognized by the League.[77] The Dutch authorities, however, agreed to forward the petition drafted by Deskaheh and Decker. As Richard Veatch has shown, the League's acting Secretary

[73] The link between Canadian membership in the League and Canadian policy to exercise actual territorial control over Iroquois territories has been suggested by Joëlle Rostowski and Grace Li Xiu Woo. Canada was anxious to benefit from League membership and sought to acquire a positive international reputation. Experiencing greater domestic autonomy at the same time that autonomy introduced new pressures to exercise actual territorial control, the Canadian government, which until then had not established formal relations with indigenous nations, presumed now to have actual control over all territories north of the boundary with the United States. See Rostowski, 'The Redman's Appeal', p. 435 and G. Woo, 'Canada's forgotten founders: the modern significance of the Haudenosaunee (Iroquois) application for membership in the League of Nations', *Law, Social Justice & Global Development Journal (LGD)*, 1 (2003) 4 (www2.warwick.ac.uk/fac/soc/law/elj/lgd/2003_1/woo/).

[74] An American lawyer from Rochester, New York, George Decker was enrolled by Deskaheh because of his experience defending Iroquois land claims: L. Hauptman, *The Iroquois struggle for survival: World War II to red power* (Syracuse University Press, 1986), pp. 4, 186.

[75] Rostowski, 'The Redman's appeal', p. 437.

[76] R. Veatch, *Canada and the League of Nations* (University of Toronto Press, 1975), p. 92.

[77] The same petition delivered to the Dutch, as well as other similar documents, had been sent by Deskaheh to the League's Secretariat with no positive result. Veatch, *Canada and the League*, p. 94.

General, Joseph Avenol (1879–1952), tried to 'bury the matter'. As an official of the Political Section, he thought unlikely that members of the Council would ask the matter to be put on the agenda: 'The question would be completely buried and never likely to be resuscitated'.[78] However, in August 1923, the letter by the Government of the Netherlands to the Council, the petition by the Six Nations and the reply by the Canadian government were distributed to the members of Council of the League.[79]

The petition reads as an accurate articulation of the central elements required in order to be admitted to the League of Nations. It begins with a simple statement about the Six Nations: 'We are an organized and self-governing people'.[80] The petition then invoked a series of treaties concluded first with the Dutch and then with the British Crown that recognized Iroquois independence.[81] In particular, the petition explained that, having entered into alliance and assisted British forces against the colonies that had revolted, the Six Nations were offered by King George III 'to accept a home beyond the limits of the new United States, on the banks of the Grand River, in place of our guaranteed home-lands then lost to our people'. Ever since, the petition stresses, Iroquois have 'enjoyed home rule in those lands as a separate people'.[82] Finally, recounting the unsuccessful efforts to achieve protection of Iroquois sovereignty by peaceful means, the petition concludes with a warning – 'we have abstained as yet from forcible resistance of these intruders' – and an appeal for League intervention, accepting for that purpose, membership in the League of Nations and the obligations that it carries.[83]

The Canadian response came without delay: 'The claim that the Six Nations are an organised and self-governing people so as to form a political unit apart from Canada is to anyone acquainted with the actual conditions, an absurd one.'[84] The response by the Canadian Under-Secretary of State for External Affairs, Joseph Pope (1854–1926), emphasized the fact that Iroquois were under Canadian jurisdiction: 'The position of the Indians as British subjects resident for a long period of years within the unquestioned jurisdiction and recognised boundaries of Canada, subject

[78] G. H. F. Abraham to Van Hamel, 31 July 1923, LoN Archive 11/29540/28075, quoted in Veatch, *Canada and the League*, p. 94.

[79] 'Petition to the League of Nations from the Six Nations of the Grand River, communicated by the Government of the Netherlands', LoN Doc C.500.1923.VII.

[80] *Ibid.*, p. 2.

[81] 'The British, who came later, in turn recognised us as a confederacy of independent states': *ibid.*

[82] *Ibid.*, p. 3. [83] *Ibid.*, pp. 3–4. [84] LoN Doc C.154.M.34.1924.VII, p. 6.

to and protected by Canadian laws is a matter of public knowledge.'[85] For Pope, in consequence, the issue was a domestic affair in relation to which the League has no competence: 'Equally absurd, therefore is it to suggest the possibility of war in the only sense which would justify the intervention of the League of Nations... in the dispute with the Indians no military force has been employed, violations of the law where necessary having been sufficiently dealt through the police forces of the Dominion.'[86]

Had Deskaheh not continued the diplomatic offensive, in the absence of any Council member interested in taking up the issue, the whole matter would have been put to rest. Against all odds, Deskaheh and Decker travelled to Geneva to carry on with the diplomatic offensive and to campaign before the General Assembly to obtain League involvement.[87] Again, Deskaheh sought to be heard directly by the League, and again the League's Secretariat refused to hear petitions by non-members. Deskaheh also followed the trend we have seen in so many semi-peripheral delegations that published their demands in preparation of their efforts to break into international conferences, from Paris to Geneva. Deskaheh published the Six Nations' petition with a title suggesting a wider representation of the indigenous cause: 'The Redman's Appeal for Justice'.[88] Again Deskaheh tried to get support by member states to be heard, and again the Iranian delegation, represented by Arfa-ed-Dowleh, was one of the delegations offering support.

The Appeal rehashed the ideas exposed in the previous petition about the autonomy of the Six Nations based on treaties and recognition and added a more detailed argument about the justification for involvement by the League. Joëlle Rostkowski, in her study about Deskaheh's diplomatic mission in Geneva, explains that Deskaheh and Decker, after consulting the Information Section of the League, decided not to seek membership in the League.[89] Instead, the Appeal invoked Article 17 of the Covenant dealing with disputes between members and states that are not members of the League. Although bypassing the process of admission, the Redman's Appeal spelled out the same requirements we have seen to develop in the questionnaire and the process of admission. The Appeal's

[85] *Ibid.* [86] *Ibid.*

[87] Although, as we have seen, semi-peripherals' peregrination to Paris and then Geneva was not uncommon, Deskaheh's mission was unique and inaugurated later attempts by indigenous peoples to harness the international sphere to resist.

[88] 'The Redman's appeal for justice', LoN Archive 11/28075/30626.

[89] Rostkowski, 'The Redman's appeal', p. 440.

starting point was that the Six Nations was a league of states, a league of 'organized and self-governing peoples, respectively, within domains of their own'. In fact: 'the oldest League of Nations'.[90] The Appeal also makes reference to treaties and recognition granted by 'Great Britain, France and the Netherlands'.[91]

Once the elements of statehood were asserted, Deskaheh's Appeal could then describe Canadian exercise of jurisdiction as 'imposing . . . Dominion rule upon neighboring Red men . . . in violation of Six Nations Laws'.[92] Moreover, the Appeal could represent Canadian measures 'taken without the consent of the Six Nations . . . and with the manifest purpose . . . to destroy all de jure government of the Six Nations' as resulting in a situation 'constituting a menace to international peace'.[93] Canadian interventions, the Appeal protested, culminated in the 'hostile invasion of the Six Nations domain, wherein the Dominion Government then established an armed force which it has since maintained'.[94]

In September 1923, a joint letter by the delegates of Ireland, Panama, Persia and Estonia was sent to the President of the Assembly demanding a new appeal by the Six Nations to be communicated to the Assembly and suggesting that the Council request the PCIJ to give an advisory opinion on the pertinence of the Six Nations' petition under Article 17 of the Covenant.[95] Arfa-ed-Dowleh followed up with other communications demanding that the Six Nations' Appeal be discussed by the Council. What followed was a strong reaction against Deskaheh and against his mission before the League. Richard Veatch has described in detail the intricate manoeuvrings intended to bury the matter, not just by Canada and Great Britain, but also and more surprisingly by League of Nations officials.[96] When Arfa-ed-Dowleh insisted on referring the matter to the Council and insisted on the request for an advisory opinion, Secretary General Drummond took the unusual step of asking the President of the Council to challenge the Iranian delegate and inquire whether he was acting officially on behalf of the Persian Government.[97] Arfa-ed-Dowleh was thus

[90] 'The Redman's appeal for justice', p. 1. [91] *Ibid.*, p. 2.

[92] *Ibid.*, p. 4 (referring to the Enfranchisement Act and the imposition of Canadian property law).

[93] *Ibid.*, p. 4. [94] *Ibid.*, p. 5.

[95] Veatch offers a possible explanation for theses states' support of the Six Nations, noting that two days before the letter, delegates of Panama, Persia and Estonia had opposed Canada's effort to reinterpret Article 10 of the Covenant, reducing the scope of collective security: Veatch, *Canada and the League*, p. 95.

[96] *Ibid.*, pp. 96–100. [97] *Ibid.*, p. 97.

forced to refer the matter back to Teheran. In the meantime Britain exercised diplomatic pressure against Panama and Estonia, as well as Iran, cautioning that pursuing the matter further would amount to an impertinent interference in the domestic affairs of the British Empire.[98] Canada drafted an official response, which, unlike the Six Nations' petition, was published in the League's Official Journal.[99] Deskaheh personally suffered the consequences of his challenge. The Canadian government retaliated replacing the traditional governance system of the Six Nations that had Deskaheh as its Chief, with an elected Council. Deskaheh's challenge, Rostkowski argues, speeded up Canadian assimilation and enfranchisement. After more than a year in Geneva, Deskaheh returned to Canada emotionally destroyed and unwelcomed by the new indigenous authorities and died less than a year after his return.[100]

Thus 1923 was the year Ethiopians were admitted and the Six Nations rejected. Although League membership offered no consolation to an Ethiopia invaded by Italy, I have argued that Ethiopian membership was part of the trend securing more inclusive rules for admission, for statehood replaced the standard of civilization. Even the failure of the diplomatic offensive by Deskaheh illustrates this shift. Deskaheh's attempt was defeated, but this was a political defeat. It did not stop the transformations in the doctrinal structure of international law, transformations carried out in great part by semi-peripherals. Canada and Britain had to resort to behind-the-scenes machinations to forestall League intervention, rather than opting for what would earlier have been the most obvious strategy, namely invoking a standard of civilization against indigenous tribes. In 1923, this standard seemed no longer part of modern international law.

Some have interpreted statehood as a new standard of civilization.[101] This interpretation stresses the continuities between two modes of regulating exclusion and inequality. True, every standard of membership and inclusion will effect the exclusion of those polities not satisfying the set requirements. Notwithstanding the new grounds for exclusion, statehood was a semi-peripheral conquest in relation to the dissolution of the standard of civilization. At the level of ideas, with the emergence of a standard of statehood, the path to sovereignty became clear. In this process, the standard of civilization disappeared. Then, foreign – colonial, mandate, or protectorate – rule lost its justification and self-determination

[98] *Ibid.*, p. 98. [99] LoN, *Official Journal*, 5 (1924), 829–42.

[100] Rostowski, 'The Redman's appeal', p. 436.

[101] E.g. Gong, *The standard of 'civilization'*, p. 26.

could re-emerge as the right of polities fighting for territorial control. This finally occurred much later, with a change in international politics, during decolonization, but the intellectual seed had been sown before, during the interwar.

The dissolution of the standard of civilization was an important intellectual victory; though it was a victory with considerable costs, as the defeat of Deskaheh and the destiny of the Six Nations shows. Statehood both accelerated a policy of assimilation of indigenous tribes and the exercise of effective territorial control over their territories by Canada, hindering any prospect of indigenous sovereignty in the absence of territorial control. Acquiring territorial control by force therefore became a factual condition for acquiring sovereignty. As a result, international law rules governing armed resistance by polities fighting for self-government and regulating repression by military forces became extremely important; these rules thus became another subject for contestation between core and semi-periphery.

Acquiring statehood by force: the Syrian uprising and the French bombardment of Damascus

The political defeat of a right to self-determination in Paris and the subsequent rise of a formal concept of statehood requiring territorial control created a double incentive in favour of the resort to collective violence. On the one hand, peoples fighting for independence had to acquire territorial control in order to attain statehood and consequently in order to obtain self-determination. On the other hand, as we saw in the example of the Six Nations, states like Canada were pushed to extend and exercise effective control over territories with peoples aspiring to obtain political independence. When armed resistance was followed by a crackdown, it became crucial to determine the legal status of those resisting foreign rule with armed force as well as to determine the legality of military measures adopted by the mandatory or protecting power. Did insurgents and the civilian population under foreign rule enjoy humanitarian law protections, or were humanitarian protections limited to war between civilized combatants? Was military repression in a protectorate or in a mandate within or beyond the competence of modern international law? Let me explore these questions in relation to the 1925 rebellion in the Syrian mandate, and with some brief reference to the Bondelswarts incident in South West Africa and the war of the Rif in the Spanish and French protectorates in Morocco.

Between 18 and 20 October 1925, French forces bombarded the city of Damascus.[102] Five years earlier in 1920, having obtained the mandate at the San Remo Conference, France invaded Syria, captured Damascus and dissolved Faysal's kingdom, which had declared Syrian independence after the Great War. The French ruled by exploiting religious and ethnic differences, creating an autonomous Lebanon and further fragmenting Syria by giving administrative autonomy to Aleppo and Damascus, as well as to an Alawi coastal state and to the Jabal Druze. The French also ruled with brutality, exiling nationalist activists under the threat of capital punishment and allowing the *Services Speciaux*, a military intelligence unit, to acquire far-reaching influence in the Mandate.[103]

In 1925 the French faced a general rebellion. The five years between the French invasion of Syria and the general insurrection were not peaceful. While the traditional Damascene elite oscillated between accommodating to French rule and resisting by appealing to the French government and the League of Nations, Syrians of more modest and rural background were willing to oppose French rule by force. As Michael Provence has shown, the coalition of Syrian nationalist forces opposing French rule included Druze leaders and some Damascene merchants, peasants and workers, as well as some Bedouin and Christian villagers.[104]

The revolt started in the Ḥawrān, the region controlled by the Druze, with two decisive victories over the French in the battles of al-Kafr and al-Mazra'a.[105] The French High Commissioner responded, not only adopting severe repressive measures, such as press censorship, the banning of political parties and public gatherings, and incarceration and deportation of political figures, but also waging war against insurgents. French battalions charged rebels on the ground, while aeroplanes fought them from the skies, bombarding villages that had been accused of having 'harboured' or 'assisted' insurgents.[106]

The rebellion reached national scale when the most radical Damascene and Druze leaders decided to bring the revolt to Damascus. By October 1925, unable to control insurgency within the city, the French, supported by aircraft, tanks and artillery decided to confront the rebels in the villages

[102] There is a large literature on the uprising leading to the bombardment. I have relied mostly on Michael Provence's work: M. Provence, *The great Syrian revolt and the rise of Arab nationalism* (Austin: University of Texas Press, 2005).

[103] W. L. Cleveland, *Islam against the West: Shakib Arslan and the campaign for Islamic nationalism* (Austin: University of Texas Press, 1985), p. 46, citing A. Hourani, *Syria and Lebanon, a political essay* (Oxford University Press, 1946), pp. 170–9.

[104] Provence, *Syrian Revolt*, p. 67 and *passim*. [105] *Ibid.*, p. 61. [106] *Ibid.*

surrounding Damascus. After looting and burning villages and executing villagers, French soldiers returned to Damascus with prisoners and corpses as trophies. When prisoners were executed in the main square and mutilated corpses of rebels were put on display, Damascus rose up in arms.[107] While police and gendarmes abandoned their posts, insurgents reached the vicinity of the palace occupied by the French and looting spread over the bazaar. On 18 October, the uprising of the city as well as the general Syrian revolt was swiftly quashed by a massive bombardment of Damascus. The French High Commissioner, before the rebellion reached Damascus, had already decided how to respond to the uprising. Without warning to residents, Damascus witnessed two full days of French firepower. Complete quarters of the old city, including residences and Mosques, were destroyed by the bombardment. Nearly 1,500 people, including men, women and children were killed.[108] As insurgents left Damascus, Damascene notables, who disavowed responsibility for the uprising, negotiated an end to the bombardment, the French demanding payment of a fine in Turkish gold lira and in rifles.

The bombardment of Damascus was yet another instance in the long and bloody list of atrocities committed by Western forces during the history of colonial domination. And it was not the first time an insurrection in a colony, mandate or protectorate was suppressed with military violence and specifically with aerial force, as the Bondelswarts affair showed.[109] After the bombardment of Damascus a debate on the legality of the military operation and in general on the laws applicable to warfare pitting forces of 'civilized states' against forces of 'less-advanced', or 'savage' peoples, ensued on the pages of the *American Journal of International Law*. An American international lawyer, Quincy Wright (1890–1970) wrote a comment somewhat critical of the French, while a lesser-known figure, a US captain named Elbridge Colby (1891–1982), responded to Wright invoking the classical standard of civilization to argue that the rules governing

[107] Q. Wright, 'The bombardment of Damascus', *AJIL*, 20 (1926), 263–80, 264; Provence, *Syrian revolt*, p. 102.

[108] These numbers are taken from P. Khoury, *Syria and the French Mandate: the politics of Arab nationalism, 1920–1945* (Princeton University Press, 1987), p. 178. Quincy Wright believed causalities to be between 500 and 1,000: Wright, 'The bombardment', 264. On the contrary, French representatives to the League's PMC special session to discuss the bombardment, maintained that only between 150 and 200 people died during the bombardment: PMC, Minutes of the eighth session (extraordinary), Rome, February, 1926, LoN Doc C.174.M.65. 1926 VI, pp. 152–3.

[109] See e.g. D. Omissi, *Air power and colonial control: the Royal Air Force 1919–1939* (New York: St Martin's Press, 1990).

combat between civilized states do not apply in a military confrontation between a 'civilized state' and 'savage peoples'.[110]

Quincy Wright, then a young professor at the University of Chicago, during the Second World War became adviser to the US Department of State and after the war became US adviser to the International Military Tribunal in Nürnberg. Wright had written his doctoral dissertation on the League's mandate system as a new form of international administration, had travelled extensively through the Middle East while conducting research for his dissertation and visited Damascus after the French attack. Unlike captain Colby who framed the question in terms of the civilized status of the opponents, Wright examined the legality of the bombardment within the broader issue of determining international law's scope of validity. Is the use of force to suppress a rebellion a domestic or international affair? Is military force part of the matters traditionally considered the exclusive competence of the territorial state? This was a typically modern topic. If classical international law provided sovereigns with a shield to protect their autonomy, modern scholars believed that there was no domain out of the reach of international law, for as Pillet, Scelle and others had been arguing for decades, it is not the state, but the individual who is the real and ultimate subject and end of international law.

Wright explained that Syrians 'look upon the situation as one of warfare . . . astonished [about the League's inaction] they think that the laws of war should be applicable and that these laws forbid the bombardment of undefended towns'.[111] The French, on the other hand, conceive the uprising as a problem of 'banditry or brigandage . . . the activity of her forces as police measures outside of international law'.[112] Wright thought that there were two possible theories explaining the positions held by the Syrian and the French. Based on the standard of civilization, the French position conceives repression of the Syrian uprising outside the realm of international law. Commenting on the French position and not entirely discarding the standard, Wright notes that the old standard is no longer understood as drawing an absolute dividing line between civilized and savage peoples: 'perhaps . . . Syria would come better under the head of "nonage" or immaturity' which was precisely – as Wright points out – the 'theory of "tutelage"' adopted by the Covenant of the League when establishing the mandate system. Wright, however, opposed this interpretation.

[110] E. Colby, 'How to fight savage tribes', *AJIL*, 21 (1927), 279–88; Wright, 'The bombardment'.

[111] Wright, 'The bombardment', 265. [112] *Ibid.*

Although many authors quote the standard – Wright observes – it is not clear what rules of general international law would be subtracted, that is, would not apply in relation to non-civilized peoples. In this respect Wright is absolutely clear: neither 'the different culture' nor 'the fact of tutelage would withdraw Syrians from the protection of the law of war . . . '[113]

In 1926, the standard of civilization – Wright thinks – was no longer credible. The French – Wright notes – should in consequence use another theory to justify the resort to armed force in the mandate. The French considered the repression of the uprising as domestic violence outside the realm of international law. Wright, however, as a modern international lawyer, was committed to the project of international law serving individuals rather than states. Moreover, in light of the modern idea that law imposes limits on sovereignty, Wright declares: 'France has no powers in Syria other than those conferred by the mandate'.[114]

French international lawyers, not in any way different from other Western jurists at the core, remained unapologetic about colonialism and silent about its darker episodes.[115] French internationalists, as we have seen, were at the forefront of the modern internationalist legal discourse. Therefore, they probably were uninterested in openly voicing a nationalist defence of the French position. Rather, French lawyers understood the problem of armed resistance as a technical jurisdictional issue, which explains their general silence in relation to the bombardment. Nathaniel Berman, in his study of French 'colonial desires' in relation to the war of the Rif, has shown that Western interwar lawyers placed the regulation of violent rebellions against Western rule outside the realm of international law. Let us remember that combat between Riffian forces and the Spanish and French military forces preceded and then overlapped with the Syrian Revolt. Berman notes that 'no major French, American or British international law journal published an article about this war'.[116] In fact, Berman quotes no other than Georges Scelle – the leading French international lawyer we have encountered in Part III – in order to explain international

[113] *Ibid.*, 265. [114] *Ibid.*, 268.

[115] The *Revue*, for example, published nothing about the bombardment; although a short review of Wright's article was included, it did not comment on the legality of French action. Moreover, French studies about the mandate system were generally doctrinal and formalist: see e.g. P. Pic, *Le régime du mandat d'après le traité de Versailles, son application dans le proche Orient: mandat français en Syrie, anglais en Palestine et Mésopotamie* (Paris: A. Pédone, 1923).

[116] N. Berman, '"The appeals of the Orient": colonized desire and the war of the Riff' in K. Knop (ed.), *Gender and human rights* (Oxford University Press, 2004), pp. 195–230, 202.

lawyers' silence. Berman explains that only after having been consulted by the French Human Rights League, Scelle gave an opinion about the Rif, affirming that the war was outside the competence of international law. The following passage is quoted by Berman in translation:

> The Rif, the Riffians, Abd-el-Krim, have no international personality of any degree. Morocco is a country under protectorate with two protecting States and the League of Nations has no capacity to intervene in the domain of a protectorate . . . legally, one cannot even say that there is a war – an international war, of course, because there is a war in the larger sense of the term . . .[117]

Since French international law scholars remained mostly silent, the French position referred to by Wright was the position adopted by the French government, forced by the League's PMC to defend the use of armed force in the Syrian Mandate. However, the silence of French lawyers turned out to reflect a similar position to that of the French government forced to speak out. French officials did not argue that humanitarian protections in armed combat were inapplicable regarding combatants that did not meet the standard of civilization. Rather, like Scelle who argued that repressive measures in a protectorate, namely armed force against Riffian rebels in the French protectorate of Morocco, were outside the purview of international law, French officials maintained that armed repression in Syria re-established order in the mandate. However, limiting the scope of international law to exclude the regulation of war was a very conventional position to take; remember that Lapradelle and Basdevant, for instance, argued that interventions in China and Venezuela were justified since modern international law protects, in the name of humanity, the interests of individuals rather than the rights of sovereigns.[118]

Arguing that armed repression in a protectorate was beyond the competence of international law, was probably a plausible though conservative argument to make in the interwar period, but arguing that armed repression in a mandate was beyond the competence of international law, was unsustainable. For the mandate system was not just a regime established by the League, but a regime in which the mandatory power acted 'in behalf of the League', and in which the League retained wide powers to advise, cooperate, censure and supervise the mandate.[119] In fact, as we will see, the French government defended military force to repress the Syrian

[117] G. Scelle, 'Rapport', *Les Cahiers des droits de l'homme*, 25 (1925), 496 in Berman, 'Appeals of the Orient', p. 202.

[118] A. de Lapradelle, 'La question chinoise' and Basdevant, *L'action anglo-germano-italienne*.

[119] Wright, *Mandates*, p. 191 and see in general chs. 7 and 14.

revolt as a proportionate measure within the limits of the mandatory power's authority over mandated communities.

The ward no longer wants to collaborate

Robert de Caix (1869–1970), former Secretary-General of the French High Commissariat for Syria and Lebanon, addressing the PMC as delegate of France, explained that the administration of a Mandate, especially an A Mandate, was 'as thorny a problem as its principle was easy to formulate'. For, the 'collaboration of the ward was very often lacking'.[120]

Under the League's Mandate system – specifically, according to Article 22 of the Covenant – as the mandatory power in Syria, the French government had to prepare an annual report in reference to the territory committed to its charge. The body responsible for receiving and examining the annual reports and for supervising the fulfilment of the obligations that the Mandate imposed on the mandatory power was the PMC. The French government had the obligation to explain and justify before the PMC the repressive measures adopted against Syrian rebels.

While the French were bombarding Damascus, the PMC was holding its seventh session in Geneva. The Chairman, Marquis Theodori, informed his colleagues that he had received a vast number of telegrams and letters protesting about the situation in Syria.[121] Following existing rules of procedure to handle petitions, the PMC did not discuss the content of the petitions and passed the information to the mandatory power.[122] Accordingly, the French government prepared a response and an extraordinary session was scheduled for February 1926 to meet in Rome.[123] In this extraordinary

[120] PMC, Minutes of the eighth session, p. 131.

[121] PMC, Minutes of the seventh session of the Permanent Mandates Commission, held Oct. 19–30, 1925, LoN Doc C.P.M.328, p. 129. During the days following the bombardment, the Chairman was flooded with telegrams and letters sent by Syrian organizations from around the world. Among others: Members of the Syrian Colony, Valparaiso, [Chile] Telegram of 29 October 1925; Members of the Syrian Association, Paris, Telegram of 22 October 1925; Members of the Syrian Society of America, New York, Telegram of 8 November 1925; Telegram of 22 October 1925. For a full list see *ibid.*, Annex 2, pp. 171–3.

[122] *Ibid.*, pp. 129, 133. On the procedural rules to be adopted by the PMC to handle petitions, see A. Momirov, 'The individual right to petition in internationalized territories: from progressive thought to an abandoned practice', *Journal of the History of International Law*, 9 (2007), 203–31.

[123] The PMC held one annual session and, after 1923, two sessions during the year. The Commission decided to hold a third extraordinary session on Syria during the winter of 1926. Although with some objections about expenses and potential political costs, the Commission decided, because of the milder weather, to meet in Rome rather than

session the PMC would discuss the French annual Report of 1924 and a new preliminary Report of 1925 in light of the 'recent disturbances' and in view of the numerous appeals, petitions and protests denouncing French repression of the uprising.[124] Among these, the petitions drafted by Shakib Arslan, envoy of the Syro-Palestinian Congress, as well as countless protests and memoranda sent by organizations like the National Lebanon League and the Syrian American Society of the United States.[125]

In September 1921, a group of Syrian exiles organized in Geneva a Syro-Palestinian Congress, in order to formulate a coherent response against the French Mandate and decide on the best strategies to procure League support.[126] Michel Luftfallah, a Greek-Orthodox from a wealthy merchant-landowner family of the Syrian community in Egypt, was the driving force and financier of the Congress and was appointed its president. A Lebanese Druze, Shakib Arslan was selected as member of a permanent delegation established to represent the cause in Europe and before the League.[127] In 1925, when the rebellion escalated, the Congress was reactivated and Arslan moved from Turkish exile to Switzerland.

On the eve of the bombardment, the Syro-Palestinian Congress drafted an appeal addressed to the League's General Assembly, to inform about 'the unhappy position of the Syro-Palestinian people' as well as their 'grievances and aspirations'.[128] The Congress neither challenged the League's authority, nor the mandate system itself. Rather, the Syro-Palestinian Congress requested the League's 'assistance, help and protection'. For, in light of the way in which the mandate had been applied, the

in Geneva: Wright, *Mandates*, p. 144. Members of the Commission did not regret their choice. At the close of the session they expressed gratitude for Italian hospitality. They were delighted by the 'tranquility' of the 'magnificent palace' of the Minister for the Colonies where they met and the opportunity of being presented to the King of Italy and Mussolini. PMC, Minutes of the eighth session (extraordinary), Rome, Feb. 16, March 6, 1926, LoN Doc C.174.M.65. 1926 VI, p. 170.

124 PMC, Ordre du Jour de la VIII-me Session (Extraordinaire) de la Commission Permanente des Mandats, LoN Doc C.P.M. 370.

125 PMC, Minutes of the eighth session, pp. 8–9. For a full list of petitions received during the eighth session with regard to the situation in Syria see PMC, LoN Doc C.P.M. 508 and Memorandum of the Syrian American Society, registered by the PMC in Rome on 18 February 1926 as LoN Doc C.P.M. 373.

126 Cleveland, *Islam against the West*, p. 49.

127 *Ibid.*

128 Due to its importance, the PMC decided to include the document as an Annex to the minutes of the eighth session. See Executive Committee of the Syro-Palestinian Congress, Appeal addressed to the Sixth General Assembly of the League of Nations, Cairo, September 29, 1925: PMC, Minutes of the eighth session, pp. 174–86.

French had prevented the attainment of 'the praiseworthy ends aimed at by the League', leading Syria to 'political and economic retrogression'.[129] French administration – the appeal explains – was far from being the 'advanced nation' that according to Article 22 of the Covenant of the League would show the Syrian people how to withstand the 'strenuous conditions of the modern world'.[130] The French mandate – the Syro-Palestinian appeal declared – was nothing but bad and backward administration. French advisers, who are attached to almost all administrative departments 'do not possess qualifications required for the performance of their duties and have not the necessary competence'.[131] Some are simply soldiers, 'quite ignorant of administrative procedures', others inexperienced officers. Though for both everything is foreign: the language, custom, history and mentality of the country.[132] They accept 'tips' and, worst of all, base their actions on the reports, full of 'lies and calumnies', sent in by 'hundreds of spies', 'creatures without law or God', 'men lost to all honor'. The appeal summarizes the argument linking bad administration to the rebellion: it was the 'tyranny and brutality' of Captain Carbillet, the Governor of the Jebel Druze, that sparked the rebellion of 1925.[133]

Rather than enlightened and modern government, the Syro-Palestinian Congress saw everywhere signs of backward administration. The very same division of Syria, to start with, followed sectarian considerations, a policy without 'precedent even in the Middle Ages'.[134] Breaking Syrian

129 *Ibid.*, p. 174.

130 The first two paragraphs of Article 22 of the Covenant of the LoN establish the central principles of the mandate system:

> To those colonies and territories which as a consequence of the late war have ceased to be under the sovereignty of the States which formerly governed them and which are inhabited by peoples not yet able to stand by themselves under the strenuous conditions of the modern world, there should be applied the principle that the well-being and development of such peoples form a sacred trust of civilisation and that securities for the performance of this trust should be embodied in this Covenant.
>
> The best method of giving practical effect to this principle is that the tutelage of such peoples should be entrusted to advanced nations who by reason of their resources, their experience or their geographical position can best undertake this responsibility, and who are willing to accept it, and that this tutelage should be exercised by them as Mandatories on behalf of the League.

131 Syro-Palestinian Congress, 'Appeal', p. 176. 132 *Ibid.*, p. 177.

133 *Ibid.*, p. 176; the 'situation becoming intolerable, it was natural that delegations should be formed to protest against the present regime and to lay before the French High Commissariat the complaints of the population': *ibid.*, p. 185.

134 *Ibid.*, p. 175.

unity was achieved by stirring up religious antagonism.[135] French policy in the mandate, in areas like finance, education or culture, did not fare better. Here the appeal brought together a wide array of examples showing backward policies. For instance, instead of financial assistance to modernize Syria, French authorities have taken gold reserves out of the country, tying the Syrian currency to the Franc, with disastrous economic consequences. Moreover, all French expenditure has been limited to maintaining an 'army of occupation', which has 'terrorized the population . . . preventing popular manifestations'.[136] Without formal permits, French societies have carried out archaeological excavations, the destiny of the objects discovered being unknown and only a small part of them given to the Syrian Museum. Although both Arabic and French are official languages, since French officials do not speak Arabic, French has acquired a privileged status. Similarly, French schools teaching French as well as fidelity to France, receive special treatment from the High Commissariat, while intriguing against other local schools.[137]

In 'essence' the mandate 'is a system of colonization pure and simple'. The appeal concludes declaring that 'Syria is making no progress' and asking the PMC to send a mission of inquiry to Syria.[138] The drafters of the appeal invoked here the distinction between classical international law's exploitative colonialism and modern international law's commitment to the administration of territories formerly under colonial rule as a 'sacred trust of civilization'. In relation to communities formerly part of the Turkish Empire that have reached 'a stage of development where their existence as independent nations can be provisionally recognized', Article 22 of the League determined the establishment of a mandate, to provide 'administrative advice and assistance . . . until such time as they are able to stand alone'.[139] In the words of the Syro-Palestinian appeal, the mandatory power has no right to exploit the land in its own benefit, but to help 'these countries towards the attainment of the dearest of their aspirations – *complete independence*'.[140]

135 *Ibid.*, pp. 175, 181. 136 *Ibid.*, pp. 175–81. 137 *Ibid.*, pp. 175–81.

138 *Ibid.*, pp. 174, 186.

139 Covenant LoN, Article 22, para. 4: 'Certain communities formerly belonging to the Turkish Empire have reached a stage of development where their existence as independent nations can be provisionally recognized subject to the rendering of administrative advice and assistance by a Mandatory until such time as they are able to stand alone. The wishes of these communities must be a principal consideration in the selection of the Mandatory.'

140 Syro-Palestinian Congress, 'Appeal', p. 174 (emphasis in the original).

Mandate rule: indirect and temporary, or direct and brutal?

Modern semi-peripheral lawyers and advocates would not settle for less than independence, but it was not absolute sovereignty that they aspired to obtain. Semi-peripherals strived to obtain an internationalized sovereignty, namely autonomy guaranteed by the international community. The Syro-Palestinian appeal, for instance, affirmed: 'We are convinced that after reading this statement you will agree that the best course would be to leave us full freedom to govern ourselves without foreign interference, and to draw up our constitution on the lines of modern institutions under the protection of the League of Nations'.[141]

But determining the exact scope and nature of the protection the League should afford would depend on the answer given to a number of other questions: what is the nature of the mandate itself? What is the nature of the authority and competences of the PMC? These were questions formulated by the League's PMC, by other mandatory powers as well as by the very same peoples under the mandates system. For the rules of the Covenant as well as the treaties instituting each mandate were full of broad standards and vague concepts in need of interpretation. For example, the Syrian petitions, as we will see, read Article 22 of the Covenant emphasizing the expression 'able to stand alone' as 'complete independence', while members of the PMC read the expression 'administrative advice and assistance' as 'indirect and temporary rule', while mandatory powers like France read the expression as conferring a 'right of administration' including a right to legislate, levy taxes and most importantly ensure defence and maintain order.

The interpretation of indirect rule was discussed by the PMC on various occasions, including the extraordinary session on Syria held in Rome in February 1926. Here again, the symbolic differentiation between old and new colonialism acquired concrete relevance to sustain a distinction between direct rule associated with the colonial past and indirect rule associated with modern international law. At the first meeting of the extraordinary session, after a long presentation and discussion of the French Report of 1924 and the preliminary Report of 1925, which specifically dealt with the uprising, and after a long discussion on procedure, including the decision to follow a questionnaire to guide the interrogation of the mandatory power's representative, based on the precedent of the Bondelswarts affair, the Dutch member of the PMC, D. F. W. van Rees

[141] *Ibid.*

(1863–1934), addressed Robert de Caix, the French delegate and former French official in the Mandate of Syria and Lebanon.

Finding the French report wholly inadequate, van Rees redirects the discussion to general questions about the French understanding about its mission in Syria.[142] What is the French idea of the powers accorded to her in the administration of a mandate? – van Rees asks bringing into discussion an article published in the *RGDIP* by Paul Pic, a French international law professor. In his article, Pic not only argued that the right of administration included the right to legislate and to levy taxes, to ensure defence and maintain order in the mandate, and therefore, the right to occupy the mandate with armed forces and to organize local militia under French control. But also, Pic maintained that the mandate imposes on France only a 'moral obligation to respect as far as possible local autonomies'.[143] The view supported by Professor Pic is misleading – van Rees reproached the French delegates. The mandate is a 'custodian' who has the obligation to refrain from 'direct administration and from any interference in the local native organizations'.[144] In fact, the PMC believed that the more commitment to temporary and indirect rule is shown 'in each act of administration', the deeper will 'inhabitants be imbued with the same doctrine and the more speedily and more completely will peace be established in Syria'.[145]

Caix replied with nothing but the conventional line. However, it was a line that finally conceded the validity of temporal and indirect rule, departing from the views like the one supported by Pic. It was therefore a welcomed declaration registered by the Commission with 'very great satisfaction' and included in the PMC's Report to the League.[146] Caix stated:

The mandate is a provisional system designed to enable populations which, politically speaking, are still minors to educate themselves so as to arrive one day at full self-government. This presupposes that the mandatory power will gradually create native organizations in the mandated territory such as may, when complete be able to ensure entirely the government of the country and such as may,

[142] Actually, in the final Report to the League the PMC regrets the 'inadequacy of the written documentation supplied by the mandatory Power': PMC, Minutes of the eighth session, p. 201.

[143] P. Pic, *Le régime du mandat d'après le traité de Versailles: son application dans le proche Orient, mandat français en Syrie, anglais en Palestine et Mésopotamie* (Paris: A. Pédone, 1923), p. 43 and PMC, Minutes of the eighth session (extraordinary), Rome, LoN C.174.M.65 1926 VI, p. 47.

[144] PMC, Minutes of the eighth session, p. 47. [145] *Ibid.*, p. 202. [146] *Ibid.*, p. 202.

if they carry out their duties in a proper manner, render the intervention of the Mandatory unnecessary.[147]

The declaration of the French delegate, as the PMC noted, restated the doctrine of indirect rule, the commission's official interpretation regarding the rights of the mandatory power. Once Caix declared commitment to what the PMC believed to be the letter and spirit of Article 22 and of the rules contained in the mandate of Syria and Lebanon, discussing whether the mandate authorised direct or indirect, permanent or temporal rule was no longer part of the debate. Instead, the discussion was now centred on defining indirect and temporal rule, defining the rights that the mandatory power enjoyed under indirect rule and determining specifically the type of coercive measures it could adopt to secure order in the mandate.

Armed repression: proportionality rather than civilization

In plain terms, once the French declaration restated the idea that peoples under mandate are like 'minors' in need of 'tutelage', the discussion shifted to determining the best pedagogy 'in the interest of the minor'.[148] It was clear for Caix, clear from the point of view of the French that the tutor had powers not only to 'give advice', but also to 'correct the work of the native government and even to make up for their deficiencies' and that for this reason the mandate required an 'organization of tutelary nature, possessing the necessary authority to ensure the good government and progress of the country'.[149] The Swiss member of the PMC, William Rappard (1883–1958) agreed in principle with Caix. Rappard – a renowned internationalist who would later co-found and direct the *Institut des Hautes Études Internationales* in Geneva – using a similar metaphor to describe the mandatory power's mission, affirmed: 'if children asked their father to help them in performing their tasks, there was for the father a middle course between himself performing them and leaving the children entirely to themselves. The policy . . . to recommend was neither revolutionary nor one of immobility, but a progressive educational policy'.[150]

[147] *Ibid.*, p. 45.

[148] Caix recognized that Syrians were 'independent and sovereign but were in the same position as a minor who had virtually all his rights, the free exercise of which was merely postponed': *ibid.*, p. 61. Rappard, the PMC member, responded with a number of problematic metaphors about the responsibilities of the father on the education of children: *ibid.*, pp. 51, 130 and *passim*.

[149] *Ibid.*, p. 45. [150] *Ibid.*, p. 130.

Was armed repression included among the powers that the French 'tutor' had in Syria?

Although the PMC agreed that 'correction' and 'tutelage' corresponded to a standard of indirect rule, members of the PMC expressed utter discontent with the lack of evidence in the French reports. Without concrete evidence, van Rees complained that it is impossible to determine if the incidents in Syria followed actually from 'direct administration' or 'guardianship'. The reports seem to be written for a political body, regarding political exigencies, but this is not a political, but a technical body – van Rees insisted. Rappard joined van Rees, pointing out that supervising the 'good execution of the mandate' was impossible when, 'particularly anxious concerning the interests of the minor', the PMC listens only to the guardian, while 'the minor is absent', and the PMC 'only knows about grievances through documents it cannot check'.[151]

Rappard was referring to the grievances in the countless petitions and memoranda by Syrian organizations we have seen above, of which he probably knew not only in writing but probably also personally from Shakib Arslan, who had travelled to Rome with hopes of being heard by the PMC. We know from the Bondelswarts affair that the PMC regarded its supervisory role to be different from the role of a commission of inquiry and that in consequence it neither visited mandates, nor heard directly individuals from the mandates or their representatives.[152] However, similar to the Bondelswarts affair where the PMC discussed the incident following reports by the Anti-Slavery Society, during the Rome meeting, members of the PMC followed petitions closely and explicitly during the discussion of the Syrian revolt. In fact, the French delegate Caix was warned not to continue repeating the facts from the 'French side', and was directed to address the complaints mentioned in the petitions.[153]

In addition to inquiring about the causes of the revolt, the PMC interrogated Caix about the role of the secret services, the use of black and Algerian troops, the use of aeroplanes, the use of gas and the civilian casualties inflicted by the bombardment of Damascus, among other grievances that had been raised by the Syrian petitions. When it came to the question of the repression of the uprising, Caix responded: 'The incidents of 1925 were a question of proportion'.[154] In light of the contested nature

[151] *Ibid.*, p. 51.

[152] Rappard himself mentioned that the position of the PMC was 'extraordinary delicate' because while receiving petitions and transmitting them to the French government, it can only hear and accept the replies from the mandatory power: *ibid.*

[153] *Ibid.*, p. 53. [154] *Ibid.*, p. 131.

of the rules regulating warfare against non-Western combatants, as we have seen in the divergent positions held by Wright, Colby and Scelle, this answer was significant. Caix's declaration neither invoked a standard of civilization to argue that international law protections did not apply to Syrian rebels, nor maintained that French repression in the mandate was beyond the purview of international law.[155] Rather, foreshadowing the modern trend to regulate through broad standards, it claimed repression of the Syrian uprising to have been proportional. Once again, it is worth mentioning that the introduction of a proportionality test did not mean that modern international law represented progress or a necessary improvement in the rules applicable to semi-peripheral polities. Recalling the exchange between French officials, the PMC and Syrian activist, simply suggests that the legal language changed both for legitimizing Western domination and for articulating semi-peripheral resistance.

In fact, and rather unsurprisingly, core actors interpreted the new standard in ways that were detrimental to peripheral polities. Invoking a standard of proportionality, Caix assumed – and the PMC accepted – that to maintain law and order the mandatory power had a right to resort to force. The legality of measures for the 'suppression' of a revolt and to maintain order had already been enunciated a few years before by the PMC during the discussion of the Bondelswarts incident.[156] Assuming that force to maintain law and order has to be proportional in order

[155] The exact scope and nature of humanitarian law protections that The Hague regulations included in the case of non-international conflicts and in relation to aerial warfare was far from being clear. For example, the 'Rules concerning the control of wireless telegraphy in time of war and air warfare', drafted in 1923 by the Commission of Jurists at The Hague, included norms relevant to the repression of the Syrian uprising and to the use of force in the semi-periphery. For example, Article 22: 'Any air bombardment for the purpose of terrorizing the civil population or destroying or damaging private property without military character or injuring non-combatants, is forbidden.' Article 24: 'Aerial bombardment is legitimate only when directed at a military objective, that is to say, an object of which the destruction or injury would constitute a distinct military advantage to the belligerent . . . The bombardment of cities, towns, villages, dwellings, or buildings not in the immediate neighborhood of the operations of land forces is prohibited. In cases where the objectives specified in paragraph 2 [military targets] are so situated, that they cannot be bombarded without the indiscriminate bombardment of the civilian population, the aircraft must abstain from bombardment.' The rules in the draft never came into force as a treaty; their standing as customary law, as an emerging state practice or as moral humanitarian principles remained disputed.

[156] During the examination of the questionnaire drafted to guide the discussions with the South African government regarding the Bondelswarts affair, van Rees explained: 'If a revolt occurred, it was evident that the re-establishment of order demanded a suppression of that revolt in the common interest': PMC, *Minutes of the third session*, p. 68.

to be lawful, left a malleable margin to regard repressive measures as unlawful, because entailing disproportionate or unreasonable force. An incipient test of proportionality and reasonableness was adopted by the PMC in order to assess the mandatory power's responsibility in relation to 'measures of suppression' against the Bondelswarts.[157] In the hands of Caix, the standard became so malleable that if not for the gravity of the issue, it would look like a comical manipulation of proportionality. While the principle of distinction between combatants and civilians was already an established principle of humanitarian law in the Hague regulations, according to which military operations should be limited to military targets and to obtain a military advantage, Caix defended the opposite, lack of precision as meeting the standard of proportionality. The French aerial bombardment 'was not a particularly barbarous method of repression, as the people could almost always hear the aeroplanes coming and had time to take shelter; further, the bomb-throwing was extremely inaccurate'.[158]

Standards like proportionality presented semi-peripherals with a great challenge. Making use of relatively indeterminate standards, powerful actors were left with ample room for choosing between multiple potential outcomes – arguing that inaccurate bombing is proportional, for instance. But there was an additional and more serious problem. Broad standards interact with relatively determinate rules. If rules were disadvantageous for the periphery, we can only expect the articulation of broad standards to reflect rather than resist this structural imbalance. If standards were articulated from the particular standpoint of core states, without rules to dispute the 'French side', the series of assumptions from which the dominant standpoint is framed will remain undisputed. Freire d'Andrade, the Portuguese member of the PMC, noted that aeroplanes may be used to 'impress natives', but warned Caix that 'bombardment may claim victims among women and children'. Caix replied that using ground forces would claim 'more casualities among soldiers'. Choosing air over ground forces seems only a plausible and proportional choice from the 'French side' and in relation to background rules that were disadvantageous to the peripheries. If we accept the metaphor used by French officials and the

157 Van Rees also argued: 'If, however, that suppression was carried out in a manner as harsh as it appeared in the case under discussion, the government could only escape responsibility if it were clearly proved that measures of suppression of a less drastic nature were impossible, either from a military point of view, or from the view of its internal policy.' *Ibid.*

158 PMC, *Minutes of the eighth session*, p. 148.

PMC and accept that the French is a tutor over minors in need of education, and that the tutor has power to discipline mischievous students, then the rules sanctioning the mandate and the mandatory power's right to impose law and order – even if we also believe that the mandate is in the ward's own interest – would probably tolerate the French not deploying ground forces and legitimately avoiding, as Caix put it, incurring 'greater sacrifices' and encountering 'greater difficulties'.[159] We would probably also regard the use of aeroplanes proportional by South African forces – as it was actually argued – because of the economic expediency when operating in vast territories.[160] Casualties seemed in this context almost inevitable and most unfortunate, as Caix concluded: 'war in which the operations were being conducted against people who were not in uniform might invoke very unfortunate consequences'.[161]

The small number of international rules that could be clearly appealed to in order to defend the interests of semi-peripheral polities limited the positive impact that the substitution of civilization with proportionality could have yielded. The absence of rules, for example, sanctioning armed resistance to obtain self-determination, or concrete *lege lata* rules prohibiting aerial bombardment of civilians in non-international conflicts, limited the potential for PMC supervision and semi-peripheral activism. Actually, both the South African delegate answering questions posed by the PMC regarding the Bondelswarts affair and Caix answering for the French repression in Syria pointed out the right to maintain law and order and the use of aeroplanes to repress insurgents.[162] Regarding the protection of civilians during the suppression of an uprising, immunity was a humanitarian privilege not granted to 'villagers' who 'consented to receive' or 'collaborated with' rebels, 'an attitude which . . . justified repression'.[163]

As semi-peripheral international lawyers appropriated the modern discourse, as they skilfully produced modern arguments advancing the interests of their polities, semi-peripherals realized they had reached a dead-end. Were international law to continue offering avenues for semi-peripheral resistance, they realized that many existing rules had to change and new rules had to be enacted. This is what semi-peripheral lawyers

[159] *Ibid.*, pp. 148–9. [160] PMC, *Minutes of the third session.*
[161] PMC, *Minutes of the eighth session*, p. 151.
[162] '. . . repressive measures taken by aeroplanes were not . . . exceptional; such measures were frequently taken in similar cases – for example, in Iraq': *ibid.*
[163] *Ibid.*

and diplomats, especially Latin Americans, sought to achieve by codifying modern international law. The codification of new laws of war, specifically in relation to non-international armed conflict against colonial rulers, had to wait until the second post-war, until the Geneva Conventions. However, what semi-peripherals achieved during the interwar was not insignificant. At the third Hague Conference they blocked the codification of state responsibility, because it could grant to foreign residents a standard of protection higher than to nationals. At Montevideo, among other new rules, semi-peripherals obtained a formal definition of statehood and non-intervention.

9 Codifying American international law: statehood and non-intervention

Codifying international law was, during the first decades of the twentieth century, part of a concerted effort, by scholars, governments and scientific associations, to modernize the classical legal order inherited from the previous century. International lawyers strived to bring international law up to date. Not only laying down, systematically and comprehensively, existing law, but also formulating the new rules that would allow for the progressive development of international law. The interwar codification effort yielded, however, only modest results. At the first codification conference convened at The Hague in 1930, states failed to pass any codification project.[1]

Seen from the perspective of the semi-periphery, however, codification involved more than restating old law and laying down new rules. Codification opened a precious opportunity for discussing and changing the basic structure of international law. Semi-peripherals, and in particular Latin Americans, rose up to the challenge. Although among the many projects drafted only few became law, the history of codification between the 1900s and the 1930s witnessed a great semi-peripheral victory. More than enacting a few new rules, Latin Americans transformed the structure

[1] For example, a United Nations report taking stock of the history of codification, recounts the pessimistic views expressed by many governments at the final Assembly of the 1930 Hague Conference. Among others, the report quotes a British delegate stating: 'the Conference failed to reach agreement even on the most fundamental point'. See 'United Nations documents on the development and codification of international law', *AJIL*, 41 (1947) (supplement), 29–148, 82. Moreover, Manley Hudson, the Harvard professor who had not only led a codification research group, but also submitted many of its own projects to the Conference, stated: 'The results achieved are somewhat meagre': M. Hudson, 'The first conference for the codification of international law', *AJIL*, 24 (1930), 447–66, 447.

of international law. This chapter looks at the codification effort to explore and in part explain this transformation, expressed, in the shift from a universal international law to regional international legal orders, from the standard of civilization to formal statehood and a declarative doctrine of recognition, and from intervention to non-intervention.

At the Seventh Pan-American Conference held in Montevideo in 1933, the nineteen states of Latin America and the United States adopted the 'Convention on Rights and Duties of States'. Up until today, international lawyers looking for an authoritative definition of statehood quote Article 1 of the Montevideo Convention:

> The state as a person of international law should possess the following qualifications: a) a permanent population; b) a defined territory; c) government; and d) capacity to enter into relations with the other states.[2]

To our contemporary eyes, Article 1 appears as either a mere *lege lata* restatement, or a formalist conception of statehood demanding an update. Conversely, in the eyes of Latin American publicists contemporary to the negotiations, the Montevideo Convention culminated in a more than thirty years long effort to codify and transform international law. For them, the Montevideo Convention represented an immense accomplishment, not just because of the new definition of statehood, but mainly because the adoption of a formal conception of statehood was accompanied by a declaratory doctrine of recognition and followed by an enumeration of the fundamental rights enjoyed by states, including sovereign autonomy and equality. Most importantly among these: non-intervention.

In historical hindsight, although forgotten beyond Article 1, the Montevideo Convention marked a definite departure from classical international law, not least because the signatories included, in addition to all the states of Latin America, the United States, the central force behind the reconstruction of the international order after the Great War.[3]

[2] Convention on Rights and Duties of States, Montevideo, 26 December 1933.

[3] The centrality of the United States is generally missed because of the European bent of most histories of international law. The rise of the US, as Benjamin Coates has shown, came at the turn of the twentieth century with the foundation of professional organizations, like the American Society of International Law, that harnessed a new consciousness of national power and the availability of vast funds provided by the Carnegie Endowment for International Peace, with an American mission to expand international law and institutions: B. Coates, 'Transatlantic advocates: American international law and US foreign relations, 1898–1919', PhD dissertation, Columbia University (2010), pp. 68–9, 84 ff, 193 ff and *passim*. The active involvement of the United States in the development of modern international law makes the passage of

A formal conception of statehood marked a radical departure from classical international law's substantive standard of civilization. More significant for what it excluded than for what it required, a formal definition of statehood struck a potent blow to the doctrine of the standard of civilization. A formal conception excluded any substantive criterion within the definition of statehood. It excluded all substantive qualifiers that had previously been considered relevant to attribute sovereignty. Including, for instance, reference to the race, religion or culture of the population, to the size of the territory, to the nature of the government, or to the type of relations – equal or unequal – non-Western states had established with Western states.

According to classical international law, as we have seen, international personality and membership in the international community depended on the capacity of a state to meet the standard of civilization. Introducing a declarative doctrine of recognition, Articles 3 and 4 of the Montevideo Convention delivered a final blow to the standard of civilization. 'The political existence of the state is independent of recognition by the other states' – affirms Article 3. The simple conjunction of the elements listed in Article 1 – population, territory, government and capacity to enter interstate relations – gives rise to international personality, and bestows all the rights that emanate from sovereignty. States enjoy these rights 'even before recognition' – Article 3 insists – 'upon the simple fact of its existence as a person under international law' – concludes Article 4.

These two doctrines – statehood and recognition – were not new. Many scholars, like the very same Antoine Pillet, one of the precursors of the modern sensibility, had already identified the elements of the statehood as territory, people and government. On the other hand, Lassa Oppenheim, in the first edition of his treatise, affirmed that new members of the 'family of nations' are 'not born into that community' but admitted 'into it through recognition'.[4] Pillet, however, identified the elements of statehood in the context of existing states and the functions they have to secure for self-preservation.[5] Pillet, moreover, reaffirmed the

US–Latin-America relations explored here relevant for the global history of international law.

[4] Oppenheim, *International law*, vol. I, p. 16; 'those States which have hitherto formed the Family of Nations must expressly or tacitly consent to the reception of the new member': *ibid.*, p. 32.

[5] In the context of a discussion of the right to self-preservation, Pillet declares that 'the content of this right or function of internal preservation is of tacit analysis. One knows the elements of which a state is essentially composed: these are territory, people and a

conventional nineteenth-century view according to which membership in the international community and enjoyment of rights depended on people's level of civilization.[6] Pillet discussed the elements of statehood assuming the existence of a state. Similarly, Oppenheim believed that 'statehood alone does not imply membership in the Family of Nations'.[7] Membership depends on both civilization and recognition.[8]

The novelty of Montevideo rests therefore on how it combined statehood and recognition as formal statehood and declaratory recognition in order to decouple sovereignty from civilization. In fact, compared to the standard developed by the League of Nations to decide on the admission of new states, Montevideo introduced another fundamental innovation. And again the novelty came from what Montevideo excluded. As we have seen in the previous chapter, the standard for admission developed by the League required the applicant, in accordance to Article 1 of the League's Covenant, not only to be 'self-governing', but also to have been de jure and de facto recognized by a significant number of states, that is, it required a level of independence as well as a constitutive doctrine of recognition. Montevideo, conversely, excludes both the criterion of independence, replacing it with 'government', and the constitutive doctrine, replacing it with a declaratory doctrine of recognition.

The writings of semi-peripheral scholars arguing for the dissolution of the standard of civilization appropriated the language of modern international law. This intellectual work paid off in the concrete rules enacted by the Montevideo Convention. In this regard, the Convention should

distinctive political organisation. The completeness of these three elements assures the preservation of the state. Maintaining this completeness constitutes the first duty of the State'. A. Pillet, *Recherches sur les droits fondamentaux des états dans l'ordre des rapports internationaux et sur la solution des conflits qu'ils font naître* (Paris: A. Pédone, 1899), p. 79.

6
> ... there is no equal rights between the civilised states and the uncivilised or less civilised states. The former handle their relations with the latter as superiors responsible for making them enter willingly or by force in the ways of civilisation: on this basis they arrogate to themselves certain rights to direct, to control and sometimes to administer, that without these they would not have them in any way against them. Between the status of one and the other, there is flagrant inequality, and this inequality is in fact the real basis of their relationship.

Ibid., p. 25.

7 Oppenheim, *International law*, vol. I, p. 108.

8 'As the basis of the Law of Nations is the common consent of civilised States, statehood alone does not include membership of the Family of Nations ... For every State that is not already, but wants to be, a member, recognition is therefore necessary. A State is and becomes an International Person through recognition only and exclusively': *ibid.*, pp. 108–9.

be considered as a unique offspring of the modern semi-peripheral sensibility. Latin American international lawyers and diplomats who had been drafting and negotiating codification projects for decades, probably indifferent about intellectual affiliations, were most satisfied with what they believed was Montevideo's greatest achievement, the recognition of non-intervention in Article 8: 'No state has the right to intervene in the internal or external affairs of another'.[9]

Codifying non-intervention was a great achievement because Article 8 did not lay down existing law, but created new law. According to general public international law and specifically according to the corollary to the Monroe doctrine, the United States enjoyed a right to intervene coercively in another state to protect its nationals or national interest, to recover public debt and other pecuniary claims based on injuries suffered by its nationals.[10] Signing the convention, the United States renounced for the first time the right it had defended and invoked when intervening in Latin America. It is therefore understandable that Latin Americans thought that the most important aspect of Montevideo was the inclusion of the fundamental rights derived from statehood. The fundamental rights of states are absolute (Article 5). Juridical equality does not depend on the power of the state. All states enjoy the same rights and have the same capacity to exercise them (Article 4). Sovereign autonomy is also absolute. Not only have states no right to interfere in the internal and external affairs of other states, but also the state has absolute jurisdiction over all inhabitants within its territory, thus foreign residents cannot claim rights more extensive than those of nationals (Articles 8 and 9).[11]

The recognition of absolute sovereign autonomy and equality, achieved by the Montevideo Convention, had been a central goal for semi-peripheral publicists of the classical period. Let us remember the bold, though unsuccessful, defence of sovereign equality by Barbosa at the Second Hague Conference and by Pueyrredón at the League of Nations. Let us remember that Drago's plea for sovereign autonomy by proscribing intervention was only partially adopted at the Second Hague Conference in 1907. Montevideo realized non-intervention, sanctioning the Drago doctrine thirty

[9] Convention on Rights and Duties of States, Montevideo, 26 December 1933.

[10] Only a few years before Montevideo, the Department of State published a Memorandum prepared in 1928 by undersecretary J. Reuben Clark containing the traditional view on the legality of American interventions in Latin America: J. R. Clark, *Memorandum on the Monroe doctrine* (Washington: Government Printing Office, 1930).

[11] Convention on Rights and Duties of States, Montevideo, 26 December 1933.

years after its first formulation in 1902. In relation to its greatest achievements, the Montevideo Convention may therefore look anachronistic. It either appears to have recognized sovereign rights too late, or perhaps to have recognized sovereignty for semi-peripheral states too early. Let me explain.

Recognizing absolute sovereignty during the interwar years, a period characterized, on the one hand, by the need to limit sovereignty to make room for the first permanent international organization, the League of Nations, and on the other hand, by the modernist anti-formalist disaggregation of sovereignty, in 1933 Montevideo may already seem passé. Alternatively, if foreshadowing the return to sovereignty prompted by the Third World movement's revival of legal formalism after decolonization, the Montevideo Convention came too early into life.[12] This anachronism may explain the relative absence of the Montevideo Convention from our historical memory.

This anachronism is both correct and inaccurate. It may seem anachronistic from the point of view of Western history of international law, but in fact the Montevideo Convention expressed and was one of the high points of the modern international law sensibility as articulated in the semi-periphery. This chapter explains why. The history leading to Montevideo suggests that codification advocated by Latin Americans expressed the modern semi-peripheral sensibility that, rather than disowning sovereignty, repositioned the demands for autonomy and equality in modern terms. The rules codified in Montevideo had a massive impact: if not on the unequal distribution of power and resources that characterizes international relations, it transformed the normative structure on the basis of which powerful states seek to justify and stabilize the exercise of international power and weaker states seek to resist. They put an end to the classical legal order. Rules on statehood and recognition marked the dissolution of the standard of civilization. Rules enunciating the rights and duties of states gave form to the modern regime governing semi-peripheral sovereignty.

Why to codify under modern international law?

In 1923, ten years before the signing of the Montevideo Convention, and long twenty-three years before his tenure at the ICJ, before becoming the

[12] On the reappearance of the language of absolute sovereignty and the apparent resurgence of legal formalism, see Becker Lorca, 'Eurocentrism'.

Court's most famous dissenter, Alejandro Alvarez presented to the Fifth Pan-American Conference held in Santiago a project to codify 'American international law'.[13] Otherwise remembered as one of the most prominent anti-formalist international lawyers, Alvarez produced during the first decades of the twentieth century a vast literature on codification as well as numerous codification projects.[14] Why was Alvarez along with other interwar modernist scholars interested in codifying international law?

The codification movement of the interwar years was part of the wider effort to renew international law in the aftermath of the crisis brought by the First World War.[15] After the Great War, as we have seen, the classical sensibility of the nineteenth century centred on the absolute sovereign autonomy and equality of states was superseded by a modernist, cosmopolitan sensibility that limited sovereignty in the name of a stronger international legal order.

The modernist jurist thought that the centrality that their classical predecessors had ascribed to state sovereignty imposed an insurmountable obstacle to the development of institutions capable of representing the interest of a much stronger and interdependent international society. They believed that sovereignty made the conclusion of treaties enacting rules to limit state behaviour so difficult that the legal order inherited from the previous century had a fundamental problem: international law contained only a handful of rules. Interwar scholars advocated for the reconstruction of international law. They thought that a legal order capable of securing international peace had not only to contain more rules, but also rules that reflected not just the interests of states but the interest of the international community. Were international law to be renewed

[13] A. Alvarez, *La codificación del derecho internacional en América* (Santiago de Chile: Imprenta Universitaria, 1923).

[14] For example, A. Alvarez, *La codification du droit international, ses endances – ses bases* (Paris: A. Pédone, 1912); A. Alvarez, *La conférence des juristes de Rio de Janeiro et la codification du droit international américain* (Paris: A. Pédone, 1913); A. Alvarez, *Rapport-questionnaire et projets présentés à la deuxième session de l'institut américain de droit international à la Havane* (Washington: Institut américain de droit international, 1917); A. Alvarez, *Le nouveau droit international public et sa codification en Amérique plan développé des matières d'un ouvrage en 2 volumes, devant paraître sous ce titre, et être présenté à l'Assemblée des juristes américaines, à Rio de Janeiro en 1925, pour la codification du droit international* (Paris: A. Rousseau, 1924).

[15] For an example of the connection between codification and modernist renewal during the interwar period see e.g. G. Guerrero, *La codification du droit international: la première conférence (La Haye, 13 mars–12 avril 1930)* (Paris: A. Pédone, 1930), pp. 9–10. For contemporary analysis, see O. Diggelmann, *Anfänge der Völkerrechtssoziologie*.

beyond the shortsighted interests of states, modern scholars believed that codification had to be led by the League of Nations and scientific organizations, rather than by states.[16]

Thus, the codification of international law, which had been advocated since the times of Bentham, did not begin until international law became also a profession. General codification efforts did not really take off until 1873, year of the foundation of the *Institut de Droit International* in Ghent and the International Law Association in Brussels. Both professional associations were created to contribute to the progress of international law. In both associations, the advantages of codification were discussed. In both, scientific meetings, in which specific aspects of international law were studied – from the establishment of a prize tribunal to the regulation of warfare – were followed by codification proposals. Some of these projects were in fact adopted by the First and Second Peace Conferences convened in The Hague.[17]

However, most codification drafts prepared by scholars and then taken up by states in the Hague Conferences were not adopted into law. The project of the 'men of 1873', as Koskenniemi has called them, to civilize the behaviour of nations through law faced a number of difficulties. Reconciling the rights of the sovereign with the obligations imposed in the name of the international community, reconciling realism with idealism,

[16] For example, the Committee of jurists advising the League on the drafting of the Statute of the PCIJ advocated for the codification of international law, suggesting that a number of scientific organizations should be invited to prepare codification projects. The American lawyer and head of the international law section of the Carnegie Endowment, James Brown Scott, commented: 'The experience that the world has had with the Conference at Paris, composed of nationally-minded instead of internationally-minded men, has suggested in more than one quarter the advantage of consulting members of scientific bodies . . . ' J. B. Scott, *The project of a permanent court of international justice and resolutions of the advisory committee of jurists: report and commentary by James Brown Scott* (Washington: The Endowment, 1920), p. 138. Similarly, Alejandro Alvarez thinks that jurists are better equipped because they will not just recognize the rights of states, but also the obligations and limitations imposed on sovereignty by international solidarity, by the needs of an interdependent international community: A. Alvarez, *Exposé de motifs et déclaration des grands principes du droit international moderne (approuvée par l'Académie diplomatique internationale, l'Union juridique internationale et l'International Law Association)* (Paris: Les Éditions Internationales, 1936).

[17] On the rise of international law as a profession see Koskenniemi, *Gentle civilizer*, pp. 39 ff. The profession's engagement with codification began in 1866, at the meeting of the British Association for the Promotion of Social Science, in which David Dudley Field proposed the appointment of a committee to prepare the outlines of an international code, and with the publication of Bluntschli's *Das moderne Völkerrecht* in 1868. See, E. Nys, 'Codification of international law', *AJIL*, 5 (1911), 871–900, 887.

was not easy. The failure of the Hague conferences were for the most part attributed to the persisting classical preference given to the interest of sovereigns above the interest of the international community, to high politics above the progress of international law.[18]

The liberal internationalist of the beginning of the twentieth century identified a defence of sovereignty with the classical sensibility, and saw both sovereignty and classical legal thinking as great obstacles to the development of international law. However, the challenge that the modern language of international law was bringing to the classical paradigm, redefining and to some extent eroding states' absolute sovereignty to carve out room for international organizations, echoed in the semi-periphery as an articulation of new forms of inequality for smaller states. For example, we have seen that Brazilian delegate Ruy Barbosa and others perceived that the greater privileges given to the Western great powers to determine the Court's composition was the most controversial aspect of the proposal to create a permanent international court at the Second Hague Conference. During the negotiations of the Covenant of the League of Nations, Japanese delegates Nobuaki Makino and Sutemi Chinda deemed unacceptable to include in the Covenant a clause recognizing religious equality at the same time that the equality of all states and races was excluded. Argentinean delegate to the first Assembly of the League of Nations, Honorio Pueyrredón, also regarded unacceptable that the Council of the League of Nations was formed not only by members elected by the Assembly, but also by permanent members, dropping Argentina out of the League when his motion, including among others the democratic election of all members of the Council by the Assembly, was not taken up by the Assembly.

At the Second Hague Conference of 1907 and during the negotiations leading to the League, semi-peripherals saw their most cherished positions either defeated or upheld at great costs. Semi-peripheral jurists learnt from these experiences. Having openly, in publications and academic gatherings, articulated the modern discourse of international law, semi-peripheral lawyers were ready and awaiting the next codification opportunity to reframe the demand of sovereign autonomy and equality

[18] The renowned German liberal internationalist Walther Schücking, for example, laments German opposition to compulsory arbitration at the Second Hague Conference. Though opposition to arbitration was celebrated in Germany, Schücking condemns this 'reactionary attitude' that forestalled the development of international law: Schücking, *Die Organisation der Welt*, pp. 605–6.

in the modern vocabulary. This opportunity came when the codification project resurfaced during the interwar years.

Codifiers at the centre and the semi-periphery: the 'crisis of codification'

Modern jurists thought that the centrality that their classical predecessors had bestowed to sovereignty imposed an insurmountable obstacle to the development of rules and institutions capable of representing the interest of a much stronger and interdependent international community. Absolute sovereignty, more specifically the 'will theory', permeating the doctrine of sources of international law with a contractual image, subordinated rules limiting state behaviour to states' explicit or implicit consent, to the conclusion of a treaty or to the finding of common state practice. These arguments that had been expressed by international lawyers since the turn of the century, acquired renewed force after the First World War. To the modern international lawyer, classical international law's old structure explained the scarcity of international rules, in particular rules limiting the powers of sovereigns to go to war, and showed that codification was the best answer not just for moving international law forward by enacting more rules, but also for renewing international law and securing international peace.

After the Great War, it was clear that a stronger international order would require not only a permanent international organization and a permanent court of justice, but also new rules of international law. The Advisory Committee of Jurists that prepared the Statute of the PCIJ, for example, worried that the potential of a future Court would be hampered by the absence of clear rules of international law for the Court to apply in the resolution of disputes. In a resolution presented to the Assembly of the League, the Committee suggested resuming the Hague Codification Conferences.[19] A Third Codification Conference to be convened in 1915, as decided by the Second Hague Conference, never met because of the outbreak of the war. After the war, in 1924, the Assembly of League of Nations resolved to call for a Third Codification Conference to be held in

[19] The Committee advocated codification to restate and clarify existing law as well as to reconcile divergent rules and formulate new ones in areas where rules became obsolete after the Great War and the transformations of international life. Moreover, in the interest of international justice, the Committee considered codifying new subjects not regulated by international law. Scott, *The project of a permanent court*, pp. 133–4.

1930 and appointed a Committee of Experts to carry out the preparatory work.[20] Semi-peripheral jurists saw another opportunity opened with the resumption of the codification effort.

In 1924, Latin American lawyers were ready to participate in the debate on codification, now speaking the language of modern international law. After various rounds of negotiations and disagreement about codification, at each of the Pan-American Conferences convened since 1889, Latin Americans enjoyed a head start.[21] By then, Alejandro Alvarez for instance, had presented numerous codification projects and published a vast literature on codification.[22] In fact, Alvarez was among the first international lawyers to frame the codification of international law in modern terms. In 1912, on the occasion of the first meeting of the Rio Committee of Jurists – a group of experts commissioned by the Third Pan-American Conference to study and draft codification proposals – Alvarez published *La codification du droit international, ses tendances – ses bases* bringing codification up to date by transforming it into an anti-formalist legal technique to renew international law.[23]

Alvarez was in a privileged position. Professionally based in Paris it was easier for him to be versed in the modern legal discourse, to befriend modern jurists and penetrate professional circles at the core. At the same time, Alvarez was politically and normatively situated in Latin America, for which rather than discounting sovereignty, equality and non-intervention he reinserted these aspirations within the modern discourse.[24]

Thus, on the one hand, Alvarez appropriated the conventional dichotomy that modern jurists had constructed between an old and a new social order and between a classical and a modern law. The transition from 'a system of pure individualism and anarchy in international relations' into a 'system of solidarity' brought the classical international

20 *Ibid.*, p. 133.

21 The First International Conference of the Americas, or Pan-American Conference met in Washington in 1889. By 1924, American states had organized five continental conferences, namely Mexico City 1902, Rio de Janeiro 1906, Buenos Aires 1910 and Santiago 1923.

22 Between 1912 and 1924 Alvarez had published a book and various articles on codification. Alvarez was in a better position than many renowned Western scholars. For example, Manley Hudson's work on codification leading the 'Harvard Research in International Law' project was inspired by Alvarez's work, although this influence was not openly acknowledged by Hudson. See Becker Lorca, 'Alvarez situated', 922–6.

23 Alvarez, *Codification du droit.*

24 On Alvarez's double position, as central and semi-peripheral, see Becker Lorca, 'Alvarez situated'.

law fashioned after a 'naturalist metaphysic' into crisis.[25] The crisis was aggravated – Alvarez insists – by publicists' inability to recognize the emergence of a new modern law reflecting social interdependence and based on positive observation of the new conditions of modern life. Instead, old publicists continue conceiving the international society as an 'aggregate of sovereign and independent states' and believe that international law is a 'set of rules that civilised states should follow in their mutual relations'.[26] To put an end to the discredit of international law, Alvarez proposes studying the classical foundations of international law and revising them in accordance to the basis of modern international life. Codification should be enlisted in this reconstruction. Codification – Alvarez believed – entails more than drafting rules: it should begin with the exploration of the fundamental basis of international life, it should be subjected to rigorous criticism in order to reflect the new conditions of modern life. Modern life has transformed the basis of international law, for states are immersed in a regime of interdependence and solidarity.[27]

While repeating the conventional critique of classical international law, Alvarez, on the other hand, is distinctively semi-peripheral when rooting in Europe the elements of the old regime that persist in spite of the efforts to renew international law: imperialist and nationalist competition and the European balance of power. In contrast, Alvarez places high hopes on the renewal of international law in the new world. Latin American codification should therefore itself become a modern legal tool. Alvarez advised the Pan-American Committee of Jurists, which had been given the task of preparing a draft code, not to undertake a codification effort like a classical private law project. Instead of drafting one code, in Alvarez's proposal, the Committee would periodically submit to states new projects and modifications to existing projects, so that the Committee becomes the continent's legislative power, adapting international law to the necessities of modern life, at a moment in which – Alvarez insisted – we live in an epoch of transition from *individualism* into solidarity.[28]

[25] Alvarez, *Codification du droit*, pp. 122–3 and *passim*. [26] *Ibid.*, p. 7. [27] *Ibid.*, *passim*.

[28] Junta Internacional de Jurisconsultos, *Actas, resoluciones y documentos: primera reunión en Rio de Janeiro, 26 de junio–29 de junio de 1912* (Rio de Janeiro, 1914), at pp. 47–51, 51–76; A. Alvarez, *La codificacion del derecho internacional en América: trabajos de la tercera Comisión de la Asamblea de Jurisconsultos reunida en Santiago de Chile* (Santiago de Chile: Imprenta Universitaria, 1923), pp. 26–7.

State responsibility: the Hague Conference again blocked by the semi-peripherals

The Conference was least successful in its work on the responsibility of states. The Committee informed the Conference that it

> was unable to complete its study of the question of the responsibility of States for damage caused on their territory to the person or property of foreigners, and accordingly was unable to make any report to the Conference . . .

This failure was all the more surprising as this subject appeared before the Conference to be ready for codification.[29]

Given Alvarez's prolific writing on codification, it is not surprising that by 1924, when the League decided to resume codification, other semi-peripheral lawyers were able to reframe the old demand for autonomy and equality in the modern legal vocabulary. Were modern international lawyers from the semi-periphery more successful than Barbosa, Drago or Makino, who articulated similar demands in classical terms? Gustavo Guerrero (1876–1958), a Salvadorian jurist who later became judge and president of both the PCIJ and the ICJ, had the opportunity to test the limits of the modern international legal discourse.[30] The Committee of Experts for the Progressive Codification of International Law had decided to study codification in four different areas. One of them was the responsibility of states for damages done in their territories to the person or property of foreigners.[31] This was not only a very delicate issue for

[29] 'United Nations documents on the development and codification', 82.

[30] Gustavo Guerrero was born in 1876 in the capital of El Salvador, San Salvador and died in Nice, France in 1958. Guerrero displayed early his rebellious character as a law student in El Salvador. Publishing a few articles criticizing the government, Guerrero had to finish his studies in Guatemala. Back in El Salvador, Guerrero entered the Foreign Service and went off to Europe, occupying consular positions in France and Italy, becoming then ambassador in Paris where he befriended the Parisian cosmopolitan community of international lawyers. In 1927 he returned to El Salvador to serve as Minister of Foreign Affairs, and, as we will see, heading the Salvadorian delegation to the Pan-American Conference in Habana. In Habana, Guerrero led the anti-imperialist legal backlash against the United States, for which he lost his position as minister. Guerrero returned to Europe representing Salvador before the League, becoming president of the League's Tenth Assembly, and later on judge and president of both the PCIJ and the ICJ. See 'Gustavo Guerrero, 1876–1958, in memoriam', *Revue Internationale française du Droit des Gens*, 28 (1959), 5–8; A. Martínez Moreno, Alfredo, 'José Gustavo Guerrero, caballero andante de derecho' in A. A. Cançado Trindade and A. Martínez Moreno (eds.), *Doctrina latinoamericana del derecho internacional* (San José: Corte Interamericana de Derechos Humanos, 2003), pp. 9–32.

[31] As Alan Nissel has shown, one of the historic roots of contemporary state responsibility was the nineteenth-century US diplomatic practice regarding the protection of

semi-peripheral states with Western residents in their cities and ports, as the Venezuelan blockade or the Boxer intervention in China showed, but also state responsibility, as a contemporary commentator put it, 'involves principles that underlie the whole fabric of public international law'.[32] The Committee appointed a Sub-Committee to prepare a report. Gustavo Guerrero was appointed Rapporteur.[33]

The Guerrero report

Similar to Alvarez, before discussing which rules to codify, Guerrero begins his report with an exposition of the bases of codification.[34] Guerrero presents the sovereign rights semi-peripheral states should enjoy in modern terms. The 'absolute need of social intercourse' – Guerrero repeats the modern mantra – 'creates the need for law'.[35] When states realize that they have interests in common – Guerrero explains in his report – states not only organize themselves into an international community, combining their wills in 'one common will' that creates international law, but also subordinate the authority of each of them to the 'higher authority of the international community'. Although international law's binding force is based on consent, Guerrero concludes affirming that consent is not given by states considered individually, but by the collective will of all states: 'the wills of separate States coalescing in one single will'.[36]

These statements were truly in line with the modern sensibility, affirming that the rules proposed in his report reflect the collective will of

investments of American citizens abroad and the rules that evolved to regard a state responsible for the violation of the interests of foreign investors: A. Nissel, 'The duality of state responsibility', *Columbia Human Rights Law Review*, 44 (2013), 793–858.

32 'To the international lawyer . . . the Responsibility of States for Damage Caused in Their Territory to the Person or Property of Foreigners, involves principles that underlie the whole fabric of public international law. There is perhaps no subject of international law so constantly and so actively before the nations, nor one which so vitally affects them, as that of Responsibility of States.' H. Green, 'Responsibility of states for damages caused in their territory to the person or property of foreigners', *AJIL* 24 (1930), 500–516, 500, quoted in Nissel, 'The duality', 21.

33 G. Guerrero, 'Questionnaire no. 4: responsibility of states for damage done in their territories to the person or property of foreigners', *AJIL* (supplement), 20 (1926), 176–203.

34 According to Diggelmann, engaging in theoretical discussions was a characteristic common to modern international lawyers who reacted against the excessive descriptivism and positivism of their classical predecessors: Diggelmann, *Anfänge*, pp. 24–31.

35 Guerrero, 'Questionnaire', 178. 36 *Ibid.*, 178–9.

the international community, rather than the particular interest of semi-peripheral states. But at the same time, Guerrero deploys the modern legal discourse selectively, discounting the centrality of writings by jurists as sources of international law. Guerrero explains that studying the question of state responsibility, and in particular the recourse to coercion when responsibility is established, one should not consider the domestic law of some nations to look at the rights and duties states have vis-à-vis foreign residents and nationals residing abroad. States are free to enact domestic rules and bestow rights to individuals, though these rights are not valid at the international level, for international law governs interstate relations, and individuals are not international law subjects.[37] Nor should one look at international rules, customary or conventional, that govern the relations of some states and are in opposition to the collective will of the international community.[38] Moreover, only marginal appreciation should be given to the views held by scholars, since doctrine 'has no power to determine what is the unanimous will of nations'.[39]

Guerrero had good reasons to limit the sources relevant for codification. Foreign residents frequently invoked diplomatic protection and Western states routinely invoked injury to their nationals to intervene abroad. Some claims were based on custom, others were written in unequal treaties between Western and non-Western states and there was lots of writing by scholars from the core gathering support in favour of intervention. At the time of the Hague Conference, Edwin Borchard, an American professor at Yale, for example, had written a book about diplomatic protection.[40] Borchard's book contained a defence of state responsibility for damages against foreigners; as strong as vehement was his reaction against Guerrero's report:

> Perhaps that [Hague] Conference was handicapped from the start by the fact that the Guerrero report . . . departed materially, in some of its fundamental postulates and premises (representing minority views) from the subsequent Bases of Discussion, which reflected the views of the majority of the replying governments.[41]

[37] *Ibid.*, 179. Recognizing rights 'would be tantamount to reverting to universal relations under *jus naturale*': *ibid.*, 180.

[38] *Ibid.*, 179–80. [39] *Ibid.*, 181. [40] Borchard, *The diplomatic protection.*

[41] E. Borchard, '"Responsibility of states" at the Hague Codification Conference', *AJIL*, 24 (1930), 517–40, 517 (parenthesis in the original). Borchard participated in the Conference as one of the American delegates and was appointed to the drafting committee of the Third Committee dealing with state responsibility. Borchard was not happy. Guerrero's report was blamed for the failure of the Conference, a report that

Borchard had good reasons to be displeased: distinguishing between domestic and international law, between the will of some states and the common will of the international community, and disregarding the work of eminent scholars, Guerrero's report widens the autonomy of smaller states by limiting their scope of responsibility. Thus, Guerrero challenged the nineteenth-century American diplomatic practice of protecting investments by Americans abroad.[42] Although Guerrero admits that the international community has recognized the existence of certain basic rights to all individuals, rights that have therefore become the minimum protection states should afford to foreign residents. But these rights – Guerrero's report warns – do not include a right to claim more favourable treatment than is accorded to nationals. The maximum the foreigner can claim is civil equality with nationals. Guerrero, however, notes that national treatment is not part of customary international law. The obligation to grant national treatment therefore needs to be explicitly established by a treaty.[43]

First in the report and then in the meetings of the Third Committee at the Codification Conference, Guerrero, supported by other delegates from states of the semi-periphery, argued that responsibility should be predicated upon the infringement of an international legal obligation positively established by treaty or custom and not on the basis of obligations deduced by analogy from domestic law.[44] Guerrero's report concludes:

contradicted Borchard's own ideas. While he had advocated the pre-eminence of the consequential duty to repair for injuries, Guerrero emphasized the breach of an obligation under an existing international rule. See Nissel, 'The duality', 819.

42 See Nissel, 'The duality'.

43 Moreover, Guerrero makes it plain that it is only the territorial state that affords protection and that the territorial state is free to decide how to afford that protection: Guerrero, 'Questionnaire', 182–4.

44 Unlike contemporary international law, according to which state responsibility can be established in relation to any breach of an international obligation, Guerrero's report defined and listed the specific violations eliciting responsibility: political crimes (only when the state fails to act in due diligence); illegal acts of officials (acting within their powers, when the state fails in its duty to prevent the action or does not take adequate measures thereafter) and denial of justice (when the state refuses to grant foreigners free access to the courts). In relation to the latter, Guerrero knew that he was arguing against the view held by many publicists who found states responsible for judicial error or for decisions that were manifestly unjust. Guerrero supported his position both in terms of the sovereign autonomy of judicial decisions and on the common will of the international community. Guerrero excluded from state responsibility acts by officials committed outside their scope of competence and, most importantly, acts of privates, including damage caused during riots, revolutions or civil war, cases in which the state becomes responsible only if it denies access to courts. *Ibid.*, 185–93.

Since international responsibility can only arise out of a wrongful act, contrary to international law, committed by one State against another State, damage caused to a foreigner cannot involve international responsibility unless the State in which he resides has itself violated a duty contracted by treaty with the State of which the foreigner is a national, or a duty recognized by customary law in a clear and definite form.[45]

In consequence, international responsibility arises not from the injury sustained by foreigners, but from an action or inaction imputable to a state. From this conclusion, Guerrero deduces another consequence that is particularly important to semi-peripheral states. Until all means of pacific settlement have been exhausted, the state seeking redress is barred from using coercion.[46] If responsibility arises between states in relation to events happening within the jurisdiction of one state, international law should offer a peaceful avenue for states to investigate and determine the facts involving the wrongful act contrary to international law. Guerrero notes that this instance already exists in a number of treaties establishing the compulsory intervention of an 'international commission of enquiry'. Guerrero finally advocates for including this obligation in a general international convention. Most important of all, according to Guerrero, this convention would proscribe the use of coercion before and after the formation of the commission of enquiry.[47]

The semi-peripheral challenge: Guerrero, Sipsom and Wu

The Guerrero report was circulated among governments, League members and others participating at the Hague Conference. Some participants gave comments, on the basis of which the committee of experts drafted the 'bases of discussion', containing a number of propositions to guide the deliberations at the conference.[48] This document departed substantially from the Guerrero report. With the appointment of Jules Basdevant from France as Chairman and Charles de Visscher (1884–1973) from Belgium as Rapporteur, the Third Committee opened the floor for discussion. Delegates from semi-peripheral states immediately took the opportunity to disagree with the general principles contained in the bases of discussion.

45 *Ibid.*, 201. 46 *Ibid.*, 198–200. 47 *Ibid.*, 199.

48 League of Nations, *Act of the Conference for the Codification of International Law, The Hague, 1930, vol. IV, Minutes of the Third Committee* (Geneva: League of Nations, 1930), bases of discussion, annex 1, pp. 198 ff.

Constantin Sipsom (1875–1960), the Rumanian delegate, pointed out that if responsibility will be recognized when a state infringes an international obligation towards foreign subjects: 'it would have been preferable to invert the order of the factors and to start by determining the obligations towards foreigners'. Under customary international law – Sipsom argued – it is far from clear what rights foreigners enjoy and what obligations states have regarding foreign residents.[49] In the same vein, Guerrero defended the main points of his report. As soon as the discussion of the articles began, specifically regarding Basis of Discussion No. 2 on responsibility for the 'enactment of legislature incompatible with its international obligations, resulting from treaty or otherwise', Guerrero warned: 'everything will depend on our definition of international obligation'.[50]

Disagreements like this resurfaced throughout the discussion. During deliberations about the definition of obligation, local remedies, denial of justice or responsibility for acts of officials, delegates were divided, mostly between core and semi-periphery.[51] For example, the demand, by the Salvadorian and Rumanian delegates, Guerrero and Sipsom, to clearly define the obligations generating responsibility (Basis No. 2), was firmly opposed by delegates from the core. W. E. Beckett, the British delegate, affirmed that codification should not cover all obligations, leaving room for a general custom as a source of obligation.[52] Others believed that it was not necessary to determine the international obligations of states, since it was not the role of the conference to become the codifier of the law applicable to foreign residents.[53] The attempt to reach a compromise on the basis of defining the sources of international law obligations, rather than the obligations themselves, also failed.[54]

[49] *Ibid.*, pp. 18–19. [50] *Ibid.*, p. 27.

[51] Semi-peripherals advocated for the exhaustion of local remedies as a strict requirement, while delegates from the core argued for a broad notion of denial of justice. Moreover, responsibility for acts of officials outside their duties was firmly opposed by Latin-American delegates. *Ibid.*, pp. 87–8.

[52] *Ibid.*, p. 34.

[53] This group included an Italian, Cavaglieri, a Belgian, de Visscher, a Swiss, Dinichert and a Greek, Politis.

[54] While some delegates, including Politis, pointed at Article 38 of the Statute of the PCIJ, Guerrero replied that Article 38 only guides the PCIJ to find the sources of law to apply in the resolution of controversies and not to determine international obligations, in which case the rule has to be 'indisputably admitted by the international community': *ibid.*, p. 44. Moreover, Sinpsom contested the use of Article 38, requiring instead that custom, general principles and the doctrine of jurists be explicitly accepted by states for the purposes of responsiblity: *ibid.*, p. 54.

The committee appointed a sub-committee to solve the impasse.[55] By the time the third committee had reached its fifteenth meeting, disagreement turned into stalemate. At the fifteenth session, the discussion on responsibility for damage caused to foreigners by private persons brought about another division and a final setback to the negotiations. Bases of Discussion 10, 17 and 18 had established responsibility according to a standard of due diligence expected from 'civilised States'.[56] Although reservations about the term 'civilised' were voiced, the basic point of a minimum standard of diligence was upheld. A joint declaration by the Estonian, Latvian and Finnish delegations affirmed: 'while admitting that the term "civilised State" is open to criticism, and that a better term may be found ... It is also recognised that there is a minimum standard of conduct which may reasonably be expected from every country'.[57] Thus, the Committee considered a joint proposal submitted by a number of states, mostly from the core, which based responsibility on states failing 'to take such measures as in the circumstances should normally have been taken to prevent, make reparation or inflict punishment for the acts causing damage'.[58] This proposal, which could be interpreted as sanctioning unequal treatment between foreign residents and nationals, a problem so critical to nations still subjected to unequal treaties, was unacceptable to Chao-Chu (Chaoshu) Wu (1887–1934), the Chinese delegate to the conference and the League, a former minister of foreign affairs, who had graduated from the University of London.

Wu submitted an alternative draft recognizing responsibility only when states 'manifestly failed to take such preventive or punitive measures as in the circumstances might reasonably be expected of it had the persons injured been its own nationals'.[59] In contrast to a standard of due diligence based on 'normal circumstances' or 'reasonableness', Wu defended national treatment: the 'treatment accorded to a nation's own nationals' is the only criterion that does not leave matters to the judgement of

[55] When the issue came up for a vote, Guerrero insisted: 'I shall be compelled to vote against all the articles, until I know how international obligations are to be defined'. Guerrero's position was supported among others by the delegate of Czechoslovakia: *ibid.*, p. 46.

[56] Basis 10 established responsibility as the result of failure to 'show such diligence in the protection of foreigners as, having regard to the circumstances and to the status of the person concerned, could be expected from a civilised State': *ibid.*, p. 200.

[57] *Ibid.*, p. 185.

[58] Submitted by the Greek, Italian, British, United States and French delegates: *ibid.*, p. 175.

[59] *Ibid.*, p. 185.

the state exercising protection. Applying automatically as the standard of protection afforded in each country, national treatment is the best rule in abstract. But noting that the problem in everyone's mind is about Western nationals residing abroad, Wu reminded that the rule he advocates would be the best rule globally, for also China has millions of people residing around the world.[60]

Politis defended the joint proposal against Wu's alternative draft, pointing out that the text of the proposal was taken from a resolution passed by the *Institut de Droit International*. Although recognizing that the joint proposal could be read as granting foreigners, in exceptional circumstances, better treatment than nationals, Politis argued that the Chinese proposal clearly and expressly rejects this possibility, establishing national treatment as the only standard of protection and responsibility. If 'a purely scientific association like the *Institut*' could neither affirm that international law recognizes national treatment, nor establish that foreigners may be entitled to better treatment, Politis contended that it was better for a codification conference 'not to reach agreement' and thus adopt the joint proposal, which 'has the merit of leaving the question open'.[61]

Wu's proposal was voted and defeated seventeen to twenty-three, very much along the lines dividing central and semi-peripheral states. However, this vote was followed by another vote approving the draft text in the joint proposal by only a margin of twenty-one to seventeen votes. With almost the same seventeen states voting in favour of Wu's proposal and against the draft, everyone realized that semi-peripheral states had congealed into a strong minority block that prevented reaching the two-thirds majority required on a second reading of the draft articles. Everyone realized that the codification of international responsibility had failed.[62]

Borchard, the American professor, was ready to blame semi-peripherals for their intransigence. In addition to his criticism against Guerrero and Sipsom, Borchard believed Wu's proposal to be 'too absolute'. Citing his own work on diplomatic protection, Borchard affirmed the legality of a

[60] *Ibid.*, pp. 186–7. Wu's argument was cast in the modern language. Rather than invoking sovereign equality to support equal treatment, equal treatment is presented as the best rule itself in relation to the vague standards of due diligence.

[61] *Ibid.*, p. 186.

[62] *Ibid.*, pp. 189–90. The seventeen delegations, mostly states of the semi-periphery, voting against the draft were: Brazil, Chile, China, Colombia, Czekoslovakia, Free City of Danzig, Hungary, Mexico, Nicaragua, Persia, Poland, Portugal, Rumania, Salvador, Turkey, Uruguay and Yugoslavia. With the exception of Hungary, the same sixteen states in addition to Egypt voted in favour of Wu's proposal.

standard of due diligence to determine responsibility, even if nationals may not have access to local remedies, when injury to foreigners follows a contravention of the 'requirements of *civilised* justice or administration'. Insisting on a categorical rule of equal treatment, which is only possible in states satisfying 'the requirement of *civilised* justice' – Borchard concludes – the minority prevented the adoption of the convention.[63]

Conventionally, international lawyers have seen the increase of rules of international law as a sign of progress, arduously accomplished by overcoming the narrow interests of states.[64] They have also seen the failure to pass new rules and institutions as a capitulation to sovereignty. Unsurprisingly, when semi-peripherals were believed to be responsible for the failure of the codification conference, they were also held responsible for slowing down progress. This view, expressed by someone like Borchard right after the conference, continued long after 1930. In 1951, for example, another Yale Professor, Percy Ellwood Corbett believed that opposition explaining the failure of a 'long and careful attempt to codify', explaining the 'fiasco of The Hague', came from the 'weakness of the sense of community' of 'a strong minority of the Latin American and certain European States [that] refused to subscribe to a general standard of *civilised* justice and instead that no injury was suffered by an alien who received the same treatment as nationals'.[65]

We can only realize Corbett's misinterpretation if we realize that semi-peripherals neither blocked progress, nor simply invoked sovereignty. Rather, articulating the modern discourse of international law, Guerrero, Sipsom and Wu defended their own interpretations against jurists from the core. During the interwar, defending semi-peripheral interpretations of international law had become easier. Unlike their classical predecessors who were newcomers to the profession, Guerrero, Sipsom, Wu and others, as part of a second generation of semi-peripherals, were in a stronger position to withstand criticism.[66] Moreover, while arguments pursued

63 Borchard, 'Responsibility of states', 537–8 (italics added).

64 Kennedy, 'When renewal repeats', and T. Skouteris, *The notion of progress in international law discourse* (The Hague, T. M. C. Asser Press/Cambridge University Press, 2010).

65 P. E. Corbett, *Law and society in the relations of states* (New York: Harcourt, Brace and Co., 1951), pp. 48–9 (emphasis added).

66 As we have seen in Part III, classical semi-peripheral foregrounded absolute sovereignty to back the demand for autonomy and equality and when they did so – let us remember the aftermath to the Second Hague Conference – they were harshly criticized not just because of articulating a discourse based on sovereignty and individualism that was rapidly becoming obsolete, but also because they were seen as responsible for blocking the creation of new international institutions.

by modern semi-peripherals became stronger, the criticism they received from core jurists became weaker. Delegates from the semi-periphery did not try to limit state responsibility by deducing rules from sovereignty. Guerrero's report proposed rules that were rooted in the 'common will' of the international community. Sipsom's objections were framed as an effort to further develop the law, defining and giving content to international obligations. Wu defended equal treatment because it was the best rule, considered from a global perspective. More importantly, it was now Borchard the American professor who looked utterly old-fashioned defending the standard of civilization.

If in 1907 semi-peripherals had been blamed for the failure of the Second Hague Conference, in 1930, to some extent, roles reversed. At the end of the conference, some delegates from core countries ended up expressing no regrets about the outcome of the conference and played down the role of codification in the development of international law.[67] Semi-peripherals, on the other hand, turned the situation in their favour, defending codification and concluding their participation with a note of confidence. Alvarez called attention to the codification work undertaken in the new world. Guerrero proposed the appointment of delegates from small nations in the committee of experts to be created in order to continue the progressive codification of international law. Both declarations were greeted with affirmations of the importance of codification in the new world, with declarations endorsing Alvarez's work, recognizing his 'propaganda work for codification' and with assurances that future commissions of experts would have wide representation. Any doubt about the responsibility of semi-peripherals' contributions in the failure of the codification Conference was thus dispelled.[68]

The failure of universal codification in 1930, however, reinforced semi-peripheral scepticism regarding the ability of Western scholars to overcome imperialism and the European balance of power. It emboldened Latin Americans to concentrate forces in the pan-American context. The project of codifying 'American international law' at the Seventh Pan-American Conference, meeting in 1933 in Montevideo, provided the right opportunity.

[67] During the plenary meeting at the closing of the conference, the British delegate Beckett affirmed: 'we must not . . . run away with the idea that codification is the only method by which the law may be developed'. League of Nations, *Act of the Conference for the Codification of International Law, The Hague, 1930, vol. I, Plenary meetings* (Geneva, 1930), p. 47.

[68] *Ibid.*, pp. 45–50.

Codifying international law in the new world: the long road to Montevideo

In the American continent, codifying international law had been an idea present since the times of independence. Simón Bolivar, one of the leading intellectual and political figures of the independence movement against Spain, had thought about codification as part of his dream of continental unity. Codification was therefore discussed in 1826 at the American Congress of Panama, a meeting of former Spanish-American colonies that inaugurated a system of conferences, and at the First Pan-American Conference held in Washington in 1889, which created the Pan-American Union, a regional international organization including Latin American states and the United States.[69] In 1902, at the Second Pan-American Conference convened in Mexico City, the Brazilian delegation presented a proposal to create a Committee of Jurists in charge of studying and preparing a code of public and private international law. New negotiations at the Third Conference, held in Rio de Janeiro in 1906, led to the conclusion of a convention establishing a Committee of Jurists based in Rio. In 1912, the Committee of Rio met for the first time. At this meeting, Epitácio Pessôa (1865–1942), on behalf of the Brazilian government, presented his own codification draft. Inspired by classical international law, Pessôa's draft, centred on the absolute sovereign autonomy and equality of states, sounded like a classical law document.[70]

The Pessôa code satisfied the aspiration of many Latin-American publicists. But in 1912, five years after semi-peripherals had been blamed for the failure of the Hague Conference, a younger generation of Latin Americans embracing the modern sensibility had begun to replace those who had participated at The Hague. As an alternative to Pessôa, Alejandro Alvarez, representing Chile, Costa Rica and Ecuador, submitted to the Rio Committee a proposal based on his work on codification. In a book written in preparation for the 1912 meeting, Alvarez argued that, before drafting articles, the method and purpose of codification should

[69] See A. Bustamante, *Los progresos de la codificación bajo los auspicios de la Unión panamericana* (Habana: El siglo XX, 1926); Alvarez, *La codificación*, pp. 7–20; and for contemporary analysis, J. Esquirol, 'Latin America' in B. Fassbender and A. Peters (eds.), *The Oxford handbook of the history of international law* (Oxford University Press, 2012), pp. 553–77, 560–2.

[70] E. Pessôa, *Projecto de código de direito internacional publico* (Rio de Janeiro: Imprensa Nacional, 1911).

be elucidated. Unlike private law codification, which Alvarez describes as once-and-for-all rationalization of past rules, public international law codification should be gradual and progressive.[71] Accordingly, Alvarez proposed that the Committee of Jurists should periodically submit new projects and modifications to existing projects. The Committee would thus become the legislative body of the American continent, in charge of adapting international law to the necessities of modern life.[72]

The Rio Committee decided not to take a stance regarding the proposals submitted by Pessôa and Alvarez, but to divide the work in six sub-commissions to study different areas to be codified. Although the discussion of the preliminary projects prepared by the sub-commissions was halted by the outbreak of the First World War, codification in the Americas had gained inexorable momentum, including the support of states as well as professional organizations. In 1912, James Brown Scott and Alejandro Alvarez founded the American Institute of International Law, a scientific organization devoted to the study and progress of international law in the Americas.[73] In 1915, in its first meeting in Washington, Scott as President of the institute presented the 'Declaration of rights and duties of states'. In 1917, at the second meeting of the institute in Habana, Alvarez presented the first version of a codification project he then continued reworking during the interwar years. The existence of these two alternative projects by Scott and Alvarez would later become relevant in the long road to Montevideo.[74]

In 1923, the interstate codification effort was resumed at the Fourth Pan-American Conference held in Santiago, Chile. This time Alvarez presented a number of projects he had been working on over the past decade, in addition to the preliminary projects he had prepared for the sub-commission

[71] Alvarez, *Codification du droit*, p. 277.

[72] Junta Internacional de Jurisconsultos, *Actas, resoluciones y documentos: primera reunión en Rio de Janeiro, 26 de junio–29 de junio de 1912* (Rio de Janeiro, 1914), pp. 47–51, 51–76; Alvarez, *La codificación*, pp. 26–7.

[73] Financially supported by the Carnegie Endowment for Peace, the American institute included members from the United States (e.g. Elihu Root and Scott), Central America and the Caribbean (e.g. Luis Anderson and Antonio Bustamante) and South America (e.g. Alvarez).

[74] E. Root, 'The declaration of the rights and duties of nations adopted by the American Institute of International Law', *AJIL*, 10 (1916), 211–21; A. Alvarez, *Rapport-questionnaire et projets présentés à la deuxième session de l'Institut américain de droit international à la Havane* (Washington: Institut américain de droit international, 1917). As we will see, at the Pan-American conference of 1928, Scott's project was revived because it did not contain the principle of non-intervention.

on the rights and duties of states. The conference decided to resume the work of the Rio Committee of Jurists, adopting Alvarez's codification project as a basis for future discussions.[75]

The projects that Alvarez submitted to the Santiago Conference in 1923 appeared fully modern. On the one hand, rights of states were seen as rights recognized in the interest of the international community. On the other hand, codification itself was conceived as part of the modern effort to renew international law: specifically, it was part of the effort to create an 'American international law'.[76] Codification in the Americas would produce a distinctive 'American Code' – Alvarez's report argues – not only because it would govern relations between the states of the Americas, declaring the principles of public law governing matters of continental interest, but also because on matters of global interest the code would embrace the particular doctrines, precedents and state practices adopted in the Americas, which are more 'simple, just and liberal' than those professed in the 'old world'.[77] If on matters of global interest, the states of the American continent follow their own doctrines, precedents and state practices, they may end up codifying rules that diverge from those in effect between European states. To avoid this 'anomaly', namely international law having contradictory rules in each continent, Alvarez suggests submitting the discussion of these matters to world conferences, either to harmonize rules or to confirm the existence of a continental divergence.

As early as 1912, in his work on codification prepared for the Second Pan-American conference and then in an article published in 1913 in the *Revue Générale*, Alvarez argued that if a new rule of international law is codified in the Americas contradicting an existing rule in force between European states, the older European rule would lose its universal character and in consequence become a continental or particular rule of international law.[78] Alvarez insisted that recognizing international law regimes of continental scope, and in particular an 'American international law', was

[75] United States, *Report of the delegates of the United States of America to the fifth International Conference of American States held at Santiago, Chile, March 25 to May 3, 1923 with appendices* (Washington: Government Printing Office, 1924).

[76] The project of an 'American international law' had been advocated by Alvarez since the publication in 1910 of *Le droit international américain, son fondement – sa nature d'après l'histoire diplomatique des états du nouveau monde et leur vie politique et économique* (Paris: A. Pédone, 1910); see Esquirol, 'Latin America', 562–6.

[77] Alvarez, *La Codificación*, p. 30; Alvarez, *La Conférence des juristes*, p. 48.

[78] Alvarez, *Codification du droit*, pp. 196 ff; Alvarez, *La Conférence des juristes*, p. 51.

neither intended to break the universality of international law in matters of global interest, nor to draft a code with the purpose of enacting rules in contradiction to those in effect in Europe.[79] However, given that the basis of international law, and thus the basis of codification, is the actual international life of nations, divergent practices between American states in relation to matters of global interest can lead to the emergence of rules that are in conflict with existing rules reflecting international life in Europe.[80] In the article published in 1913, Alvarez explicitly favoured submitting these matters to the upcoming Third Hague Conference, scheduled to convene in 1914. The Conference was postponed because of the war. When the Codification Conference of 1930 resumed the work of The Hague, the ideas expressed by Alvarez in 1913 became incredibly timely, foreshadowing the conflict between Guerrero and core jurists we saw above.

Alvarez's ideas about American international law and codification enunciated during the first decade of the century were closely followed during the pan-American conferences of the interwar years.[81] Latin Americans concentrated all their efforts in enacting continental rules, some of which clearly diverged from the rules of international law followed by European states: most importantly, non-intervention; the proscription of coercion to recover public debt or other pecuniary compensations; a declaratory rule of recognition; compulsory arbitration; and a strong regime of neutrality. Let me take neutrality as a brief illustration before exploring non-intervention in greater detail. One of the projects presented by Alvarez to the American Institute in 1917 was a codification draft on maritime neutrality. Alvarez's draft borrowed many rules from the Convention adopted at the Second Hague Conference of 1907. But while The Hague regulations gave pre-eminence to the rights of belligerents, Alvarez shifted the emphasis towards the rights of neutrals. This shift would arguably favour Latin American states, which, not directly

[79] Alvarez, *Codification du droit*, p. 196; Alvarez, *La Conférence des juristes*, pp. 48–9, 52.

[80] In line with his modern sensibility, Alvarez was an antiformalist (rather than a classical formalist) international lawyer, who believed that international law does not emerge from state consent, but reflects the life of peoples, their common history, culture and psychology: A. Alvarez, 'Latin America and International Law', 269–353, 273–4.

[81] On the debate regarding the existence of an American or Latin American international law, see C. D. Burnett, 'Contingent constitutions: empire and law in the Americas', PhD thesis, Princeton University, (2010), ch. 4, pp. 283–334 and J. Esquirol, 'Alejandro Alvarez's Latin American law: a question of identity', *Leiden Journal of International Law*, 19 (2006), 931–56.

participating in war between great powers, would try, as they did during the Great War, to maintain trade relations with both sides of the conflict. Instead of foregrounding the benefits of neutrality for smaller states, as a good modern jurist, Alvarez argued that a strong regime of neutrality reflects the interest of the international community to limit the scope of hostilities and the number of states involved in war. But at the same time, as a modern jurist, Alvarez does not want to give new rights to individual sovereigns, but rather he internationalizes sovereign rights. Alvarez's draft proposes that an assembly of neutral states should have powers to enforce the rights and duties regarding both belligerents and neutrals. Among these rights, and specially important to semi-peripheral nations, Alvarez recognized freedom of commerce.[82]

The article published in 1913 was also timely in 1930 because Alvarez offered a way out to the stalemate between core and semi-peripheral states that, as we have seen, actually occurred at the Hague Conference. What would happen – Alvarez asked in 1913 – if at a codification conference the states of the Americas advocate for rules that they consider crucial to their existence and development, but that European states refuse to recognize? If one admits that new usage can abrogate existing rules, it is clear that when a whole continent has followed a new practice and adopts a new rule, the old rule will no longer be a universal rule of international law. An old rule, the principle of intervention recognized in Europe – cunningly introduced by Alvarez as an example – can no longer be regarded a universal rule from the moment it has been rejected by the American continent. If this divergence is not resolved by a world conference – Alvarez warns – the states of the Americas will no longer have the right to impose the new rule beyond the continent, but at the same time the old rule invoked by European states would no longer be a rule of international law valid in the American continent.[83]

Alvarez's achievement was not insignificant. Thus far and in accordance to classical international law, non-intervention had been supported by deducing it from the principle of sovereign autonomy, most notoriously by Calvo and Drago. We have seen that modern jurists like Politis and Lapradelle recognized new grounds for intervention. Alvarez reinstalled a rule of non-intervention on modern grounds. The difference between Drago and Alvarez therefore reflects the difference between

[82] Alvarez reworked the project for the Fifth Pan-American Conference of 1923. A Convention was then adopted in 1928 at the Sixth Conference in Habana.

[83] Alvarez, *La Conférence des juristes*, pp. 50–1.

the classical and modern legal sensibilities in Latin America. This is why, I would suggest, Alvarez criticized Drago's doctrine for being too absolute.[84]

But there was one big problem in Alvarez's plan. Codifying American international law and then opposing these rules against European states, in order to turn universal rules into rules with a regional scope of validity, required enacting truly continental rules. Latin Americans had to enlist the United States in the codification project. The problem was that the divergence Alvarez presented between an international life of peoples organized around the balance of power and international life based on solidarity and interdependence, did not exactly match the divergence between the old and new worlds. The United States, as we have seen, sided with other core states against semi-peripherals. The US defended inequality at the Second Hague Conference and supported, against Guerrero, an expansive doctrine of responsibility at the Third Hague Conference. And as we will see, the United States was not willing to relinquish the special rights to intervene in the region under Roosevelt's corollary to the Monroe doctrine.[85]

Alvarez was well aware of this problem. One alternative to tackle it, followed by Alvarez and others, was precisely to consider the United States included in and thus bounded by American international law. The boundaries of foreign policies reflecting the interests of the United States like the Monroe doctrine were in consequence considered redefined by American international law. Alvarez affirmed that recognizing both the 'solidarity

[84] Alvarez, *Droit international américain*, p. 335, but other scholars, like Jorge Esquirol, see this same passage as expressing Alvarez's ambivalence regarding the Latin American law project: Esquirol, 'A question of identity', 931–56, 947. Christina Burnett, on the other hand, in the context of her investigation of Alvarez's interpretation of the Monroe doctrine, reaches a conclusion similar to the one I have suggested above. Burnett believes that considering Drago's doctrine 'too "absolute" is consistent with Alvarez's efforts to distinguish "modern" and evolving political sciences from the "static, natural law vision" of law': Burnett, 'Contingent constitutions', p. 411 note 175, also making reference to C. Landauer, 'A Latin American in Paris: Alejandro Álvarez's Le droit international américain', *Leiden Journal of International Law*, 19 (2006), 957–81, 960.

[85] The Monroe doctrine recognized the right of independence of the states of the Americas, by proscribing interventions by European powers and the recolonization of the American continent. See Burnett, 'Contingent constitutions', pp. 335–416. At its inception, the Monroe doctrine did not give a right to intervene coercively in a Latin American state, to protect its nationals or national interest, to recover public debt and other pecuniary claims based on injuries suffered by its nationals. The legality of these rights was only asserted by the 1904 corollary: see e.g. J. R. Clark, *Memorandum on the Monroe doctrine* (Washington: Government Printing Office, 1930).

of interests' and 'independence' between the states of the Americas, Monroe's declaration 'did not do more than serve as an echo of the sentiment that then predominated in all the republics' of the Americas: 'whether the famous message of 1823 had been written or not, the principles contained in it would always have been sustained in the New World. In this sense, it may be said, and not without a certain amount of truth, that the Monroe Doctrine is neither doctrine nor of Monroe.'[86]

In order to exclude America's interpretation when exceeding the proper continental meaning of the doctrine, namely, in order to exclude Roosevelt's corollary, Alvarez, without even explicitly mentioning the corollary, characterizes it as an 'extension' not part of the doctrine itself, but as 'hegemony of the United States'. Unlike the doctrine, Alvarez insists that the extension has not been formulated 'as one piece nor at one time or in a solemn manner . . . it is even more curious – Alvarez observes – that the United States did not appeal to the doctrine during the time when it was strictly applying the principles contained therein, and that it has appealed to it when its application was not in point and when the act in question was one of hegemony'.[87]

Claiming that American international law was neither American nor Latin American but continental, was a strategy that included the United States in a regional order that would limit the scope for unilateral justifications of American foreign policy. The final step in this strategy was to lock this arrangement by internationalizing it. Alvarez, in consequence, believed that the inclusion of the Monroe doctrine in Article 21 of the Covenant of the League of Nations did not signal American hegemony, but international recognition of American international law.[88] Alvarez believed that the strategy behind the idea of an American international law extended also to codification. Because of its continental nature, pan-American codification offered an alternative to bring Americans into the project while offering Latin Americans assurances that codification would not to be entirely controlled by the United States. Alvarez believed that the United States would accept Latin American unity and the codification of divergent rules like non-intervention, in exchange for removing the spectre of European interventions in the continent.[89] The outcome,

86 Alvarez, 'Latin America', 311.

87 Alvarez, 'Latin America', 318 and Burnett, 'Contingent constitutions', 411.

88 Alvarez, *La Codificación*, p. 53.

89 Becker Lorca, 'Alvarez situated' and F. Pike, *Chile and the United States, 1880–1962: the emergence of Chile's social crisis and the challenge to United States diplomacy* (University of Notre Dame Press, 1963), pp. 222–3.

an American international law code with rules diverging from European international law, would have to be accepted by Europe, because of the support and participation of the United States, while the rules themselves would limit American foreign policy protecting Latin America.

When the Hague Conference of 1930 ended in a deadlock, Latin Americans might not have experienced the setback as a complete defeat. The deadlock could be explained as a verification of a continental divergence between American and European rules of international law. But this only increased the pressure to get rules passed within the pan-American context, for only if adopted among American states could these rules be invoked as divergent continental rules of international law. In effect, after 1930, Latin Americans turned all their attention to the next Pan-American Conference, the Montevideo Conference of 1933.

Pan-American codification

Before Montevideo, in one pan-American Conference after the other and in the meetings of the Rio Committee of Jurists of 1906, 1912 and 1927, Latin Americans fought arduously for the rules finally enacted in Montevideo. While the goals and rules advocated remained relatively constant, there was a shift in the framework through which Latin Americans pursued their demands. The demand for sovereign autonomy and equality, first advocated in terms of absolute rights belonging to the essence of statehood, was progressively framed in a modern language. Let me briefly illustrate this shift by contrasting the codification projects submitted by Pessôa in 1912 and Alvarez in 1923.

The codification project Epitácio Pessôa prepared for the first meeting of the Rio Committee of 1912 articulated the classical sensibility. The code starts defining statehood and then enumerating the rights and obligation of states.[90] Though classical, it would be inaccurate either to characterize the Pessôa draft as outmoded, or to imply that its rules had a particularly conservative bent. On the contrary, before the war only a minority of international lawyers had followed the French sociological school's call for recognizing solidarity and interdependence between states. Moreover, some rules in Pessôa's draft, though in a classical vocabulary,

[90] The Pessôa code was divided in seven sections (*livros*). The first section deals with states as international persons (it defines states, and regulates the recognition and extinction of states and changes in territory) and the second section deals with state sovereignty: Pessôa, *Projecto de código*.

anticipated future codifications. For example, a formal definition of statehood anticipated the dissolution of the standard of civilization.[91] Among other provisions, the draft included an absolute principle of non-intervention (including the prohibition of interventions by an invitation extended by a government facing a revolution), state equality and the proscription of conquest as a lawful title to acquire territory.[92]

Pessôa's 1912 draft is a classical code, not so much because of the content of its rules, but because of how rules are organized in the code. Sovereignty is at the centre and from that centre a space of sovereign autonomy is deduced, announcing the *Lotus* principle before it was formulated by the *PCIJ*.[93] After presenting his draft code, Pessôa continued to be involved in the codification effort leading to Montevideo and participated in the shift towards codification in modern terms, which, pushing for very similar rules, embedded sovereignty within the discourse of solidarity, interdependence and internationalism. The codification project submitted by Alvarez in 1923 maintains many of the rules recognized by Pessôa but inverts the structure of the 1912 draft.[94] Instead of starting with a definition of sovereignty, Alvarez's Project number 1 starts off affirming that the society of states is governed by international law. The formation and interpretation of the rules of international law – Alvarez's project affirms – should be 'inspired by a notion of international obligation, solidarity and general interest'.[95] Rather than sovereignty, at the centre of Alvarez's project is an international society governed by law, a society in which states are the primary but not the only international

91 'For the purpose of this Code, a State is a permanent grouping of individuals that inhabit a defined territory and obey the same government that is in charge of the administration of justice and the preservation of order.' *Ibid.*, Article 1.

92 'States are equal': *ibid.*, Article 17; 'No State can intervene in the domestic affairs of another': *ibid.*, Article 19; 'A territory cannot be acquired by conquest': *ibid.*, Article 43.

93 'The State is the preeminent international person': *ibid.*, Article 2; 'The exercise of the rights expressed in the previous articles have no other limitation than the exercise of the rights of other States, the provisions of this code, of private international law and of treaties': *ibid.*, Article 18.

94 Alvarez's 1923 report contained five projects, four of which were of his own authorship and that had already been presented in 1917 at the meeting of the American Institute of International Law in Habana: Project number 1, regarding the fundamental bases of international law; Project number 2, regarding the fundamental rights of the American continent; Project number 3, regulation of neutrality in naval war; Project number 4, declaration of rights and duties of states (by James Scott); Project number 5, declaration of rights and duties of nations. American Institute of International Law, *Acte final de la session de la Havane: (deuxième session de l'institut) 22–27 janvier 1917; résolutions et projets* (Oxford University Press, 1917).

95 Project number 1, Articles 1 and 19.

law subjects.[96] The modern form of the draft allowed Alvarez to argue for continental rules that diverged from European international law, rules that judged only by their content would have appeared as classical rather than modern rules and thus more difficult to justify.

Given that international law governs an international society that is not only universal but also regionally diverse, Alvarez reaffirms the right of the American states to have a distinctively continental international law.[97] Alvarez drafted an entire and separate section devoted to 'American public international law'. Project number 2 recognized many of the rules long sought after by Latin American publicists, from rules defending sovereign autonomy, including for instance non-intervention, to sovereign equality, including for instance national treatment, namely a rule granting foreign residents the same rights enjoyed by nationals. These rules, demanded by Latin Americans since the time of classical law, adopted with Alvarez modern form. Neither autonomy nor equality were considered as absolute rights.

Sovereign autonomy protects American states from foreign intervention. Project number 2 imposes on extra-continental powers an absolute prohibition to interfere with the enjoyment of freedom and independence of the states of the Americas as well as a prohibition to interfere in their domestic or international affairs. Even with their consent, extra-continental powers have no right to occupy American territory.[98] But sovereignty is not absolute, as members of the international society states are subject to duties, legal duties sanctioned by law and moral duties sanctioned by public opinion.[99] Sovereign equality also protects American states from foreign intervention by limiting diplomatic protection to

[96] For example, according to Project number 1, Article 2, international law governs not only interstate relations, but also the international rights of individuals and associations. According to Project number 1, Article 6, customary rules have to be recognized not only by states, but also by the public opinion of the world or a continent.

[97] Project number 1, Article 5 and Article 6 regulate the scope and sources of the rules of international law, recognizing universal and continental rules. Project number 1, Article 10 establishes that continental rules apply in each continent but to all states of the world, including those who have not recognized or objected to those rules. Project number 2, Article 1 affirms that the states of America have the right to determine the continental rules, especially those expressing the foundations of the American international society, according to its historical past, needs and aspirations.

[98] Project number 2, Articles 3, 4 and 5. Moreover, Article 6 declares that all American states should be supportive [*solidarios*] in the defence and preservation of these rights.

[99] Project number 5, Articles 8–10.

harm suffered by foreign residents determined according to national treatment. Since foreign residents have no right to a higher standard of protection than nationals, diplomatic protection can only be invoked after a denial of justice. But again, sovereign equality is not absolute, for national treatment comes with a correlative international obligation to grant and respect rights of individuals and associations; civil and political rights that Alvarez's project enumerates.[100]

Unlike Pessôa's draft code, in the projects prepared by Alvarez sovereignty is no longer an absolute right. Assessed in abstract, the rules contained in the Pessôa code could have been more beneficial to Latin American states than the rules in Alvarez's projects. But it would have been very difficult in 1923 to support a code drafted in the language of classical international law. Thus, neither explicitly rejecting, nor explicitly endorsing absolute sovereignty, Alvarez believed that the autonomy of Latin American states could be defended by embedding states' rights within international regimes. Here the jurisprudential point about the 'eclectic' nature of international law proved useful. The modern law of nations – Alvarez argued – emerged when individualism, at the basis of national and international life since the French revolution, gradually disappeared to be gradually replaced by a regime of cooperation and solidarity. But this replacement was never complete. Some rules of international law remained reflecting the interest of states while others advanced the collective interest of the international society. Modern international law is thus a 'melange', requiring a modern jurist to mediate between 'individualism and solidarity'.[101] It was the eclectic nature of the modern discourse that Latin Americans exploited to support classical rights in modern form.

Formal statehood and declaratory recognition

The Pan-American Conference of 1923 adopted the projects drafted by Alvarez to guide future codification. The Conference restored the Rio Committee of Jurists that had been inactive since the war and instructed

[100] Project number 2, Articles 7–10.

[101] A. Alvarez, 'Le nouveau droit de gens et le projet d'une école internationale de droit international', *RDI*, Tr. Série, T.I (1920), 154; on this aspect of Alvarez, see L. Obregón, 'Noted for dissent: the international life of Alejandro Álvarez', *Leiden Journal of International Law*, 19 (2006), 983–1016.

the Committee to meet in 1927 in order to prepare drafts to be submitted to the Fourth Pan-American Conference, to be held in Habana in 1928.[102] In 1927, the Rio Committee appointed a sub-commission to discuss the codification of public international law and to study the revised versions of the codification projects Alvarez and the American Institute of International Law had submitted in 1923.

It is in these projects that the definition of statehood resurfaced. Article 1 of Project number 2 defined the state as a people in a territory with a constituted government, capacity to enter in relations with other states and a degree of civilization that enables it to observe the principles of international law.[103] With the exception of the last requirement this is practically the same definition of statehood adopted five years later in Montevideo. And it was precisely this last requirement that elicited discussion at the meeting of the Rio Committee. The Colombian member, Jesús María Yepes (1892–1962) asked:

> Who will determine the achievement of this level of civilisation? Any powerful state that has a particular concept of civilisation, can decide that a specific human group is not sufficiently civilised as to fall under the jurisdiction of the rules of international law. It is what has happened in Europe in relation to Africa and Asia. European states have a Western concept of culture; saw that the states of Asia and Africa did not share those concepts and did not recognize them as states.[104]

Alvarez responded to Yepes, affirming that the level of civilization is not a matter depending on European evaluation but that it is determined by the criteria established in Article 1, which only requires a state to be able to observe the principles of international law. Unconvinced, Yepes rejoined: 'what if tomorrow a European state says that small states in the Americas have not the required degree of civilisation and that therefore they will not grant them recognition?' Alvarez answered: 'If the states of the Americas have enacted a code of public international law, that

[102] After the Santiago Conference, the Pan-American Union requested the American Institute of International Law to draft a number of codification projects to be submitted to the meeting of the Rio Committee: Bustamante, *Los progresos de la codificación*, pp. 10–11. These projects were drafted in Paris during the European summer of 1924 by Alvarez, Bustamante, Scott and Luis Anderson from Costa Rica: *ibid.*, pp. 11–12.

[103] A. Alvarez, *Considérations générales sur la codification du droit international américain (code de droit international des états américains). Mémorial présentée à la deuxième Commission de juristes réunie à Rio de Janeiro le 18 avril 1927* (Rio de Janeiro: Imprensa Nacional, 1927).

[104] International Commission of Jurists, *Comisión Internacional de Jurisconsultos Americanos: reunión de 1927* (Rio de Janeiro: Secretaría General, 1927), p. 95. See also Yepes' account of the meeting in J. M. Yepes, *La codificación del derecho internacional americano y la conferencia de Rio de Janeiro* (Bogotá: Imprenta nacional, 1927).

sole fact testifies to their state of civilisation and protects them from any doubt'.[105]

This was certainly not a convincing answer for those struggling for self-government in Africa, Asia and the Middle East, but in the Latin American context, a reference to civilization was understood not as a requirement determining membership, but as a requirement to observe international obligations. The provision was approved with no changes and thus included in the draft project to be submitted to Habana in 1928.[106] The exchange between Alvarez and Yepes, who were not only colleagues but also close friends, shows that among Latin Americans the standard of civilization had been displaced to a secondary role. Transforming the standard of civilization into an element of statehood, Alvarez could deprive it of its classical role to determine membership in the international community, a role that would be fulfilled by a declaratory doctrine of recognition. Relegated to this secondary role, the removal of the reference to civilization from the definition of statehood occurred uneventfully after Habana and in preparation to the Montevideo Conference, then statehood was finally defined in purely formal terms.[107]

The shift from the standard of civilization to the doctrine of recognition had been announced and defended by Alvarez more than a decade before, in the book written in 1912 on occasion of the second meeting of the Rio Committee. On the one hand, and not without ambivalence, Alvarez seems to suggest that a standard of civilization is no longer pertinent in a universal international community in which all classes of peoples are members and subjects of international law.[108] On the other hand, it is the reality of independence that characterizes the state and that gives rise to its international personality, with all the rights and duties

[105] International Commission of Jurists, *Reunión de 1927*, p. 95.

[106] *Ibid.*, p. 96 and International Commission of Jurists, *Public international law, projects to be submitted for the consideration of the Sixth International Conference of American States*, (Washington: Pan-American Union, Government Printing Office, 1927).

[107] As explained below, the codification project adopted in 1927 by the Rio Committee and then submitted to the Habana Conference of 1928 was rejected in Habana. After 1928, in the draft prepared by the American Institute to be submitted to the next Conference in Montevideo the reference to civilization disappeared.

[108] 'We will not talk about tribes and savage populations, because we no longer believe that in our days they still exist from the perspective of international law; they are all under the dominion of civilised states. But if they exist, their recognition as subjects of international law would be needed, because they are members of the international community.' Alvarez, *Codification du droit*, p. 81.

attached to statehood.[109] Alvarez admits that states will seek and consider recognition by other states as very useful, though not to bestow on them sovereign rights, but only to establish official and stable foreign relations. Since the emancipation of the Americas, it takes only the proclamation of independence, without the need of recognition, to be a sovereign state. Since the independence of the Americas international law has adopted a declaratory doctrine of recognition.[110]

These ideas about recognition were reproduced in the project submitted to the Committee in 1927. Project number 2, Article 2 on juridical equality, establishes that the rights of each state do not depend on the existence of the state as an international legal person. Moreover, Article 5 declares the political existence of the state to be independent from recognition. This provision was approved without changes in 1927 and was then adopted as Article 3 of the Montevideo Convention.[111] Once recognition was limited to a declaratory function, Latin Americans tried also to limit the prerogative of states to grant recognition. At the meeting of the Rio Committee, Abel Nicolas Léger (1886–1948) from Haiti introduced an amendment to make recognition irrevocable. Luis Anderson (1873–1948), from Costa Rica, proposed the granting of recognition to be unconditional.[112]

Anderson stayed firm during the discussions following the introduction of the two amendments. If recognition were allowed to be conditional what would happen if the conditions were not fulfilled? Would states be allowed to withdraw recognition? If allowed to be conditional – Anderson insists – a state could extort another state in order to grant recognition.[113] Most importantly, in order to link the concept of legal personality to the reality of statehood rather than to recognition, Anderson declares that legal personality materializes from the state's

[109] *Ibid.*, p. 79.

[110] Alvarez recognizes the division between declaratory and constitutive doctrines, but favours the former: *ibid.*, pp. 79–80.

[111] 'The political existence of the state is independent of recognition by the other states. Even before recognition the state has the right to defend its integrity and independence, to provide for its conservation and prosperity, and consequently to organize itself as it sees fit, to legislate upon its interests, administer its services, and to define the jurisdiction and competence of its courts.'

[112] International Commission, *Reunión de 1927*, pp. 102, 105.

[113] Moreover, Anderson remarks: 'Would European powers destroy again Poland if it does not respect the minority protections, that is, the conditions under which it was recognized?' 'When the Allies offered Russia recognition in exchange for recognizing debt, it was a matter of interest not of law.' *Ibid.*, 105.

own conditions of existence, 'when a state emerges with its territory, population and government' – note the absence of any reference to civilization.[114]

Jesse Reeves (1872–1942), an academic and member of the Rio Committee from the United States, opposed the two amendments. Pessôa, presiding the meeting, anticipated the dangers of achieving too much at the drafting stage. Adopting strong rules protecting the sovereignty of Latin American states could come at the cost of alienating the United States. Pessôa tried to moderate the demands of his Latin American colleagues, reminding them of the great conquest that, as we will see, they had obtained at the Rio meetings, namely the recognition of non-intervention. Arguing against the amendments, Pessôa explained that the drafting committee rejected unconditional recognition because it would have the unintended consequence of states withholding recognition. Requiring recognition to be irrevocable would make cordial relations between American states more difficult.[115] In spite of Pessôa's warnings, the amendments passed nine votes to seven. And Pessôa's worries were confirmed the following year when the public international law code drafted in Rio was submitted and rejected in Habana.[116] At the Sixth Pan-American Conference in Habana the whole project to codify American international law failed spectacularly. The main cause was not the passing of these two amendments, but the rule regarded by Pessôa as the main achievement of the 1927 meeting of the Rio Committee, namely, non-intervention.

Non-intervention

In Rio, during the discussion of Project number 2, Luis Anderson offered a rallying cry for non-intervention. Article 2 of Project number 2 recognized that all states enjoy the same rights. Anderson affirmed with eloquence that the most immediate consequence of the principle that all states have the same sovereign rights, is that their internal and external relations should be respected.[117] By virtue of sovereign equality, Anderson proposed

[114] *Ibid.*, p 105. [115] *Ibid.*, pp. 101, 104 and 108.

[116] On the other hand, a Code of Private International Law prepared by Bustamante was adopted in Habana, thereafter known as the Bustamante code.

[117] International Commission, *Reunión de 1927*, p. 97. Research by Salisbury has shown that Anderson's proposal was of his own rather than Costa Rican initiative and that it took the conference by surprise: R. Salisbury, *Anti-imperialism and international competition in Central America, 1920–1929* (Wilmington, DE: SR Books, 1989), p. 114.

the following amendment: 'no state has the right to intervene in the internal affairs of another'.[118]

Pessôa, as president of the meeting, turned immediately to Reeves, asking the American delegate if he agreed with Anderson's amendment. 'Yes, mister President. It is a general principle' – replied Reeves. Not without surprise, Latin Americans rejoiced and decided on the spot to vote on the amendment as a separate provision. Saavedra Lamas, the Argentinean delegate, reaffirmed the status of non-intervention as an immutable principle of Argentinean foreign policy, the Cuban delegate proposed approving the provision by acclamation and the Peruvian delegate Víctor Maúrtua (1865–1937) requested unanimity to be expressly recorded in the proceedings of the meeting. The proceedings reported: 'all delegates stand up and applause, the article, being this way approved'.[119]

118 International Commission, *Reunión de 1927*, p. 98. Non-intervention had been included in the codification projects of both Pessôa and Alvarez, but it had been taken away from the draft discussed at the plenary session of the Rio Committee. Saavedra Lamas, the Argentinean member of the Committee, explained that the drafting committee discussed a wide rule of non-intervention, namely the one contained in the Pessôa code of 1912. Pessôa himself explained that his article included a general prohibition of interventions as well as a prohibition of interventions by treaty or by invitation. When opposition to the second type of prohibition by most delegates led to a stalemate regarding non-intervention as a whole, the drafting committee decided to exclude the article altogether. *Ibid.*

119 *Ibid.*, pp. 98–9. Why did Reeves concede? I will explore below the broader question about the reasons for the change in American foreign policy regarding non-intervention. In relation to the position adopted by Reeves in 1927, let me only point out that professional lawyers and scholars who supported the creation of a permanent international court and the League of Nations and participated in the drafting of codification proposals at the American Institute and the Harvard Research initiative (in which Reeves participated as a reporter) were much more committed to liberal internationalism than isolationist Republican lawyers appointed at the State Department after Republicans came to power in 1920. I would suggest that Reeves might have simply followed his own professional judgment in the context of a state department disinterested in Pan-Americanism and in codification. Charles Evans Hughes, secretary of state under President Harding, refused to attend the Pan-American Conference held in Santiago in 1923, where Latin American states criticized American foreign policy and where it was decided to resume codification and instruct the Rio Committee to meet in 1927. But Republican administrations' disinterest in pan-American codification was also accompanied, as Joseph Smith has argued, with a less forceful policy towards Latin America: J. Smith, *The United States and Latin America: a history of American diplomacy, 1776–2000* (London: Routledge, 2005), pp. 84–5. This disinterest and a more conciliatory policy could explain why Reeves might have been sent to Rio without explicit instructions to oppose codification. As we will see, it was only after Rio and in the wake of the Habana Conference of 1928 that the state department became aware of the dangers of codification, changed course and prepared an offensive against non-intervention.

The codification projects approved in 1927 by the Committee of Rio were submitted by the Pan-American Union to the Sixth Pan-American Conference, meeting in Habana in 1928.[120] In Habana, as soon as the Peruvian delegate Maúrtua began his exposition, all the excitement of the previous year vanished. The report, prepared by Maúrtua as the rapporteur to the second commission in charge of studying the codification of the rights and duties of states, departed substantially from the projects drafted and approved in Rio.[121] Instead, after pompous declarations about the role of 'natural justice', the 'juridical sentiment of civilised peoples' and the 'essential principles of international life', Maúrtua revived the old project drafted in 1916 by the American Institute of International Law for the second meeting of the Rio Committee, which contained none of the rules passed by the Committee in 1927; most significantly, it did not include the proscription of intervention.[122] Charles Evans Hughes (1862–1948), head of the American delegation then took the stand after Maúrtua and praised him for a 'luminous report'.[123]

Why did a Peruvian support the American position? David Sheinin and Joseph Smith have argued that, previous to Habana, fearing a coalition of Latin American nations to coalesce around an anti-American agenda, secretary of state Kellogg organized a diplomatic offensive to secure the support of some friendly Latin American governments against those 'making trouble for the United States'.[124] And Peru had its own reasons.[125] Kellogg's fears were in fact confirmed when the head of the

120 International Commission of Jurists, *Sixth International Conference*.

121 Secretaría de Relaciones Exteriores, *La participación de México en la Sexta Conferencia Internacional Americana. Informe general de la delegación de México* (México, 1928), p. 48.

122 *Ibid.*, pp. 50–8. Maúrtua justified his choosing of the 1916 document stating that his own report had not to create a declaration of the rights and duties of states because a declaration already existed: 'It had been presented to the New World in 1916 by the American Institute. Yet neither had the Institute created it. Its content and expression are in the juridical sentiment of the civilised peoples.' *Ibid.*, p. 52.

123 Secretaría de Relaciones Exteriores, *La participación de México*, pp. 58–9.

124 D. Sheinin, 'Argentina and the United States at the Sixth Pan American Conference (Habana 1928)', Research Paper No. 25, Institute of Latin American Studies, University of London (1991). Smith quotes Kellogg communicating his apprehensions to the state department. 'There is no use disguising the fact that there are liable to be elements going to the next Conference purely for the purpose of making trouble for the United States. You know how difficult it was to suppress some of this even at Santiago, where there was a much better feeling towards us than there is now.' Smith, *A history of American diplomacy*, p. 87.

125 According to Salisbury, quoting the Spanish minister in Habana, Peru helped the United States in order to obtain American support against Chile on the question of the partition of Tacna and Arica: R. Salisbury, *Anti-imperialism*, p. 120.

Argentinean delegation Pueyrredón, disobeying instructions from his government, led the attack against the American position regarding tariffs and non-intervention.[126]

As part of Kellogg's diplomatic offensive, President Coolidge attended the opening ceremony at Habana in order to 'impress and conciliate the Latin American delegates'.[127] Unlike previous meetings that he had refused to attend, this time Hughes agreed to participate and head the American delegation. And this time Americans were ready to blockade the codification projects prepared in Rio. That Hughes was chosen to head the American delegation and that he accepted, is an indication of the importance that Coolidge and the state department attributed to the Conference. But that the state department was no longer disinterested in pan-American codification did not mean that Republican isolationist international lawyers abandoned their general mistrust regarding the project of codification. Among these lawyers, Hughes was the most prominent pick possible to lead the American delegation. Hughes was a Republican politician who lost the presidential election to Wilson, he had been secretary of state until 1925 and president of ASIL since 1920. A few months after Habana he was appointed judge to the PCIJ and later became chief justice of the American Supreme Court. He was also the state department's perfect pick because, unlike James Scott who had been an active supporter of codification, Hughes as president of ASIL had demonstrated no particular sympathy regarding codification.[128]

A successful codification should be strictly limited to the fundamental principles of international law, Hughes affirmed in Habana, warning that

126 See Sheinin, 'Argentina and the United States'.

127 Smith, *A history of American diplomacy*, p. 87.

128 According to Frederic Kirgis, in 1909 ASIL voted to embark on an ambitious codification project 'close to Scott's heart'. ASIL's early efforts, however, 'came to naught'. In 1924, when the League of Nations resumed the codification effort, it sent a request to different professional organizations, including ASIL, inviting them to contribute. ASIL treated the invitation as a 'hot potato'. After discussions on the authority of the Executive Committee to undertake the study of codification without full membership approval at the Annual Meeting, ASIL at the end did not participate. Although Hughes as president did not block the codification initative and expressed the view that the Executive Committee could undertake the project, Kirgis argued that 'there may well have been a lingering unease about proceeding with anything more ambitious than a watching brief in the absence of an explicit delegation of authority from the membership at large': F. Kirgis, *The American Society of International Law's first century: 1906–2006* (Leiden: Martinus Nijhoff, 2006), pp. 30–1 and 91–6. Delegation from full membership was never given, the codification effort in the United States was in consequence not undertaken by ASIL, but led by members of ASIL under the auspices of other initiatives like Manley Hudson's Harvard Research in international law project and Scott's American Institute of International Law.

codifying other principles 'would be to wreck a project before it began'. It would amount to a change of the fundamental principles of international law, which would turn discussions into a 'maze of juridical controversy', requiring furthermore new diplomatic negotiations that are beyond the scope of the Conference. 'The only success we can have is to come together in common accord, and after consideration agree in a statement of the principles that underlie all possible applications.' Hughes was indeed pleased with the exclusion of the projects adopted in Rio: 'in searching for a statement which would be fundamental, comprehensive – not fragmentary and therefore impossible – Dr. Maúrtua has taken the declaration of the American Institute . . . I congratulate him upon that'.[129]

That Maúrtua and Hughes defended the same position was no coincidence. Gathering support, a few friendly Latin American governments responded to Kellogg's diplomatic strategy before Habana. The President and the secretary of state reciprocated Peruvian support, receiving Maúrtua in Washington. A few weeks later, Scott sent a telegram to Augusto Leguia, president of Peru, congratulating Maúrtua for his work at the Conference. Scott pointed out that the President and the secretary of state personally conveyed to Maúrtua 'the inestimable value of his services, as a Peruvian, jurist, internationalist and statesman, if I may venture to say so, to Panamericanism'.[130] Leguia replied thanking Scott for his appreciation of the Peruvian delegates and declared his firm policy supporting 'the civilising action of the United States in favour of the peoples of the Americas, whose freedom defends and development protects, without ulterior motives'.[131] American and Peruvian delegates defended their position in classical legal language. They both invoked the idea of civilization to argue that conduct by a government in violation of a standard of appropriate behaviour would justify intervention. Hughes, for example, stated:

> The fundamental conception is that we are a family of States; that we are all bound together, in a conception of the relations of civilised nations. That conception of a

[129] 'Remarks of the Honorable Charles E. Hughes, at the meeting of the Committee No. 2, Public International Law, February 4, 1928', in Sixth International Conference of American States, Minutes and Reports of Committees (Part 1) 1928, Columbus Memorial Library, Organization of American States.

[130] Papers of the American Institute of International Law, Carnegie Endowment for International Peace, Subseries IV.A, Division of International Law, General, Rare Book & Manuscript Library, Columbia University, Scott to Leguia, B 38 1151, March 10, 1928.

[131] Papers of the American Institute of International Law, Carnegie Endowment for International Peace, Subseries IV.A, Division of International Law, General, Rare Book & Manuscript Library, Columbia University, Leguia to Scott, B 38 1152, April 6, 1928.

fundamental unity is the very postulate upon which we must erect our structure of juridical exposition. We cannot enter into this family of nations, we cannot perform our duties as civilised States in our relations with each other, unless we have an appreciation of the principles which govern our action.[132]

And it was this mode of arguing that caused the most controversy in Habana. Towards the end of the conference, Maúrtua and Guerrero immerse themselves in a final row over the use of the notion of civilization, Maúrtua affirming that:

it is necessary because of the honour of the civilisation of the Americas that the nations so protective of their independence, respectfully bow in front of justice and international obligations. It is not a gesture that would be applauded by the civilised world, that the Americas would cling to a wild [*selvática*] independence, silencing that they have obligations ... It is necessary that someone has the courage to say it ... and it is said by a weak ... but a civilised nation like Peru.[133]

In 1928, however, this mode of arguing by Hughes and Maúrtua had become out of date. Rising anti-American sentiment united Latin Americans in a common front against intervention. During the 1920s, Republican administrations sought to improve relations with Latin America. The sugar intervention in Cuba ended in 1922, but the Platt Amendment, giving special rights to the United States in Cuban affairs, had not yet been repealed. American marines withdrew from the Dominican Republic in 1924, but American financial supervision remained. American occupation in Haiti also remained unchanged and, most significantly, American marines withdrew from Nicaragua in 1925 only to return in 1926 in support of a conservative government and to fight rebel forces led by Augusto César Sandino, who became – along with Abd-el-Krim – a symbol of anti-imperialism globally.[134]

Latin American international lawyers like Guerrero harnessed the reigning anti-imperialist sentiment. Guerrero answered Maúrtua, disputing any differentiation between civilized and uncivilized nations: 'the weakest people of the American continent is as civilised as the strongest nation of this continent ... and proof of that is that they came to ask their

[132] 'Remarks of Hughes'.

[133] International American Conference, *Diario de la sexta conferencia internacional americana, Habana, 1928* (Habana: Imprenta de Rambla, Bouza y ca., 1928), p. 538.

[134] For an example of these connections, see R. Melgar Bao, 'The anti-imperialist league of the Americas between the East and Latin America', *Latin American Perspectives*, 35 (2008), 9–24.

rights to be recognized'.[135] Moreover, Guerrero had opposed Maúrtua's report since the beginning. As soon as Maúrtua had finished his exposition Guerrero expressed surprise: 'Dr. Maúrtua has not given us the reasons he had for completely forgetting the work accomplished by the Committee of American Jurists'.[136] Guerrero reminded his colleagues that Maúrtua had not only participated at the meeting of the Committee, but also asked for the unanimous vote in favour of non-intervention to be recorded in the proceedings. And now instead – Guerrero reproaches – he brings something very different that does not express the 'juridical sensibility of the continent'. Guerrero proposed instead that the project approved in Rio be adopted as the basis for discussion.[137] A long debate followed over two sessions in which many delegates supported Guerrero's motion and in which it was finally decided to appoint a sub-commission to study both projects.

The sub-commission did not reach agreement and drafted a resolution postponing the discussion about codification to the next Pan-American Conference. At the Plenary Session, when the resolution presented by the sub-commission was read to the Assembly, most delegates voiced dissatisfaction and reaffirmed their absolute commitment to non-intervention.[138] Delegates repeated these statements one after the other until Bernardo Alvarado from Guatemala noted that most delegations had just revealed a consensus to codify. Alvarado therefore asked the commission to explain the reasons for having postponed the discussion to the next Conference. As president of the sub-commission, Guerrero responded recognizing that agreement was not reached. But seizing the opportunity and pointing out that a new consensus had just formed, Guerrero proposed the immediate passing of a vote against interventions.[139]

135 International American Conference, *Diario de la sexta conferencia*, p. 538.

136 Secretaría de Relaciones Exteriores, *La participación de México*, p. 61.

137 *Ibid.*, pp. 61–2. 'It is because of this original vice that the project departs from universal codification.'

138 Delegates from Argentina, El Salvador, Mexico, República Dominicana, Ecuador, Haiti, Guatemala and Colombia reaffirmed the principle unequivocally. Only Hughes and Maúrtua lamented the outcome but defended the resolution, hoping that in the future an agreement on codification could be reached. They were seconded by the delegates from Nicaragua and Cuba, which were under governments backed by American forces. Unsurprisingly, both Nicaragua and Cuba were vocal when changing their position in Montevideo. The rest of the governments of the Americas reaffirmed their support to non-intervention and lamented the outcome, which was mostly explained due to the impossibility to draft a formula gathering unanimous support. International American Conference, *Diario de la sexta conferencia*, pp. 527–30.

139 *Ibid.*, p. 530.

When the president of the Assembly asked Guerrero to draft a proposal, he presented the same non-intervention article introduced by Anderson and approved in 1927 by the Rio Committee. The debate that ensued re-enacted the divisions that had marked the discussions in the commission and sub-commission. With the exception of the Peruvian delegation, all Latin Americans favoured non-intervention. This time, however, some states, principally among them Brazil, expressed concern that the deep divisions that had surfaced between states could break down the pan-American movement.[140] Other delegates defended a stronger position.[141] And finally an exasperated Hughes took the stand to express what would later become one of the most quoted defences of the legality of American imperialism.

Hughes resumed his defence, noting that at the root of the problems faced during codification was the difficulty his colleagues had to distinguish between international law and political doctrine – a reaffirmation of the classical distinction between law and politics that Latin Americans were no longer willing to accept as a correct legal argument, Guerrero for instance having defended the Rio draft as reflecting the 'juridical sensibility of the continent'. But Hughes did not stop there. Probably reassured by his diplomatic victory, once it was clear that Guerrero's proposal had no chance to succeed, Hughes insisted on getting to the real causes of the discussion and expressed what he so far had not dared to explicitly voice, namely, his belief that interventions were actually lawful. 'I have never shun away from this discussion, . . . there is nothing to hide' – a now outspoken Hughes explains. The 'real difficulty' is not intervention, is not 'external aggression'. The real problem is an 'internal difficulty'. There are situations 'in which sovereignty is suspended, in which there is no government . . . and there is no possibility to exercise the function of sovereignty and independence'.[142] Displaying unusual candour,

140 The Brazilian delegate, Raúl Fernandes, clarified that although the principle of non-intervention had always been recognized by Brazil, it would abstain from voting Guerrero's proposal, because not creating continental fracture and rivalry was also a long-standing Brazilian policy. The Commission's unanimous vote, Fernandes pointed out, was a compromise leaving the discussion for the next conference and preserving the work done so far. *Ibid.*, p. 533.

141 E.g. Eduardo Alvarez, from El Salvador, asked why wait, if Pan-Americanism is the sentiment of peace, why not protect the weaker in front of the powerful, why not do so in the name of justice, not for the Americas but for the world. Then the Mexican delegate proposed to widen the prohibition to include interventions in external affairs. *Ibid.*, pp. 534–5.

142 *Ibid.*, pp. 536–7.

betraying a sense of security as well as betraying his diplomatic skills, Hughes concludes with an outright defence of intervention:

> What are we to do when the government breaks down and the lives of American citizens are in danger? Are we to stand by and see them killed because a government, in circumstances they cannot control and for which it may not be responsible, can no longer afford reasonable protection?... Now, it is a principle of international law that in such case a government is fully justified in taking action, in what I would call an interposition of a temporary character for the purpose of protecting the lives and property of its nationals. I could say that this does not constitute an intervention... but some day I could be accused of bad faith... As it is natural, The United States cannot renounce to the right to protect its nationals... International law cannot be changed by resolutions of this Conference.[143]

At the end of the plenary session Guerrero withdrew his proposal, not before a final row with Maúrtua, which highlighted not only the conceptual rift separating the ways in which both framed their arguments, but also the political differences and personal animosity between the Peruvian delegate and most Latin Americans present in Habana.[144] According to Richard Salisbury, the exchange escalated, into a 'bitter polemic' characterized by terms and expressions that were neither 'cordial nor diplomatic'. 'The exchanges were so sharp that the president of the session expunged some particularly inflammatory remarks from the official conference records.'[145]

Montevideo, 1933

Final success came at the Seventh Conference, in Montevideo. Secretary of state Cordell Hull, the American delegate declared: 'under our support of the general principle of non-intervention, as has been suggested, no government need fear any intervention on the part of the United States under Roosevelt Administration'.[146] The shift in the American position, from Habana to Montevideo, concluding in the signing of the Convention of Rights and Duties of States, was certainly remarkable. To explain this shift, historians of foreign relations have emphasized changes in American domestic politics. The 'good neighbour' policy towards Latin America, announced first by Hoover and incorporated into official policy

[143] *Ibid.*, p. 537. [144] *Ibid.*, p. 540. [145] R. Salisbury, *Anti-imperialism*, p. 121.
[146] Séptima Conferencia Internacional Americana, *Primera, segunda y octava comisiones, actas y antecedentes, Montevideo 1933* (Montevideo, 1933), pp. 122, 126.

in Roosevelt's inaugural address, explains the change of attitude in Montevideo. Although with reservations, the codification of non-intervention was now supported by the United States.[147] The election of Roosevelt was important, not only because the 'good neighbour' policy obtained official recognition, but also because a conservative politician like secretary of state Hughes was replaced by a more progressive politician like secretary of state Hull. This interpretation assumes that having blocked non-intervention in Habana was an American diplomatic victory, a policy then reversed in Montevideo in light of political changes coming from within the United States.[148]

Seen from the point of view of Latin America, however, Habana was anything but a defeat. It rather marked a turning point. A strong and united Latin American front in defence of non-intervention coalesced in Habana. Unity paid off in Montevideo.[149] Success in Montevideo could only happen because, at the point in which the foreign policy of the United States changed, the projects discussed in previous Pan-American Conferences and meetings of the Rio Committee, could be easily and swiftly harnessed by Latin Americans into a codification draft.[150] At the same time, the way in which Latin Americans framed these projects, in particular the Rio draft of 1927, defending non-intervention as a consequence of equality (rather than sovereign autonomy) and as a rule reflecting an internationalist juridical consciousness, made it more difficult for the United States to continue supporting the legality of unilateral interventions based on a standard of civilized conduct. Hughes' defence of intervention in 1928 sounded definitively outmoded, if not desperate.

147 For example, S. Bemis, *The Latin American policy of the United States* (New York: Harcourt, Brace and Co., 1943). Cordell Hull lamented the lack of time to give adequate interpretation to the principle, thus signed the convention with a reservation that declares that non-intervention will be interpreted in accordance to President Roosevelt's address of March 4th of 1933. Séptima Conferencia Internacional Americana, *Montevideo*, pp. 122, 126. The United States only committed to non-intervention without reservations in 1938.

148 Salisbury has argued that contemporary American commentators believed that Hughes' impressive performance explained the diplomatic victory at Habana: Salisbury, *Anti-imperialism*, p. 122.

149 Salisbury has also noted that Latin Americans saw Habana as a victory, since American interventionist policies came under 'sharp and embarrassing scrutiny' and since Hughes' speeches seemed rather defensive: *ibid.*, p. 120.

150 Raimundo Rivas, the Colombian delegate to Montevideo and rapporteur on the project on rights and duties of states, insisted that the report was not original and that the draft convention was based on the project adopted by the Committee of Rio in 1927. Moreover, expressions of gratitude were offered to Alejandro Alvarez. Séptima Conferencia Internacional Americana, *Montevideo*, p. 103.

In 1933, Latin American delegates knew very well that the groundwork for codifying non-intervention had been laid down before. 'The material is exhausted and the juridical consciousness of America may already seek conscious and definite guidance' – declared the rapporteur presenting the codification draft to be discussed in Montevideo.[151] In light of total Latin American unity in Montevideo, delegates also knew that the final step was to get the United States to approve the codification draft. Delegates knew as well that this time conditions were much more auspicious than in Habana.[152] Latin Americans thus continued reproducing the arguments they had been putting forward for two decades: 'The principle of non-intervention is a fundamental American thought, and expression of the collective conscience that desires continental solidarity based on justice.'[153]

Anderson's proposal adopted in 1927, which included a prohibition to intervene in internal affairs, was under Argentinean initiative enlarged to include also external affairs.[154] In addition to a broad right of non-intervention, the Convention on Rights and Duties of States contained a list of other old Latin American aspirations. Montevideo included a formal definition of statehood, non-recognition of territorial acquisitions obtained by force, equality between states and a declaratory, unconditional and irrevocable doctrine of recognition.[155] Considered together, these rules changed the structure of modern international law. But the legacy of Montevideo went beyond these rules. Delivering a concrete triumph, Montevideo strengthened Latin American international lawyers' confidence. It was this confidence that opened new and more complex arguments and agendas beyond non-intervention. For example, at the end of the meeting the Cuban delegate denounced the treaty with the United States and the Platt Amendment, because they were extracted by coercion.[156]

A renewed sense of confidence might also have allowed Latin American lawyers to express a more particularistic and confrontational attitude.

[151] *Ibid.*, p. 103.

[152] For example, the Mexican delegate José Puig Casauranc affirmed: 'this session is free from the subterfuges and the timidities of Habana and possesses something better.' *Ibid.*, p. 107.

[153] Statements by Dominican delegate Tulio Cestero, *ibid.*, p. 104.

[154] According to the Argentinean proposal, Séptima Conferencia Internacional Americana, *Montevideo*, p. 104.

[155] Articles 1–11, Convention on Rights and Duties of States, Montevideo, 26 December 1933.

[156] Séptima Conferencia Internacional Americana, *Montevideo*, pp. 104–5.

Antoine Pierre-Paul, the Haitian delegate in Montevideo, for example, criticized Western lawyers – mentioning David Dudley Field, among others – who regard the work of the jurists of the Americas at the Rio Committee to be redundant, because of the belief that beyond their thinking about the rights of peoples there is 'nothing more than a vain and useless super-impregnation'.[157] Are we here to prove them right? Are we to show that Pan-Americanism is only to be interpreted in the interest of the strong? – asked Pierre-Paul. Foreshadowing the confrontational attitude that characterized semi-peripheral lawyers' sensibilities after the Second World War, Pierre-Paul highlighted the contradictions at the heart of American foreign policies:

> let us consider the imperialistic extension of the Monroe Doctrine . . . its abusive interpretation has caused the smaller nations of this hemisphere to shed so many tears and so much blood . . . These smaller nations have been impoverished and enslaved by Uncle Sam at the self-same moment that our 'dear relative' has proclaimed before the civilised world the right of the smaller countries to govern themselves.[158]

[157] *Ibid.*, p. 106. [158] *Ibid.*

Conclusion

It was 1933, and we see Pierre-Paul in Montevideo with his indictment of Field and American imperialism coming a long way from 1878, where we began the history of peripheral appropriations of international law, when for the first time we saw a Chinese and a Japanese delegate attending a meeting of the International Law Association. Pierre-Paul's defiance contrasts the deferential attitude Guo and Ueno displayed at the meeting where Field invoked the standard of civilization to defend unequal treatment in relation to China and Japan. The signing of the Montevideo convention marked the culmination of an era. The shift from deference to defiance was important but not the only change that Montevideo marked in the history of international law. Montevideo represented a more profound transformation.

We began our exploration in 1842, with the signing of the treaty of Nanjing following the defeat of China in the First Opium War. Nanjing was part of the globalization of international law. It represented the global expansion of international law's geographical scope of application. We began exploring nineteenth-century international law as a set of rules and doctrines governing not only relations between Western sovereigns, but also governing relations between states from the core and states formally recognized as sovereigns from the semi-periphery. We also saw international law developing rules regulating and legitimizing domination by core states over polities from the periphery.

We began examining international law as rules that, as the nineteenth century progressed, enlarged their geographic scope of application. However, up to mid nineteenth century, international law could be described as Western, that is, a regional legal regime and legal tradition articulated by Western international lawyers and with rules and doctrines favouring Western powers: the standard of civilization, for example, as one of the doctrines determining unequal treatment of peripheral polities. We ended this exploration in Montevideo, with an international law of global geographical scope, in which some peripheral peoples acquired formal statehood while others had to continue the struggle for self-determination. But by 1933, the discourse of international law, through which both domination by core states and resistance by peripheral polities was articulated, justified and contested, no longer was the purely European discourse we encountered at the beginning of the nineteenth century. The semi-peripheral appropriation of classical international law during the nineteenth century and the irruption of peripheral lawyers, politicians and activists advancing modern legal arguments during the first three decades of the twentieth century transformed Western international law into a *mestizo* international law.

International law became *mestizo* when the locations where legal ideas, doctrines and arguments were produced and shaped expanded to include the peripheries of the globe. International law became *mestizo* when in the interwar period and specifically after Montevideo, new and basic rules and doctrines emerged with peripheral origins, as we have seen in the last part of the book, when, for example, formal statehood substituted the standard of civilization and non-intervention substituted intervention to protect nationals abroad.

The new rules and doctrines that emerged during the interwar period and that were enacted in Montevideo did not transform the nature of the international order and did not change the power dynamics between core and periphery, but offered semi-peripheral international lawyers new arguments to resist core states' power. The era that witnessed the globalization of international law, the appearance of non-Western international lawyers and the rise of the peripheries as one of the locations where international law was articulated, came to an end with the outbreak of the Second World War. But as the structure and institutions of a new international order were discussed and built after the war, politicians, diplomats and lawyers from the peripheries sought again to secure sovereign autonomy and equality, non-intervention and self-determination. Like in Paris of 1919, peripherals' envoys arrived in 1945 at San Francisco, where the Charter of the United Nations was negotiated. Like in the interwar period, post-war peripherals appealed to the new international institutions to pursue their goals. As the agendas and strategies to resist were shaped by peripheral experiences accumulated until the war and to the extent that peripherals of the second post-war, like their pre-war predecessors, partially succeeded in securing formal autonomy and equality, the peripheral histories of international law explored in this book are part of the history of the international order we live in today.

Appendices

Map 1 shows that, during the 151 years between 1648 and 1799, Great Britain (England and after 1707 Great Britain) concluded 70 treaties with non-European states. The United States is excluded. Multilateral treaties concluded between Great Britain and other European states are counted. Note that most of these treaties were concluded with Russia and a great number of the remaining treaties were signed with North-African Sovereigns.

Map 2 shows that, during the nineteenth century, during the 100 years between 1800 and 1899, Great Britain concluded 474 treaties with non-European states. The United States is excluded. Multilateral treaties concluded between Great Britain and other European states and non-European states are counted. Note the expansion of treaty relations to Asia, Africa and Latin America (after the independence from Spain and Portugal).

Map 1: Treaties signed by Great Britain, 1648–1799

Map 2: Treaties signed by Great Britain, 1800–1899

Map 3: Classical international lawyers mentioned in the book

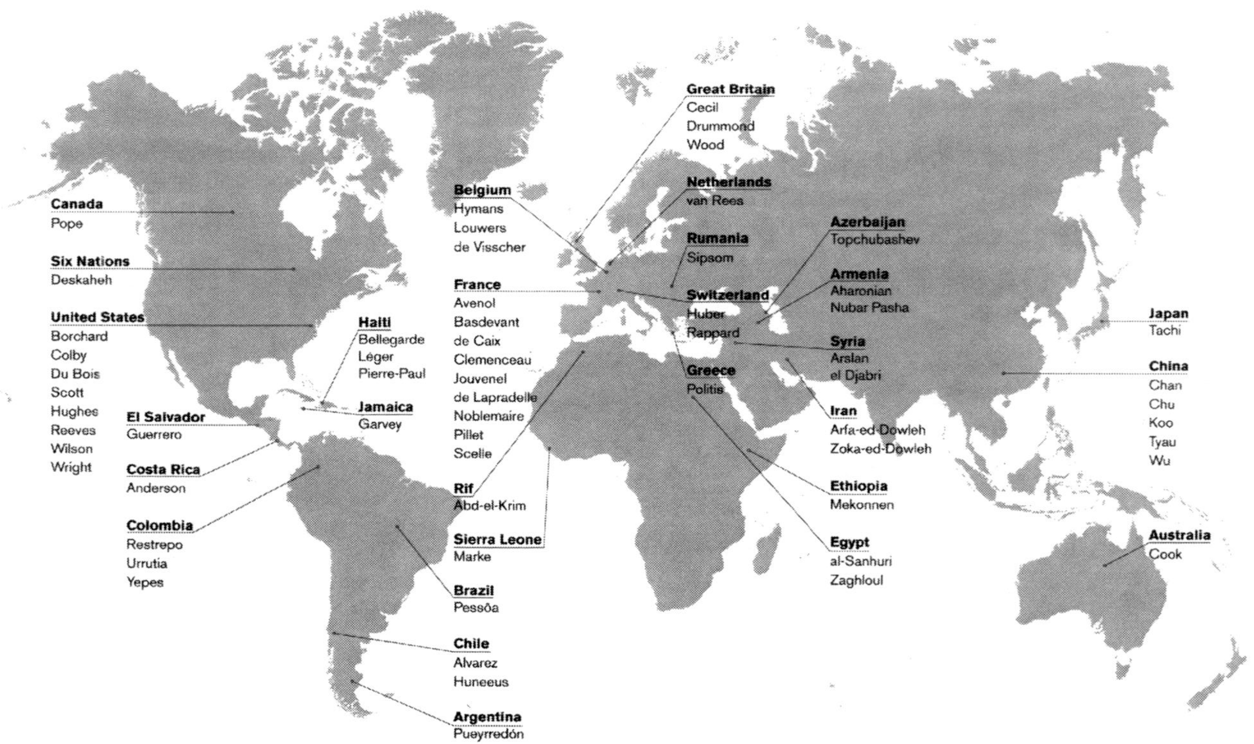

Map 4: Modern international lawyers, diplomats, politicians and activists mentioned in the book

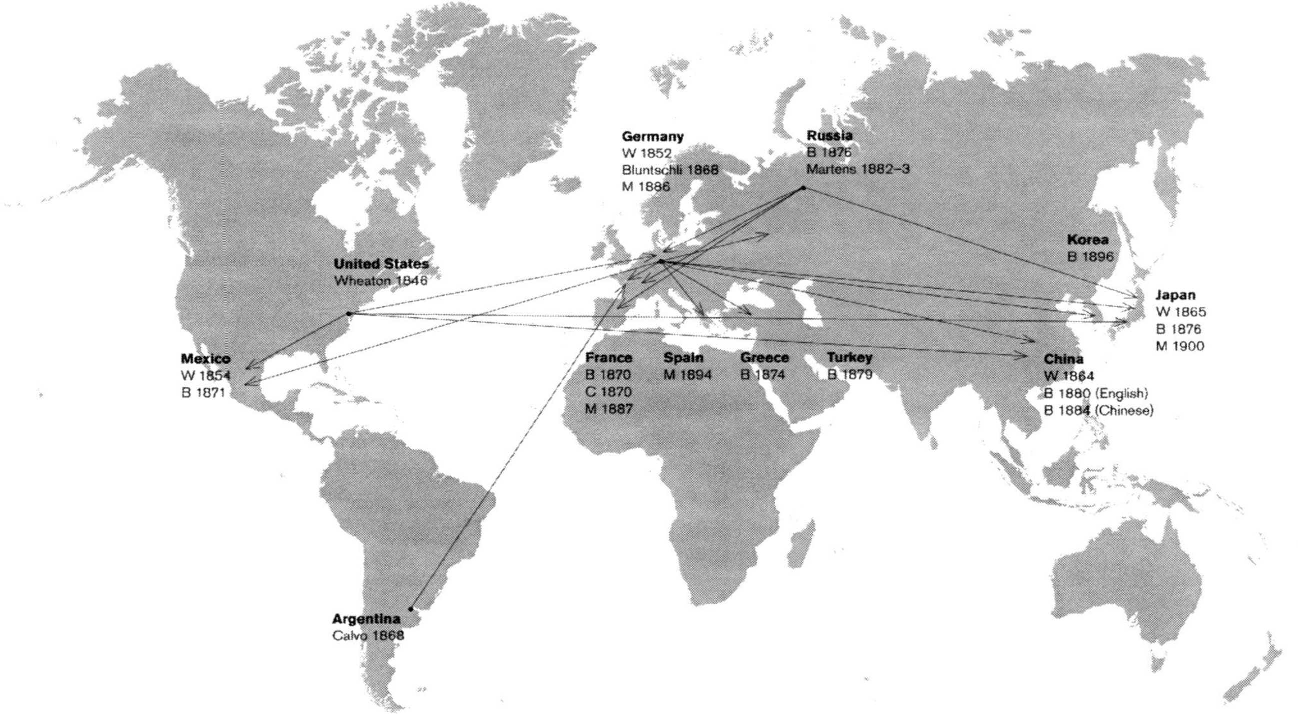

Map 5: Translations of Bluntschli (1856), Wheaton (1836), Martens (1882–3) and Calvo (1868)

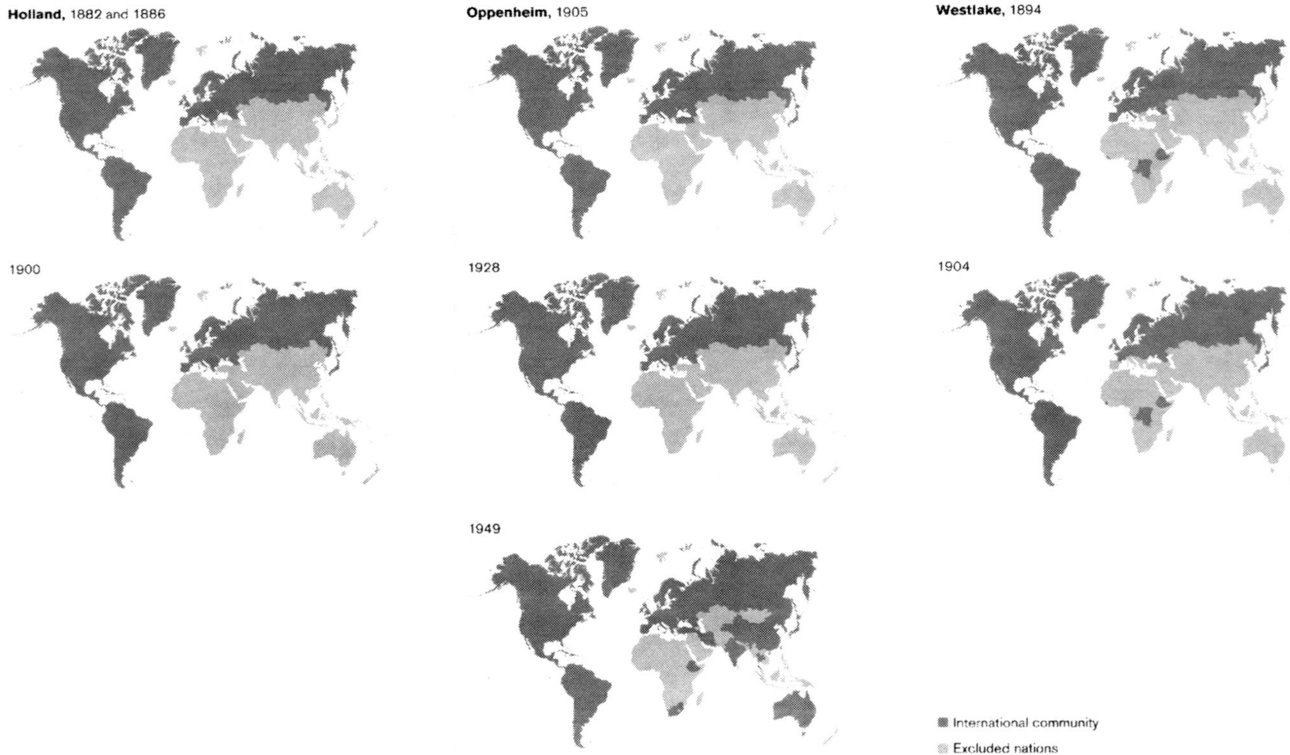

Map 6: The expansion of international law in the treatises by Holland, Oppenheim and Westlake

Bibliography

ARCHIVAL MATERIALS

General, Rare Book & Manuscript Library, Columbia University

Leguia to Scott, B 38 1152, April 6, 1928, Papers of the American Institute of International Law, Carnegie Endowment for International Peace, Subseries IV.A, Division of International Law, General, Rare Book & Manuscript Library, Columbia University

Scott to Leguia, B 38 1151, March 10, 1928, Papers of the American Institute of International Law, Carnegie Endowment for International Peace, Subseries IV.A, Division of International Law, General, Rare Book & Manuscript Library, Columbia University

Pan-American Union

International American Conference, *Diario de la sexta conferencia internacional americana, Habana, 1928* (Habana: Imprenta de Rambla, Bouza y ca., 1928)

International Commission of Jurists, *Comisión Internacional de Jurisconsultos Americanos: Reunión de 1927* (Rio de Janeiro: Secretaría General, 1927)

Public international law, projects to be submitted for the consideration of the Sixth International Conference of American States (Washington: Pan American Union, Government Printing Office, 1927)

Junta Internacional de Jurisconsultos, *Actas, resoluciones y documentos. Primera reunión en Rio de Janeiro, 19 de junio–26 de junio de 1912* (Rio de Janeiro, 1914)

Remarks of the Honorable Charles E. Hughes, at the meeting of the Committee No. 2, Public International Law, February 4, 1928, Sixth International Conference of American States, Minutes and Reports of Committees (Part 1) 1928, Columbus Memorial Library, Organization of American States

Secretaría de Relaciones Exteriores, *La participación de México en la Sexta Conferencia Internacional Americana. Informe general de la delegación de México* (México, 1928)

Séptima Conferencia Internacional Americana, *Primera, Segunda y Octava Comisiones, Actas y Antecedentes, Montevideo 1933* (Montevideo, 1933)

Sixth International Conference of American States, Minutes and Reports of Committees (Part 1), unpublished document 1928, Columbus Memorial Library, Organization of American States

United States, *Report of the delegates of the United States of America to the Fifth International Conference of American States held at Santiago, Chile, March 25 to May 3, 1923 with appendices* (Washington: Government Printing Office, 1924)

League of Nations

Abd-el-Krim, To the Civilised Nations, 1922 LoN Archive, 11/23217/12861

Executive Committee of the Syro-Palestinian Congress, Appeal Addressed to the Sixth General Assembly of the League of Nations, Cairo, September 29th, 1925, PMC, Minutes of the Eighth Session

G. H. F. Abraham to Van Hamel, 31 July, 1923, LoN Archive 11/29540/28075

League of Nations, *Act of the Conference for the Codification of International Law, The Hague, 1930, vol. I, Plenary meetings* (Geneva, 1930)

Act of the Conference for the Codification of International Law, The Hague, 1930, Vol. IV, Minutes of the Third Committee (Geneva: League of Nations, 1930)

'Admission of the Azerbaidjan Republic to the League', LoN Document de l'Assemblée 20/48/68

Official Journal, Special Supplement, 19 (1923), 17

Records of the First Assembly. Meetings of the Committees (Geneva, 1920)

Records of the First Assembly. Plenary Meetings (Geneva, 1920)

Records of the Second Assembly. Meetings of the Committees (Geneva, 1921), vol. I

Records of the Third Assembly. Plenary meetings (Geneva, 1922)

'Request from Armenia for Admission to the League of Nations', LoN Document de l'Assemblée 20/48/33

'Organizing Committee of the Independent Movement, The Grievances of the Korean People and the bad government of Japan', 1920 LoN Archive, 11/4515/302

Permanent Mandates Commission, Memorandum of the Syrian American Society, registered by the PMC in Rome on 18th February 1926, LoN Doc CPM 373

Minutes of the Third Session, held at Geneva July 20th to August 10th, 1923. LoN Doc A.19.1923 VI

Minutes of the Seventh Session of the Permanent Mandates Commission, held Oct. 19/30 1925, LoN Doc CPM 328

Minutes of the Eighth Session (extraordinary) Rome, Feb. 16, March 6, 1926, LoN Doc C.174.M.65. 1926 VI

Ordre du Jour de la VIII-me Session (Extraordinaire) de la Commission Permanente des Mandats, LoN Doc CPM 370

'Petition to the League of Nations from the Six Nations of the Grand River, Communicated by the Government of the Netherlands', LoN Doc C.500.1923.VII.

Republic of Azerbaidjan, 'Letter from the President of the Peace Delegation of the Republic of Azerbaidjan', LoN Document de l'Assemblée 206, December 1920

Secretary General, 'Memorandum on the admission of Azerbaijan', LoN Document de l'Assemblée 20/48/108, 1920

'The Redman's Appeal for Justice' LoN Archive 11/28075/30626

'To the International Court, by order of the Moroccan People' 1925, LoN Archive, 11/41616/12861

Universal Negro Improvement Association (UNIA), 'Petition of the Universal Negro Improvement Association League to the League of Nations, The Hague', LoN Archive, 1/22354/21159

US National Archives

'Letter sent to certain leaders of public opinion about the Egyptian Question by H. Y. Awad, May 1st 1919, USNA, RG 256, 883.00/159

Paiz, O., December 8th 1920, USNA, 500C001/157

W. E. B. Du Bois Papers, Special Collections and University Archives, University of Massachusetts Amherst Libraries

Du Bois, W. E. B., 'Letter from W. E. B. Du Bois to Premier of France (1918)', *W. E. B. Du Bois Papers* (MS 312). Special Collections and University Archives, University of Massachusetts Amherst Libraries

'Letter from W. E. B. Du Bois to President Woodrow Wilson, ca. November 1918', *W. E. B. Du Bois Papers* (MS 312). Special Collections and University Archives, University of Massachusetts Amherst Libraries

OTHER PRIMARY SOURCES

Adas, Michael, 'Contested hegemony: the Great War and the Afro-Asian assault on the civilizing mission ideology', *Journal of World History*, 15 (2004), 31–63

'Address to the nations of the world' in L. J. Ayodele Langley, *Ideologies of liberation in Black Africa, 1856–1970: documents on modern African political thought from colonial times to the present* (London: R. Collings, 1979) pp. 738–40

Ago, Roberto, 'Pluralism and the origins of the international community', *Italian Yearbook of International Law*, 3 (1977), 3–33

Aharonian, Avetis and Nubar, Boghos, *The Armenian question before the Peace Conference* (New York: Press Bureau, the Armenian National Union of America, 1919)

Ahmad, Feroz, 'Ottoman perceptions of the capitulations 1800–1914', *Journal of Islamic Studies*, 11 (1) (2000), 1–20

Akashi, Kinji, 'Japanese "acceptance" of the European law of nations: a brief history of international law in Japan' in M. Stolleis and Y. Masaharu (eds.), *East Asian and European perspectives on international law* (Baden-Baden: Nomos, 2004) pp. 1–21

Akehurst, Michael Barton and Malanczuk, Peter, *Akehurst's modern introduction to international law*, 7th edn (London: Routledge, 1997)

Akhundov, Fuad, 'Democratic Republic of Azerbaijan leaders (1918–1920), Alimardan Topchubashev – Minister of Foreign Affairs (1862–1934)', *Azerbaijan International*, 6 (1998), 31–3

Alcorta, Amancio, *Cours de droit international public*, E. Lehr trans. (Paris: Larose et Forcel, 1887) , vol. I, pp. 202–13

'El derecho internacional en las antiguas civilizaciones americanas', *Nueva Revista de Buenos Aires*, 1 (1881), 82

Alexandrowicz, Charles Henry, *An introduction to the history of the law of nations in the East Indies: (16th, 17th and 18th centuries)* (Oxford: Clarendon Press, 1967)

'Doctrinal aspects of the universality of the law of nations', *BYIL*, 37 (1961), 506–15

'The Afro-Asian world and the law of nations (historical aspects)', *Recueil des Cours de l'Académie de Droit International de La Haye*, 123 (1968), 117–214

Alvarez, Alejandro, *Considérations générales sur la codification du droit international américain (code de droit international des états américains). Mémorial présentée à la deuxième Commission de juristes réunie à Rio de Janeiro le 18 avril 1927* (Rio de Janeiro: Imprensa Nacional, 1927)

Exposé de motifs et Déclaration des grands principes du droit international moderne (approuvée par l'Académie diplomatique internationale, l'Union juridique internationale et l'International Law Association) (Paris: Les Éditions Internationales, 1936)

La codificación del derecho internacional en América: trabajos de la tercera Comisión de la Asamblea de Jurisconsultos reunida en Santiago de Chile (Santiago de Chile: Imprenta Universitaria, 1923) 26–27

La codification du droit international, sestendances – ses bases (Paris: A. Pédone, 1912)

La conférence des juristes de Rio de Janeiro et la codification du droit international américain (Paris: A. Pédone, 1913)

'Latin America and international law,' *AJIL*, 3 (1909), 269–353

Le droit international américain, son fondement – sa nature d'après l'histoire diplomatique des états du nouveau monde et leur vie politique et économique (Paris: A. Pédone, 1910)

'Le nouveau droit de gens et le projet d'une école internationale de droit international', *RDI*, Tr. Série, T.I (1920), 154

Le nouveau droit international public et sa codification en Amérique plan développé des matières d'un ouvrage en 2 volumes, devant paraître sous ce titre, et être présenté à l'Assemblée des juristes américaines, à Rio de Janeiro en 1925, pour la codification du droit international (Paris: A. Rousseau, 1924)

Rapport-questionnaire et projets présentés à la deuxième session de l'institut américain de droit international à la Havane (Washington: Institut Américain de Droit International, 1917)

American Institute of International Law, *Acte final de la session de la Havane: (deuxième session de l'institut) 22–27 janvier 1917; résolutions et projets* (Oxford University Press, 1917)

Anand, R. P., 'Family of "civilised" states and Japan: a story of humiliation, assimilation, defiance and confrontation', *Journal of the History of International Law*, 5 (2003), 1–75

'Sovereign equality of states in international law', *RdC*, 197 (1986-II), 9–228

Anghie, Antony, *Imperialism, sovereignty, and the making of international law* (Cambridge University Press, 2005)

Annuaire de l'Institut de droit international, 43 Tome II (1950)

Anzilotti, Dionisio, 'La responsibilité internationale des etats a raison des dommages soufferts par des étrangers', *RGDIP*, 13 (1906), 5–28, 285–309

Ariga, Nagao, 'De la protection accordée aux chinois résidant au Japon pendant la guerre sino-japonaise', *RGDIP*, 2 (1895), 577–583

La guerre sino-japonaise au point de vue du droit international (Paris: Pédone, 1896)

Armitage, David, *Foundations of modern international thought* (Cambridge University Press, 2013), p. 18

Association for the Reform and Codification of the Law of Nations Report of the Conference, 1 & 2 (1873–1874)

Association for the Reform and Codification of the Law of Nations Summary of the Proceedings 3 (1875)

Association for the Reform and Codification of the Law of Nations Report of the Conference 6 (1878)

Auslin, Michael R., *Negotiating with imperialism: the unequal treaties and the culture of Japanese diplomacy* (Cambridge: Harvard University Press, 2004)

Aydin, Cemil, *The politics of anti-Westernism in Asia: visions of world order in pan-Islamic and pan-Asian thought* (New York: Columbia University Press, 2007)

Baker, Betsy, 'The method behind Bluntschli's "Modern" International Law', *Journal of the History of International Law*, 4 (2002), 249–92

Bandeira Galindo, Rodrigo, 'Martti Koskenniemi and the historiographical turn in international law', *European Journal of International Law*, 16 (2005), 539–59

Barbosa, Ruy, *The equality of sovereign states* (The Hague, 1907)

Basdevant, J., *L'action coercitive anglo-germano-italienne contre le Vénézuéla, 1902–1903* (Paris: A. Pédone, 1904)

'L'action coercitive anglo-germano-italienne contre le Vénézuéla, 1902–1903', *RGDIP*, 11 (1904), 362–458

Becker Lorca, Arnulf, 'Alejandro Alvarez situated: subaltern modernities and modernisms that subvert', *Leiden Journal of International Law*, 19 (2006), 879–930

'Eurocentrism in the history of international law' in B. Fassbender and A. Peters (eds.), *The Oxford handbook of the history of international law* (Oxford University Press, 2012), pp. 1034–57

'International law in Latin America or Latin American international law? Rise, fall, and retrieval of a tradition of legal thinking and political imagination', *Harvard Journal of International Law*, 47 (2006), 283–305

'Rules for the "global war on terror": implying consent and presuming conditions for intervention', *New York University Journal of International Law and Politics*, 45 (2012), 1–95

Bellegarde-Smith, Patrick, 'Dantes Bellegarde and pan-Africanism', *Phylon*, 12 (1981), 233–44
Bello, Andrés, *Principios de derecho de jentes* (Santiago de Chile: Imprenta de la Opinión, 1832)
Bemis, S., *The Latin American policy of the United States* (New York: Harcourt, Brace and Co., 1943)
Benton, Lauren, *Law and colonial cultures: legal regimes in world history, 1400–1900* (Cambridge University Press, 2001)
Bergbohm, Carl, *Staatsverträge und Gesetze als Quellen des Völkerrechts* (Dorpat: C. Mattiesen, 1877)
Berman, Nathaniel, '"The appeals of the Orient": colonized desire and the war of the riff' in Karen Knop (ed.), *Gender and human rights* (Oxford University Press, 2004), 195–230
Bethell, Leslie, 'Britain and Latin America in historical perspective' in V. Bulmer-Thomas (ed.), *Britain and Latin America: a changing relationship* (Cambridge University Press, 1989), pp. 1–24
Bluntschli, Johann Caspar, *Bluntschli's International law*, C. Lardy, W. A. P. Martin trans. (Beijing: Tung Wên College Press, 1880)
Das moderne Völkerrecht der civilisirten Staten als Rechtsbuch dargestellt (Nördlingen: Beck, 1868)
El derecho internacional codificado, José Díaz Covarrubias trans. (Mexico: Impr. J. Batiza, 1871)
Gong fa hui tong, W. Martin trans. (Beijing: Tong wen guan, 1884)
Ho diethnes kodix (Athenai, 1874)
Hukuk-ı beyneddüvel-i kanunu (İstanbul: Vakit Gazetesi Matbaası, 1879)
Kokuhō hanron, Hiroyuki Katō trans. (Tōkyōfu: Kondō Keizō, 1876)
Kongpop hoet'ong, 1896 Chaeju chongnija p'an, W. A. P. Martin trans. (Hansŏng: Hakbu P'yŏnjipkuk, 1896)
Le droit international codifié, C. Lardy, É. Laboulaye trans. (Paris: Guillaumin, 1870)
Sovremennoe mezhdunarodnoe pravo tsivilizovannykh gosudarstv, izlozhennoe v vidie kodeksa (Moskva: Indrikh, 1876)
Bluntschli, Johann Caspar and Seyerlen, Rudolf, *Denkwürdiges aus meinem Leben* (Nördlingen: Beck, 1884)
Bogdandy, Armin and Dellavalle, Sergio, 'Universalism and particularism as paradigms of international law', IILJ Working Paper 2008/3, 1, 57
Bonfils, Henry, *Manuel de droit international public* (Paris: Rousseau, 1898)
Boogert, Maurits H. van den, *The capitulations and the Ottoman legal system qadis, consuls, and beraths in the 18th century* (Leiden: Brill, 2005)
Borchard, Edwin, '"Responsibility of states" at the Hague Codification Conference', *AJIL*, 24 (1930), 517–40
The diplomatic protection of citizens abroad; or, the law of international claims (New York: The Banks Law Pub. Co., 1922).
Brett, Oliver, Cecil, Robert and Phillimore, Walter, *The first Assembly; a study of the proceedings of the first Assembly of the League of Nations* (London: Macmillan, 1921)

Brown, Philip Marshall, *Foreigners in Turkey; their juridical status* (Princeton University Press, 1914)

Brownlie, Ian, 'The expansion of international society: the consequences of the law of nations' in H. Bull and A. Watson (eds.) in *The expansion of international society* (Oxford: Clarendon Press, 1984), pp. 357–69

'The President's roundtable', *American Society International Law Proceedings*, 13 (2001), 13, 14

Burkman, Thomas, *Japan and the League of Nations: empire and world order, 1914–1938* (Honolulu: University of Hawaii Press, 2008)

Burnett, Christina Duffy, 'Contingent constitutions: empire and law in the Americas', PhD thesis, Princeton University (2010)

Bustamante y Sirvén, Antonio Sánchez de, *Los progresos de la codificación bajo los auspicios de la unión panamericana* (Habana: El siglo XX, 1926)

Butler, William, *Russia and the Law of Nations in historical perspective* (London: Wildy, Simmonds & Hill, 2009)

Calvo, Carlos, *Annales historiques de la révolution de l'Amérique latine, accompagnées de documents à l'appui. De l'année 1808 jusqu'à la reconnaissance par les états européens de l'indépendance de ce vaste continent*, 5 vols. (Paris: A. Durand, 1864–7)

Derecho internacional teórico y práctico de Europa y América (Paris: D'Amyot, 1868)

Le droit international théorique et pratique: précédé d'un exposé historique des progrès de la science du droit des gens (Paris: A. Rousseau, 1896), vol. I

'Polémica Calvo-Alcorta', *Nueva Revista de Buenos Aires*, 7 (1883), 629

Recueil complet des traités, conventions, capitulations, armistices et autres actes diplomatiques de tous les états de l'Amérique latine, compris entre le golfe du Mexique et le cap de Horn, depuis l'année 1493 jusqu'à nos jours (Paris: A. Durand, 1862)

Cançado Trindade, Antônio, 'The presence and participation of Latin America at the Second Hague Peace Conference of 1907' in Y. Daudet (ed.), *Topicality of the 1907 Hague conference, the second peace conference (Actualité de la conférence de La Haye de 1907, deuxième conférence de la paix)* (Leiden: Nijhoff, 2008), pp. 51–84

Carathéodory, Etienne, *Du droit international concernant les grands cours d'eau: étude théorique et pratique sur la liberté de la navigation fluviale* (Leipzig: Brockhaus, 1861)

Cardoso, Fernando Henrique and Enzo Faletto, *Dependency and development in Latin America* (Berkeley: University of California Press, 1979)

Carrillo Salcedo, Juan Antonio, 'Aspectos doctrinales del problema de la universalidad del derecho de gentes', *Revista española de derecho internacional*, 17 (1964), 3–15

Cassel, Pär, 'Excavating extraterritoriality: the "judicial sub-prefect" as a prototype for the mixed court in Shanghai', *Late Imperial China*, 24 (2003), 156–82

Cassese, Antonio, *Self-determination of peoples: a legal reappraisal* (Cambridge University Press, 1995)

Chan, Chung Sing, *Les concessions en Chine* (Paris: Les presses universitaires de France, 1925)

Chang, Richard, *The justice of the Western consular courts in nineteenth-century Japan* (Westport: Greenwood Press, 1984)

Cheng, Tiqiang, 'The people's republic of China and international law', *Dalhousie Law Journal*, 8 (1984), 3–31
Chinese Delegation, 'Memorandum, The claim of China for the direct restitution to herself of the leased territory of Kiaochow, the Tsingtao-China Railway and other German rights in the respect of Shantung Province', *Chinese Social and Political Science Review*, 5 (1920), 15–115
'Questions for adjustment, submitted by China to the Peace Conference', *Chinese Social and Political Science Review*, 5 (1920), 116–61
Chinese delegation to the Peace Conference, *The claim of China: submitting for abrogation by the Peace Conference the treaties and notes made and exchanged by and between China and Japan on May 25, 1915* (Paris: Impr. de Vaugirard, 1919)
Questions for readjustment submitted by China to the Peace Conference (Paris: Impr. de Vaugirard, 1919)
Chinese National Welfare Society in America, *The Shantung question, a statement of China's claim together with important documents submitted to the Peace Conference in Paris* (San Francisco: Chinese National Welfare Society in America, 1919)
Chiu, Hungdah, 'Comparison of the nationalist and communist Chinese views of unequal treaties' in J. A. Cohen (ed.), *China's practice of international law: some case studies* (Cambridge, MA: Harvard University Press, 1972), pp. 239–67
'The development of Chinese international law terms and the problems of translation into English' in J. A. Cohen and Harold J. Berman (eds.), *Contemporary Chinese law: research problems and perspectives* (Cambridge: Harvard University Press, 1970), pp. 139–57
Chu, Chao-Hsin, *Revision of unequal treaties. China appeals to the League of Nations. Official text of the speeches of Mr. Chao-Hsin Chu, and press comments thereon* (London, London Caledonian Press, 1926)
Chu, Pao-chin, *V. K. Wellington Koo: a case study of China's diplomat and diplomacy of nationalism, 1912–1966* (Hong Kong: Chinese University Press, 1981)
Clark, J. Reuben, *Memorandum on the Monroe Doctrine* (Washington: Government Printing Office, 1930)
Cleveland, William L., *Islam against the West: Shakib Arslan and the campaign for islamic nationalism* (Austin: University of Texas Press, 1985)
Coates, Benjamin, 'Transatlantic advocates: American international law and US Foreign Relations, 1898–1919', PhD dissertation, Columbia University (2010)
Colby, Elbridge, 'How to fight savage tribes', *AJIL*, 21 (1927), 279–88
Conférence de la paix, *Pétition présentée par la Délégation Coréenne* (Paris, 1919)
Conférence intergouvernementale, *Observations présentées par la délégation Ottomane à la Conférence de la Paix* (Versailles, 1920)
Congrès Syrio-Palestinien (Genève 25 août–21 sept. 1921), *Appel adressé à l' Assemblée Générale de la Société des Nations* (Impr. Tribune de Genève, 1921)
Corbett, Percy Ellwood, *Law and Society in the Relations of States* (New York: Harcourt, Brace and Co., 1951)
Craven, Matthew, 'What happened to unequal treaties? The continuities of informal empire' in M. Craven and M. Fitzmaurice, *Interrogating the treaty:*

essays in the contemporary law of treaties (Nijmegen, The Netherlands: Wolf Legal Publishers, 2005), pp. 43–80

'Introduction' in M. Craven, M. Fitzmaurice and M. Vogiatzi (eds.), *Time, history and international law* (Dordrecht: Martinus Nijhoff, 2007)

Crawford, Neta, *Argument and change in world politics: ethics, decolonization, and humanitarian intervention* (Cambridge University Press, 2012), p. 276

Daudet, Y. (ed.), *Topicality of the 1907 Hague conference, the second peace conference (Actualité de la conférence de La Haye de 1907, deuxième conférence de la paix)* (Leiden: Nijhoff, 2008)

Davey, A. M., *The Bondelzwarts affair: a study of the repercussions, 1922–1959* (Pretoria: University of South Africa, 1961)

Davis, Calvin DeArmond, *The United States and the Second Hague Peace Conference: American diplomacy and international organisation, 1899–1914* (Durham, NC: Duke University Press, 1974), p. 94

Davis, John R., 'Britain and the European balance of power' in Chris Williams (ed.), *A companion to nineteenth-century Britain* (Oxford: Blackwell Publishing, 2006), pp. 34–52

Davis, Mike, *Late Victorian holocausts: el niño famines and the making of the third world* (London: Verso, 2001)

Davison, Roderic H., 'Ottoman diplomacy and its legacy' in Carl L. Brown, *Imperial legacy: the Ottoman imprint on the Balkans and the Middle East* (New York: Columbia University Press, 1996), pp. 174–99

de Groot, Alexander H., 'The historical development of the capitulatory regime in the Ottoman Middle East from the fifteenth to the nineteenth centuries', *Oriente Moderno*, 83 (2003), 575–604

Diggelmann, Oliver, *Anfänge der Völkerrechtssoziologie: die Völkerrechtskonzeptionen von Max Huber und Georges Scelle im Vergleich* (Zürich: Sculthess, 2000)

Don D. F. Sarmiento to Señor Ribeyro, Inclosure 1 in No. 7, Accounts and papers of the House of Commons, State Papers, vol. 32 (1864), p. 15

Drago, Luis Maria, 'Les emprunts d'état et leurs rapports avec la politique internationale', *RGDIP*, 14 (1907), 251–87

'Letter of Dr. Luis Drago, Minister of Foreign Relations of the Argentine Republic, to Mr. Mérou, Argentine Minister to the United States, December 29, 1902' in A. Alvarez, *The Monroe Doctrine, its importance in the international life of the states of the New World* (New York: Oxford University Press, 1924), 187–92

'State loans in their relation to international policy', *AJIL*, 1 (1907), 692–726

Du Bois, W. E. B., 'The African roots of war', *Atlantic Monthly*, 115 (1915), 707–14

'Memorandum to M. Diagne and others on a Pan-African Congress to be held in Paris in February, 1919', *Crisis*, 17 (1919), 224–5

Duxbury, Alison, *The participation of states in international organisations: the role of human rights and democracy* (Cambridge University Press, 2011)

Elias, Taslim Olawale, *Africa and the development of international law* (Leiden: A. W. Sijthoff, 1972)

Elleman, Bruce A., *Wilson and China: a revised history of the Shandong question* (Armonk, NY: M. E. Sharpe, 2002)

Esquirol, Jorge, 'Alejandro Alvarez's Latin American law: a question of identity', *Leiden Journal of International Law*, 19 (2006), 93–156

'Latin America' in B. Fassbender and A. Peters (eds.), *The Oxford handbook of the history of international law* (Oxford University Press, 2012), pp. 553–77

Eyffinger, Arthur, 'A highly critical moment: role and record of the 1907 Hague Peace Conference', *Netherlands International Law Review*, 54 (2007), 197–228

Fairbank, John King, 'The early treaty system in the Chinese world order' in J. K. Fairbank and Ta-tuan Ch'en (eds.), *The Chinese world order; traditional China's foreign relations* (Cambridge: Harvard University Press, 1968), pp. 257–75

Trade and diplomacy on the China coast: the opening of the treaty ports, 1842–1854 (Cambridge: Harvard University Press, 1964), p. 317

Fassbender, Bardo and Peters, Anne, 'Introduction: towards a global history of international law' in B. Fassbender and A. Peters (eds.), *The Oxford handbook of the history of international law* (Oxford University Press, 2012), pp. 3–24

Fauset, Jessie, 'Impressions of the Second Pan-African Congress', *The Crisis*, 23 (1921), 12–18

Fisch, Jörg, *Das Selbstbestimmungsrecht der Völker oder die Domestizierung einer Illusion: Eine Geschichte* (Munich: C. H. Beck, 2010)

Die europäische Expansion und das Völkerrecht: Die Auseinandersetzungen um den Status der überseeischen Gebiete vom 15. Jahrhundert bis zur Gegenwart (Stuttgart: Steiner, 1984)

'Power or weakness? On the causes of the worldwide expansion of European law', *Journal of the History of International Law*, 6 (2004), 21–6

Frank, Andre Gunder, *ReOrient: global economy in the Asian age* (Berkeley: University of California Press, 1998)

Frodsham, J. D., *The first Chinese embassy to the West; the journals of Kuo-Sung-T'ao, Liu Hsi-Hung and Chang Te-Yi*, translated by J. D. Frodsham (Oxford: Clarendon Press, 1974)

Fuji, Ito, 'One hundred years of international law studies in Japan', *Japanese Annual of International Law*, 13 (1969), 19–34

Garvey, Marcus, 'Christian Boers of South Africa use airplanes to bomb Hottentots', *The Negro World*, Saturday, June 17, 1922, p. 1

Gaurier, Dominique, *Histoire du droit international: auteurs, doctrines et développement de l'antiquité à l'aube de la période contemporaine* (Presses universitaires de Rennes, 2005)

Goldschmidt, Arthur, *Biographical dictionary of modern Egypt* (Boulder, CO: Lynne Rienner, 2000)

Gong, Gerrit, *The standard of 'civilization' in international society* (Oxford: Clarendon Press, 1984)

Grant, Colin, *Negro with a hat. The rise and fall of Marcus Garvey* (Oxford University Press, 2008)

Grewe, Wilhelm, *The epochs of international law* (trans. and rev. Michael Byers, Berlin: Walter de Gruyter, 2000)

'Vom europäischen zum universellen Völkerrecht', *Zeitschrift für Ausländisches Öffentliches Recht und Völkerrecht*, 42 (1982), 449–79

Guerrero, Gustavo, *La codification du droit international: la première conférence (La Haye, 13 mars–12 avril 1930)* (Paris: A. Pédone, 1930)
'Questionnaire no. 4: responsibility of states for damage done in their territories to the person or property of foreigners', *AJIL* (supplement), 20 (1926), 176–203
Guggenheim, Paul, 'Das Jus publicum europeum und Europa', *Jahrbuch des Öffentliches Rechts der Gegenwart*, 3 (1954), 1–14
'Gustavo Guerrero, 1876–1958, in memoriam', *Revue Internationale française du Droit des Gens*, 28 (1959), 5–8
Hanke, Lewis, *All mankind is one; a study of the disputation between Bartolomé de Las Casas and Juan Ginés de Sepúlveda in 1550 on the intellectual and religious capacity of the American Indians* (Northern Illinois University Press, 1974)
Hauptman, Laurence, *The Iroquois struggle for survival: World War II to red power* (Syracuse University Press, 1986)
Heffter, August and Geffcken, Friedrich, *Das europäische Völkerrecht der Gegenwart auf den bisherigen Grundlagen* (Berlin: H. W. Müller, 1882)
Hershey, Amos, 'The Calvo and Drago doctrines', *AJIL*, 1 (1907), 26–45
Hicks, Fredrick, 'The equality of states and the Hague Conferences,' *AJIL*, 2 (1908), 530–61
Higgins, Rosalyn, 'The Hague Peace Conference as a milestone in the development of international law' in Y. Daudet (ed.), *Topicality of the 1907 Hague conference, the second peace conference (Actualité de la conférence de La Haye de 1907, deuxième conférence de la paix)* (Leiden: Nijhoff, 2008), pp. 29–40
Hill, Robert (ed.), *The Marcus Garvey and Universal Negro Improvement Association papers* (Berkeley: University of California Press, 1983), vol. IV
The Marcus Garvey and Universal Negro Improvement Association papers: Africa for the Africans June 1921–December 1922 (Berkeley: University of California Press, 1995), vol. IX
Hill, Robert (ed.), *The Marcus Garvey and Universal Negro Improvement Association papers* (Berkeley, University of California Press, 2011), vol. XI
Holland, T.E., 'Frederic de Martens', *Journal of the Society of Comparative Legislation*, 10 (1909) 10–12
The elements of jurisprudence, 2nd edn (Oxford: Clarendon Press, 1882)
The elements of jurisprudence, 3rd edn (Oxford: Clarendon Press, 1886)
The elements of jurisprudence, 9th edn (Oxford: Clarendon Press, 1900)
Holquist, Peter, 'The Russian Empire as a civilised state: international law as principle and practice in imperial Russia, 1874–1878', National Council for Eurasian and East European Research (2004), available at www.ucis.pitt.edu/nceeer/2004_818-06g_Holquist.pdf
Holtzendorff von, Franz, *Handbuch des Völkerrechts: auf Grundlage europäischer Staatspraxis*, 4th edn (Berlin: Habel, 1889)
Hood, Miriam, *Gunboat diplomacy, 1895–1905: great power pressure in Venezuela*, 2nd edn (London/Boston: Allen & Unwin, 1983)
Hoover War Library, *A catalogue of Paris Peace Conference delegation propaganda in the Hoover War Library* (Stanford University Press, 1926)

Horowitz, Richard, 'International law and state transformation in China, Siam, and the Ottoman Empire during the nineteenth century', *Journal of World History*, 15 (2004), 445–86

Hourani, Albert, *Syria and Lebanon, a political essay* (Oxford University Press, 1946)

Howland, Douglas, 'Japan's civilised war: international law as diplomacy in the Sino-Japanese War (1894–1895)', *Journal of the History of International Law*, 9 (2007), 179–201

Hsieh, Pasha L., 'The discipline of international law in Republican China and contemporary Taiwan', unpublished paper (2013)

Hsü, Immanuel C. Y., *China's entrance into the family of nations: the diplomatic phase, 1858–1880* (Cambridge, MA: Harvard University Press, 1960), p. 121

Hu, H., *Le problème coréen* (Paris: A. Pédone, 1953)

Huber, Max, *Die Gleichheit der Staaten*, offprint from *Juristische Festgabe des Auslandes zu Josef Kohlers 60. Geburtstag*, ed. F. Berolzheimer (Stuttgart: Enke, 1909)

Die soziologischen Grundlagen des Völkerrechts (Berlin-Grunewald: W. Rothschild, 1928)

Hudson, Manley O., 'The First Conference for the Codification of International Law', *AJIL*, 24 (1930), 447–66

Hueck, Ingo 'The discipline of the history of international law. New trends and methods on the history of international law', *Journal of the History of International Law*, 3 (2001)

Hurewitz, J. C., 'Ottoman diplomacy and the European state system', *Middle East Journal*, 15 (1961), 141–52

İnalcık, Halil, '*Imtiyāzāt*' in P. J. Bearman and Marc Garborieau (eds.), *Encyclopaedia of Islam*, 2nd edn (Leiden: Brill Online)

India Home Rule League of America, *Self-determination for India* (New York: India Home Rule League of America, Paris Peace Conference, 1919)

International Peace Conference, *The proceedings of the Hague Peace conferences: translation of the official texts*, prepared in the Division of International law of the Carnegie Endowment for International Peace, under the supervision of James Brown Scott et al. (repr. Buffalo, NY: W. S. Hein, 2000)

Jacobini, H. B., *A study of the philosophy of international law as seen in works of Latin American writers* (The Hague: Nijhoff, 1954)

Japan, *The case presented by the imperial Japanese government to the Tribunal of Arbitration constituted under section 1 of the protocol concluded at Tokio, August 28, 1902, between Japan and Germany, France and Great Britain* (1904)

Jennings, Robert, 'Universal international law in a multicultural world' in M. Bos and I. Brownlie (eds.), *Liber amicorum for the Rt Hon. Lord Wilberforce* (Oxford: Clarendon Press, 1987)

Johansen, Bruce and Pritzker, Barry, 'Deskaheh' in *Encyclopedia of American Indian history* (Santa Barbara, CA: ABC-CLIO, 2007), pp. 712–13

Jones, Llewellyn, 'Military occupation of alien territory in time of peace', *Transactions of the Grotius Society*, 9 (1923), 149–63

Kaapanda, Mekondjo, 'The pan-African movement' (unpublished paper)

Kaneko, K. 'Les institutions judiciaires du Japon', *RDI*, 25 (1893), 338–56

Karady, Victor, La migration internationale d'étudiants en Europe, 1890–1940, *Actes de la Recherche en Sciences Sociales*, 145 (2002), 47–60
Kazemzadeh, Firuz, *Russia and Britain in Persia, 1864–1914: a study in imperialism* (New Haven: Yale University Press, 1968)
Kebedgy, Michel, 'Principes du droit des gens', *Zeitschrift für Schweizerisches Recht*, 19 (1900), 84
Kennedy, David, 'International law and the nineteenth century: history of an illusion', *Nordic Journal of International Law*, 65 (1996), 385–420
International legal structures (Baden-Baden: Nomos, 1987)
'The move to institutions', *Cardozo Law Review*, 8 (1986), 841–987
The rise and fall of classical legal thought (Washington DC: Beard Books, 2006 [1975])
'When renewal repeats: thinking against the box', *New York Journal of International Law and Politics*, 32 (2000), 335–500
Kentaro Kaneko, 'Les institutions judiciaires du Japon', *Revue de droit international et de législation comparée*, 25 (1893), 338–56
Khoury, P., *Syria and the French Mandate: the politics of Arab nationalism, 1920–1945* (Princeton University Press, 1987), p. 178
Kingsbury, Benedict, 'The international legal order' in P. Cane and M. Tushnet (eds.), *Oxford handbook of legal studies* (2003), pp. 271–97
Kirgis, Frederic L., *The American Society of International Law's first century: 1906–2006* (Leiden: Martinus Nijhoff, 2006)
Klüber, Johann Ludwig, *Europäisches Völkerrecht* (2nd edn, by Carl Morstadt, Schotthausen, Hurter, 1851)
Kohen, Marcelo, 'La contribución de América Latina al desarrollo progresivo del derecho internacional en materia territorial', *Anuario de derecho internacional*, 17 (2001), 57–77
Koo, V. K. Wellington, *The status of aliens in China* (New York: Columbia University, 1912)
Koskenniemi, Martti, *From apology to utopia: the structure of international legal argument* (Helsinki: Finnish Lawyers' Pub. Co., 1989)
'Histories of international law: dealing with Eurocentrism', *Rechtsgeschichte*, 19 (2011), 152–76
The gentle civilizer of nations: the rise and fall of international law, 1870–1960 (Cambridge University Press, 2002)
Kroll, Stefan, *Normgenese durch Re-Interpretation: China und das europäische Völkerrecht im 19. und 20. Jahrhundert* (Baden-Baden: Nomos, 2012)
Kunz, J., 'Natural-law thinking in the modern science of international law', *AJIL*, 55 (1961), 951–8
Landau, Jacob M., '*Mu'ahada*' in P. J. Bearman and Marc Garborieau (eds.), *Encyclopaedia of Islam*, 2nd edn (Leiden: Brill Online), http://brillonline.nl/entries/encyclopaedia-of-islam-2/muahada-COM_0766
Landauer, Carl, 'A Latin American in Paris: Alejandro Álvarez's le droit international américain', *Leiden Journal of International Law*, 19 (2006), 957–81

Långström, Tarja, *Transformation in Russia and international law* (Leiden: M. Nijhoff, 2003)

Lapradelle, Albert Geouffre de, 'La question chinoise', *RGDIP*, Part 1, 8 (1901), 272–340; Part 2, 9 (1902), 49–115; Part 3, 9 (1902), 367–405; Part 4, 10 (1903), 742–99

Maitres et doctrines du droit des gens (Paris: Les Editions internationals, 1950)

Lapradelle, Albert Geouffre de and Politis, Nicolas, 'La deuxième conference de la paix', *RGDIP*, 16 (1909), 385–437

Recueil des arbitrages internationaux (Paris: Pédone, 1923), vol. II

Lapradelle, Albert Geouffre de and Stowell, Ellery C., 'Latin America at the Hague Conference', *The Yale Law Journal*, 17 (1908), 270–80

Lauterpacht, Hersch, *The function of law in the international community* (Cambridge University Press, 1933)

Lawrence, T. J., *Essays on some disputed questions in modern international law* (Cambridge: Deighton, Bell, 1885)

The principles of international law (Boston: D. C. Heath, 1895)

Leben, Charles, 'The changing structure of international law revisited. By way of introduction', *EJIL*, 8 (1997), 399

Li, Zhaojie, 'International law in China: legal aspect of the Chinese perspective of world order', unpublished SJD dissertation, Toronto University (1995)

Liu, Lydia, 'Legislating the universal: the circulation of international law in the nineteenth century' in L. Liu (ed.), *Tokens of exchange: the problem of translation in global circulations* (Durham, NC: Duke University Press, 1999)

The clash of empires: the invention of China in modern world making (Cambridge: Harvard University Press, 2004)

Lobban, Michael, 'English approaches to international law in the nineteenth century' in Matthew Craven et al. (eds.), *Time, history and international law* (Leiden: M. Nijhoff, 2007), pp. 65–90

Lorimer, James, *The institutes of law: a treatise of the principles of jurisprudence as determined by nature* (London: W. Blackwood & Sons, 1880)

The institutes of the law of nations: a treatise of the jural relations of separate political communities (London: W. Blackwood and Sons, 1883)

Low, Maurice, 'Venezuela and the powers', *The American Monthly Review of Reviews*, 27 (1903), 39–43

MacDonald, Ronald St John, 'Introduction: Wang Tieya: persevering in adversity and shaping the future of public international law' in R. St J. MacDonald (ed.), *Essays in honour of Wang Tieya* (Dordrecht: Martinus Nijhoff, 1994), pp. 1–30

MacMillan, Margaret, *Paris 1919: six months that changed the world* (New York: Random House, 2002)

McNair, Arnold, 'Aspects of state sovereignty', *British Yearbook of International Law*, 26 (1949), 6–47

Magalhães Júnior, Raymundo, *Rui, o homen e o mito* (Rio de Janeiro: Civilização Brasileira, 1979)

Mälksoo, Lauri, 'The history of international legal theory in Russia: a civilizational dialogue with Europe', *European Journal of International Law*, 19 (2008), 211–32

'The science of international law and the concept of politics. The arguments and lives of the international law professors at the University of Dorpat/Iur'ev/Tartu 1855–1985', *British Yearbook of International Law*, 76 (2005), 383–502

Manchester, Alan K., 'The recognition of Brazilian independence', *The Hispanic American Historical Review*, 31 (1951), 80–96

Manela, Erez, *Wilsonian moment: self-determination and the international origins of anticolonial nationalism* (Oxford University Press, 2007)

Marburg, Theodore, *Development of the League of Nations idea* (New York: Macmillan, 1932)

Martens, Fedor Fedorovich, *Das Consularwesen und die Consularjurisdiction im Orient*, H. Skerst trans. (Berlin: Weidmannsche buchhandlung, 1874)

Par la justice vers la paix. Annexe: doctrine de Drago, ou note diplomatique du gouvernement argentin du 29 décembre 1902 (Paris: H. Charles-Lavauzelle, 1906)

Russie et l'Angleterre dans l'Asie centrale (Gand: I. S. Van Doosselaere, 1879)

Traité de droit international, A. Leo trans. (Paris: Librairie Marescq Aine, 1887)

Völkerrecht: das internationale Recht der Civilisirten Nationen: systematisch dargestellt, C. Bergbohm trans. (Berlin: Weidmann Buchhandlung, 1886)

Martínez Moreno, Alfredo, 'José Gustavo Guerrero, caballero andante de derecho' in A. A. Cançado Trindade and A. Martínez Moreno (eds.), *Doctrina latinoamericana del derecho internacional* (San José: Corte Interamericana de Derechos Humanos, 2003), pp. 9–32

Melgar Bao, Ricardo, 'The anti-imperialist league of the Americas between the East and Latin America', *Latin American Perspectives*, 35 (2008), 9–24

Meron, Theodor, 'The Martens clause, principles of humanity, and dictates of public conscience', *AJIL*, 94 (2000), 78–89

Miller, David, *The drafting of the Covenant* (New York: G. P. Putnam's Sons, 1928), vol. II

Miyasaki, Shigeki, 'History of the law of nations regional development: Far East' in R. Bernhardt et al. (eds.), *Encyclopaedia of public international law* (Amsterdam: North-Holland, 1995), vol. II, pp. 802–9

Momirov, Aleksandar, 'The individual right to petition in internationalized territories: from progressive thought to an abandoned practice', *Journal of the History of International Law*, 9 (2007), 203–31

Munro, Dana Gardner, *Intervention and dollar diplomacy in the Caribbean, 1900–1921* (Westport: Greenwood Press, 1980)

Murase, Shinya, 'The presence of Asia at the 1907 Hague Conference' in Y. Daudet (ed.), *Topicality of the 1907 Hague conference, the second peace conference (Actualité de la conférence de La Haye de 1907, deuxième conférence de la paix)* (Leiden: Nijhoff, 2008), pp. 88–101

Myers, Denys, 'The origin of the Hague Arbitral Courts', *AJIL*, 10 (1916), 270–311, 279

Myles, Eric, '"Humanity", "civilization" and the "international community" in the late imperial Russian mirror: three ideas "topical for our days"', *Journal of the History of International Law*, 4 (2002), 310–34

Naff, Thomas, 'The Ottoman Empire and the European states system' in H. Bull and A. Watson (eds.), *The expansion of international society* (Oxford: Clarendon Press, 1984), pp. 143–70

Neuhaus, Rupert, *Das Rechtsmissbrauchsverbot im heutigen Völkerrecht: eine Untersuchung zur Entwicklung und Anwendbarkeit eines Begriffes* (Berlin: Duncker & Humblot, 1984), pp. 25–6

Niboyet, Jean-Pauline, 'Antoine Pillet (1857–1926)' in *Mélanges Antoine Pillet* (Paris: Sirey, 1929), vol. I, pp. 3–15

Nippold, Otfried, *Die Gestaltung des Völkerrechts nach dem Weltkriege* (Zürich: Orell Füssli, 1917)

Wanderungen durch Japan: Briefe und Tagebuchblätter (Jena: Mauke, 1893)

Nissel, Alan, 'The duality of state responsibility', *Columbia Human Rights Law Review*, 44 (2013), 793–858, 819

Noradounghian, Gabriel, *Recueil d'actes internationaux de l'Empire Ottoman* (Paris: F. Pichon, 1897)

Note from Mr Seward, Sec. of State, to Mr Burton, Min. to Colombia (Apr. 27, 1866) in J. B. Moore and F. Wharton, *A digest of international law* (Washington: Government Printing Office, 1906), p. 660

Nussbaum, Arthur, *A concise history of the law of nations* (New York: Macmillan, 1954)

Nuzzo, Luigi, *Origini di una scienza: diritto internazionale e colonialismo nel XIX secolo* (Frankfurt am Main: Vittorio Klostermann, 2012)

Nys, Ernest, 'Codification of international law', *AJIL*, 5 (1911), 871–900

Oblas, Peter, 'Treaty revision and the role of the American foreign affairs adviser, 1909–1925', *Journal of the Siam Society*, 60 (1976), 171–86

Obregón, Liliana, 'Completing civilization: nineteenth century *criollo* interventions in international law', unpublished SJD dissertation, Harvard University (2002)

'Noted for dissent: the international life of Alejandro Álvarez', *Leiden Journal of International Law*, 19 (2006), 983–1016

'The civilised and the uncivilised' in B. Fassbender et al. (eds.), *The Oxford handbook of the history of international law* (Oxford University Press, 2012), pp. 919–39

ol-Memalek, Mochaver, *Claims of Persia before the Conference of the Preliminaries of Peace at Paris* (Paris: Paris Peace Conference, 1919)

Omissi, David, *Air power and colonial control: the Royal Air Force 1919–1939* (New York: St Martin's Press, 1990)

Onuma, Yasuaki, 'Japanese international law in the prewar period: perspectives on the teaching and research of international law in prewar Japan', *Japanese Annual of International Law*, 29 (1986), 23–47

Onuma, Yasuaki, 'When was the Law of International Society Born?' *Journal of the History of International Law*, 2 (2000), 1–66

Oppenheim, Lassa, *International law, a treatise*, 1st edn, 2 vols. (London: Longmans, 1905), vol. I

Oppenheim, Lassa and Lauterpacht, Hersch, *International law, a treatise*, 7th edn, 2 vols. (London: Longmans, 1948), vol. I

International law, a treatise, 8th edn, 1 vol. (London: Longmans, 1955)

Oppenheim, Lassa and McNair, Arnold, *International law, a treatise*, 4th edn, 2 vols. (London: Longmans, 1928)

Oppenheim, Lassa, Jennings, Robert and Watts, Arthur, *Oppenheim's international law*, 9th edn, 2 vols. (London: Longmans, 1996)

Örücü, Esin, 'The impact of European law on the Ottoman Empire and Turkey', in W. J. Mommsen and J. de Moor, *European expansion and law: the encounter of European and indigenous law in 19th- and 20th-century Africa and Asia* (Oxford: Berg, 1991), pp. 39–58

Ota Mishima, Maria Elena, *México y Japón en el siglo XIX: la política exterior de México y la consolidación de la soberanía japonesa* (Tlatelolco, México: Secretaría de Relaciones Exteriores, 1976)

Otsuka, Hirohiko, 'Japan's early encounter with the concept of the "law of nations"', *Japanese Annual of International Law*, 13 (1969), 35–65

Owada, Hisashi, 'Japan, international law and the international community' in N. Andō (ed.), *Japan and international law: past, present and future* (The Hague: Kluwer Law International, 1999), pp. 347–78

Özsu, Umut, 'Ottoman Empire' in Fassbender and Peters, *Oxford handbook*, pp. 429–48

Panaite, Viorel, H-Net Reviews 2 (2003), www.h-net.org/reviews/showrev.php?id=7325

'Notes on the Islamic-Ottoman law of peace', *Revue des Études Sud-est Européennes*, 41 (2003), 191–206

The Ottoman law of war and peace: the Ottoman Empire and tribute payers (Boulder: East European Monographs, 2000)

Parfitt, Rose, 'Empire des nègres blancs: the hybridity of international personality and the Abyssinia Crisis of 1935–36', *Leiden Journal of International Law*, 24 (2011), 849–72

Paris Peace Conference, *Claims of the peace delegation of the republic of Caucasian Azerbaidjan presented to the Peace conference in Paris* (Paris: Robinet-Houtain, 1919)

Paris Peace Conference, Egyptian Delegation, *The Egyptian national claims: a memorandum presented to the Peace Conference by the Egyptian delegation charged with the defence of Egyptian independence* (Paris: Imprimerie artistique Lux, 1919)

Paternostro, Alessandro, 'La revision des traités avec le Japon au point de vue du droit international', *Revue de droit international et de législation comparée*, 23 (1891), 176–200

Pears, Edwin, 'Turkish capitulations and the status of British and other foreign subjects residing in Turkey', *Law Quarterly Review*, 21 (1905), 408–25

Pélissié du Rausas, Gérard, *Le régime des capitulations dans l'Empire Ottoman*, 2 vols. (Paris: A. Rousseau, 1902)
Pellet, Alain, 'The role of the international lawyer in international litigation' in C. Wickremasinghe (ed.), *The international lawyer as practitioner* (London: British Institute of International and Comparative Law, 2000)
Pessôa, Epitácio, *Projecto de código de direito internacional publico* (Rio de Janeiro: Imprensa Nacional, 1911)
Peters, Anne, 'Unequal treaties' in W. Rüdiger (ed.), *The Max Planck encyclopedia of public international law* (Oxford University Press, 2012), pp. 38–50
Pic, P., *Le régime du mandat d'après le traité de Versailles, son application dans le proche Orient: mandat français en Syrie, anglais en Palestine et Mésopotamie* (Paris: A. Pédone, 1923)
Pike, Fredrick B., *Chile and the United States, 1880–1962: the emergence of Chile's social crisis and the challenge to United States diplomacy* (University of Notre Dame Press, 1963)
Pillet, Antoine, 'Cases on international law during the chino-japanese war (Cas de droit international pendant la guerre sino-japonaise)', *RGDIP*, 6 (1899), 335–6
'Le droit international public, ses éléments constitutifs, son domaine, son objet', *RGDIP*, 1 (1894), 1–32
Les conventions de La Haye du 29 juillet 1899 et du 18 octobre 1907: étude juridique et critique (Paris: A. Pédone, 1918)
Recherches sur les droits fondamentaux des états dans l'ordre des rapports internationaux et sur la solution des conflits qu'ils font naître (Paris: A. Pédone, 1899)
'Recherches sur les droits fondamentaux des états dans l'ordre des rapports internationaux et sur la solution des conflits qu'ils font naître' (Part 1), *RGDIP*, 5 (1898), 66–89
Platt, D. C. M., 'The allied coercion of Venezuela, 1902–3 – a reassessment', *Inter-American Economic Affairs*, 15 (1961), 3–28
Politis, Nicolas, 'Le problème des limitations de la souveraineté et la théorie de l'abus des droits dans les rapports internationaux', *RdC*, 6 (1925-I) 1–121
Les nouvelles tendances du droit international (Paris: Hachette, 1927)
Preiser, Wolfgang, *Frühe völkerrechtliche Ordnungen der außereuropäischen Welt: Ein Beitrag zur Geschichte des Völkerrechts* (Wiesbaden: F. Steiner, 1976)
'History of the law of nations: basic questions and principles' in R. Bernhardt et al. (eds.), *Encyclopaedia of public international law* (Amsterdam: North-Holland, 1984), vol. VII, pp. 126–32
'Protest der Syrer Berlin, Heftiger Protest gegen die barbarischen Schandtaten der Franzosen in Syrien', *Die Welt des Islams*, 8 (1926), 133
Provence, Michael, *The great Syrian revolt and the rise of Arab nationalism* (University of Texas Press, 2005)
Pustogarov, V. V., *Our Martens: F. F. Martens, international lawyer and architect of peace*, W. E. Butler ed. trans. (The Hague: Kluwer Law International, 2000)
Rajagopal, Balakrishnan, *International law from below development, social movements, and Third World resistance* (Cambridge University Press, 2012)

Rappard, William, 'Germany at Geneva', *Foreign Affairs*, 4 (1926), 535–46
Ratner, Steven and Slaughter, Anne-Marie, 'Appraising the methods of international law: a prospectus for readers', *AJIL*, 93 (1999), 291
Redslob, Robert, 'Völkerrechtliche Ideen der französischen Revolution' in O. Mayer, *Festgabe für Otto Mayer zum siebzigsten Geburtstag, 29 März 1916* (Tübingen: Mohr, 1916), pp. 273–301
Reibstein, Ernst, *Völkerrecht; eine Geschichte seiner Ideen in Lehre und Praxis* (Freiburg: K. Alber, 1958)
Richardson, Henry J., *The origins of African-American interests in international law* (Durham, NC: Carolina Academic Press, 2008)
Rippy, Fred, 'Antecedents of the Roosevelt corollary of the Monroe doctrine', *The Pacific Historical Review*, 9 (1940), 267–79
Rivier, Alphonse, 'Notice nécrologique sur M. Saripolos par M. Rivier', *Annuaire de l'Institut de Droit International*, 10 (1888), 52
Robertson, William Spence, *France and Latin-American Independence* (Baltimore: Johns Hopkins Press, 1939)
Rodríguez O., Jaime, E., *The emergence of Spanish America: Vicente Rocafuerte and Spanish Americanism, 1808–1832* (Berkeley: University of California Press, 1975)
Rolin-Jaequemyns, Gustave, 'Derecho internacional teórico y práctico de Europa y América, por Carlos Calvo', *Revue de Droit International et de Législation Comparée*, 1 (1869), 294–6
Root, Elihu, 'The declaration of the rights and duties of nations adopted by the American Institute of International Law', *AJIL*, 10 (1916) 211–21
Rosenne, Shabtai, *The Hague Peace Conferences of 1899 and 1907 and international arbitration: reports and documents* (The Hague: T. M. C. Asser, 2001)
Rostkowski, Joëlle, 'The Redman's appeal for justice: Deskaheh and the League of Nations' in C. F. Feest (ed.), *Indians and Europe: an interdisciplinary collection of essays* (Aachen: Edition Herodot, 1987), pp. 435–53
Salisbury, Richard V., *Anti-imperialism and international competition in Central America, 1920–1929* (Wilmington, DE: SR Books, 1989)
Sanhuri, Abdel-Razzak al-, *Le califat, son évolution vers une société des nations orientales* (Paris: P. Geuthner, 1926)
Saripolos, Nicolas, 'La question gréco-turque après l'acte final de la conférence de Berlin', *Revue de Droit International et de Législation Comparée*, 13 (1881), 231–45
'La question gréco-turque, ses commencements, ses progrès, et son état actuel', *Revue de Droit International et de Législation Comparée*, 11 (1879), 119–43
Sasse, Dirk, *Franzosen, Briten und Deutsche im Rifkrieg 1921–1926: Spekulanten und Sympathisanten, Deserteure und Hasardeure im Dienste Abdelkrims* (München: Oldenbourg, 2006), p. 82
Sayre, Francis Bowes, 'The passing of extraterritoriality in Siam', *AJIL*, 22 (1928), 70–88
Scelle, Georges, *Annuaire de l'Institut de Droit International*, 43 II (1950), 492–5
Précis de droit des gens; principes et systématique (Paris: Librairie du Recueil Sirey, 1932)

'Rapport', *Les Cahiers des Droits de l'Homme*, 25 (1925), 496 in Berman, 'Appeals of the Orient', p. 202
Schachter, Oscar, 'The invisible college of international lawyers', *Northwestern University Law Review*, 72 (1977–8), 217
Schmitt, Carl, *Der Nomos der Erde im Völkerrecht des Jus Publicum Europaeum: Im Völkerrecht des Jus Publicum Europaeum* (Berlin: Duncker, 1988)
'Die Auflösung der europäischen Ordnung im "International Law" (1890–1939)' in C. Schmitt, *Staat, Großraum, Nomos. Arbeiten aus den Jahren 1916–1969* (Berlin: Duncker, 1995), pp. 372–87
'Raum und Großraum im Völkerrecht' in C. Schmitt, *Staat, Großraum, Nomos. Arbeiten aus den Jahren 1916–1969* (Berlin: Duncker, 1995), pp. 234–68
Schücking, Walther, *Die Organisation der Welt* (Tübingen: J. C. B. Mohr, P. Siebeck, 1908)
The international union of the Hague conferences, Work of the Hague, C. G. Fenwick, trans., 2 vols. (Oxford: The Clarendon Press, 1918)
Schwarzenberger, Georg, *The League of Nations and World Order* (London: Constable, 1936)
'The rule of law and the disintegration of the international society', *AJIL*, 33 (1939), 56–77
'The standard of civilisation in international law', *Current Legal Problems*, 8 (1955), 212–34
Scott, James Brown, *The Hague Peace Conferences of 1899 and 1907; a series of lectures delivered before the Johns Hopkins University in the year 1908* (Baltimore: The Johns Hopkins Press, 1909)
The project of a permanent court of international justice and resolutions of the advisory committee of jurists: report and commentary by James Brown Scott (Washington: The Endowment, 1920)
'The work of the Second Hague Peace Conference', *AJIL*, 2 (1908), 1–28
Scully, Ellen. P, *Bargaining with the state from afar: American citizenship in treaty port China, 1844–1942* (New York: Columbia University Press, 2001)
Segesser, Daniel Marc, '"Unlawful warfare is uncivilised": the international debate on the punishment of war crimes, 1872–1918', *European Review of History*, 14 (2007), 215–34
Senga, Tsurutaro, *Gestaltung und Kritik der heutigen Konsulargerichtsbarkeit in Japan*, (Berlin: R. L. Prager, 1897)
Sheinin, David, 'Argentina and the United States at the Sixth Pan American Conference (Habana 1928)', Research Paper No. 25, Institute of Latin American Studies, University of London (1991)
Shimazu, Naoko, *Japan, race, and equality: the racial equality proposal of 1919* (London: New York: Routledge, 1998)
Simpson, Gerry, *Great powers and outlaw states: unequal sovereigns in the international legal order* (Cambridge, UK/New York: Cambridge University Press, 2004)
Skouteris, Thomas, *The notion of progress in international law discourse* (The Hague: T. M. C. Asser Press/Cambridge University Press, 2010)

Smith, Joseph, *The United States and Latin America: a history of American diplomacy, 1776–2000* (London: Routledge, 2005)
Sonyel, Salahi R., 'The protégé system in the Ottoman Empire', *Journal of Islamic Studies*, 2 (1991), 56–66
Spiermann, Ole, *International legal argument in the Permanent Court of International Justice* (Cambridge University Press, 2010)
Steiner, W. A., 'Charles Henry Alexandrowicz', *BYIL*, 47 (1975), 269–71
Stone, Julius, *Quest for survival: the role of law and foreign policy* (Cambridge: Harvard University Press, 1961)
'Students studying in the Netherlands at the end of the Edo Period', National Diet Library Japan: www.ndl.go.jp/nichiran/e/s2/s2_6.html
Strang, David, 'Contested sovereignty: the social construction of colonial imperialism' in T. J. Biersteker and C. Weber (eds.), *State sovereignty as social construct* (Cambridge University Press, 1996), pp. 22–49
Streeter, Michael, *Epitácio Pessôa, Brazil (the makers of the modern world): the Peace Conferences of 1919–23 and their aftermath* (London: Haus Publishing, 2010)
Streit, Georgios, 'Les grandes puissances dans le droit international', *Revue de Droit International et de Législation Comparée*, 2 (1900), 5–25
'Notices nécrologiques, Etienne Carathéodory', *Annuaire de l'Institut de Droit International*, 22 (1908), 342–5
Susa, Nasīm, *The capitulatory régime of Turkey, its history, origin, and nature* (Baltimore: Johns Hopkins Press, 1933)
Svarverud, Rune, *International law as world order in late imperial China: translation, reception and discourse, 1847–1911* (Leiden: Brill, 2007)
Tachi, Sakutaro, *La souveraineté et l'indépendance de l'état et les questions intérieures en droit international* (Paris: Les Éditions internationals, 1930)
Takahashi, Sakuyei (ed.), *Aeusserungen über völkerrechtlich bedeutsame Vorkommnisse aus dem chinesisch-japanischen Seekrieg und das darauf bezügliche Werk (Cases on international law during the Chino-Japanese war)* (München: E. Reinhardt, 1900)
Takahashi, Sakuyei, *Cases on international law during the Chino-Japanese war* (Cambridge University Press, 1899)
Heiji kokusaihōron (Tōkyoō: Nihon Daigaku, 1907)
International law applied to the Russo-Japanese war: with the decisions of the Japanese prize courts (London/New York: Stevens and Sons/The Banks Law Pub. Co., 1908)
'Le droit international dans l'histoire du Japon', *Revue de Droit International et de Législation Comparée*, 3 (1901), 188–201
Thayer, Lucius Ellsworth, 'The capitulations of the Ottoman Empire and the question of their abrogation as it affects the United States', *AJIL*, 17 (1923) 207–33
The New York Times, November 8, 1903, p. 4
'The Second Peace Conference. Its results and lessons', *The London Times*, 21 October 1907, p. 3

The Venezuelan arbitration before the Hague tribunal 1903, vol. 119, *[United States] 58th Congress 3d session Senate Document* (Washington: Government Printing Office, 1905)
Thompson, Edward Palmer, *Whigs and hunters: the origin of the Black Act* (London: Penguin, 1975)
Tips, Walter, '*Gustave Rolin-Jaequemyns and the making of modern Siam: the diaries and letters of King Chulalongkorn's general adviser* (Bangkok: White Lotus, 1996)
Torres Campos, Manuel, *Elementos de derecho internacional público* (Madrid: Librería de F. Fé, 1890), pp. 58–9
Toyoda, Tetsuya, 'L'aspect universaliste du droit international européen du 19ème siècle et le statut juridique de la Turquie avant 1856', *Journal of the History of International Law*, 8 (2006), 19–37
Truyol y Serra, Antonio, 'L'expansion de la société internationale aux XIXe et XXe siècles', *Recueils des Cours de l'Académie de Droit International*, 116 (1965/I), 89–179
Tseng, Yu-hao, *The termination of unequal treaties in international law; studies in comparative jurisprudence and conventional law of nations* (Shanghai: The Commercial Press, 1933)
Twiss, Travers, *The law of nations considered as independent political communities. On the rights and duties of nations in time of peace* (Oxford: Clarendon Press, 1884)
Tyau, Min-chien T. Z., *The legal obligations arising out of treaty relations between China and other states* (Shanghai: Commercial Press, 1917)
'United Nations documents on the development and codification of international law', *AJIL*, 41 (1947) (supplement), 29–148, 82–7
Veatch, Richard, *Canada and the League of Nations* (University of Toronto Press, 1975)
Verdross, Alfred, *Völkerrecht* (Wien: Springer, 1950)
Verzijl, Jan H. W., 'Western European influence on the foundations of international law' in J. H. W. Verzijl, *International law in historical perspective* (Leiden: A. W. Sijthoff, 1968), vol. I (originally published in *International Relations*, 1 (1955))
Vincent, John Carter, *The extraterritorial system in China: final phase* (Cambridge: Harvard University Press, 1970)
Visscher, Charles de, *Théories et réalités en droit international public* (Paris: Pédone, 1953)
Waddell, D. A. G., 'International politics and Latin American independence' in L. Bethell (ed.), *The independence of Latin America* (Cambridge University Press, 1984), pp. 195–232
Wallerstein, Immanuel, *World-systems analysis: an introduction* (Durham, NC: Duke University Press, 2004)
Wang, Dong, *China's unequal treaties: narrating national history* (Lanham, MD: Lexington Books, 2005)
Wang, Tieya, 'International law in China: historical and contemporary perspectives', *RdC*, 221 (1990-II), 195–369

Wesseling, Henk L., *The European colonial empires, 1815–1919*, D. Webb trans. (Harlow: Pearson Longman, 2004)

Westlake, John, *Chapters on the principles of international law* (Cambridge University Press, 1894)

International law: Part I Peace (Cambridge University Press, 1904)

'The Hague Conferences' in *The collected papers of John Westlake on public international law* (Cambridge University Press, 1914), 531–67 (originally published in the *Quarterly Review*, 414 (1908), 224–51)

Wharton, Francis, *A digest of the international law of the United States, taken from documents issued by presidents and secretaries of state, and from decisions of federal courts and opinions of attorneys-general* (Washington: Government Printing Office, 1886)

Wheaton, Henry, *Elements of international law with a sketch of the history of the science* (Philadelphia: Carey, Lea & Blanchard, 1836)

Wheaton, Henry and Beach Lawrence, William, *Elements of international law*, 6th edn (Boston: Little, Brown, 1855)

Wheaton, Henry and Dana, Richard Henry, *Elements of international law*, 8th edn (London: S. Low, Son and Co., 1866)

Whitaker, Arthur Preston, *The United States and the independence of Latin America, 1800–1830* (New York: Russell & Russell, 1962)

Whitehead, Laurence, *Latin America: a new interpretation* (New York: Palgrave Macmillan, 2006)

Woo, Grace Li Xiu, 'Canada's forgotten founders: the modern significance of the Haudenosaunee (Iroquois) application for membership in the League of Nations', *Law, Social Justice & Global Development Journal (LGD)*, 1 (2003) (www2.warwick.ac.uk/fac/soc/law/elj/lgd/2003_1/woo/)

Wright, Quincy, *Mandates under the League of Nations* (University of Chicago Press, 1930)

'The bombardment of Damascus', *AJIL*, 20 (1926), 263–80

Yamamoto, Soji, 'Japanese approaches and attitudes towards international law', *Japanese Annual of International Law*, 34 (1991), 115–24

Yamauchi, Susumu, 'Civilization and international law in Japan during the Meiji Era (1868–1912)', *Hitotsubashi Journal of Law and Politics*, 24 (1996), 1–25

Yepes, Jesús María, *La codificación del derecho internacional americano y la conferencia de Rio de Janeiro* (Bogotá: Imprenta nacional, 1927)

'La contribution de l'Amérique latine au développement du droit international public et privé', *Recueils des Cours de l'Académie de Droit International*, 32 (1930/II), 691–799

Yılmaz, Altuğ, *Turkey and some problems of international law* (Istanbul: Yenilik Basımevi, 1958), pp. 22–31

Zea, Leopoldo, *Pensamiento positivista latinoamericano* (Caracas, Venezuela: Biblioteca Ayacucho, 1980), vol. I, p. xiv

Zhu, Jin, *The tariff problem in China* (New York: Columbia University, 1916)

Ziegler, Karl-Heinz, 'The peace treaties of the Ottoman Empire with European Christian powers' in R. Lesaffer, *Peace treaties and international law in European history: from the late Middle Ages to World War One* (Cambridge University Press, 2004), pp. 338–64

Völkerrechtsgeschichte: ein Studienbuch, 2nd edn (Munich: Beck, 2007)

Zimmern, Alfred, *The League of Nations and the rule of law, 1918–1935* (London: Macmillan, 1936)

Index

CAMBRIDGE STUDIES IN INTERNATIONAL AND COMPARATIVE LAW

Books in the series

Mestizo International Law: A Global Intellectual History 1842–1933
Arnulf Becker Lorca

Sugar and the Making of International Trade Law
Michael Fakhri

Strategically-created Treaty Conflicts and the Politics of International Law
Surabhi Ranganathan

Investment Treaty Arbitration as Public International Law: Procedural Aspects and Implications
Eric De Brabandere

The New Entrants Problem in International Fisheries Law
Andrew Serdy

Substantive Protection under Investment Treaties: A Legal and Economic Analysis
Jonathan Bonnitcha

Popular Governance of Post-Conflict Reconstruction: The Role of International Law
Matthew Saul

Evolution of International Environmental Regimes: The Case of Climate Change
Simone Schiele

Judges, Law and War: The Judicial Development of International Humanitarian Law
Shane Darcy

Religious Offence and Human Rights: The Implications of Defamation of Religions
Lorenz Langer

Forum Shopping in International Adjudication: The Role of Preliminary Objections
Luiz Eduardo Ribeiro Salles

International Law and the Arctic
Michael Byers

Cooperation in the Law of Transboundary Water Resources
Christina Leb

Underwater Cultural Heritage and International Law
Sarah Dromgoole

State Responsibility: The General Part
James Crawford

The Origins of International Investment Law
Kate Miles

The Crime of Aggression under the Rome Statute of the International Criminal Court
Carrie McDougall

Crimes against Peace and International Law
Kirsten Sellars

The Non-Legal in International Law
Fleur Johns

Armed Conflict and Displacement: The Protection of Refugees and Displaced Persons under International Humanitarian Law
Mélanie Jacques

Foreign Investment and the Environment in International Law
Jorge Viñuales

The Human Rights Treaty Obligations of Peacekeepers
Kjetil Larsen

Cyberwarfare and the Laws of War
Heather Harrison Dinniss

The Right to Reparation in International Law for Victims of Armed Conflict
Christine Evans

Global Public Interest in International Investment Law
Andreas Kulick

State Immunity in International Law
Xiaodong Yang

Reparations and Victim Support in the International Criminal Court
Conor McCarthy

Reducing Genocide to Law: Definition, Meaning, and the Ultimate Crime
Payam Akhavan

Decolonizing International Law: Development, Economic Growth and the Politics of Universality
Sundhya Pahuja

Complicity and the Law of State Responsibility
Helmut Philipp Aust

State Control over Private Military and Security Companies in Armed Conflict
Hannah Tonkin

'Fair and Equitable Treatment' in International Investment Law
Roland Kläger

The UN and Human Rights: Who Guards the Guardians?
Guglielmo Verdirame

Sovereign Defaults before International Courts and Tribunals
Michael Waibel

Making the Law of the Sea: A Study in the Development of International Law
James Harrison

Science and the Precautionary Principle in International Courts and Tribunals: Expert Evidence, Burden of Proof and Finality
Caroline E. Foster

Transition from Illegal Regimes in International Law
Yaël Ronen

Access to Asylum: International Refugee Law and the Globalisation of Migration Control
Thomas Gammeltoft-Hansen

Trading Fish, Saving Fish: The Interaction between Regimes in International Law
Margaret Young

The Individual in the International Legal System: Continuity and Change in International Law
Kate Parlett

The Participation of States in International Organisations: The Role of Human Rights and Democracy
Alison Duxbury

'Armed Attack' and Article 51 of the UN Charter: Evolutions in Customary Law and Practice
Tom Ruys

Science and Risk Regulation in International Law
Jacqueline Peel

Theatre of the Rule of Law: Transnational Legal Intervention in Theory and Practice
Stephen Humphreys

The Public International Law Theory of Hans Kelsen: Believing in Universal Law
Jochen von Bernstorff

Vicarious Liability in Tort: A Comparative Perspective
Paula Giliker

Legal Personality in International Law
Roland Portmann

Legitimacy and Legality in International Law: An Interactional Account
Jutta Brunnée and
Stephen J. Toope

The Concept of Non-International Armed Conflict in International Humanitarian Law
Anthony Cullen

The Challenge of Child Labour in International Law
Franziska Humbert

Shipping Interdiction and the Law of the Sea
Douglas Guilfoyle

International Courts and Environmental Protection
Tim Stephens

Legal Principles in WTO Disputes
Andrew D. Mitchell

War Crimes in Internal Armed Conflicts
Eve La Haye

Humanitarian Occupation
Gregory H. Fox

The International Law of Environmental Impact Assessment: Process, Substance and Integration
Neil Craik

The Law and Practice of International Territorial Administration: Versailles to Iraq and Beyond
Carsten Stahn

Cultural Products and the World Trade Organization
Tania Voon

United Nations Sanctions and the Rule of Law
Jeremy Farrall

National Law in WTO Law: Effectiveness and Good Governance in the World Trading System
Sharif Bhuiyan

The Threat of Force in International Law
Nikolas Stürchler

Indigenous Rights and United Nations Standards
Alexandra Xanthaki

International Refugee Law and Socio-Economic Rights
Michelle Foster

The Protection of Cultural Property in Armed Conflict
Roger O'Keefe

Interpretation and Revision of International Boundary Decisions
Kaiyan Homi Kaikobad

Multinationals and Corporate Social Responsibility: Limitations and Opportunities in International Law
Jennifer A. Zerk

Judiciaries within Europe: A Comparative Review
John Bell

Law in Times of Crisis: Emergency Powers in Theory and Practice
Oren Gross and
Fionnuala Ní Aoláin

Vessel-Source Marine Pollution: The Law and Politics of International Regulation
Alan Tan

Enforcing Obligations Erga Omnes *in International Law*
Christian J. Tams

Non-Governmental Organisations in International Law
Anna-Karin Lindblom

Democracy, Minorities and International Law
Steven Wheatley

Prosecuting International Crimes: Selectivity and the International Law Regime
Robert Cryer

Compensation for Personal Injury in English, German and Italian Law: A Comparative Outline
Basil Markesinis,

Michael Coester,
Guido Alpa,
Augustus Ullstein

Dispute Settlement in the UN Convention on the Law of the Sea
Natalie Klein

The International Protection of Internally Displaced Persons
Catherine Phuong

Imperialism, Sovereignty and the Making of International Law
Antony Anghie

Necessity, Proportionality and the Use of Force by States
Judith Gardam

International Legal Argument in the Permanent Court of International Justice: The Rise of the International Judiciary
Ole Spiermann

Great Powers and Outlaw States: Unequal Sovereigns in the International Legal Order
Gerry Simpson

Local Remedies in International Law
C. F. Amerasinghe

Reading Humanitarian Intervention: Human Rights and the Use of Force in International Law
Anne Orford

Conflict of Norms in Public International Law: How WTO Law Relates to Other Rules of International Law
Joost Pauwelyn

Transboundary Damage in International Law
Hanqin Xue

European Criminal Procedures
Edited by
Mireille Delmas-Marty and
John Spencer

The Accountability of Armed Opposition Groups in International Law
Liesbeth Zegveld

Sharing Transboundary Resources: International Law and Optimal Resource Use
Eyal Benvenisti

International Human Rights and Humanitarian Law
René Provost

Remedies Against International Organisations
Karel Wellens

Diversity and Self-Determination in International Law
Karen Knop

The Law of Internal Armed Conflict
Lindsay Moir

International Commercial Arbitration and African States: Practice, Participation and Institutional Development
Amazu A. Asouzu

The Enforceability of Promises in European Contract Law
James Gordley

International Law in Antiquity
David J. Bederman

Money Laundering: A New International Law Enforcement Model
Guy Stessens

Good Faith in European Contract Law
Reinhard Zimmermann and
Simon Whittaker

On Civil Procedure
J. A. Jolowicz

Trusts: A Comparative Study
Maurizio Lupoi

The Right to Property in Commonwealth Constitutions
Tom Allen

International Organizations Before National Courts
August Reinisch

The Changing International Law of High Seas Fisheries
Francisco Orrego Vicuña

Trade and the Environment: A Comparative Study of EC and US Law
Damien Geradin

Unjust Enrichment: A Study of Private Law and Public Values
Hanoch Dagan

Religious Liberty and International Law in Europe
Malcolm D. Evans

Ethics and Authority in International Law
Alfred P. Rubin

Sovereignty Over Natural Resources: Balancing Rights and Duties
Nico Schrijver

The Polar Regions and the Development of International Law
Donald R. Rothwell

Fragmentation and the International Relations of Micro-States: Self-determination and Statehood
Jorri Duursma

Principles of the Institutional Law of International Organizations
C. F. Amerasinghe

Lightning Source UK Ltd.
Milton Keynes UK
UKOW05n1546260115

245144UK00001B/6/P

9 780521 763387